PIERRE TEILHARD DE CHARDIN

GARLAND REFERENCE LIBRARY
OF THE HUMANITIES
(VOL. 158)

PIERRE TEILHARD DE CHARDIN
A Comprehensive Bibliography

Joseph M. McCarthy

GARLAND PUBLISHING, INC. • NEW YORK & LONDON
1981

Library of Congress Cataloging in Publication Data

McCarthy, Joseph M., 1940–
  Pierre Teilhard de Chardin : a comprehensive
bibliography.

  (Garland reference library of the humanities ;
v. 158)
  Includes indexes.
  1. Teilhard de Chardin, Pierre—Bibliography.
I. Title. II. Series.
Z8863.78.M37 [B2430.T374]   016.56   78-68299
ISBN 0-8240-9783-1   AACR2

Printed on acid-free, 250-year-life paper
Manufactured in the United States of America

CONTENTS

10-12-81

PREFACE

Twenty years ago, I paid fifty cents for a twelve-page, mimeographed Teilhard bibliography by Robert T. Francoeur and Judith Visyak (Item 1545 in this compilation). Since that time, I've consulted a number of other Teilhard bibliographies in order to try to keep abreast of the flood of publications by and about Teilhard. Of these bibliographies, I found two to be of central importance: that by Joan Jarque i Jutglar (Item 2068) and Laszlo Polgar's annual compilation of teilhardiana (Item 3205). The former, now more than a decade old, made no attempt to cover works by Teilhard, while the latter is available only in annual cumulations in *Archivum Historicum Societatis Iesu*. Therefore, it has seemed worthwhile to compile an up-to-date bibliography including works both by and about Teilhard, with the most comprehensive possible coverage.

In the quarter-century since his death, Teilhard has been hailed as the Copernicus of a new theological understanding and damned as a singularly dangerous heretic. This distinguished paleontologist, unknown in his lifetime outside a small circle of friends and fellow professionals, burst upon the consciousness of the world at large with the posthumous publication of his *Le phénomène humain* (Item 4702). His conception of teleological evolution thrilled those who saw it as a means of understanding man's destiny or of reconciling Catholicism and the scientific age, at the same time that it horrified others who saw it as pseudoscientific nonsense or as a fatal concession to the encroachment of science upon theology. The result has been a debate of fierce intensity in which all too many of the contributions on both sides have lacked objectivity, clarity and charity. A noticeable cooling of tempers in recent years affords the hope that future studies may be characterized by less heat and more light. In the hope of encouraging such future studies, I offer this tool.

Some years ago, Rev. John J. Connelly gave me my first opportunity to lecture on Teilhard and quickened a spark of interest without which this compilation might never have occurred or appealed to me, and I am grateful for his encouragement. My greatest debt of gratitude is to my wife and children, who, despite having had to share me with this project for so long, have always been generous in encouraging my scholarly interests.

Joseph M. McCarthy
Suffolk University
Boston, Mass.
Easter Sunday, 1980

NOTE TO THE USER

The bibliography is in two sections: Part I, Works About Teilhard de Chardin, and Part II, Works By Teilhard de Chardin.

The first part, arranged alphabetically by author, cites works in the language of original publication; where useful, titles are translated into English and placed in square brackets following the foreign-language title. Any subsequent editions and/or translations of the work are then listed chronologically.

The second section lists Teilhard's works alphabetically by title. Works produced in collaboration with others are listed at the end, alphabetically by the name of the first coauthor. Typescripts and manuscripts cited as located in Paris are at the Fondation Teilhard de Chardin, 38 rue Geoffroy St.-Hilaire, Paris 5e.

In both sections, shorter works are cross-referenced to and from anthologies where they are collected. Within periodical citations, the first number following the colon is, in most cases, the volume number, with subsequent numbers referring to pages. Where only one number or number run follows the colon, this is the page reference.

There are comprehensive subject indexes to the two sections.

Works About Teilhard de Chardin

1. A.F.T. "Recherches paléo-anthropologiques en Afrique."
   Revue Teilhard de Chardin (1962): 10, 23-26.

2. "A propos du Père Teilhard de Chardin." *Cahiers d'action
   littéraire* (1958): 22, 6.

3. Aarts, L.M. "De verwachting van de parousie." *Ons
   Geestelijk Leven* (1964-65): 41, 361-367.

4. Abad, Miguel Angel. "La cosmosgenesis en Teilhard de
   Chardin." *Ensayos* (1966): 44, 8-12.

5. Abascal Cobo, Manuel A. *Cosmología evolutiva: (filosofía
   dinámica de Teilhard de Chardin*. Santander: Instituto
   Cultural de Cantabria, Instituto Prehistoria y
   Arqueología Sautuola, Disputación Provincial de Santander, 1974.

6. Abendroth, Walter von. "Das denkerische Abenteuer
   Teilhard de Chardins." *Die Zeit* (1964): 5, 21.

7. Abraham, Pierre. "Notes de carnet." *Europe* (1965):
   431/432, 3-11.

8. Abrami, Vittorio. "Mlle. Mortier de Chardin." *La fiera
   letteraria*, February 10, 1966.

9. Abril Castelló, Vidal. "Teilhard de Chardin, filósofo
   del derecho (Possibilidades de su pensamiento jurídico."
   Anales de la filosofía del derecho (1970): 15, 139-196.

10. Adalberto da Postioma, Fr. "Il concetto di storia in
    Teilhard de Chardin." *Tempo e storicità dell'uomo*.
    Atti del Terzo Convegno nazionale dei docenti di
    filosofia. Padova: Gregoriana, 1971, pp. 145-151.

11. Adams, D. "Christ and the Possible Future." *Listening*
    (1972): 7, 63-73.

12. Adams, James J. "St. Paul and Teilhard de Chardin."
    Item 607, pp. 1-9.

13. Adisusanta, Francis. "Teilhard's Idea of Man." *Anjali*
    (1967): 18, 33-41.

14. Admetller, J. "El fenómeno teilhardiano." *El ciervo*
    (1969): 182, 16-17.

15. Ágh, Attila. "Anthropologische Voraussetzungen der
    Konvergenz." *Acta teilhardiana* (1970): 7, 19-23.

16. ————. "Filosofskaja antropologija Teilharda de Chardina."
    Voprosy filosofii (1970): 175-179.
    "Die philosophische Anthropologie Teilhard de Chardins."
    Perspektiven der Zukunft (1971): 5, 3-5.

17. ————. "Formirovanije filosofkoj antropologii Teilharda
    de Chardina." [Formation of the Philosophical Anthro-
    pology of Teilhard de Chardin.] *Filosofskije nauki*
    (1969): 141-148.

18. ————. "Teilhard de Chardin filózofiai antropológiá-
    jához." [Concerning Teilhard de Chardin's Philosophical
    Anthropology.] *Világosság* (1967): 4, 11-21.

19. ————. "'Tudományos' istenkeresés és antropológiai
    kutatás Teilhard de Chardin munkásságaban." ["Scientific
    Search for God and Anthropological Research in the
    Work of Teilhard de Chardin.] *Magyar Filozófiai Szemle*
    (1968): 12, 1-61.

20. Agretti Aquino, Francisco. "A humanidade a caminho de
    Deus." *Convivium* (1965): 3, 66-86.

21. Aguilera, César. "Perspectivas historico-religiosas
    sobre el pensamiento de Teilhard de Chardin." Item
    745, pp. 132-169.

22. Aguirre, Emiliano. "Entre lo nuevo y lo eterno." *La
    estafeta literaria* (1964): 290, 9-10.

23. ————. "El legado del P. Teilhard de Chardin." *Revista
    de Antropologia y Etnologia* (1955): 9, 9-21.

24. ————. "El mañana de la evolución." *Cuadernos his-
    panoamericanos* (1966): 199, 5-19.

25. ————. "Nuevas trayectorias paleontólogicas." *Proyección*
    (1955): 7, 38-41.

26. ———. "Teilhard de Chardin." *La estafeta literaria*
(1963): 280, 2.

27. Aimond, Charles-Eugène. "Comment le Père Teilhard de
Chardin, soldat et philosophe, vécut la guerre." *Ecclesia* (1965): 198, 53-54.

28. Albert de l'Annonciation, Fr. "Autour de Teilhard de
Chardin." *Carmel* (1968): 145-150.

29. Alberti, Ottorino. "L'opera scientifica di Teilhard de
Chardin." *Aquinas* (1969): 12, 369-396.
Also in Item 33.

30. ———. "Osservazioni sulla genesi del pensiero teilhardiano." *Aquinas* (1969): 12, 123-157.
Also in Item 33.

31. ———. "Riflessioni su Teilhard de Chardin en merito al
recente volume di P. Philippe de la Trinité." *Divinitas* (1968): 12, 581-600.

32. ———. "Rilievi critici sul pensiero di Teilhard de
Chardin." *Aquinas* (1969): 12, 469-517.
Also in Item 33.

33. ———. *La scienza nel pensiero di Teilhard de Chardin.*
Roma: Lateran University Press, 1969. Contains Items
29, 30, 32.

34. Alçada Baptista, Antonio. "Notas para una moral activa."
O tempo e o modo (1966j: 37, 456-465.

35. ———. "Reflexão sobre a democracia em Teilhard de
Chardin." *O tempo e o modo* (1963): 9, 1-9.

36. Alemany, Carlos. "A los quince años de su muerte. 'El
fenomeno Teilhard' visto per Mlle. Mortier." *Hechos y
dichos*, October, 1970, pp. 35-37.

37. ———. "La nueva frontera de la humanidad en Teilhard de
Chardin." *Ensayos* (1968): 53, 35-41.

38. Alessandrini, Ludovico. "Il 'caso' Teilhard de Chardin."
Orizzonti (1965): 20, 6-8.

39. Alexander, Thomas. "Declaration of Cosmic Interdependence:
An Introduction into 'Teilhardian Perspective.'" *The
Teilhard Review* (1971): 6, 46-50.

40. ———. *The Vision of Teilhard de Chardin Programmed for
     V.I.P.'s.* New York: Vantage Press, 1969.

41. Alioto, Joseph L. "Teilhard and Political Determinism."
     Item 528, pp. 53-63.

42. Allard, Guy-H. "Teilhard de Chardin." *Maintenant* (1965):
     42, 191-193.

43. Allegra, Gabriele. *Il primato di Cristo in S. Paulo e in
     Duns Scoto. Dialogo col P. Teilhard de Chardin SJ.* Pa-
     lermo: Crociata del Vangelo, 1966.
     *My Conversations with Teilhard de Chardin on the Primacy
     of Christ, Peking 1942-1945.* Chicago: Franciscan Herald
     Press, 1971.

44. Aller, Catherine. *The Challenge of Pierre Teilhard de
     Chardin.* New York: Exposition Press, 1964.
     Also 2d ed., 1967.

45. Allesandri, M. "Il pensiero de Pierre Teilhard de Chardin."
     Divinitas (1959): 3, 345-364.

46. Almagno, Romano S. *A Basic Teilhard Bibliography.* New
     York: American Teilhard de Chardin Association, 1968.
     Bibliografia teilhardiana, 1955-1970. Firenze: Centro
     di studio e di ricerca Teilhard de Chardin, Istituto
     Stensen, 1970.
     A Basic Teilhard Bibliography. Item 2196, pp. 145-
     165.

47. ———. "Emmanuel de Breuvery, S.I." *Acta teilhardiana*
     (1970): 7, 89.

48. Almeida Sampaio, Laura F. "Teilhard nos fala de felici-
     dade." *Convivium* (1965): 3, 87-96.

49. Almquist, Kurt. "Aspects de l'idolâtrie teilhardienne."
     Études traditionelles (1968): 69, 251-260.

50. Alonso, Aurelio. "Ustedes, nosotros, la fe. Aurelio
     Alonso responde a 'Mundo católico.'" *El caimán barbudo*
     (1966): 9, 2-5.

51. Altner, Günter. *Schöpfungsglaube und Entwicklungs
     gedanke in der protestantischen Theologie zwischen
     Ernst Haeckel und Teilhard de Chardin.* Zürich: E.V.G.,
     1965.

52. Álvarez Álvarez, José L. "Teilhard de Chardin, profeta o
    hereje? Una visión objetiva de su pensamiento a través
    de sus críticos y de sus defensores." *Vida nueva* (1968):
    626, 15-22.

53. Álvarez de Juan, Manuel. *Ciencia, humanismo, transcendencia
    (Reflexiones en torno a Teilhard de Chardin)*. Calahorra:
    Alvarez, 1977.

53a. ———. "Ciencia y humanismo." *Revista augustiniana de
    espiritualidad* (1975): 16, 363-373.

54. ———. "Ética y ciencia. Valor humano de la investiga-
    cion en Tielhard de Chardin." *Revista augustiniana de
    espiritualidad* (1975): 16, 103-113.

55. ———. "La formación del científico y Teilhard de Chardin."
    Typescript. Universidad de Valencia, 1972.

56. Alvergnat, Louis. "Extrait du courrier reçu au sujet de
    Claude Tresmontant sur 'Le Père Teilhard de Chardin et la
    Théologie.'" *Lettre* (1962): 52, 24-25.

57. Alves, Vittorino de Sousa. "O conceito de pessõa no fenomen-
    ologia." *Revista portuguesa de filosofia* (1972): 28, 299-
    323.

58. Amaral, Yvette. "O outro Teilhard." *Semana católico*, July
    9, 1967, p. 3.

59. Amato, Angelo. "La cristologia cosmica di Teilhard de Char-
    din." *Problemi attuali di cristologia*. Roma: Libreria
    Ateneo Salesiano, 1975, pp. 95-124.

60. Amato, Franz. "Un maestro della cultura contemporanea:
    Teilhard de Chardin." *Quarta generazione* (1963): 5, 50-
    56; 9, 57-62; 11, 55-60.

61. Ambacher, Michel. "Réflexions sur la 'Physique général-
    isée' du P. Teilhard de Chardin." *Dialogue* (1964-65):
    3, 353-362.

62. Amen, Mark. "Teilhard de Chardin's conception of man."
    Duns Scotus Philosophical Association (1967): 31, 132-155.

63. Amidei, V.B. "Il modernismo di Teilhard de Chardin." *Ad-
    veniat regnum tuum* (1967): 5, 33-60.

64. Ancona, Leonardo. "Le dimensioni psichologiche del Milieu divin." Item 2744, pp. 109-120. Also in *Testimonianze* (1965): 8, 744-755. "Les dimensions psychologiques du Milieu divin." Item 2744 trans., pp. 102-113.

65. Anderson, James F. "Teilhard's Christianized Cosmology." *Heythrop Journal* (1972): 63-67.

66. ———. "Teilhard's Cosmological Kinship to Aristotle." *New Scholasticism* (1971): 45, 584-589.

67. Anderson, John Joseph. "Eros in Teilhard de Chardin. A Study in the Function of Eros in the Evolution of Love-Energy in Ultimate Christian Moral Motivation." Doctoral dissertation, Fordham University, 1971.

68. André, Paul. "La féconde expérience de Teilhard de Chardin." *Hôtel-Revue*, January, 1961, p. 27.

69. André-Vincent, I. "La synthèse cosmogénétique de Teilhard de Chardin et le droit." *Archive de philosophie du droit* (1965): 10, 33-63.

69a. Anér, Kerstin. "Teilhard de Chardin, en presentation." Item 1944, pp. 12-29.

70. Aninat de V.R., Andrés. *El cristianismo en óptica de evolución. Apuntes teológicos inspirados en las doctrinas de Teilhard de Chardin.* Valparaíso: Universidad Católica de Valparaíso, 1973.

71. Anthony, G.F.P. "Whither Evolution? Some Questions to Teilhard de Chardin." *International Philosophical Quarterly* (1975): 15, 75-82.

71a. Antolović, Josip. "Teilhard de Chardin i pobožnost Srcu Isusovu." [Teilhard de Chardin and the Cult of the Sacred Heart.] *Obnovljeni Život* (1978): 33, 356-361.

72. Antunes, Manuel. "Teilhard de Chardin." *Grandes contemporaneos.* Lisboa: Verbo, 1973, pp. 93-105.

73. ———. "Teilhard de Chardin dez anos depois." *Broteria* (1965): 80, 451-460.

74. Apollonia, Luigi d'. "Note sur Pierre Teilhard de Chardin SJ." *Relations* (1958): 18, 206-209.

75. ———. "Le Saint-Office, le P. Teilhard et ses disciples." *Relations* (1962): 22, 254.

76. Ara, Masahito. "Mokujirokuteki uchûron. [Apocalyptic Cosmology.] *Misuzu* (1964): 17-19.

77. Aragonnès, Claude. "Extraits de lettres de voyage et carnets de route du Père Teilhard de Chardin." *Prestige français* (1956): 15, 41-43, 70.

78. ———. "Introduction à 'Genèse d'une pensée.'" Item 4490, pp. 35-32.

79. ———. "Lettres de voyage et de séjour du Père Teilhard de Chardin." *Revue de Paris* (1957): 9, 19-32.

80. ———. "Le 'Milieu divin' du Père Teilhard de Chardin." *Revue de Paris* (1958): 10, 132-135.

81. ———. "Le Pére Teilhard de Chardin et le Phénomène Humain." *L'Auvergne littéraire, artistique et historique* (1956): 151, 1-7.

82. ———. "Pierre Teilhard de Chardin." *Revue de Paris* (1959): 164-166.

83. ———. "Pierre Teilhard de Chardin à Sarcenat." *L'Auvergne littéraire, artistique et historique* (1957): 156, 7-13. Also Item 3292, pp. 79-88.

84. ———. "Pierre Teilhard de Chardin. Lettres du front (1914-1918)." *Revue Teilhard de Chardin* (1960): 1/2, 2-10.

85. ———. "Le voyageur et l'explorateur." *La table ronde* (1955): 90, 25-28.

86. Arata, Rodolfo. *L'eterno nella coscienza.* Roma: Cinque Lune, 1972.

87. Arboleda, Alirio. "Mensaje de Teilhard de Chardin (Visión de conjunto)." *Universidad de Antioquia* (1969): 45, 587-604.

88. Archambault, Liette. "Humanisme scientifique. 'L'energie humaine' par Teilhard de Chardin." *Collège et famille* (1965): 22, 63-70.

89. Archanjo, José Luiz. "O 'anti-evolucionismo' de Teilhard." *Revista portuguesa de filosofia* (1972): 28, 332-354.

90. ———. "A hiperfísica de Pierre Teilhard de Chardin."
     Doctoral thesis, Pontifical Catholic University of São
     Paulo, 1974.

91. Arcidiacono, Salvatore. "Energia radiale e tagenziale."
     Il fuoco (1961): 4, 3-6.

92. ———. "Entropía y sintropía." *Folia humanistica* (1972):
     10, 429-440.

93. Ardusso, Franco, et al. *Introduzione alla teologia contempor-
     anea. Profilo storico e antologia.* Torino: Società Edi-
     trice Internazionale, 1972. See pp. 269-287.

94. Arfel, Alla. "Pierre Teilhard et Jean-Paul Sartre devant
     la vie." *Revue Teilhard de Chardin* (1964): 20/21, 41-44.

95. Arias, Isidro. "Cristo, primer querido y punto Omega del
     universo. El cristocentrismo en Duns Escoto y en Teilhard
     de Chardin." *Reflejos* (1965): 59-103.

96. Armagnac, Christian d'. "Bulletin d'études teilhardiennes."
     Études (1965): 322, 664-668; (1969): 330, 449-453; (1970):
     332, 615-622; (1977): 347, 695-699.

97. ———. "De Bergson à Teilhard. La nature, l'homme et Dieu."
     Études (1964): 320, 166-177.

98. ———. "De Blondel à Teilhard: Nature et Intériorité."
     Archives de philosophie (1958): 21, 298-312.

99. ———. "Epistémologie et philosophie d'évolution." *Ar-
     chives de philosophie* (1960): 23, 153-163.

100. ———. "Études récentes sur le Père Teilhard." *Civitas*
     (1963): 18, 379-389.
     Also *Études* (1963): 316, 52-64.

101. ———. "Études teilhardiennes." *Études* (1966): 325, 131-
     135.

102. ———. "Nouveaux commentaires sur Teilhard." *Etudes*
     (1967): 327, 422-429.
     "Neue Bücher über Teilhard." *Dokumente* (1967): 23,
     73-76.

103. ———. "Pascal et Teilhard, témoins de Jesus-Christ."
     Christus (1968): 15, 281-284.

104. ———. "La pensée du Père Teilhard de Chardin comme apologetique moderne." *Nouvelle revue théologique* (1962): 6, 598-621.
Also *Études teilhardiennes* (1968): 1, 61-89.
"El pensamiento de Teilhard de Chardin como apologetica moderna." *Selecciones de teologia* (1963): 5, 45-55.

105. ———. "Il pensiero teologico nel Milieu divin." Item 2744, pp. 63-84.
"Les fondaments philosophiques et théologiques du Milieu divin." Item 2744 trans., pp. 56-78.

106. ———. "Le phénomène humain." *Journal A.C.*, January, 1956, pp. 5, 11.

107. ———. "Philosophie de la nature et méthode chez le Père Teilhard de Chardin." *Archives de philosophie* (1957): 20, 5-41.

108. ———. *Pierre Teilhard de Chardin témoin de la foi*. Paris: Bloud & Gay, 1966.

109. ———. "Le premier Teilhard: le Christ et le Monde." *Études* (1965): 322, 652-663.
Also in *Perspectives* (1965): 23, 22-30.
"Teilhard elsö tanulmányai." *Merleg* (1965): 2, 91-95.

110. ———. "Réflexions sur deux aspects complémentaires du vivant: insertion et émergence." *Recherches et débats* (1964): 48, 172-178.

111. ———. "Teilhard de Chardin est-il gidien?" *Les études philosophiques* (1966): 21, 533-537.

112. Armand, Louis. "Dix ans apres." Item 1259, pp. 61-67.

113. Arnaud, Joseph. "Tâches humaines, espoirs humains et espérance chrétienne chez Teilhard et Moltmann." *Recherches et réflexions sur l'espérance chrétienne aujourd'hui*. Paris: Editions ouvrières, 1974, pp. 79-116.

114. ———. "Teilhard est-il matérialiste? Le 'dedans,' le 'radial' et le 'tangentiel' chez Teilhard de Chardin (Essai d'interprétation)." *Impacts* (1968): 5-35.

115. Arnoux, Jacques d'. *Nouvelles paroles d'un revenant.*
      Justice pour Dieu. Paris: Nouvelles éditions latines,
      1965. See pp. 145-148.

116. Aron, Robert. "Pierre Teilhard de Chardin." *Prestige*
      français (1965): 15, 38-40.

117. ————. "Teilhard de Chardin ou le génie contagieux."
      Les nouvelles littéraires, April, 1965, p. 3.

118. Arroyo, Ana. "Et par terre gisait un manteau...."
      Rencontre Orient-Occident, January/February, 1958,
      pp. 19-20.

119. Arrupe, Pedro. "La Compagnie de Jésus devant les pro-
      blemes du collége chrétien." *La documentation catho-*
      lique, September 19, 1965, pp. 1601-1606.

120. ————. "Sobre Teilhard de Chardin (Respuesta a la
      prensa)." *Corporación* (1968): 81, 9.
      Also *Saint-Luc (1965)*: 10, 579-580.

121. Arsenault, F. "L'éthique sociale chez Teilhard de
      Chardin." *Studies in Religion* (1971): 1, 25-44.

122. Artero Bernad, Félix. "Reflexiones y proyectos para
      'Comunidad,' por una integración de la ciencia social."
      Comunidad (1968): 13, 309-316.

123. Artur, Jules. "A propos de P. Teilhard de Chardin. En
      relisant Edouard Schuré." *Pensée catholique* (1966):
      102, 52-60.

124. ————. "Le dernier ouvrage sur Teilhard de Chardin."
      Pensée catholique (1969): 123, 97-115.

125. Aubert, Jean-Marie. "Amiguïté de Teilhard de Chardin."
      Prêtres diocesains (1963): 307-316.

126. ————. *Philosophie de la nature.* Paris: Beauchesne,
      1965. See pp. 313-314.

127. ————. *Recherche scientifique et foi chrétienne.*
      Paris: Fayard, 1962.

128. ————. "Teilhard de Chardin est-il hérétique?" Mimeo-
      graphed. Toulouse: Centre culturel catholique, 1963.

129. Aubry, Joseph. "Teilhard de Chardin: avventuriero o esploratore?" *Dimensioni* (1965): 2, 1-5, 42. Also in Item 130.

130. ———. "Teilhard de Chardin. Le idee e l'uomo: l'universo teso al punto Omega. Ombre e luci: avventuriero e esploratore." *Uomini come segni.* Torino: Edizioni Periodici SEI, 1968, pp. 7-22. Re-edition of Item 129 and Item 131.

131. ———. "Teilhard de Chardin: l'universo teso al punto Omega." *Dimensioni* (1965): 1, 1-6. Also in Item 130.

132. Auersperg, Alfred von. "Genetisch-interpretierte Informationstheorie und kybernetisch-orientierte Informationstheorie im Lichte der Energielehre von Teilhard de Chardin." *Jahrbuch für Psychologie, Psychotherapie und medizinische Anthropologie* (1967): 15, 88-99.

133. ———. "Die Krise in der Biologie." *Jahrbuch für Psychologie, Psychotherapie und medizinische Anthropologie* (1967): 77-82.

134. ———. "Kritische vorbemerkungen zur Lekture Pierre Teilhard de Chardin 'Le phénomène humain.'" *Der Nervenarzt* (1961): 32, 229-230.

135. ———. *Poesie und Forschung: Goethe, Weizsäcker, Teilhard de Chardin.* Stuttgart: Enke, 1965.

136. ———. "Teilhard de Chardin und die moderne Anthropologie." *Hippokrates* (1963): 111-143.

137. ———. "Versuch einer anthropologischen Deutung des Selectionsprinzipes im Sinne Teilhard de Chardins." *Jahrbuch für Psychologie, Psychotherapie und medizinische Anthropologie* (1964): 169-171.

138. ———. "Vorläufige und rückläufige Bestimmung in der Physiogenese." *Jahrbuch fur Psychologie, Psychotherapie und medizinische Anthropologie*

139. August, Eugen R. "Tennyson and Teilhard: The Faith of In Memorian." *Publications of the Modern Language Association of America* (1969): 84, 217-226. Also Item 607, pp. 31-56.

140. Aumont, Michèle. "Teilhard ce constructeur." Revue Teil-
     hard de Chardin (1968): 36, 47-50.

141. Ausprenger, Franz. "Für Teilhard ist die Menschheit jung."
     Europa (1961): 12, 56-57.

142. "Autour de 'teilhardogenèse'?" Ephemerides carmeliticae
     (1964): 15, 190-223.
     Also Pensée catholique (1964): 89. 49-88.

143. Ayala, F.J. "The Evolutionary Thought of Teilhard de
     Chardin." Colloquium (1967): 207-216.

144. ────. "A Note on Evolution and Religion in the Light
     of Teilhard's 'Divine Milieu.'" Zygon (1968): 3, 426-
     431.

145. Bablon, René. Évolution, révolution: ou, Teilhard n'avait
     pas voulu ça. Paris: La Pensée Universelle, 1974.

146. Babolin, Albino. Il Movimento di Gallarte. I convegni
     dal 1966 al 1970. Padova: Editrice Gregoriana, 1971.
     See pp. 43-59.

147. Babosov, E.M. "Teilhardismus. Versuch einer Synthese
     zwischen Wissenschaft un Christentum." Perspektiven
     der Zukunft (1971): 5, 6.

148. ────. Teilhardizm. Popytka sinteza nauki i khristian-
     sivo. [Teilhardism: An Attempt at Synthesis of Science
     and Christianity.] Minsk: Vysheishaya Shkola, 1970.

149. Bacot, Jacques. "Autour du Congrès Universel des Croy-
     ants." Item 3292, pp. 143-150.

150. Badacz, B. "Dialogue entre Blondel et Teilhard de Chardin."
     Résurrection (1962): 22, 42-54.

151. Bagdanavicius, Vytautas. "Teilhard de Chardin apie
     zmogaus veiksmu sudievinima." [Teilhard de Chardin
     on the Consecration of Human Effort.] Aidai (1964):
     10-16.

152. Balari, Juan. "Teilhard de Chardin: Un hijo muy ilustre
     de la Iglesia." Mensajero (1975): 35-37.

153. Balducci, Ernesto: "Evoluzionismo e cristianesimo."
     Testimonianze (1959): 15, 428-436.

154. Balek, Richard W. "The Birth of Life and Consciousness." Item 1544, pp. 92-97.

155. Ball, R.E. "Teilhard de Chardin and the Invisible." *The Teilhard Review* (1969-70): 4, 86-92.

156. Ballester Escalas, R. *Teilhard de Chardin*. Barcelona: Toray, 1967.

157. Ballivián Calderón, René. *Relaciones humanas en una nueva dimension, a la luz de las ideas de Teilhard de Chardin*. La Paz: Librería Editorial Juventud, 1974.

158. Baltasar, Hans Urs von. "The Achievement of Henri de Lubac." *Thought* (1976): 51, 7-49.

159. ————. "Ein folgenschweres protestantisches Werk über Teilhard de Chardin." *Civitas* (1969): 5, 434-437. See Item 1075.

160. ————. *Das Ganze im Fragment. Aspekte der Geschichtstheologie*. Einsiedeln: Benziger-Verlag, 1963.

161. ————. "Die Spiritualität Teilhards de Chardin." *Wort und Wahrheit* (1963): 18, 339-350
"La espiritualidad de Teilhard de Chardin." *Orbis catholicus* (1964): 7, 220-237.
"A espiritualidade do Teilhard de Chardin." *Vozes*. (1964): 58, 352-367.

162. Baltazar, Eulalio R. *Teilhard and the Supernatural*. Baltimore: Helicon, 1966.

163. ————. "Teilhard de Chardin: A Philosophy of Processionism." *Continuum* (1964-65): 2, 87-97.
Also *New Theology*. New York: Macmillan, 1965, vol. 2, pp. 134-150.

164. Balzan, Paul. "Le chemin de l'esprit." *Citadelle* (1963): 4, 7-8.

165. Banka, Jozef. "Metodologiczne aspekty dziela Teilharda de Chardin." [Methodological Aspects of the Thought of Teilhard de Chardin.] *Kwartalnik Historii Nauki i Techniki* (1967): 12, 557-570.

166. Barbour, George H. "At Work in the Field." Item 1544, pp. 24-34.

167. ————. "The Future of Man by Pierre Teilhard de Chardin."
      Union Seminary Quarterly Review (1965): 2, 198-200.

168. ————. "A Geologist in the Field." Item 501, pp. 32-39.
      Also Item 497. pp. 32-39.

169. ————. *In the Field with Teilhard de Chardin.* New York:
      Herder and Herder, 1965. Contains Items 4553, 4566.
      Teilhard de Chardin sur le terrain. Paris: Sueil,
      1965.
      *Unterwegs mit Teilhard de Chardin. Auf den Spuren
      des Lebens in drei Kontinenten.* Freiburg-im-Breisgau
      & Olten: Walter-Verlag, 1967.
      Het vereldwerk van Teilhard de Chardin. Utrecht:
      Spectrum, 1967.

170, ————. "Memorial to Pierre Teilhard de Chardin SJ (1881-
      1955)." *Proceedings of the Geological Society of Amer-
      ica* (1956): 169-176.

171. ————. "Obituary of P. Teilhard de Chardin." *Proceed-
      ings of the Geological Society of London* (1955): 132-133.

172. ————. "Pierre Teilhard de Chardin." *Report of the Third
      Pan-African Congress on Prehistory.* London: Chatto &
      Windus, 1957, pp. 28-29.

173. ————. "Sur le terrain avec Teilhard de Chardin." *Ec-
      clesia* (1965): 195, 117.

174. ————. "Teilhard de Chardin." *Journal of the Paleonto-
      logical Society of India* (1957): 2, 21-23.

175. ————. "Teilhard de Chardin as a Geologist in the Field."
      Week-end Magazine, July 17, 1965, p. 1.

176. ————. "Unterwegs mit Teilhard de Chardin." *Litterarium*
      (1967): 15, 20-21. Excerpt from Item 169.

177. ————. "With Teilhard in China." *Catholic Digest*, Sep-
      tember, 1965, pp. 94-101. Excerpt from Item 169.

178. Barbour, Ian. "Five Ways of Reading Teilhard." *Teilhard
      Review* (1968): 1, 3-20.
      Also *Soundings* (1968): 115-145.

179. ————. *Issues in Science and Religion.* London: SCM
      Press, 1966. See pp. 394ff.

180. ———. "The Significance of Teilhard." *The Christian Century* (1967): 84, 1098-1102.

181. ———. "Teilhard's Process Metaphysics." *Journal of Religion* (1969): 49, 136-159.

182. Baresta, Luc. "Gespräch mit einem Thomisten." *Dokumente* (1967): 23, 52-57.

183. ———. "Teilhard malgre le teilhardisme ou: difficultés d'une saisie totale du réel." *La France catholique*, December 16, 1966, p. 6.

184. Barga, Luis de la. "La Compañia de Jesús desea el diálogo." *El correo catalán*, June 15, 1965, p. 3.

185. Bariège, Joan. "Un jésuite vous dévoile le secret de l'homme." *Constellation* (1961): 157, 133-139.

186. Barjon, Louis. "L'appel de Pâques." *Revue Teilhard de Chardin* (1963): 17, 13-18. Contains Item 4558.

187. ———. *Le combat de Pierre Teilhard de Chardin.* Québec: Les Presses de l'Université Laval, 1971.

188. ———. "Fidélité chrétienne et religieuse du Père Teilhard de Chardin." *Foi vivante* (1963): 4, 70-82.

189. ———. "Le monde en expansion--Pierre Teilhard de Chardin." *Mondes d'écrivains--Destinées d'hommes.* Paris: Casterman, 1960, pp. 211-243.

190. ———. "Le Père Teilhard de Chardin." Typescript. 2 vols.; Paris: Fondation Teilhard de Chardin, 1956.

191. ———. "Teilhard de Chardin. Goût de réel." *Vie enseignante* (1966): 183, 17-19; 185, 1, 12. Also Item 1259, pp. 86-89.

192. ———. "Teilhard de Chardin ou l'univers réconcilé." *Union des religieuses enseignantes* (1966-67): 3, 9-24.

193. ———, and Pierre Leroy. *La carrière scientifique de Pierre Teilhard de Chardin.* Monaco: Rocher, 1964. Contains Item 4742.
La carriera scientifica di Teilhard de Chardin. Roma: Paoline, 1966.
A carriera científica de Teilhard de Chardin. Lisboa: Livraria Morais, 1965.

194. Barmann, Lawrence F. "Some Recent Teilhardiana." *Clergy Review* (1969): 54, 124-129.

195. ——. "The Teilhard Syndrome. Damnation by Insinuation." *The Tablet*, February 12, 1966, pp. 185-186. See also February 19, 1966, p. 226.

196. Barnello, George. "Planetary Citizenship: New Hope for Humanity." *International Foundations of Education Quarterly* (1974): 1, 143-146.

197. Baron, Enrique. "Cristocentrismo en Teilhard de Chardin. Selección de textos." *Proyección* (1974): 21, 104-112.

198. Baron, Jacques. "Les leçons d'une carrière à l'américaine." *Enterprise* (1961): 641, 45, 47, 49, 51, 53.

199. Barral, M. Louis. *Eléments du bati scientifique teilhardien.* Monaco: Rocher, 1964.
    Fundamentos científicos de Teilhard de Chardin. Lisboa: Livraria Morais, 1965.

200. Barreau, Hervé. "Signification religeiuse de l'oeuvre de Teilhard de Chardin: christianisme, esotérisme ou évolutionnisme." *Akten des XIV. Internationalen Kongresses für Philosophie.* Wien: Herder, 1970, vol. 5, pp. 394-396.

201. Barrio, J.L. "La socialización en P. Teilhard de Chardin." *Casiciaco* (1971): 24, 168-177.

202. Barthélemy-Madaule, Madeleine. "Ambiente mistico e Ambiente divino." Item 2744, pp. 36-45.
    "Milieu mystique et Mileiu divin." Item 2744 trans., pp. 36-45.

203. ——. "A propos du travail de Cl. Tresmontant 'Le Père Teilhard de Chardin et la théologie.'" *Lettre* (1962): 52, 26-27.

204. ——. *Bergson et Teilhard de Chardin.* Paris: Seuil, 1963.
    Bergson und Teilhard de Chardin. Die Anfänge einer neuen Welterkenntnis. Olten & Freiburg im Breisgau: Walter-Verlag, 1970.

205. ——. "Bergson et Teilhard de Chardin." Item 3041, pp. 116-131.
    Also *Les études bergsoniennes* (1960): 5, 65-81.

206. ———. "Comment le Père Teilhard a jugé le marxisme."
     Témoignage chrétien, December 5, 1958.

207. ———. "La démarche teilhardienne et la notion de struc-
     ture." *Études teilhardiennes* (1969): 2, 6-12.

208. ———. "L'energie humaine par P. Teilhard de Chardin."
     L'éducation nationale (1962): 29, 21.

209. ———. "En quel sens peut-on dire que Teilhard soit
     philosophe?" *Livres de France* (1966): 4, 16-20.
     "La vision teilhardienne est-elle un philosophie?"
     Item 3903, pp. 155-175.
     "In welchem Sinne kann man von einer Teilhardischen
     Philosophie sprechen?" Item 1213, pp. 53-65.

210. ———. "L'homme et son prochain dans l'univers du Père
     Teilhard de Chardin." *Actes du 8e Congrès des Sociétés
     de philosophie de langue française, Toulouse 6-9 9˙1965.*
     Paris: Le Congrès, 1956, pp. 255-256.

211. ———. *L'idéologie du hasard et de la nécessité.* Paris:
     Seuil, 1972. See pp. 127-146.

212. ———. "Introduction à la methode chez Bergson et Teil-
     hard de Chardin." *Actes du 10e Congrès des Sociétés
     des philosophie de langue française.* Paris: Le Congrès,
     1959, pp. 211-216.

213. ———. "Introduction à un rapprochement entre Henri
     Bergson et Pierre Teilhard de Chardin." *Les études
     bergsoniennes* (1960): 5, 63-81.

214. ———. "La montée du mouvement social." Item 741, pp.
     57-74.

215. ———. "Morale chrétienne et morale marxiste." *Les
     Livres* (1961): 4, 32.

216. ———. "Mystique et recherche scientifique." *Études
     teilhardiennes* (1968): 91-106.

217. ———. "Notes à l'article 'Teilhard et l'histoire de
     G. Ronay." *Europe* (1965): 431/432, 128-130. See
     Item 3432.

218. ———. "La pensée politique de Teilhard de Chardin."
     France-forum (1958): 11, 16-20.

219. ———. "La personne dans la perspective teilhardienne."
     Recherches et débats (1962): 40, 66-78.

220. ———. *La personne et le drame humain chez Teilhard de
     Chardin.* Paris: Seuil, 1966.
     Also Paris: Seuil, 1967.

221. ———. "La perspective teilhardienne et l'action."
     Europe (1965): 431/432, 70-88.

222. ———. "Perspektiven Teilhard de Chardins." In Item
     1213.

223. ———. "Pierre Teilhard de Chardin. Une perspective
     phénoménologique." *Histoire de la philosophie euro-
     péene. II. Tableau de la philosophie contemporaine,*
     by A. Weber and D. Huisman. Paris: Fischbacher, 1957,
     pp. 263-276.

224. ———. "Pierre Teilhard de Chardin: La vision du passé."
     L'éducation nationale (1958): 14, 20-21.

225. ———. "La plus grande oeuvre de l'homme: L'hominisa-
     tion de sa propre espèce dans un universe personnalisé."
     Les études philosophiques (1957): 3, 153-156.

226. ———. "Pour dissiper quelques malentendus." Item
     1284, pp. 369-384.
     "Para dissipar algunos malentendias." Item 1284
     trans., pp. 113-133.
     "Per dissipare alcuni malentesi." *Nuovo osserva-
     tore* (1965): 6, 385-392.

227. ———. "Première thèse en Sorbonne sur le P. Teilhard
     de Chardin." *Union catholiques des scientifiques
     français. Bulletin* (1963): 74, 8-12.

228. ———. "Présence de Teilhard de Chardin." *Coopera-
     tion* (1967): 12, 5.

229. ———. "Prophétie, providence et histoire." *L'avenir,
     Semaine des intellectuels catholiques 1963.* Paris:
     Fayard, 1964, pp. 129-141.

230. ———. "Réflexions sur la methode et la perspective
     teilhardienne." *Les études philosophiques* (1966):
     21, 510-552.

231. ————. "Le sens mystique chez le Père Teilhard de Chardin." *L'âge nouveau* (1960): 110, 79-84.

232. ————. "Sur Teilhard de Chardin." *Les Livres* (1961): 8, 42.

233. ————. "Synthèse de l'esprit et de la matière." *Le Figaro littéraire*, September 17, 1960, p. 10.

234. ————. "Teilhard bafoué." *Témoignage chrétien*, November 29, 1966, p. 19.

235. ————. "Teilhard de Chardin." *La Cooperazione* (1967): 19, 12.

236. ————. "Teilhard de Chardin et l'amour du prochain." *Foi vivante* (1964): 18, 44-49.

237. ————. "Teilhard de Chardin, Neo-Marxism, Existentialism, a Confrontation." *International Philosophical Quarterly* (1961): 4, 648-667. Also Item 607, pp. 57-78.

238. ————. "Teilhard reconnu." *Témoignage chrétien*, October 13, 1966, pp. 25-26.

239. ————. "Teilhards wereldbeschouwing en de hedendaagse stromingen." Item 3724, pp. 52-72.

240. ————. "Trois ouvrages sur Pierre Teilhard de Chardin." *L'education nationale* (1959): 10, 18-19.

241. Bartnik, Czeslaw. "Extrait du précis de la methodologie teilhardienne d'histoire universelle." Item 3950, pp. 136-157.

242. ————. *Problem historii uniwersalnej w teilhardyzmie.* [The Problem of Universal History in Teilhard.] Lublin: Towarzystwo Naukowe Katolickiego Uniwersyteto Lubelskiego, 1972.

243. ————. *Teilhardowska wizja dziejow* [The Teilhardian Vision of History.] Lublin: Towarzystwo Naukowe Katolickiego Uniwersyteto Lubelskiego, 1975.

244. Basile, Joseph. *La formation culturelle des cadres et des dirigeants.* Belgique: Marabout, 1965. See pp. 77-83.

245. ———. *Teilhard de Chardin. Explication générale de
     l'univers et destin de l'homme.* Liege: Desver, 1961.

246. Bastaire, Jean. "Teilhard l'impatient." *Cahiers
     universitaires catholiques* (1965-66): 3/4, 146-159.

247. ———. "Teilhard vu par Henri de Lubac." *Esprit*
     (1962): 310, 512-513.

248. Bastide, Georges. "Correspondance." *Les études philo-
     sophiques* (1966): 4, 33.

249. ———. "Naturalisme et spiritualité: Le statut de
     la réflexion dans la pensée de Teilhard de Chardin."
     Les études philosophiques (1965): 20, 409-447.

250. Battaglia, F. "Evoluzionismo e Teilhard de Chardin."
     Evoluzionismo e storia umana. Brescia: Morcelliana,
     1968, pp. 62-67.

251. Baudiquey, Paul. "Comprende, aimer, adorer. La vision
     panchristique du Père Teilhard." *Rencontre* (1965):
     3-11.

252. ———. "Vers un nouveau type d'homme: Marx ou Teil-
     hard?" *Rencontre* (1964): 10-11, 14-16.

253. Baudry, Gérard-Henry. "L'apport de Teilhard à la thé-
     ologie contemporaine." *Revue Teilhard de Chardin*
     (1976): 65, 11-17.

254. ———. *Ce que croyait Teilhard.* Tours: Maine, 1971.
     Il credo di Teilhard. Torino: Editorial SFI:
     1972.

255. ———. *Cosmos et poésie. Essai sur Teilhard de Char-
     din.* Lille: G.-H. Baudry, 1976.

256. ———. "De la futurologie à l'eschatologie." *Revue
     Teilhard de Chardin* (1976): 67/68, 42-46.

257. ———. *Dictionnaire des correspondants de Teilhard de
     Chardin, suivi du répertoire chronologique des lettres
     publiées.* Lille: Cedex, 1974.

257a. ———. "Les grands axes de l'eschatologie teilhardienne
     (1946-1955)." *Mélanges de science religieuse* (1977):
     34, 213-235; (1978): 35, 37-71.

258. ———. "L'homme acteur de l'évolution: La nature hom-
      inisée." *Revue Teilhard de Chardin* (1975): 61/62, 65-
      73.

259. ———. "Mao et Teilhard, d'un petit livre rouge à
      l'autre." *Facultés catholiques de Lille. Bulletin*
      (1972): 1, 11-21.
      Also *Revue Teilhard de Chardin* (1973): 56, 13-17;
      57, 28-33.

260. ———. "La mystique de la recherche selon Teilhard."
      Revue Teilhard de Chardin (1974): 58/59, 49-56.

261. ———. "Péguy et Teilhard de Chardin, prophètes de
      l'espérance." *Facultés catholiques de Lille. Bul-
      letin* (1973): 2, 71-80.
      "Teilhard et Péguy: prophètes de l'espérance."
      Revue Teilhard de Chardin (1974): 60, 25-33.

262. ———. *Pierre Teilhard de Chardin: Bibliographie
      (1881-1972).* Lille: Facultés Catholiques, 1972.

263. ———. "Le problème de Dieu dans la philosophie de
      Teilhard de Chardin (Étude génétique). Mimeographed.
      Nantes: Faculté des lettres et sciences humaines de
      l'Université de Nantes, 1969.

264. ———. *Qui était Teilhard de Chardin? Introduction à
      sa vie et à son oeurve.* Lille: G.-H. Baudry, 1972.

265. ———. "La vie intérieure de Pierre Teilhard." *Revue
      Teilhard de Chardin* (1977): 70, 1-6.

266. Baum, Gregory. "Warning on Teilhard." Mimeographed.
      Paris: Fondation Teilhard de Chardin, 1962.
      Also *Catholic Messenger*, July 26, 1962, p. 10.

267. Baumer, Franz. *Teilhard de Chardin.* Berlin: Colloquium
      Verlag, 1971.

268. Baumer, Iso. "Pascal, Newman, Teilhard de Chardin."
      Orientierung (1962): 26, 204-208.

269. "Sprache und Denkstil bei Teilhard de Chardin."
      Schweizer Rundschau (1962): 61, 561-567.

270. Baumgartner, Friederich. "Eine Erschütterung geht durch
     die Christenheit. Die revolutionären Ideen des
     Jesuitenpaters Pierre Teilhard de Chardin, des
     Brückenbauers zwischen Religion und Naturwissen-
     schaften." *Die andere Welt* (1964): 15, 577-579.

271. Bausch, Horst. "Frohe Botschaft für das Atomzeitalter:
     Der Mensch wird gut." *Kristall* (1964): 26, 26-30.

272. Bavaud, Georges. "Comment comprendre le christologie de
     Pierre Teilhard de Chardin." *Civitas* (1966): 3, 114-
     120.
     "Come capire la cristologia di Teilhard de Chardin."
     Humanitas (1967): 22, 341-349.

273. Bavouzet, I., and I. Heckenroth. *Aggiornamento ou muta-
     tion?* St. Etienne (Loire): Dumas, 1965.

274. Bayce, Beatriz. *Aproximación a Teilhard de Chardin.*
     Montevideo: Arca, 1965.

275. Beaufrère, Marie-Noëlle. "Immanence et transcendance
     chez Teilhard de Chardin." Thesis for Diplome d'études
     supérieures de philosophie. Mimeographed. Paris:
     Université de Paris, 1965.

276. Beaujon, Edmond. "Teilhard de Chardin et la totalité."
     Journal de Genève, December 11, 1959, p. 3.

277. Beckmann, H.J. "Das Bild des Menschen nach Pierre Teil-
     hard de Chardin unter besonderer Berücksichtigung
     seines Werkes: 'Der Mensch im Kosmos.'" *Anzeiger für
     die katholische Geistlichkeit* (1961): 70, 370-390.

278. Beer, Jean de. "Au 'Colloque Teilhard' de Vézelay.
     L'union créatrice." *Le Monde*, September 10-11, 1967,
     p. 6.

279. ———. "L'émerveillement teilhardien." *Cahiers de
     vie franciscaine* (1960): 27, 176-181.

280. ———. "Glosy o Teilhardzie de Chardin." [Views on
     Teilhard de Chardin.] *Znak* (1962): 92/93, 247-250.

281. ———. "Hommage à Teilhard de Chardin. Une quinzaine
     à France-culture." *Le Monde*, April 1, 1965, p. 10.

282. ———. "Imaginaires, réalités et nourritures eucharistiques." Item 3093, pp. 257-274.

283. ———. "Le Milieu divin e i gentili." Item 2744, pp. 49-55.
"Le Milieu divin et les gentils." Item 2744 trans., pp. 46-51.

284. ———. "Une remarque sur l'espérance." *Europe* (1965): 431/432, 131-140.

285. ———. "Teilhard de Chardin: O cosmogonie extrem de originala." *Viaţa românesca* (1965): 12, 178-188.

286. ———. "Teilhard et l'espérance." *Cahiers littéraires* (1965): 13, 5-7.

287. ———. "Témoignage." Item 3292, pp. 173-178.

288. Bégouën, Max-Henri. "A la mémoire de Marguerite Teilhard-Chambon." Item 3041, pp. 46-49.

289. ———. "Ce que je dois au Père Teilhard de Chardin." *Europe* (1965): 431/432, 49-63.

290. ———. "1915. Au Front avec Teilhard de Chardin." *La table ronde* (1955): 90, 60-64.

291. ———. "Témoignage." Item 3292, pp. 15-38.

292. Belin-Milleron, J. "L'homme et le monde chez le P. Teilhard de Chardin." Typescript. Paris: À la Fondation Teilhard de Chardin, 1958.

293. ———. "Vers une morale commune des 'Rameux humains.'" Item 3041, pp. 84-94.

294. Bellofiore, Luigi. "Il dramma di Pierre Teilhard de Chardin (1881-1955)." *Prospettive* (1966): 287-293.

295. ———. "Il messagio di Pierre Teilhard de Chardin." *Prospettive* (1967): 1-30.

296. ———. "Il problema del mondo e Dio in Teilhard de Chardin." *Prospettive* (1966): 348-358.

297. ———. "Teilhard de Chardin." *Prospettive* (1967): 81-96.

298. Beltran de Guevara, J.M. "Teilhard de Chardin o la
      pasión de síntesis." *Sic* (1965): 28, 174-178.

299. Bendaña, Ricardo. "Aproximación al pensamiento ético
      de Teilhard de Chardin." *Estudios centroamericanos*
      (1969): 25, 229-232.

300. Bendlová, Peluška. *Člověk a moderní katolicismus.
      Krize katolického humanismu.* [Man in Modern Catholi-
      cism. The Crisis of Catholic Humanism.] Praha: Svo-
      bodné slovo, 1965. See pp. 69-91, 106-125.

301. ————. "Teilhard de Chardin a soudobý katolický per-
      sonalismus." [Teilhard de Chardin and Contemporary
      Catholic Personalism.] *Filosoficky casopis* (1965):
      702-721.

302. ————. *Teilhard de Chardin, nová naděje katolicismu?*
      [Teilhard de Chardin, New Hope of Catholicism?] Praha:
      Svoboda, 1967.

303. Bengoechea, José Luis. "La socialización en Teilhard
      de Chardin." *Ensayos* (1966): 44, 28-30.

304. Benoit, Raymond. "The Alchemy of Teilhard." *Con-
      tinuum* (1969): 7, 218-220.

305. ————. "Whitman, Teilhard and Jung." Item 607, pp.
      79-89.

306. Benz, Ernst. *Schöpfungsglaube und Endzeiterwartung.
      Antwort auf Teilhard de Chardins Theologie der
      Evolution.* München: Nymphenburger Verlagshandlung,
      1965.
          *Evolution and Christian Hope: Man's Concept of the
      Future from the Early Fathers to Teilhard de Chardin.*
      Garden City, N.Y.: Doubleday, 1966.
      Also London: V. Gollancz, 1967.

307. ————. "Teilhard de Chardin." *Zeitschrift für
      Religions- und Geistesgeschichte* (1962): 14, 209-216.

308. ————. "Teilhard de Chardin und die Zukunft der
      Menschen (Zur Stellung Teilhard de Chardins in der
      Theologiegeschichte des 19. und 20. Jahrhunderts)."
      Zeitschrift für Religions- und Geistesgeschichte
      (1962): 14, 316-333.

309. ————.' "Teilhard de Chardin und Sri Aurobindo." Item 1213, pp. 80-123.

310. ————. *Die Übermensch*. Zurich: Rhein-Verlag, 1962.

311. ————. "Die Zukunft des Menschen bei Teilhard de Chardin." Item 1331, pp. 27-49.

312. ————. "Zum theologischen Verstandnis der Fvolutionslehre." Item 1213, pp. 13-52.

313. Bergé, Louis. "A propos du Milieu divin de Teilhard de Chardin." *Revue de Paris* (1967): 74, 91-104.

314. Bergenthal, Ferdinand. "Die Berufung des Denkers im Zusammenbruch der Weltanschauungen. Eine Vor-Besinnung zu Teilhard de Chardin." *Wissenschaft und Weisheit* (1969): 32, 113-122.

315. ————. "Das Denken des Menschen und die Selbstbezeugung der Wahrheit. (Die transzendental-philosophischen Voraussetzungen für ein kritisches Verständnis Teilhards de Chardin)." *Memorias del XIII Congreso internacional de Filosofía*. Toluca: Universidad Nacional Autonoma de Mexico, 1963, pp. 74-84.

316. ————. "Transsubstantiatio. Zur Inerpretation Teilhards de Chardin." *Wissenschaft und Wahrheit* (1968): 31, 115-120.

317. Berger, Gaston. "L'idée d'avenir et la pensée de Teilhard de Chardin." *Phénoménologie du temps et prospective*. Paris: Presses Universitaires de France, 1964, pp. 237-254.
Also *Revue Teilhard de Chardin* (1973): 54/55, 32-50.

318. ————. "Teilhard de Chardin. L'humanité va vers sa jeunesse." *Arts* (1961): 819, 1, 4.

319. Bergeron, Marie-Ina. *La Chine et Teilhard*. Paris: Éditions Universitaires, 1976.

320. ————. "La Chine et Teilhard." *Revue Teilhard de Chardin* (1977): 69, 4-17. Except from Item 319.

320a. ————. "L'homme et sa parole." *Revue Teilhard de Chardin* (1978): 74, 9-19. Excerpt from Item 319.

321. ———. "Le Père Teilhard de Chardin et la Chine."
      Revue Teilhard de Chardin (1976): 65, 3-5. Excerpt
      from Item 319.

322. Bergeron, Philippe. *L'action humaine dans l'oeuvre de
      Teilhard de Chardin*. Montréal: Fides, 1969.

323. Bergier, Jacques. "L'astronomie neutrique va-t-elle
      réaliser un grand rêve de Teilhard de Chardin?" *Re-
      vue Teilhard de Chardin* (1961): 6, 7-8.

324. Bergounioux, Frédéric-Marie. *L'âme sacerdotale du Père
      Teilhard de Chardin*. Toulouse: Privat, 1956.
      Also Item 3292, pp. 71-78.
      "The Priestly Soul of Father Teilhard de Chardin."
      In Item 2723.

325. ———. "Données nouvelles en paléontologie humaine."
      Bulletin de littérature ecclésiastique (1955): 2,
      100-106.

326. ———. "Le Père Teilhard de Chardin a-t-il été un
      faussaire?" *Frères du monde* (1963): 21, 24-34.

327. ———. "Le Père Teilhard de Chardin et la convergence
      christique." *Frères du monde* (1963): 21, 9-23.

328. ———. "Pour lire Teilhard de Chardin." *Frères du
      monde*(1963): 21, 34-40.

329. ———. *La préhistoire et ses problèmes*. Paris:
      Fayard, 1958.

330. ———. "Recherches préhistoriques en Fxtrême-Orient
      d'après le. R.P. Teilhard de Chardin." *Bulletin de
      littérature ecclésiastique* (1969): 92-99.
      Also Item 4669, vol. 7, pp. 3093-3100.

331. Berlincourt, Serge. "Une gloire fulgurante et mon-
      diale: P. Teilhard de Chardin." *L'école bernoise*,
      November 12, 1966, pp. 803-804, 813; November 19,
      1966, pp. 829-831; November 26, 1966, pp. 847-849.

332. Bernal Amezquita, Carlos. "The Phenomenolopy of Psy-
      chosocial Evolution in Pierre Teilhard de Chardin, as a
      Basis for a Theory of Personality." Doctoral dis-
      sertation, St. Louis University, 1971.

332a. Bernhard, Augustin. "L'ouverture du Musée Huang-ho-Pai-ho à Tientsin." *Chine-Ceylan-Madagascar* (1924): 65, 163-165.

333. Bernard-Maitre, Henri. "Pierre Teilhard de Chardin, 1881-1955. Son oeuvre scientifique en Extrême-Orient presentée par lui-même." *Journal of Oriental Studies* (1956): 318-321.

334. Bernharda, Agnes. "Die 'Mystik der Arbeit' nach Teilhard de Chardin." *Der katholische Erzieher* (1964): 17, 222-228.

335. Bernier, R. "Recherche sur les notions de phylétisations, d'orthogénèse et de finalité chez Teilhard de Chardin." *Physis* (1966): 8, 317-331.

336. Bernoville, G. "Contemporary Trends in Catholic Thought in France." *Dublin Review* (1950): 224, 13-31.

337. Berry, Thomas. "The Threshold of the Modern World." Item 3247, pp. 57-59.

338. Berset, Bernard. *Incarnation ou eschatologie?* Paris: Cerf, 1964.

339. Berthault, Guy. "Teilhard et l'illusion évolutioniste." *Dieu n'échoue pas* (1968): 31-43.

340. Bertrand, Guy M. "Pierre Teilhard de Chardin et son oeuvre." *Liberté* (1961): 3-7.

341. Bertrand-Serret, René. "Déterminisme et finalité, entropie et syntropie." *La pensée catholique* (1958): 7-16.

342. Bethge, Hildburg. "Die Zukunft der Menschheit in der Sicht Pierre Teilhard de Chardins." *Stimme der Gemeinde zum kirchlichen Leben, zur Politik, Wirtschaft und Kultur* (1965): 17, 743-758.

343. Bétinas, Marcel. *Introduction à l'organisation évolutive.* Annonay: Bétinas, 1965.

344. Bettiza, Enzo. "Teilhard de Chardin profeta anche in URSS." *La Domenica de Corriere*, December 11, 1966, p. 25.

345.   *Between Two Cities: God and Man in America.* New York: America Press, 1962.

346.   Beutler, W. "Bewusstsein auf der Höhe der Zeit. Ansatzpunkte einer Auseinandersetzung mit Teilhard der Chardin." *Werkhefte katholischer Laien* (1961): 15, 143-150.

347.   "Bibliografia polacca sul Padre Teilhard de Chardin." *La vita cattolica in Polonia* (1966): 4, 55-60.
       "Bibliographie polonaise du Père Teilhard de Chardin." *La vie catholique en Pologne* (1966): 4, 57-63.

348.   Bielawski, Józef. "Teilharda wizja dziejów." [Teilhard's Vision of History.] *Więź* (1976): 130-134.

349.   Biéville, L. de. "A la découverte de Pierre Teilhard de Chardin." *Le christianisme au XXe siècle*, September 16, 1965, p. 43.

350.   ————. "Le milieu divin: Pierre Teilhard de Chardin." *Christianisme social* (1960): 3-12.

351.   Biffi, Inos. "La prospettiva del male ne Le Milieu divin e le condizioni per la sua intelligenza." Item 2744, pp. 191-195.
       "La perspective du mal dans le Milieu divin et les conditions nécessaires à la compréhension du mal." Item 2744 trans., pp. 181-185.

352.   Bilaniuk, Petro. "The Christology of Teilhard de Chardin." In Item 3247.

353.   Billy, André. "Les idées du P. Teilhard sur l'avenir de l'humanité." *Le Figaro*, July 29, 1959, p. 11.

354.   ————. "Le Père Teilhard au front." *Le Figaro*, November 29, 1961, p. 20.

355.   ————. "Le P. Teilhard de Chardin devant la vie et la mort." *Le Figaro*, July 26, 1965, p. 13.

356.   ————. "'Le phénomène humain' du Père Teilhard de Chardin enfin révélé au public." *Le Figaro*, November 23, 1955.

357.   ————. "Le phénomène humain par le Père Teilhard de Chardin." *Livres de France* (1956): 13-14.

358. ———. "Pour ou contre Teilhard de Chardin." *Le Figaro*, March 11, 1959, p. 16.

359. ———. "Un Teilhard de Chardin simple, clair et vivant." *Le Figaro*, October 14, 1968, p. 14.

360. ———. "Teilhard de Chardin. Tome VII." *Le Figaro*, November 20, 1963, p. 20. See Item 4322.

361. Bilot, Alain. "La déclaration sur la race et les préjugés raciaux de septembre 1967 et la complémentarité des races selon Pierre Teilhard de Chardin." *Le lien international* (1968): 14-24.

362. ———. "La socialisation chez Teilhard de Chardin et ses incidences politiques." Mimeographed. Paris: Faculté de droit et des sciences économiques de l'Université de Paris, 1968.

363. Binns, Emily M. "The Mystery of the Church." Item 2158, pp. 119-145.
"Il misterio della Chiesa." Item 2158 trans., pp. 165-203.

364. ———. "Teilhard de Chardin and the Future of the Universe." *American Ecclesiastical Review* (1971): 73-89.

365. ———. "Towards a Cosmic Church: The Implications of the Thought of Teilhard de Chardin for Contemporary Ecclesiology." Doctoral dissertation, Catholic University of America, 1970.

366. ———. "The Very Quick Life of the Church Today." *Teilhard Review* (1971-72): 84-93.

367. Biondi, A. "Teilhard and Bergson." *Teilhard Review* (1973): 82-85.

368. Biondi, Humbert. "Evoluzione e spiritualizzazione del mundo secondo Teilhard." *Futuro dell'uomo* (1977): 3-9.

369. Birmingham, William. "The Authentication of Teilhard." *Cross Currents* (1965): 252-255.

370. ———. "Teilhard." *Catholic World*, November, 1967, pp. 90-91.

371. Birx, H. James. *Pierre Teilhard de Chardin's Philosophy of Evolution.*" Springfield, Ill.: Thomas, 1972.

372. Bishop, Claire H. "Pierre Teilhard de Chardin (1881-1955)¿" *The Third Hour* (1956): 46-51.

373. ————. "Teilhard and the Cosmic Christ." Item 1544, pp. 35-38.

374. Billières, René, and Jacques Vacherot. *Science, seule espérance? Marx? Teilhard?* Paris: Editions Ouvrières, 1966. *¿La ciencia, única esperanza? ¿Marx, Teilhard?* Madrid: Gredos, 1972.

375. Blackham, H.J. "A Metaphysic of Man." *Religious Humanism* (1969): 166-168.

376. Blair, H.A. "Incarnation: The Reconciliation of the Energy." Item 1919, pp. 101-111.

377. ————. "Progress." Item 1919, pp. 79-100.

378. Blair, Thomas Albert. "Two Evolutionary Theories: Neo-Darwinism and Teilhard de Chardin." Doctoral dissertation, St. John's University, New York, 1972.

379. Blajot, J. "La cosmovisión de Teilhard de Chardin." *Semana médica* (1967): 8-9.

380. ————. "El futuro de la humanidad." *Semana médica* (1967): 8-9.

381. Blanc, Alberto Carlo. "L'avvenire dell'uomo." *Quaderni ACI* (1956): 53-73.

382. Blanchard, J.P. "De Saint Paul au Père Teilhard." *Revue Teilhard de Chardin* (1963): 5-7.

383. ————. "Imploration d'être et création." *Univers* (1965): 57-69.

384. ————. "Méthode du Père Teilhard." *Revue Teilhard de Chardin* (1962): 9-10.

385. ————. *Méthodes et principes du Père Teilhard de Chardin.* Paris: La Colombe, 1961.

386. Blanchet, André. "Propos en marge. Teilhard plus intime." *Etudes* (1972): 579-584.

387. Blanchet, Msgr. *Jésus Christ et l'Univers.* Paris: Spes, 1957. See pp. 21-28.

388. Blasi, Mario. "Ricetta per la felicità." *Città di vita* (1963): 476-480.

389. Bloch, B.G. "Koncepja ewolucji życia u H. Bergsona i P. Teilharda de Chardin." [The Concept of Evolution of Life According to Bergson and Teilhard de Chardin.] *Studia philosophiae christianae* (1969): 218-228.

390. ———. "Die phänomenologische Erfassung der Anthropogenese bei Teilhard de Chardin." *Acta teilhardiana* (1973): 29-36.
"Fenomenologiczne ujęcie antropogenezy u Teilharda de Chardin." *Ślaskie Studia Historyczno-Teologiczne* (1974): 207-214.
"La fenomenologia dell'evoluzione in Teilhard de Chardin." *Antonianum* (1977): 496-510.

391. ———. "Wizja pokojowego rozwoju ludzkości wedlug Teilharda de Chardin." [The Vision of the Peaceful Evolution of Humanity According to Teilhard de Chardin.] *Filozofia i pikoj.* [Philosophy and Peace.] Warszawa: Pánstwowe Wydawnictwo Naukowe, 1971, pp. 229-249.

392. Blouin, Jacques. "Le plérôme à travers l'oeuvre teilhardienne." Typescript. Montreal: Institut supérieur de sciences religieuses de l'Université de Montréal, 1966.

393. Bo, Carlo. "Il mondo e la mia fede." *L'Europeo* (1962): 83.

394. Boff, Leonardo. *O Evangelho do Cristo Cosmico. A realidade de um mito. O mito de uma realidade.* Petrópolis: Vozes, 1971. See pp. 17-40.

395. Bogdański, Kazimierz. "Biofizykalne aspekty filozofii Teilharda de Chardin." [Biophysical Aspects of the Philosophy of Teilhard de Chardin.] *Życie i myśl* (1969): 107-122.
Also Item 3888, pp. 59-79.

396. ———. "Biostruktury i kompleksykacja." [Biostructure
      and Complexity.] *Życie Warszawy* (1967): 4.

397. Bogliolo, Luigi. "Scienza e filosofia in Teilhard de
      Chardin alla luce del tomismo." *Euntes docete* (1964):
      177-191.

398. Boillot, Louis. "La théorie de l'évolution selon le P.
      Teilhard de Chardin." *Académie des sciences, belles-
      lettres et arts de Besançon. Procès verbaux et
      mémoires* (1964-65): 217-225.

399. Boisdeffre, Pierre de. "L'accélération de l'histoire."
      Revue Teilhard de Chardin (1963): 14-15.

400. ———. "Angoisse d'aujourd'hui, espérance de demain.
      Des télécommunications au service d'un monde uni."
      Item 1259, pp. 174-197.

401. ———. "Faut-il brûler Teilhard de Chardin?" *Combat*,
      October 1, 1959.

402. ———. "Une histoire vivante de la littérature d'au-
      jourd'hui." *Le livre contemporain* (1958): 212-215.
      Also *Une histoire vivante de la littérature d'au-
      jourd'hui.* Paris: Perrin, 1964, pp. 270-273.

403. ———. "Le message teilhardien et la radiodiffusion
      française." *Cahiers littéraires* (1965): 2-4.

404. ———. "L'oeuvre du Père Teilhard de Chardin." *Com-
      bat*, January 24, 1957, p. 7.

405. ———. "Problèmes actuels et pensée teilhardienne."
      Revue générale belge (1961): 15-38.

406. ———. "Ouelques réflexions sur le 'teilhardisme.'"
      La Croix, October 9-10, 1960, p. 4.

407. ———. "Teilhard de Chardin." *Dictionnaire de littér-
      ature contemporaine.* Paris: Éditions Universitaires,
      1962, pp. 606-611.

408. Bolle, Jacques. "Le phénomène spirituel." *Le Phare
      dimanche*, April 2, 1961, p. 6.

409. ———. "Pour Teilhard de Chardin." *Les beaux-arts*,
      May, 1951, pp. 1-2.

410. Bon, Michel. "Les savants, la morale et Dieu. Teilhard de Chardin." *Horizons* (1962): 4, 6.

411. Boné, Édouard. "L'apparition de l'homme et la vision du passé." *Nouvelle revue théologique* (1957): 984-985.

412. ————. "In memoriam Pierre Teilhard de Chardin." *South African Journal of Science* (1955): 16-18.

413. ————. "L'oeuvre paléontologique de Pierre Teilhard de Chardin." *Revue des questions scientifiques* (1964): 47-76; (1965): 90-104.

414. ————. "Pierre Teilhard de Chardin, prêtre et savant." *Radio-Télévision catholique belge* (1961): 2-5.

415. ————. "Pierre Teilhard de Chardin, SJ." *Revue des questions scientifiques* (1956): 90-104.

416. ————. "Teilhard de Chardin." *New Catholic Encyclopedia.* New York: McGraw-Hill, 1967, vol. 13, pp. 977-978.

417. Bonjean, François. "Carnets." *Confluent* (1961): 254-262.

418. Bonnot, Gerard. "L'hérésie de Teilhard de Chardin." *Express* (1965): 47-50. "Teilhard de Chardin no itan." *Misuzu* (1965): 71-75.

419. "Books of Kaiser, Rynne, Kung and Teilhard Banned from Catholic Bookstores in Rome." *Commonweal*, October 18, 1963, p. 88.

420. Bordet, Charles. *Teilhard de Chardin, l'actualité de son message.* Paris: Éditions Ouvrières, 1965. *La actulidad del mensaje de Teilhard de Chardin.* Barcelona: Betis, 1968.

421. Borkowska, Ada. "Dzielo Teilharda na tle pewnych problemów wspólczesnej teologii." [Teilhard's Works and Some Contemporary Theological Problems.] *Życie i myśl* (1967): 19-26. Also Item 3888, pp. 255-266.

422. Borne, Étienne. "L'affaire Teilhard." *Forces nouvelles*, July 5, 1962, p. 10.

423. ————. "Analogies entre Teilhard et saint Thomas."
      Témoignage chrétien, January 31, 1958.

424. ————. "Ce que je dois au Père Teilhard." Item
      3292, pp. 159-160.

425. ————. "Les communistes et le P. Teilhard." *France-
      forum* (1960): 34.

426. ————. *De Pascal à Teilhard*. Clermont-Ferrand: G. de
      Bussac, 1963.

427. ————. "Hommage au Père Teilhard de Chardin." *Recherches
      et débats* (1955): 159-164.

428. ————. "Idéosophie ou philosophie." *Recherches et dé-
      bats* (1967): 231-243.

429. ————. "Littérature teilhardienne." *Forces nouvelles*,
      May 24, 1962, p. 9.

430. ————. "Maritain et Teilhard ou le dialogue impossible."
      France-forum (1967): 38.

431. ————. "Matière et Esprit dans la philosophie de Teil-
      hard de Chardin." *Recherches et débats* (1962): 45-65.

432. ————. "Un néophyte de dialogue: M. Roger Garaudy."
      Le monde, March 30, 1960.

433. ————. *Pascal*. *Textes du tricentenaire*. Paris:
      Fayard, 1963. See pp. 353-368.

434. ————. "La pensée de Teilhard constitue l'un des pôles
      de la pensée chrétienne." *Témoignage chrétien*, Decem-
      ber 22, 1955.
      Also *Témoignage chrétien*, January 31, p. 1.

435. ————. "La pensée politique de Teilhard de Chardin."
      France-forum (1958): 16-20.

436. ————. "Le Père Teilhard de Chardin. Un grand penseur
      religieux." *Le Monde*, March 13, 1955, p. 7.

437. ————. "Teilhard et Mounier." *France-forum* (1963): 4.

438. ————, Claude Cuénot, and Maurice de Gandillac. "Teil-
      hard contesté." *France-forum* (1962): 3-11.

439. Boros, Ladislaus. "Un altro libro su Teilhard de Chardin." *Osservatore romano*, December 25, 1964, p. 10.

440. ———. "Bücher von und über Teilhard de Chardin." *Orientierung* (1959): 46-47.

441. ———. "Entwicklungslehre und Glaube." *Schweizer illustrierte Zeitung* (1965): 35.

442. ———. "Evolution und Metaphysik." *Orientierung* 237-241.

443. ———. "Evolutionismus und Anthropologie. Zum Lebenswerk von Pierre Teilhard de Chardin." *Wort und Wahrheit* (1958): 15-24.

444. ———. "Evolutionismus und Spiritualität. Ein Versuch über die 'geistliche Lehre' Teilhard de Chardins." *Der grosse Entschluss* (1959/60): 254-259, 301-303, 346-350, 398-403.
"Evolutie en spiritualiteit." *Analecta voor het Bisdom Rotterdam* (1963): 211-236.

445. ———. "'Der göttliche Bereit' von Teilhard de Chardin." *Bücher der Entscheidung*. Würzburg: Echter-Verlag, 1964: pp. 142-150.

446. ———. "Die Grundlage des Denkens von Teilhard." *Orientierung* (1964): 42-45.
Also *Der grosse Entschluss* (1963/64): 408-414.

447. ———. "Offen zur Welt. Teilhard de Chardin." *Kompass* (1960): 71-73.

448. ———. "Streit um Teilhard de Chardin." *Der Männer-Seelsorger* (1963): 154-158, 176-180.

449. ———. "Teilhard de Chardin." *Kompass* (1960): 71-73.

450. ———. "Teilhard de Chardin--Der universale Christus." *Motive des Glaubens*. Hamburg: Furche-Verlag, 1968, pp. 153-160.
Also 2d ed., 1970.

451. Borowitz, Eugen B. "Teilhard de Chardin." *Judaism* (1965): 330-338.

452.   Borruso, S., and W.F. Donders. "Teilhard de Chardin."
       Afer (1965): 358-364.

453.   Bortolaso, G. "Il concetto di progresso in Teilhard de
       Chardin." *Evoluzionismo e storia umana.* Brescia:
       Morcelliana, 1968, pp. 185-188.

454.   Bosc, Jean. "A propos du P. Teilhard de Chardin." *Foi
       et vie* (1958): 469-524.

455.   Boskowits, Karl Friedrich [pseud. F.-A. Viallet]. "'Amor
       terrae.' Pierre Teilhard de Chardin, ein Künder neuen
       Weltgefühls." *Antares* (1956): 14-18.

456.   ———. "Mein Gespräch mit Teilhard de Chardin." *Per-
       spektiven der Zukunft* (1968): 2-5.

457.   ———. "Richtungen der Deutung. Ein Abschnitt aus
       dem sensationellen II. Band der Teilhard-Biographie."
       Die Besinnung (1963): 80-85.

458.   ———. *Teilhard de Chardin. I. Zwischen Alpha und
       Omega. Das Weltbild Teilhard de Chardins.* Nürnberg:
       Glock und Lutz, 1958.
       Also Zürich: Christiana-Verlag, 1958.
       Also 2d ed., 1963, with Item 459.

459.   ———. *Teilhard de Chardin. II. Zwischen Ja und Nein.
       Dialog. Dokumente. Kritik.* Nürnberg: Glock und
       Lutz, 1963, with Item 458.
       Also Zürich: Christiana-Verlag, 1963, with Item
       458.
       *Voor en tegen Teilhard. Pierre Teilhard de Chardin
       in de kritik.* Hilversum/Antwerpen: Paul Brand, 1967.

460.   ———. "Teilhard de Chardin und der Zen Buddhismus."
       Perspektiven der Zukunft (1970): 11-14.

461.   ———. *L'univers personnel de Teilhard de Chardin.*
       Paris: Amiot-Dumont, 1955.

462.   ———. *L'univers personnel de Teilhard de Chardin.
       II. Le dépassement.* Paris: Librairie Fischbacher,
       1961. Contains Item 4804.

463.   ———. "Versuch eines persönlichen Universums."
       Neues Abendland (1955): 565-567.

464. ————. "Die Weigerung. Zur Situation Teilhard de Chardins." *Die Besinnung* (1963): 235-241.

465. Bossio, G. "Il fenomeno umano nell'ipotesi dell'evoluzione integrale." *Civiltà cattolica* (1955): 622-631.
Also *L'Osservatore romano*, December 23, 1955.
Also *Documentation catholique*, January 22, 1956.

466. Boublik, Vladimir. "Attualità di Teilhard." *Bollettino informazioni di Centro di studi e di ricerca Teilhard de Chardin, Istituto Stensen* (1972): 1-24.

467. Boule, Marcellin. "Rapport sur l'attribution du prix Visquenel à M. l'abbé Teilhard de Chardin." *Comptes rendus sommaires de la Société géologique de France*, séance du 9 juin 1922, pp. 129-131.

468. ————. "Le 'Sinanthropus.'" *L'anthropologie* (1929): 455-460.
Also Item 4669, vol. 3, pp. 1160-1161.

469. Bounoure, Louis. "La cosmologie du P. Teilhard de Chardin devant la biologie expérimentale." *Revue des sciences religieuses* (1957): 390-392.

470. ————. *Recherche d'une doctrine de la vie*. Paris: Robert Laffont, 1964.

471. ————. "Recherches et conceptions paléontologiques de Teilhard de Chardin." *Itinéraires* (1965): 7-40.
Response to questionnaire in Item 3259.

472. Bourgault, Raymond. "Le chercheur et sa passion: l'aventure de Pierre Teilhard de Chardin." *Relations* (1972): 54-55.

473. Bourgouin-Moudrova, Hélène. "L'homme comme création de l'homme selon Engels et selon Pierre Teilhard de Chardin." *Les études philosophiques* (1967): 467-470.

474. Boutang, Pierre. "Un chevalier de l'impossible." *Le Monde*, March 11-12, 1965, p. 13.

475. Bouyer, Louis. "A propos de deux ouvrages sur le P. Teilhard de Chardin. Le malheur d'avoir des disciples." *La France catholique* (1958): 626, 8; 627, 3.

476. ———. "Réponse à C. Cuénot." *La France catholique*
     (1958): 628, 3.

477. Boyd, W.J.P. "Teilhard de Chardin and Modern Protestant
     Theology." Item 1919, pp. 113-155.

478. Boyer, Régis. "Teilhard de Chardin." *Birtingur* (1963):
     16-26.

479. ———. "Téorie ojca Teilhard de Chardin." *Życie i myśl*
     (1960): 3-15.

480. Bozóky, Maria. "Teilhard fotoarcai." [Photographs of
     Teilhard.] *Vigilia* (1969): 522-525.

481. Bracken, J. "Chardin and Royce: Toward a New Christian
     Eschatology." *American Ecclesiastical Review* (1975):
     169-175.

482. Bradet, H.-M. "Le bonheur. Les bonheurs." *Mainentant*
     (1965): 193-194.

483. Brandenstein, Bela von. "Über die Prinzipienlehre der
     Weltanschauung Teilhard de Chardins." *Wissenschaft
     und Weisheit* (1971): 30-37.

484. Braun, C. "Het goddelijk gewicht van ons hendelen."
     Ons Geestelijk Leven (1964-65): 325-333.

485. Bravo, Francisco. "Cristo en la obra del Padre Teilhard
     de Chardin." *Cristología y pastoral en América latina*.
     Barcelona: Nova Terra, 1966, pp. 99-206.
         Christ in the Thought of Teilhard de Chardin. Notre
     Dame, Indiana: University of Notre Dame Press, 1967.

486. ———. "La dialéctica en Teilhard de Chardin." *Estudi-
     os filosoficos* (1974): 9-40.

487. ———. "La fenomenologia del cosmos según Teilhard
     de Chardin." *Presente* (1965): 19-31.

488. ———. "L'histoire et son objet." *Études teilhardi-
     ennes* (1969): 25-38.

489. ———. "Pierre Teilhard de Chardin and Pastoral Re-
     newal in Latin America." *CIF Reports* (1966): 9-12.

490. ——. *Teilhard de Chardin, su concepción de la historia.* Barcelona: Nova Terra, 1970. *La vision d'histoire chez Teilhard de Chardin.* Paris: Cerf, 1970.

491. Bravo Vivar, Noé. "La conception de l'homme chez Karl Marx et Teilhard de Chardin." Typescript. Paris: Faculté de lettres et sciences humaines de l'Université de Paris, 1969.

492. Braybrooke, Neville. "C.G. Jung and Teilhard de Chardin. A Dialogue." *The Month* (1968): 96-104. Also Item 607, pp. 90-100. "C.G. Jung y Teilhard de Chardin. Un diálogo." *Arbor* (1969): 345-352.

493. ——. "The Flare-Path of Teilhard de Chardin." *Aryan Path* (1966): 494-498.

494. ——. "The Phenomenon of Teilhard de Chardin. Pilgrim of the Future." *The Southern Cross*, April 13, 1966, pp. 5, 173.

495. ——. "The Priest Who Crossed All the World's Frontiers." *The Catholic Herald*, May 28, 1965, p. 6.

496. ——. "Teilhard." *National Catholic Reporter*, November 14, 1975, p. 8.

497. ——. *Teilhard de Chardin: Pilgrim of the Future.* New York: Seabury Press, 1964. Varies from Item 501 only slightly. Contains Items 168, 913, 959, 2566, 2680, 3280, 3793, 3289, 4007, 4175, 4728 Also London: Darton, Longman & Todd, 1964.

498. ——. "The Vision of Teilhard de Chardin." Item 497, pp. 111-128. Also *Graphic*, August 30, and September 13, 1967.

499. ——. "Voices in the Desert: Jung and Teilhard." *Chicago Studies* (1966): 153-162. Also *Aryan Path* (1967): 442-449. Also *Antigonish Review* (1970): 63-71.

500. ——. "Voices in the Desert: A Radio Act of Worship." *Revue catholique de radio et de télévision* (1965): 1-4.

501. ————. *The Wind and the Rain.* Baltimore: Newman, 1962.
     Varies from Item 497 only slightly. Contains Items 168,
     198, 913, 959, 2566, 2680, 3230, 3280, 3793, 3829, 4007,
     4175, 4372, 4728, 4813.
     Also London: Warburg, 1962.

502. Bréchet, Raymond. "La vision de jeune Teilhard." *Choisir*
     (1965): 16-17.

503. Brega, Gian Piero. "Teilhard e il marxismo." *Il filo
     rosso* (1963): 48-57.

504. Brémond, H.J., and A. Brémond. *Le charme d'Athènes et
     autres essais.* Paris: Bloud et Gay, 1925. See pp.
     29-30.

505. Brennan, Martin. "The Phenomenon of Man." *Studies*
     (1960): 117-130.
     "Le phénomène humain." *Pax Romana* (1961): 17-23.

506. ————. "Teilhard de Chardin." *Feasta* (1967): 5-8.
     Also *Comharthatocht* (1967): 16-22.

507. Bret, Lucien. "Notes sur Teilhard de Chardin." *L'Au-
     vergne littéraire, artistique et historique* (1968):
     19-26.

508. Breuil, Henri. "Le double miracle dans le cas Teilhard."
     Item 3292, pp. 137-138.

509. ————. "Les enquêtes du géologue et du préhistorien."
     La table ronde (1955): 19-24.

510. ————. "Teilhard de Chardin et son 'Phénomène humain.'"
     La table ronde (1956): 109-114.
     Also *Bulletin de littérature ecclésiastique* (1956):
     38-44.

511. Breza, Tadeusz. "Une morale nouvelle." *Europe* (1965):
     158-163.

512. Brien, Paul. "De Charles Darwin à Pierre Teilhard de
     Chardin." *Synthèses* (1962): 29-42.

513. ————. "Hommage à Pierre Teilhard de Chardin." *Revue
     Teilhard de Chardin* (1961): 8-12.
     Also *Radio-Télévision catholique belge* (1965): 2-3.

514. Bright, Laurence. "Some Other Views on Teilhard." *Bulletin of the Newman Association, Philosophy of Science Group* (1960): 2-7.

515. Brillantes, Gregorio C. "The Phenomenon of Teilhard de Chardin." *Philippines Free Press* (1967): 74, 80, 121-122, 124-125.

516. Brincourt, André. "Un juste croquis de Teilhard de Chardin." *Le Figaro* (1965): 6549, 23.

517. Brincourt, J., and G. Thoyer. "Teilhard de Chardin et les voies spirituelles de l'Extrême-Orient." *Médecine de France*, July, 1969, pp. 43-50.

517a. Brion, Marcel. "Rencontre avec le Père Teilhard de Chardin." *Les nouvelles littéraires*, January 11, 1951, pp. 1, 4.

518. Briones Toledo, Hernán. *Pierre Teilhard de Chardin y otros ensayos. Rostros y rastros en el pensamiento contemporaneo.* Santiago de Chile: Andrés Bello, 1966.

519. Broch, Thomas. *Das Problem der Freiheit im Werk von Pierre Teilhard de Chardin.* Mainz: M. Grünewald, 1977.

520. Brochier, Hubert. "Het denken van Teilhard de Chardin en de wereld van thans." *De Maand* (1963): 25-34.

521. Brodrick, A. "Father of Prehistory." *Catholic Digest*, April, 1964, pp. 48-57.

522. Broker, Werner. "Aspects de l'évolution." *Concilium* (1967): 13-27.

523. ———. "Pro und Contra zu Teilhard de Chardin. Würdigung einiger neuerer Schriften." *Theologische Revue* (1966): 289-294.

524. Bronowski, J. "Where Do We Go From Here?" *A Sense of the Future: Essays in Natural Philosophy.* Cambridge, Mass.: MIT Press, 1977, pp. 155-162.

525. Brooks, Romeo Walter. "The Influence of the Spirituality of Teilhard de Chardin on Religious Life." Doctoral dissertation, Marquette University, 1971.

526.   Broucker, José de. "Le 'phénomène Teilhard.'" *Informa-
       tions catholiques internationales* (1965): 19-21, 23-29.

527.   Brown, Douglas. "The Phenomenon of Teilhard." *The Catho-
       lic Herald*, October 28, 1966, p. 5.

528.   Browning, Geraldine O. *Teilhard de Chardin: In Quest of
       the Perfection of Man.* Rutherford, Madison, Teaneck,
       N.J.: Fairleigh Dickinson University Press, 1973. Con-
       tains Items 1531, 1779, 2815, 2846, 3687, 4021.

529.   Bruch, Jean-Louis. "La pensée de Teilhard de Chardin."
       Culture française (1961): 311-312, 315-316.
       Also *Levende Talen* (1961): 511-513.

530.   Brun, Jean. "Un gnosticisme gidien: Teilhard de Chardin."
       Les études philosophiques (1965): 465-482.

531.   Brunelle, Lucien. "Le phénomène humain devant la foi et
       devant le raison." *Pensée* (1961): 118-121.

532.   Brunner, August. "Pierre Teilhard de Chardin." *Divinitas*
       (1962): 444-459.

533.   ———. "Pierre Teilhard de Chardin." *Stimmen der Zeit*
       (1959): 210-222.
       "La obra de Teilhard de Chardin." *Orbis catholicus*
       (1960): 315-331.
       "Pierre Teilhard de Chardin: A Critique." *Theology
       Digest* (1960): 143-147.

534.   Bruns, J. Edgard. "Cosmosgenesis and Theology." Item
       1544, pp. 167-185.

535.   ———. "God Up Above--Or Up Ahead?" *Catholic World*
       (1960): 323-325.

536.   ———. "On to Omega!" *Catholic World* (1970): 52.

537.   ———. "The Vision of Pierre Teilhard de Chardin."
       Catholic Book Reporter (1961): 4-5.

538.   Bruteau, Beatrice. *Evolution Toward Divinity. Teilhard
       de Chardin and the Hindu Traditions.* Wheaton, Illinois:
       Theosophical Publishing House, 1974.

539.   ———. "Sri Aurobindo and Teilhard de Chardin on the
       Problem of Action." *International Philosophical Quart-
       erly* (1972): 193-204.

540. Brynildsen, Aasmund. *Lyset og øiet. Betrakninger over Teilhard de Chardins liv og verk.* Oslo: Servolibris, 1962.

541. Bubner, Rudolf. *Evolution und Reinkarnation. Ein Dialog mit Teilhard de Chardin.* Freiburg-im-Breisgau: Die Kommenden, 1966.

542. ———. "Hundert Jahre nach Darwin: Pierre Teilhard de Chardin." *Die Drei* (1963): 2-16.

543. ———. "Der Mensch und seine zwei Naturen. Evolution, Kreation, Reinkarnation." *Perspektiven der Zukunft* (1971): 6-10.

544. ———. "La question laissée ouverte par Teilhard de Chardin." *Triades* (1963): 12-28.

545. ———. "Teilhard de Chardin als Grundlage einer Diskussion." *Die Drei* (1964): 165-176.

546. Buki, Gáboi. "Teilhard de Chardin az ellenvetések tükreben." [Teilhard de Chardin in the Light of Controversies.] *Katolikus Szemle* (1965): 213-221.

547. Bully, Philippe. "Du vivant au divin." *Arts et métiers* (1958): 53-55.

548. ———. "Noosphère et téléfinalité." *Arts et métiers* (1958): 2, 57-59.

549. Bulnes, Jose M. "El concepto de materia según Teilhard de Chardin." *Diálogos* (1965): 2, 87-109.

550. Burkhardt, W., J.F. Ewing, R. Francoeur, and J.V. Walsh. "Evolution, Science and Religion." *Jubilee*, May, 1960, pp. 1, 48-51.

551. Burkhouse, Barbara Jean. "Education for a Cosmogenesis. Implications from Teilhard de Chardin." Doctoral dissertation, Lehigh University, 1973.

552. Burkitt, M.C. "Philosophies of Pierre Teilhard de Chardin." *Nature* (1965): 207, 139-140.

553. Burney, Pierre. "Le Père Teilhard, les 'incroyants' et l'espérance. Divergences et convergences." Item 3950, pp. 68-93.

554. ————. "Sketch for a Morality of Love. A Tentative Ap-
      plication of Teilhardian Methods." *Teilhard Review*,
      (1969-70): 2, 60-71.

555. ————. "Teilhard de Chardin, allié du mondialisme."
      Monde uni (1961): 56, 4-6.

556. Bussery, H. "A propos de Teilhard de Chardin." *Alléluia.*
      Communauté catholique de l'INSA (1963): 1-9.

557. Bustumante, José María. "El fenómeno cultural Teilhard
      de Chardin." Item 745, pp. 23-57.

558. Butler, Kenneth G. "An Exposition and Critique of the
      Logical Structure and Biological Basis of the Ortho-
      genetic Theory of Pierre Teilhard de Chardin." Doctor-
      al dissertation, University of Ottawa, 1974.

559. ————. "Teilhard and a New Direction in Psychology."
      Teilhard Review (1977): 12, 85-87.

560. ————. "The Teilhardian Reconstruction of the Biosphere
      Through Analogical Inference." *Teilhard Review* (1977):
      12, 14-20.

561. Butryn, Stanislaw. "Wizja świata Teilharda de Chardin a
      fizyka współczesna." [Teilhard de Chardin's Vision of
      the World and Modern Physics.] *Czlowiek i Światopogląd*
      (1968): 53-69.

562. Buttafoco, Marguerite de. "Correspondance avec le Père
      Teilhard de Chardin." *Revue Teilhard de Chardin* (1976):
      65, 27-30; 66, 18-23.

563. Buttafuoco, Yvonne de. "Controverses philosophiques
      avec le Père Teilhard de Chardin." *Revue Teilhard de*
      Chardin (1961): 8/9, 30-33.

564. ————. "En guise d'introduction." *Revue Teilhard de*
      Chardin (1962): 10, 3.

565. Byrne, Peter. "Teilhard de Chardin and Commitment."
      Review for Religious (1971): 30, 763-774.

566. Caboara, Lorenzo. "Prima rassegna su Teilhard de Char-
      din." *Rivista internazionale di filosofia politica e*
      sociale (1965): 9, 440-446.

567. Cacho Nazábal, Ignacio. "El cristo cósmico." *Hechos y dichos* (1966): 295-301.

568. ————. "Immanencia y transcendencia del Cristo cósmico en el pensamiento de Teilhard de Chardin." Typescript. Barcelona: Facultad de teología de Barcelona, 1970.

569. Cailleux, André. "Connaissance scientifique et filiation." *Revue Teilhard de Chardin* (1965): 24-25, 20-25.

570. ————. "L'évolution du langage." *Revue Teilhard de Chardin* (1965): 22, 25-33.

571. ————. "Le Père Teilhard de Chardin, 1881-1955." *Revue de géologie dynamique* (1955): 6, 88-89.

572. Cairns, Hugh. "Model of a Man-with-a-Model. A Suggested Interpretative Model for Teilhard." *Teilhard Review* (1969-70): 2, 72-85.

573. ————. "Pleroma-Fulfillment in Teilhard." *Teilhard Review* (1974): 1, 10-16.

574. ————. "Teilhard de Chardin and the General Theory of Action." *Technology and Society* (1969): 5, 88-93.

575. Calmel, R.T. "Homme racheté ou phénomène extrahumain." *Itinéraires* (1962): 62, 181-200.

576. ————. "Lecture du livre de Henri Massis: 'Visage des idées.'" *Itinéraires* (1959): 34, 80-95. See pp. 87-92.

577. ————. "Lumière du dogme et brume du teilhardisme." *Itinéraires* (1963): 78.

578. ————. "Première approche du teilhardisme: la distinction des trois ordres ." *Itinéraires* (1962): 61, 155-163.

579. ————. "Réponse au teilhardisme." *Itinéraires* (1963): 71, 86-111. "Riposta al teilhardismo." Item 1403, pp. 89-167.

580. ————. "Teilhard et l'amour." *Itinéraires* (1967): 117, 145-154.

581. Calomino, Anna Giuseppina. "La dignità della persona in 'Le phénomène humain' di Pierre Teilhard de Chardin." Typescript. Roma: Istituto Maria Assunta, 1973.

582. Calvet, Jean. Réflexions sur le Phénomène humain de Pierre Teilhard de Chardin. Paris: Tolra, 1966.

Calvo, Dino, see Stacio, Anselmo

583. Calvo Hernando, Manuel. "Faltan 36 años par el tercer milenario." El colombiano literario (1964): 5.

584. Câmara, Helder. "Teilhard de Chardin, Man of Love." CIF Reports (1966): 2, 13-14. "Teilhard de Chardin, prophète du développement." Bible et vie chrétienne (1966): 71, 28-31. Also Pour arriver à temps. Paris: Desclée de Brouwer, 1970, pp. 177-183.

585. Camón Aznar, José. Cinco pensadores ante el espíritu. Madrid: Biblioteca de autores cristianos, 1975. See pp. 189-280.

586. Campbell, Harry M. "Teilhard de Chardin and 'The Mysterious Divinity, Evolution.'" Thomist (1972): 36, 608-615.

587. Campbell, Paul J. "Providence, Progress and Security--St. Paul-Chardin." Insight (1967-68): 6, 25-28.

588. Campbell, Peter A. "The Phenomenon of Isolation and Sin in the Perspectives of Teilhard de Chardin." Focus. A Theological Journal (1964): 1, 98-107; (1965): 2, 91-112.

589. Campion, Donald R. "The Phenomenon of Teilhard." America (1965): 12, 480-481, 696-697.

590. Campo Alange, Condesa de. Entre biologia y humanismo." La estafeta literaria (1964): 290, 5-6.

591. Campos, Henrique. "Teilhard de Chardin. Dez anos depois da morte." Itinerarium (1965): 11, 259-265.

592. Canals Vidal, Francisco. "Teilhard de Chardin." Cristiandad (1967): 441, 209.

593. Canevaro, Katy. "Teilhard, uomo e sacerdote." Il Gallo (1963): 18, 31-33, 51-53, 71-73, 91-93, 111-113.

594. ———, and Angelo Marchese. *Teilhard de Chardin figlio d'obbedienza*. Roma: A.V.E., 1965.

595. Cantoni, Agostino. *Il problemo Teilhard de Chardin: Scienze, filosofia, teologia*. Milan: Marzorati, 1969.

596. Capdevila, Vincenç-Maria. "El pecat original en la perspectiva evolucionista." *Qüestions de vida cristiana* (1969): 47, 83-89.

597. Cappelletti, Vincenzo. "Dopo Teilhard de Chardin." *Il Veltro* (1969): 13, 799-803.

598. Caprioli, Mario. "Sur un ouvrage du Père Philippe de la Trinité: Teilhard de Chardin—Étude critique." *Doctor communis* (1968): 21, 208-220.

599. Cara, Guy. "Vrais savants et faux prophètes de la vie: la 'philosophie' du biologiste Louis Bounoure." *La France catholique* (1965): 945, 2.

600. Carballo, J. "Litro y medio de cerebro posee el hombre, pero no lo sabe aprovechar." *Ya*, February 12, 1962, pp. 1-2.

601. Cardaropoli, Gerardo. "Il cristocentrismo nel pensiero di Duns Scoto e di Teilhard de Chardin." *De doctrina Joannis Duns Scoti. III. Problemata theologica*. Roma: Commissio Scotistica, 1968, pp. 259-290.

602. Cardoletti, Pietro. "L'aspirazione al tutto come chiave per la comprensione del Milieu divin, della spiritualità e della dottrina di Teilhard de Chardin." Item 2744, pp. 57-61.
  "L'aspiration au tout comme clef pour la comprehension du Milieu divin, de la spiritualité et de la doctrine de Teilhard de Chardin." Item 2744 trans., pp. 52-55.

603. ———. "Introduzione al pensiero di Pierre Teilhard de Chardin." *Letture* (1963): 18, 307-314.

604. ———. "Rassegna teilhardiana." *Letture* (1968): 23, 593-599.

605. Cardonnel, Jean. "L'heure de la foi en l'homme." *Actuelles* (1963): 2, 6.

606. Carême, Maurice. "Poème composée en hommage au Père Teil-
      hard." *Revue Teilhard de Chardin* (1962): 11, 2.

607. Cargas, Harry. *The Continuous Flame: Teilhard in the
      Great Traditions.* St. Louis: B. Herder, 1969. Con-
      tains Items 12, 139, 237, 305, 492, 1575, 1938, 2339,
      3441.

608. ────. "Teilhard de Chardin as John the Baptist."
      Way of St. Francis (1962): 18, 37-42.

609. Carles, Jules. "Le problème d'Adam." *Les Nouvelles
      littéraires* (1963): 1857, 6.

610. ────. *Teilhard de Chardin. Sa vie, son oeuvre, avec
      un exposé de sa philosophie.* Paris: PUF, 1964.
      Also 2d ed., 1971.

611. ────. "Teilhard et la notion de personne." *Les Nou-
      velles littéraires*, April 14, 1966.

612. ────. *Le Transformisme.* Paris: PUF, 1960, See pp.
      91-94.

613. Carp, Eugène Antoine Désiré Émile. *Teilhard, Jung en
      Sartre over Evolutie.* Utrecht: Spectrum, 1969.

614. Cartier, Albert. "Maurice Blondel (1861-1949). Un philo-
      sophe pour notre temps." *Lo calel* (1962): 29, 12-13.

615. Cartier, Jean-Pierre. "Un visionnaire du monde moderne:
      Teilhard de Chardin." *Paris-Match* (1965): 842, 81-99.

616. Cartier, Raymond. "L'homme, d'où vient-il? où va-t-il?"
      Paris-Match (1956): 380, 30-41.

617. Caruso, Igor A. "Teilhard de Chardin, Interpret der
      Gegenwart und Gestalter der Zukunft." *Acta teilhardiana*
      (1969): 19-26.
      Also Item 3425, pp. 65-76.

618. ────. "Teilhard war kein Teilhardist." *Neues Forum*
      (1968): 15, 174-176.

619. Carvalho, A. Mosca de. "A evolução e a história em Teil-
      hard." *Symposium* (1966): 8, 19-22.

620. Casado, Fidel. "Santiago de Viterbo ¿un evolucionista preteilhardiano en el medioevo? (Analogía entre un escolástico de s. XIII y un sabio del s. XX)." *Estudio augustiniano* (1976): 11, 115-127.

621. Casañas, Francisco. "Las visiones del Padre Teilhard de Chardin." *Ilustración del Clero* (1961): 54, 297-304.

622. Casas, José Antonio. "Sombras y luces en Teilhard de Chardin." *Revista javeriana* (1965): 64, 142-144.

623. Casasús de Sierra, Margarita. *Iluminó mi esperanza Teilhard.* México: Universidad Nacional Autonoma de México, 1970.

624. Casella, Vittorio. "L'esperienza essentiale dell'amore." *Dialogo* (1968): 74-90.

625. ————. "Teilhard de Chardin, profeta dell'amore." *Dialogo* (1964): 22, 136-142.

626. Cassa, Mario. "La 'dialettica' di Teilhard de Chardin." *Critica storica* (1963): 2, 241-249.

627. Castanos de Medicis, Stélios. "Unité-Espace-Temps." *Revue Teilhard de Chardin* (1963): 17, 23-29.

628. Castelli, Ferdinando. *Sei profeti per il nostro tempo. Volti dell'umanesimo contemporaneo.* Napoli: Edizioni Dehoniane, 1972. See pp. 335-390.

629. Castello, Pier Antonio. "Evolution et péché originel: quel est l'apport de Teilhard de Chardin?" Typescript. Milan: Facultà di teologia dell'Università di Milano, 1963.

630. Castex, M.N., and C. Benzi. "Teilhard de Chardin." *Stromata* (1966): 22, 197-202.

631. Castro, Josué de. "L'homme à l'âge atomique, une nouvelle conscience politique internationale." *Univers* (1965): 1, 95-103.

632. Catalan, Jean-Francois. "Vers un fondement 'objectif' des valeurs humaines?" *Archives de philosophie* (1958): 1, 117-122.

633. Catani, Maurizio. "L'evoluzione cosmica di Teilhard."
     Comunità (1963): 112, 83-87.

634. Catemario, Armando. "Destino cosmico e destino individuale
     dell'uomo." Item 1300, pp. 199-241.

635. Cavallero, Erminio. "Teilhard de Chardin in italiano."
     Città di vita (1969): 24, 9-22.

636. Cavanaugh, Jackie Ray. "Pierre Teilhard de Chardin: A
     Dialogue Between Science and Theology." Doctoral dis-
     sertation, School of Theology at Claremont, 1975.

637. Ceccatty, Max de. "Point de vue d'un biologiste." Item
     1330, pp. 375-380.
     "Punto de vista de un biólogo." Item 1284 trans., pp.
     65-73.

638. Celiesius, Petras. "Teilhard de Chardin." *Lux Christi*
     (1963): 46/47, 87-92.

639. Celiński, Boleslaw. "'Mój swiat' Teilharda de Chardin w
     swietle zasad tomistycznej filosofii bytu." [Teilhard
     de Chardin's "My World" in the Light of Thomist Philo-
     sophy of Being.] *Homo Dei* (1967): 36, 226-230.

640. "Le cercle d'études de la pensée du P. Teilhard de Char-
     din." *La vie catholique en Pologne* (1966): 4, 55-56.

641. Cestari, Giuseppe. "Alla ricerca di un nuovo S. Tomaso."
     Il Regno, October, 1962, pp. 9-10.

642. Ceusters, Robert. "P. Teilhard de Chardin. Weten-
     schappelijke methode en 'Wetenschap van de mens' als
     benadering van de theologie." Mimeographed. Heverlee/
     Leuven: Faculteit van theologie de Leuven, 1970.

643. Cevallos Garcia, Gabriel. "Evocación de Teilhard de Char-
     din." *Anales de la Universidad de Cuenca* (1964): 20,
     7-14.

644. Chaigne, Louis. *Les lettres contemporaines.* Paris: Del
     Duca, 1964. See pp. 552-554.

645. "The Chain of Evolution." *The Times Literary Supplement*,
     November 27, 1959, pp. 1-2.

646. Chaix-Ruy, Jules. *Le surhomme. De Nietzsche à Teilhard de Chardin.* Paris: Centurion, 1965. See pp. 249-344. *El superhombre: De Nietzsche a Teilhard de Chardin.* Salamanca: Sigueme, 1968. *The Superman: From Nietzsche to Teilhard de Chardin.* Notre Dame, Ind., University of Notre Dame Press, 1969.

647. Chanson, P., and Paul Chauchard. "J.B. Buckez, précurseur de Teilhard de Chardin." *Synthèses*, June, 1965, pp. 53-74.

648. Charbonneau, Bernard M. "Progrès et liberté." *Foi et vie* (1957): 6, 493-524.

649. ———. *Teilhard de Chardin. Prophète d'un âge totalitaire.* Paris: Denoel, 1963. See Item 4076. *Teilhard de Chardin, profeet van een totalitair tijdperk.* 's-Gravenhage: Kruseman, 1967.

650. "Chardin's Work Seen as Ground for Christian-Marxist Dialogue." *The Catholic Messenger*, November 10, 1966, p. 3.

651. Charles, F. Albert. "Nouvel humanisme et enseignement chrétien." *Orientations*, October, 1963, pp. 36-64.

652. Charlesworth, M.J. "The World of Teilhard de Chardin." *Quadrant* (1961): 19, 75-80.

653. Charon, Jean E. *La connaissance de l'univers.* Paris: Seuil, 1961.

654. ———. *De la physique à l'homme.* Genève: Éditions Gonthier, 1965. See pp. 55-58.

655. ———. *Du temps, de l'espace et des hommes.* Paris: Seuil, 1962.

655a. ———. "Une évolution néo-teilhardienne." *Revue Teilhard de Chardin* (1978): 73, 4-9.

656. ———. *L'homme à sa découverte.* Paris: Seuil, 1963.

657. Charles-Geniaux, Claire. "L'avenir de l'homme: Negation du progrès ou foi en l'avenir." *Revue du Tarn* (1960): 5, 166-169.

658. ———. "Einstein et Teilhard de Chardin annoncent une science et une religion 'cosmiques.'" *Arts* (1961): 835, 1.

659. ———. "L'être et le verbe." *Univers* (1965): 2, 49-57.

660. ———. "Glosy o Teilhardzie de Chardin." [Views on Teilhard de Chardin.] *Znak* (1962): 92/93, 238-245.

661. ———. "L'immense problème du langage." *Univers* (1964): 1, 85-98.

662. ———. "La physique montre que l'évolution a un but." *Revue Teilhard de Chardin* (1967): 30, 16-26.

663. Charrière, François. "Monitum." *La Liberté*, August 25-26, 1962.

664. Chassagneux, Albert. "La religion change-t-elle?" *Jeunes chrétiens d'Ampère* (1965): 44.

665. "La chasteté selon Teilhard." *Permanences* (1967): 44, 55-80.

666. Chatelet, François. "De l'autre côté du cheval." *Le nouvel observateur* (1966): 67.

667. Chauchard, Paul. "Actualité de Teilhard de Chardin." *Le concours médical*, July 21, 1962.
Also *Perspectives ouvrières* (1956): 80, 15-17.

668. ———. "L'amorisation: un fait, un devoir." *Revue Teilhard de Chardin* (1963): 14, 16-17.

669. ———. "L'amour, secret du monde. Pierre Teilhard de Chardin." *Balisage* (1961): 16/17, 25-27.

670. ———. "Apprendre à vivre." *Revue Teilhard de Chardin* (1968): 36, 12-14.

671. ———. "Aspects psychobiologiques de l'amour." *Education et enseignement. Revue de l'U.C.E.O.* (1960): 4, 3-10.

672. ———. "Bibliographie teilhardienne." *La table ronde*, May, 1962.

673. ————. "Biologie et neurosociologie au service de la
        connaissance de l'homme." *La table ronde* (1961): 158,
        1-20.

674. ————. "Le cerveau humain, organe de la noosphère."
        Revue Teilhard de Chardin (1960): 3/4, 15-16.

675. ————. "Claudel, Teilhard ou la convergence des con-
        traires." *La table ronde* (1964): 194, 174-180.

676. ————. "La création évolutive." *Droit et liberté*,
        April, 1956, pp. 8-14.

677. ————. "Culture et humanisme scientifique." *La
        table ronde* (1962): 169, 139-143.

678. ————. "De la matière à l'esprit." *Revue Teilhard de
        Chardin* (1962): 10, 5-7.

679. ————. "De la nature humain." *La table ronde* (1961):
        166, 65-73.

680. ————. "Deux fils de l'espérance." *La table ronde*
        (1964): 202, 79-84.

681. ————. "Deux maîtres de l'apologétique chrétienne:
        Pascal et Teilhard de Chardin." *La table ronde* (1962):
        171, 97-103.
        "Pascal e Teilhard de Chardin." *Avvento* (1965): 9,
        59-63.

682. ————. "Egalité cérébrale des races." *Revue Teilhard de
        Chardin* (1964): 19, 12-14.

683. ————. "Einheit statt Doktrin." *Dokumente* (1967): 23,
        57-58.

684. ————. "Erotisme et chasteté dans l'énergétique de
        l'amour." *Univers* (1965): 2, 79-94.

685. ————. *L'être humain selon Teilhard de Chardin*. Paris:
        Gabalda, 1959.
        *Man and Cosmos. Scientific Phenomenology in Teilhard
        de Chardin*. New York: Herder & Herder, 1965.
        Also Montréal: Palm, 1965.

686. ————. "Evolution and Aquinas." *Time*, January 11,
        1960, p. 4.

687.   ———. "L'évolution et les valeurs humaines." *L'âge nouveau* (1959): 106, 37-47.

688.   ———. "Evolutionnisme matérialiste et fixisme onto-logique dans la création évolutive." *Bulletin de la Société française de philosophie* (1959).

689.   ———. "Glosy o Teilhardzie de Chardin." [Views on Teilhard de Chardin.] *Znak* (1962): 92/93, 234-238.

690.   ———. *O Homem em Teilhard de Chardin.* São Paulo: Herder, 1963.

691.   ———. "Hommage à Ignace Lepp." *Revue Teilhard de Chardin* (1967): 30, 4-5.

692.   ———. "Importance et limites du niveau biologique d'objectivation des valeurs humaines." *Archives de philosophie* (1958): 1, 106-116.

693.   ———. "Introduction aux travaux." *Univers* (1965): 3, 3-5.

694.   ———. "Un lexique pour Teilhard." *Témoignage chréti-en* (1963): 971, 15.

695.   ———. "Le mythe d'un (certain) teilhardisme." *Revue Teilhard de Chardin* (1963): 15, 33-35.

696.   ———. "Noosphère et hygiène cérébrale." *Le phare dimanche*, April 2, 1961, pp. 5-6.

697.   ———. "Noosphère et nature humain." *Revue Teilhard de Chardin* (1961): 8/9, 20-24.

698.   ———. "L'optimisme dramatique de Teilhard est l'espér-ance chrétienne." *Revue Teilhard de Chardin* (1962): 11, 17-18.

699.   ———. *Our Need of Love.* New York: P.J. Kenedy, 1968.

700.   ———. *La pensée scientifique de Teilhard.* Paris: Éditions Universitaires, 1965.
        El pensamiento científico de Teilhard de Chardin. Madrid: Peninsula, 1966.

701.   ———. "La phénoménologie scientifique. Pierre Teil-hard de Chardin." *Balisage* (1961): 16/17, 7-8, 25-27.

702. ————. "Pierre Teilhard de Chardin." *Civiltà delle macchine* (1962): 3, 23-29.

703. ————. "Pour une convergence personnalisante: l'unité dans la diversité." *Univers* (1966): 3, 55-65.

704. ————. "Pour un front commun d'avancée humaine." *Univers* (1964): 1, 63-73.

705. ————. "Présence de Pierre Teilhard de Chardin." *Synthèses* (1961): 187, 363-366.

706. ————. "Profane et sacré." *La Croix*, May 12-13, 1968.

707. ————. "Le R.P. Teilhard de Chardin et la Phénomène humain." *Presse médicale* (1956): 64, 842-843.

708. ————. "Science et prière." *Droit et liberté*, October, 1955, pp. 107-114.

709. ————. "Scientifiques et mystiques: Pascal et Teilhard de Chardin." *Pascal, textes du tricentenaire*. Paris: Fayard, 1963, pp. 83-97.

710. ————. "Technique, sagesse, sainteté." *Revue Teilhard de Chardin* (1967): 30, 43-53.

711. ————. "Teilhard de Chardin et la conception catholique de Dieu." *L'âge nouveau* (1960): 110, 85-88.

712. ————. "Teilhard de Chardin et saint Thomas d'Aquin." *Revue Teilhard de Chardin* (1960): 1/2, 11-12.

713. ————. *Teilhard de Chardin e il fenomeno umano*. Città di Castello: Carabba, 1964.

714. ————. "Teilhard de Chardin. L'humanisme socialiste et la réconciliation des humanismes." *Synthèses* (1960): 169/170, 331-355.
"Teilhard de Chardin, het socialistisch humanisme en de verzoening der humanismen." Item 3724, pp. 73-107.

715. ————. *Teilhard de Chardin on Love and Suffering*. Glen Rock, N.J.: Paulist Press, 1966.

716. ————. *Teilhard de Chardin, un modèle et un guide pour notre temps*. Paris: Levain, 1964.
Teilhard de Chardin, voorbeeld en gids voor onze tijd. Leuven: Levain, 1969.

717. ――――. *Teilhard et l'optimisme de la croix.* Paris:
Éditions Universitaires, 1964.
Teilhard de Chardin e o otimismo da Cruz. Petró-
polis: Vozes, 1967\
Teilhard y el optimismo de la cruz. Buenos Aires:
Columbia, 1968.

718. ――――. "Teilhard, le miséricordieux." *L'Evangile de
la miséricorde,* ed. by Alphonse Goettmann. Paris:
Cerf, 1965, pp. 217-227.

719. ――――. "Teilhard le nécessaire." *Revue Teilhard de
Chardin* (1970): 42, 25-34; 43, 16-21.

720. ――――. *Teilhard, témoin d'amour.* Paris: Éditions
Universitaires, 1962.
Teilhard, getuige van de liefde. Tielt-Den Haag:
Lannoo, 1964.
Teilhard, testamunha do amor. Petropolis, Vozes,
1967.
Teilhard, testigo del amor. Buenos Aires: Columba,
1968.

721. ――――. "Valeur et limites de l'apport scientifique à
la philosophie." *Dialectica* (1959): 2, 123-143.

722. ――――. "Vers une chimie de la mémoire." *Revue Teilhard de Chardin* (1964): 18, 11-15.

723. ――――. "'La vision du passé' de Teilhard de Chardin."
Les études philosophiques (1957): 12, 362-363.

724. ――――, and Hubert Cuypers. *Für und wider Teilhard de
Chardin.* Olten: Roven, 1964.

725. Chauvin, Rémy. "Rostand et Teilhard." *Saint-Luc.
Evangile et médecine* (1965): 71, 574-578.

726. Chavaz, Edmond. "A propos du Père Teilhard de Chardin."
Le Courrier, July 15, 1962, p.1; July 16, 1962, p.1;
July 17, 1962, p. 1; July 18, 1962, p. 1; July 19,
1962, pp. 1-2.

727. ――――. "Teilhard dégage la voie de l'espérance."
Le Courrier, April 28, 1965, pp. 1-3.

728. ――――. "Teilhard donne une voix à notre angoisse."
Le Courrier, April 27, 1965, pp. 1-2.

729. ————. "Um Pater Teilhard de Chardin." *Schweizer Rundschau* (1962): 61, 546-560.

730. Cheney, Brainard. "Has Teilhard de Chardin Really Joined the Within and the Without of Things?" *Sewannee Review* (1965): 73, 217-236.

731. Chenu, M.-D. *La foi dans l'intelligence*. Paris: Cerf, 1964.

732. Chérvel, Jules. "'Le phénomène humain.'" *L'union* (1960): 4, 21-93.

733. Chevalier, Jacques. "Lettre à Claude Cuenot." Item 3041, pp. 52-54.

734. Chiari, Joseph. *Twentieth Century French Thought*. New York: Gordian Press, 1975.

735. Chibon, Pierre. "Réflexions après une conférence sur le Père Teilhard de Chardin." *Résurrection* (1956): 2, 61-66.

736. Chifflot, T.G. "Pour une vision chrétienne de l'histoire. A propos de Teilhard de Chardin." *Signes du temps* (1960): 7, 3-7.
   Also *Approches d'une théologie de l'histoire*. Paris: Cerf, 1960, pp. 105-127.

737. Choisy, Maryse. "L'amour dynamique de l'histoire et son sens nouveau chez Teilhard de Chardin." *Revue Teilhard de Chardin* (1963): 15, 2-4.

738. ————. *L'être et le silence*. Genève: Mont-Blanc, 1964. See pp. 121-123, 249-256.

738a. ————. "Mon grand ami Teilhard de Chardin n'est plus." *Combat*, April 18, 1955. See also Item 4550.

739. ————. *Teilhard et l'Inde*. Paris: Éditions Universitaires, 1963.
   Teilhard e a Índia. Petrópolis: Vozes, 1967.

739a. ————. "Teilhard et l'Inde." *Revue Teilhard de Chardin* (1978): 73, 26-29; 75/76, 51-55. Excerpts from Item 739.

740. Chombart de Lauwe, Paul. "Social Evolution and Human
      Aspirations. Teilhard de Chardin and Sociology."
      American Catholic Sociological Review (1962): 4,
      294-309, 336-337.

741. *Le Christ évoluteur. Socialisation et religion.* Paris:
      Seuil, 1966. Contains Items 214, 1254, 2076, 2279,
      2282, 4063, 4255, 4363, 4373.

742. Christophe, Lucien. "Les papiers de guerre de Teilhard
      de Chardin." *Revue générale belge* (1962): 5, 1-16.

743. "Chronique des revues: Pierre Teilhard de Chardin."
      Rencontre Orient-Occident (1955): 5, 29-30; 6, 25-26.

744. "Chronologie biographique." *Revue Teilhard de Chardin*
      (1967-68): 33/34, 78-81

745. *Ciclo de conferencias en torno a Pierre Teilhard de
      Chardin.* Santander: Anteneo de Santander, 1967. Con-
      tains Items 21, 557, 804, 937, 1701, 1885, 2481, 4098.

746. Cieszkowski, Jerzy. "Die Anthropologie in der Konzep-
      tion von Pierre Teilhard de Chardin." *Polen* (1967):
      4/5, 29-31.

747. Cione, Edmond. *Fede e ragione nella storia. Filosofia
      della religione e storia degli ideali religiose dell'Oc-
      cidente.* Bologna: Capelli, 1963.

748. Citron, Hans. "Das wissenschaftliche Werk von Armin
      Müller." *Perspektiven der Zukunft* (1973): 2, 2-4.

749. Citterich, Vittorio. "Padre de Lubac alla 'Domus
      Mariae.' L'ispirazione paolina in Teilhard de Chardin."
      L'Avvenire d'Italia, October 17, 1965, p. 3.

750. Clair, Jacques. "Dieu est-il marxiste?" *Revue Teilhard
      de Chardin* (1963): 16, 17-19.
      Also in *Paris-variétés* (1960): 85, 4, 9.

751. ————. "'Journal' d'un non-croyant." Item 1259, pp.
      114-121.

752. ————. "Teilhard de Chardin: l'avenir de l'homme."
      Paris-variétés (1960): 84, 4, 8.

753. ————. "Teilhard de Chardin: L'homme est la clef de l'univers." *Bulletin du Centre de documentation du Grand Orient de France* (1963): 37, 17.

754. ————. "Témoignage." Item 3292, pp. 179-180.

755. Clark, Mary T. "The 'Divine Milieu' in Philosophical Perspective." *Downside Review* (1962): 80, 12-25.

756. ————. "Modern Thomism and Teilhard de Chardin." *Mélanges Charles de Koninck.* Quebec: Presses de L'Université Laval, 1968, pp. 115-128.

757. Clarke, Desmond. "Original Sin in the Thought of Teilhard de Chardin." *Laurentianum* (1968): 9, 353-394.

758. ————. "Le péché originel dans les oeuvres du P. de Chardin." Typescript. Lyons: Faucltés catholiques de Lyon, 1967.

759. Clarke, Thomas E. "The Significance of Teilhard." *America* (1966): 22, 779.

760. Claude, Henri. "Sur Teilhard de Chardin." *A.F. Université* (1965): 100, 8.

761. Clavelin, Maurice. "Teilhard de Chardin (Le R.P. Pierre) (1881-1955)." *Les philosophes célèbres*, ed. by M. Merleau-Ponty. Paris: Lucien Mazenod, 1956, pp. 447-448.

762. Claverino, F. "Il lavoro dell'uomo nel pensiero di Teilhard de Chardin." *Studium* (1971): 67, 189-192.

763. Cliquet, R. "De evolutietheorie van Teilhard de Chardin met betrekking tot het vraagstuk van de hominisatie." *Handelingen van het XXVe Vlaams Filologencongres.* Zellik: Secretariaat van de Vlaamse Filologengencongressen, 1967, pp. 53-61.

764. Clouard, Henri. *Histoire de la littérature française. II. 1915-1960.* Paris: Albin Michel, 1962. See pp. 542-552.

765. ————. "Teilhard de Chardin, poète de la matière." *Les Beaux-Arts de Bruxelles*, February, 1961.

766. Coccia, Antonio. "La transformazione dell'universo in
      Teilhard de Chardin." *Città de vita* (1967): 22, 75-
      81.
      Also *Ideali politici e problemi religiosi in alcumi
      grandi filosofi*. Roma: Miscellanea Francescana, 1977,
      pp. 183-188.

767. Codaccioni, A. "Les conceptions du Père Teilhard de
      Chardin sur le groupe zoologique humain." *Informa-
      tion scientifique* (1959): 13, 23-26.

768. Coffy, Robert. *Teilhard de Chardin et la socialisme*.
      Lyon: Chronique Sociale de France, 1966.
      Teilhard de Chardin e o socialismo. Lisboa: Livrar-
      ia Morais, 1967.
      Teilhard de Chardin e il socialismo. Alba: Edizi-
      one Paoline, 1969.

769. Cognet, Louis. *Le Père Teilhard de Chardin et la pensée
      contemporaine*. Paris: Flammarion, 1952.

770. ————. "Quelques notes." *La France catholique*, Feb-
      ruary, 1951.

771. Cohen, Lionel. "La nature et l'homme dans l'oeuvre
      d'Albert Camus et dans le pensée de Teilhard de Char-
      din." Mimeographed. Jerusalem: Hebrew University,
      1972.

772. Cole, Raymond. "Información, evolución y entropía.
      (Algunos apuntes en torno a una intuición de Teil-
      hard de Chardin.)" *Logos* (1976): 11, 69-88.

773. Colin, Fernand. "Contribution du Père Teilhard de
      Chardin à la formulation de la mystique d'Occident."
      *Académie des sciences, belles-lettres et arts de
      Besançon. Procès-verbaux et memoires* (1962-63):
      175, 85-101.

774. ————. "Le Père Teilhard de Chardin et Claudel. Deux
      esprits cosmiques. Aspects sur leur mystique." *Acad-
      émie des sciences, belles-lettres et arts de Besançon.
      Procès-verbaux et memoires* (1960-61): 174, 19-34.

775. ————. "Teilhard de Chardin et Claudel." *Résonnances
      lyonnaises* (1960): 87, 30-33.

775a. Collart. Émile. "Teilhard l'anti-Pascal?" *Revue Teilhard de Chardin* (1978): 75/76, 52-53.

776. Collignon, Joseph. "Phenomenon of Teilhard." *Christian Century* (1965): 82, 426-428.

777. ————. "The Uses of Guilt." *Saturday Review*, October 31, 1964, pp. 26-27, 36.

778. Collin, Remy. *L'évolution, hypothèses et problèmes.* Paris: Fayard, 1958. *Evolution.* New York: Hawthorne, 1959.

779. Collins, James. "Darwin's Impact on Philosophy." *Thought* (1959): 133, 185-248. See pp. 245-248.

780. Collins, Peter M. "Teilhard de Chardin and Christian Schools." *Educational Theory* (1973): 267-276.

781. "Colloquium Teilhardianum: Pax Romana Meeting in Venice." *Tablet*, June 23, 1961, p. 598.

782. Colombo, Giuseppe. "La teologia del Milieu divin." Item 2744, pp. 93-97. "La théologie du Milieu divin." Item 2744 trans., pp. 85-89.

783. Colomer, Eusebio. *De la Edad Media al Renacimiento, Ramón Llull, Nicólas de Cusa, Juan Pico della Mirandola.* Barcelona: Editorial Herder, 1975.

784. ————. "Diálogo con Teilhard de Chardin." *Hechos y dichos* (1966): 495-497.

785. ————. "En torno a la concepción bíblica y científica del hombre. Diálogo entre un teilhardiano ilustrado y un teológo benévolo." *Hechos y dichos* (1969): 215-225.

786. ————. "En torno a Teilhard de Chardin: la obra y sus intérpretes." *Selecciones de libros. Actualidad bibliográfica de filosofía y teologia* (1964): 1, 26-40; (1968): 5, 11-76.

787. ————. "Entre Cristo y el hombre." *La estafeta literaria* (1964): 290, 4-5.

788. ————. "Estudi preliminar." Item 4603 trans., pp. 7-
46.

789. ————. *A Evolução segundo Teilhard de Chardin.* Oporto:
Livraria Tavares Martins, 1967.

790. ————. "Evolució, creació i providència." *Qüestions
de vida cristiana* (1969): 47, 57-82.

791. ————. "La evolución cristocéntrica de Teilhard de
Chardin." *Espíritu* (1963): 12, 112-126.

792. ————. "Evolución y cristianismo." Item 1419, pp.
853-911.

793. ————. "El fenomenon Teilhard." *Qüestions de vida
cristiana* (1965): 27, 100-109.
"El fenómeno Teilhard." *Hechos y dichos* (1966):
282-287.

794. ————. *Hombre y Dios al encuentro. Antropología y
teología en Teilhard de Chardin.* Barcelona: Herder,
1974.

795. ————. "Mundo y Dios al encuentro. El universo cristo-
céntrico de Teilhard de Chardin." *Orbis catholicus*
(1962): 3, 193-215.
Also Barcelona: Nova Terra, 1963.
Also 2d ed., 1964.
"Pierre Teilhard de Chardin verso il 'Punto Omega.'"
Digest cattolico (1963): 4, 39-48.

796. ————. *L'obra de Teilhard i els seus intèrprets.* Barcelona: Editorial 62, 1964. Also contains Item 908.

797. ————. *El pensament de Teilhard de Chardin.* Barcelona:
Bruguera, 1967.

798. ————. "Pierre Teilhard de Chardin." *Archivum Historicum Societatis Jesu* (1967): 36, 341-367.

799. ————. *Pierre Teilhard de Chardin, un evolucionisme
cristià?* Barcelona: Dalmau, 1961.

800. ————. "El problema de Dios en Teilhard de Chardin."
Revista portuguesa de filosofia (1970): 36, 51-91.

801. ———. "Proceso a Teilhard de Chardin." *Diario de Barcelona*, June 15, 1967.

802. ———. "Socialización y personalismo en Teilhard de Chardin." *Convivium* (1969): 28, 25-52. Also *Revista portuguesa de filosofia* (1969): 25, 168-201.

803. ———. "Teilhard de Chardin, diez años después." *Razón y fe* (1965): 810/811, 17-36.

804. ———. "Teilhard de Chardin filósofo." *Pensamiento* (1970): 26, 141-161.

805. ———. "Teilhard de Chardin y el ateísmo secularista." *Razón y fe* (1969): 179, 359-376.

806. ———. "Teilhard de Chardin y la crisis del humanismo." *Pensamiento* (1974): 30, 379-397.

807. ———. "Teilhard en el origen de un mundo nuevo." *Temas* (1965): 136-139. Also Item 745, pp. 231-264. "Teilhard de Chardin a l'origen d'un món neu." *Avant* (1965): 3, 7-9.

808. ———. "Teilhardiana." *Selecciones de libros* (1965): 2, 256-264.

809. ———, and A. Rubio. "Bibliografía teilhardiana." *Hechos y dichos* (1966): 326-336.

810. Combaluzier, Charles. *Introduction à la géologie.* Paris: Seuil, 1961.

811. Combes, André. "A propos de theodicée teilhardienne. Simples réflexions méthodologiques." *La pensée catholique* (1967): 108, 32-63. Also *Les études philosophiques* (1965): 20, 483-511.

812. ———. "Autour de 'teilhardogenèse'? Réponse." *La pensée catholique* (1964): 89, 61-68.

813. ———. *Teilhard de Chardin et la sainte évolution.* Paris: Seghers, 1969.

814. ————. "Teilhardogénèse." *La pensée catholique* (1963):
      84, 45–81.
      Also *Ephemerides carmeliticae* (1963): 14, 155–194.

815. Combes, Joseph. "Pour une relecture de Teilhard de
      Chardin." *Bulletin de la Faculté catholique de Lyon*
      (1969): 46, 35–40.

816. Comblin, Joseph. *Echec de l'Action catholique?* Paris:
      Editions Universitaires, 1961. See pp. 157–162.

817. ————. "Trois hommes et un renouveau théologique."
      Dictionnaire des idées contemporaines. Paris: Éditions
      Universitaires, 1964, pp. 111–165.

818. Compagnion, C. "Convergence de la science." *Isen* (1966):
      11, 14.

819. "Une conférence de l'union rationaliste sur le Père Teil-
      hard de Chardin." *Union catholique des scientifiques
      français. Bulletin* (1960): 54, 4–5.

820. Congar, Yves. "Église et monde." *Esprit*, February, 1965,
      pp. 341–342.
      "Iglesia y mundo." *Cuadernos para el diálogo* (1965):
      19, 7–11.

821. ————. "Perspectives chrétiennes sur la vie personnelle
      et la vie collective." *Socialisation et personne hu-
      maine.* Grenoble: Semaine sociale de Grenoble, 1960,
      pp. 195–221.

822. Congregation of the Holy Office. "Monitum on the Writ-
      ings of Teilhard de Chardin." *Acta Apostolicae Sedis*
      (1962): 54, 526.
      Also *American Ecclesiastical Review* (1962): 147, 134.
      Also *Irish Ecclesiastical Record* (1962): 98, 195.
      Also *Jurist* (1962): 22, 447.
      Also *Catholic Messenger*, July 5, 1962, pp. 1+.
      Also *Clergy Review* (1962): 47, 562.

823. Connolly, James M. *Le renouveau théologique dans la
      France contemporaine.* Paris/Fribourg: Éditions St.
      Paul, 1966. See pp. 134–148.

824. Conto, Galdino de. "O homen em Teilhard de Chardin."
      Anuario Riograndense de Filosofia (1967): 1, 151–161.

825. ————. "Teilhard de Chardin e a evolucão." *Vozes*
(1968): 62, 508-521, 605-622, 712-716.

826. Contri, Sirio. "Teilhard de Chardin o l'evoluzione
ideal." *Ragguaglio librario* (1965): 32, 16-18.

827. "Contribuição de Chardin ao socialismo africano." *Vozes*
(1966): 60, 670-673.

828. "Convergences. Actes du 3e Symposium international
Pierre Teilhard de Chardin." *Univers* (1964): 1-104.

829. Cony, Carlos Héctor. "Teilhard de Chardin." *Correio
da manhã*, July 31, 1963, p. 1.

830. Cop, Józef. "Nad dzielem O. Teilharda pt. 'Środowisko
Boze.'" [Regarding Père Teilhard's Work, "The Divine
Milieu."] *Collectanea theologica* (1973): 2, 158-163.

831. Copleston, Frederick. *A History of Philosophy. IX.
Maine de Biran to Sartre.* London: Search Press, 1975.
See pp. 318-339.
Also Garden City, N.Y.: Doubleday Image Books, 1977.

832. Coppieters 't Wallant, Bertrand. "Le préfixe dans 'Le
phénomène humain' du Père Teilhard de Chardin." Mimeographed. Louvain: Faculté de philosophie et lettres
de l'Université catholique de Louvain, 1969.

833. Corbishley, Thomas. *The Contemporary Christian.* London: Chapman, 1966. See pp. 83-94.

834. ————. "The Phenomenon of Teilhard de Chardin." *Wiseman Review* (1965): 238, 267-277.

835. ————. *The Spirituality of Teilhard de Chardin.* London: Collins, 1971.
Also Paramus, N.J.: Paulist Press, 1971.

836. ————. "Teilhard and the 'Eternal Feminine.'" *The
Month* (1968): 40, 86-87.

837. ————. "Teilhard and his Detractors." *The Month*
(1973): 6, 300-304.

838. ————. "Teilhard and the Original Sin." *The Teilhard
Review* (1974): 2, 36-37.

839. ————. "Teilhard the Theologian." *Tablet* (1971): 225,
      1070.

840. ————. "Teilhardism in England." *Wiseman Review* (1964–
      65).

840a. Corbo, Michele. "Genesi del personalismo di Teilhard
      de Chardin." *Studium* (1977): 73, 609–632.

840b. ————. "Scienza e storia in Teilhard de Chardin."
      Thesis, Università di Bari, 1975.

841. Cornelis, Marcel. *Sortis du ghetto. Spiritualité de
      la pré-mission. Jalons pour une spiritualité de la
      pré-mission à la lumière de Foucauld, Teilhard, Peyri-
      guère.* Paris: Éditions Cheminement, 1964.
      *Salidos del ghetto. Espiritualidad de la obra pre-
      misión. (Jalones para una espiritualidad de la pre-
      misión a la luz de Foucauld, Teilhard y Peyriguère.*
      Barcelona: Nova Terra, 1967.
      *Uit het ghetto. Richtlijnen voor een spiritualiteit
      van de premissionering, aan de hand van de Foucauld,
      Teilhard en Peyriguère.* Antwerpen: Patmos, 1967.
      Also Bilthoven: H. Nelissen, 1967.

842. Corneloup, J. "À la recherche d'un nouvel humanisme."
      Évoluer (1962): 10, 1.

843. ————. *D'Alpha à Omega. La vie. Une conception
      hylozoïste de l'évolution.* Paris: Vega, 1957.
      Also *Évoluer* (1967–68): 33/36, 1+.

844. ————. "Les francs-maçons devant la pensée de Teilhard
      de Chardin." *Grand Orient de France, Foyer philoso-
      phique* (1957): 3–7.

845. ————. "Le milieu divin." *Symbolisme* (1959): 343,
      149–160.

846. ————. "Pensée teilhardienne et humanité en progres."
      Symbolisme (1957): 332, 221–237.

847. ————. "Teilhard de Chardin et sa doctrine de l'évolu-
      tion." *Symbolisme* (1956): 320, 103–121.

848. ————. "Teilhard de Chardin et son oeuvre." *Lettres
      mensuelles*, Octobre, 1970, pp. 8–11

849. Corte, Marcel de. "Apollonius de Tyane et le P. Teil-
      hard de Chardin." Écrits de Paris, March, 1968, pp.
      13-21.

850. ———. "La religion teilhardienne." Le Vaillant (1965):
      44, 4-5.
      Also Itinéraires (1965): 91, 110-183.

851. ———. "Sociologie du teilhardisme." In Item 3744.
      Also Ordre français (1963): 7, 51-61.

      Corte, Nicholas. See Cristiani, Leon.

852. Cortellese Platania, Elena. Cristo nella materia. Rifles-
      sioni su Teilhard de Chardin. Bologna: Edizioni De-
      honiane, 1968.

853. Cortese, Alessandro. "Appunti sul senso del termine
      sforzo ('La perfection chrétienne de l'effort humain')."
      Item 2744, pp. 145-154.
      "Notes sur le sens du terme effort ('La perfection
      chrétienne de l'effort humain')." Item 2744 trans.,
      pp. 134-143.

854. Corvez, Maurice. "Creation et évolution du monde."
      Revue thomiste (1964): 64, 549-568. See pp. 558-562.

855. ———. De la science à la foi, Teilhard de Chardin.
      Tours/Paris: Mame, 1964.
      De la ciencia a la fe. Teilhard de Chardin. Bilbao:
      Mensajero, 1967.

856. "'Cosmologie de la univers.' La science des résultats
      des sciences." Rencontre (1965): 2, 20-24.

857. "Cosmos in Travail: L. Barjon's Lectures at the Ren-
      contres Chrétiennes." Tablet (1963): 217, 372.

858. Cot, J. "La pensée philosophique de Teilhard de Chardin."
      Cahiers rationalistes (1960): 187, 106-128.

859. Cotereau, J. "Autour du P. Teilhard de Chardin." La
      raison (1961): 52, 1.

860. ———. "Comment l'Église persécute ... puis exploite le
      génie." La raison (1961): 50, 1.

861. Couillard, Pierre. "Chronique teilhardienne." *Dialogue*
      (1966): 50, 644-660.

862. ————. "Notes bibliographiques." *Dialogue* (1965): 49,
      568-575.

863. ————. "La place de l'homme dans la nature." *Dialogue*
      (1964-65): 48, 314-384.

864. Courroy, Marie-Paule. "O 'amor' no pensamento do P.
      Teilhard de Chardin." *Revista portuguesa de filosofia*
      (1972): 28, 324-331.

865. Cousins, Ewert H. "Christ and the Cosmos: Teilhard de
      Chardin and Bonaventure." *Cord* (1966): 16, 99-105,
      131-136.
      "Teilhard de Chardin et saint Bonaventure." *Études
      franciscaines* (1969): 19, 175-186.
      Also Item 3950, pp. 195-211.

866. ————. *Process Theology: Basic Writings*. New York:
      Newman Press, 1971.

867. ————. "Teilhard and the Theology of the Spirit."
      Cross Currents (1969): 2, 159-177.

868. ————. "Teilhard, Process Thought and Religious Educa-
      tion." *Religious Education* (1973): 68, 331-338.

869. Coutagne, Paul-Henri. "Actualité Teilhard?" *Bulletin
      des catholiques scientifiques français* (1973): 129,
      14-27.

870. ————. "Le Christ au coeur de la matière et au coeur
      de l'histoire. La vision christique du Père Teilhard
      de Chardin." *Equipes enseignantes* (1967-68): 2, 64-
      78; 3, 70-87.
      Also *Que dites-vous du Christ? De saint Marc à Bon-
      hoeffer*. Paris: Cerf, 1969, pp. 135-180.

871. ————. "Chronique teilhardienne." *Revue des sciences
      philosophiques et théologiques* (1968): 52, 303-343.

872. ————. "Chronique teilhardienne. Teilhard en face à
      face avec l'histoire." *Revue des sciences philosophiques
      et théologiques* (1973): 57, 323-345.

873. ————. "Chronique teilhardienne. Teilhard et les voies de l'humanisme chrétien." *Revue des sciences philosophiques et théologiques* (1975): 59, 317-334.

874. ————. "L'eternel féminin." *Vie spirituelle* (1969): 120, 459-467.

875. ————. "La 'modernità' secondo Teilhard de Chardin." *Futuro dell'uomo* (1976): 3, 3-12. Also in Item 876.

876. ————. "Modernité et modernisme chez Teilhard de Chardin." *Recherches et documents du Centre Thomas More* (1975): 7, 21-45. Contains Items 875 and 881.

877. ————. "Un prophète en procès: Teilhard de Chardin." *Vie spirituelle* (1971): 125, 345-352.

878. ————. "Science et foi: de Teilhard de Chardin à Alexis Carrel." *Vie spirituelle* (1975): 129, 904-910.

879. ————. "Teilhard de Chardin." *Revue des sciences philosophiques et théologiques* (1964): 48, 160-168. Also *Vie spirituelle* (1968): 119, 96-100; (1969): 121, 154-158.

880. ————. "Teilhard de Chardin apôtre du Christ pour notre temps." *Vie spirituelle* (1970): 123, 481-485.

881. ————. "Teilhard de Chardin e il modernismo." *Futuro dell'uomo* (1976): 4, 3-16. Also in Item 876.

882. Coutinho, Auizio Bezerra. "Teilhard de Chardin: ciência e profetismo." *Estudios Universitários* (1966): 6, 39-49.

883. Cox, Harvey. "Progrès évolutionniste et espérance chrétienne." *Concilium* (1967): 26, 35-45.

884. Crabbe, Raoul. "Une conférence de Mme. Dominique de Wespin. P. Teilhard de Chardin tel que je l'ai connu." *Le Phare dimanche* (1960): 737, 5.

884a. Cracco, G. Amedeo. "De transformismo." *Dossiers de la Commission Synodale de Peiping* (1930): 5, 259-264.

885. Cranston, Maurice. "Teilhard and Tillich." *Encounter*
      (1967): 6, 83-86.

886. Cren, Pierre. "Le chrétien et le monde selon Teilhard
      de Chardin." *Concilium* (1966): 19, 61-71.
      "Christ und Welt nach Teilhard de Chardin." *Concili-
      um* (1966): 2, 689-696.
      "The Christian and the World in Teilhard de Chardin."
      Concilium (1966): 2, 38-45.
      "El cristiano y el mundo según Teilhard de Chardin."
      Concilium (1966): 2/3, 254-268.
      "De christen en de wereld volgens Teilhard de Char-
      din." *Concilium* (1966): 9, 73-86.
      "O cristão e o mundo segundo Teilhard de Chardin."
      Concilium (1966): 9, 63-74.

887. Crepin, Julien. "Zwei Vertreter der Evolutionslehre:
      Bergson und Teilhard de Chardin." *Perspektiven der
      Zukunft* (1969): 3, 5-7.

888. Crespi, Clara. "Il mundo, l'uomo, Cristo nel pensiero
      del padre Pierre Teilhard de Chardin." Laureate the-
      sis. Milano: Università degli Studi, 1961.

889. Crespy, Georges. "Le Christ du Père Teilhard de Char-
      din." *Revue de théologie et philosophie* (1959): 9,
      297-321.

890. ————. *Essai sur Teilhard de Chardin. De la science
      à la théologie.* Neuchatel/Paris: Delachaux et Niestle,
      1966.
      *Ensayo sobre Teilhard de Chardin. De la ciencia
      a la teología.* Salamanca: Sígueme, 1967.
      *Der Gott für uns. Weltbild und Theologie nach
      Teilhard de Chardin.* Stuttgart: Schwabenverlag, 1968.
      *Dalla scienze alla teologia. Saggio su Teilhard de
      Chardin.* Roma: A.V.E., 1968.
      *From Science to Theology? An Essay on Teilhard de
      Chardin.* Nashville, Tenn.: Abingdon Press, 1968.

891. ————. *Essai sur la théologie de Teilhard de Chardin.*
      Paris: Éditions Universitaires, 1961.

892. ————. "Evolution and Christology in Teilhard de
      Chardin." *Dialog* (1965): 4, 118-127.

893. ————. "Intention scientifique et vision de l'homme."
      Revue de l'évangelisation (1959): 82, 102-114.

894. ———. "L'intention théologique de Teilhard de Chardin." Item 3851, pp. 303-332.

895. ———. "La pensée du Père Teilhard de Chardin." *Cahiers de Villemétrie* (1961): 9/10, 3-19.

896. ———. *La pensée théologique de Teilhard de Chardin.* Paris: Éditions Universitaires, 1961. Contains Item 4583.
Il pensiero teologico di Pierre Teilhard de Chardin. Torino: Borla, 1963.
Das theologische Denken Teilhard de Chardins. Stuttgart: Schwabenverlag, 1964.
Het theologisch denken van Teilhard de Chardin. Utrecht/Antwerpen: Spectrum, 1966.
El pensamiento teológico de Teilhard de Chardin. Barcelona: Estela, 1970.

897. ———. "La problématique de Teilhard de Chardin." *Études théologiques et religieuses* (1961): 36, 205-244.

898. ———. "Teilhard de Chardin et l'oecuménisme." *Actuelles* (1963): 2.

899. ———. "Teilhard de Chardin et la théologie." *Christianisme sociale* (1960): 3/4, 155-163.
"Teilhard de Chardin and Theology." *Chicago Theological Seminary Register* (1964): 4, 10-14.

900. ———. "Teilhard de Chardin on Evil and the Cross." *Philosophy Today* (1964): 8, 84-100. Excerpts from Item 895.

901. ———. "The Theological Quest and the Teilhardian Tradition." *Religion in Life* (1968): 37, 334-345.

902. Crichton, J.D. "A Jesuit Tries to Grasp the Universe." *The Catholic Herald*, December 11, 1959, p. 3.

903. ———. "La théologie de Teilhard de Chardin. Conférence donnée à Faculté de théologie reformée de Bruxelles le 22 janvier 1964." Mimeographed. Paris: Fondation Teilhard de Chardin, 1964.

904. Crippa, Domingos. "A grande aventura do mundo." *Convivium* (1965): 3, 7-38.

905. Cristiani, Leon [pseud. Nicholas Corte]. Une apologé-
      tique de l'accueil: Teilhard de Chardin." *Ecclesia*
      (1964): 178, 39-44.

906. ———. "Un jugement sur le Père Teilhard de Chardin."
      L'ami du clergé (1957): 67, 665-667.

907. ———. *Nos raisons de croire. Sens et vertu de
      l'apologétique.* Paris: Fayard, 1957.
      Le ragioni della nostra fede. Catania: Edizioni
      Paoline, 1958.

908. ———. *La vie et l'âme de Teilhard de Chardin.* Paris:
      Fayard, 1957.
      Also Paris: Librairie générale française, 1963.
      La vida i el pensament de Teilhard de Chardin.
      Barcelona: Editorial 62, 1964. Also contains Item
      796.
      Pierre Teilhard de Chardin: His Life and Spirit.
      London/New York: Barrie and Rackliff, 1960.
      Also New York: Macmillan, 1960.

909. ———. "La vie et l'âme de Teilhard de Chardin."
      Union catholique des scientifiques français (1957):
      40, 17-20.

910. Cronin, Francis Raymond. "Complexity-Consciousness in
      Teilhard de Chardin." Doctoral dissertation, Fordham
      University, 1971.

911. ———. "The Scientific Phenomenology of Teilhard de
      Chardin." *The Teilhard Review* (1974): 3, 84-89.

912. ———. "Teilhard de Chardin's Centrogenetic Ontology."
      The Teilhard Review (1976): 11, 58-64.

913. Cronin, Vincent. "The Noosphere and Extra-Sensory Per-
      ception." Item 497, pp. 88-91.
      Also Item 501, pp. 88-91.

914. Crozon, Pierre. "Interrogations sur l'oeuvre de Teil-
      hard de Chardin." *Masses ouvrières* (1965): 217, 33-55.
      Also *Perspectives* (1965): 24/25, 34-49.

915. ———. "Teilhard de Chardin et son oeuvre." *Pédagogie*
      (1965): 20, 648-664.

916. Crusafont Pairó, Miguel. "Antropogénesis y cefaliz-
      ación en el sistema teilhardiano." *Revista de
      psiquiatria y psicologia médica* (1965): 7, 173-183.

917. ————. "Concepiones cosmovitalistas del evolucionismo." *Museo de la ciudad de Sabadell* (1948): 4, 5-28.

918. ————. "El cuarto aniversario de la muerte del P. Teilhard de Chardin." *Boletin informativo* (1959): 18/19, 2-3.

919. ————. "Este extrano apéndice que llamamos España." *Atlántida* (1965): 10, 1-17.

920. ————. *Evolución y ascensión.* Madrid: Taurus, 1960. See pp. 65-67.

921. ————. "El evolucionismo en el progreso." *Revista* (1957): 295, 11.

922. ————. *El fenómeno humano según los puntos de vista del P. Teilhard de Chardin.* Sabadell: Fundación Bosch y Cardellach, 1956.

923. ————. "El fenómeno teilhardiano." *La estafeta literaria* (1964): 290, 8.

924. ————. "El hombre: entre la esperanza y la nada." *Convivium* (1972): 37, 47-64.

925. ————. "L'hominisation." Item 1015, pp. 133-137.

926. ————. "La ley recurrente de complejidad-conciencia, al dia." *Memorias de la Real Academia de Ciencias y Artes de Barcelona* (1964): 4, 135-201.

927. ————. "El mensaje del Padre Teilhard." *Revista* (1956): 104, 8.

928. ————. "El microcosmos y Teilhard." *Sabadell*, May 21, 1965, p. 3.

929. ————. "Neodarwinismo y orthogeneticicismo: un intento de conciliación." *Atlántida* (1965): 16, 395-401.

930. ————. "La noosfera y el fenomeno humano según las ideas del P. Teilhard de Chardin." *Estudios Geológicos* (1953): 17, 147-153.

931. ————. "El nuevo humanismo, trascedente del Padre Teilhard." *Sesiones Científicas de la Federación Farmacéutica* (1960): 1-18.

932. ————. "La obra de Teilhard a la luz de las nuevas
adquisiciones de la ciencia." Item 1396, pp. 17-27.

933. ————. "El Oreopiteco y su significación en la filo-
genia humana." *Orbis catholicus* (1959): 1, 97-112.

934. ————. "Paleontogia y evolución. Résumé d'une conférence donnée au Colego Mayor Loyola de Barcelona le 28
fevrier 1964." Mimeographed. Paris: Fondation Teilhard de Chardin, 1964.

935. ————. "El pensamiento científico del P. Teilhard de
Chardin." *Estudios Geológicos* (1956): 31/32, 343-375.

936. ————. "Problemàtica de la evolució." *Qüestions de
vida cristiana* (1969): 47, 5-17.

937. ————. "El proceso de la antropogénesis en la prob-
lemática teilhardiana." Item 745, pp. 115-132.

938. ————. "Proteognosia 'versus' evolucionismo." *Orbis
catholicus* (1964): 6, 482-504.

939. ————. "La quinta semana sobre Teilhard de Chardin en
Vézelay (Francia)." *Arbor* (1965): 230, 87-96.

940. ————. "La semana guerrero." *Tele-exprés*, January 26,
1968.

941. ————. "Singularidad bio-espiritual del hombre."
Boletin del Instituto de Estudios Asturianos (1963):
6, 1-28.

942. ————. "La síntesis del P. Teilhard y la singularidad
del hombre." *Enlace* (1964): 49, 5.

943. ————. "Teilhard: compendio, síntesis y convergencia."
Hechos y dichos (1966): 247-256.

944. ————. "Teilhard entre nosotros." *Sabadell*, October
28, 1967, p. 9.

945. ————. "El universo es centrado, su centro es Cristo."
Revista (1959): 376, 6.

946. ————. "Variations sur un thème et dans le ton teilhardiens. Décade dévouée au P. Teilhard à Vézelay."
Typescript. Paris: Fondation Teilhard de Chardin, 1960.

947. Csikszentmihalyi, Mihaly. "Sociological Implications in the Thought of Teilhard de Chardin." *Zygon* (1970): 5, 130-147.

948. Cuadrado, Leandro. "Teilhard de Chardin 'en' Salamanca." *El adelanto*, March, 1968.

949. Cubillo, Luis. "El evolucionismo en Teilhard de Chardin." *Religión y cultura* (1965): 10, 353-377.

950. Cuénot, Claude. "A propos de 'Science et foi.'" *Études teilhardiennes* (1968): 1, 143-148.

951. ———. "L'angoisse contemporaine: un essai de réponse." *Cahiers de vie franciscaine* (1962): 33, 2-31.

952. ———. "Appel aux bonnes volontés." *Revue Teilhard de Chardin* (1960): 1/2, 30-31.

953. ———. "L'apport scientifique de Pierre Teilhard de Chardin." *L'information scientifique* (1963): 18, 13-14.

954. ———. "Autour du P. Teilhard de Chardin." *La raison* (1961): 52.

955. ———. *Aventura e visão de Teilhard de Chardin*. Lisboa: Livraria Morais, 1966.

956. ———. *Ce que Teilhard a vraiment dit*. Paris: Stock, 1972.
Also Verviers: Gérard, 1973.
Lo que verdaderamente dijo Teilhard. México: M. Aguilar, 1974.

957. ———. "Coloquio veneziano su Teilhard de Chardin." *Leggere* (1962): 8/9, 1-3.

958. ———. "De l'anthropologie à l'anthropogénèse." *Synthèses* (1958): 13, 258-266.

959. ———. "Enfance prédestinée." Item 497, pp. 21-31.
Also Item 501, pp. 21-31.

960. ———. "La espiritualidad de Teilhard de Chardin." *Cuadernos para el diálogo* (1965): 17, 10-14.

961. ———. "Esprit et matière dans la philosophie de Pierre Teilhard de Chardin." Item 1015, pp. 67-85.

962. ————. "État present des études teilhardienne." *Cité libre* (1963): 56, 20-21.

963. ————. "L'être humain selon Teilhard de Chardin. Ses aspects complémentaires dans la phénoménologie scienfique et la pensée chrétienne." *Rencontre Orient-Occident* (1960): 3, 7-12.

964. ————. "Faith Seeking Understanding." *Frontier* (1967): 10, 220-222.

965. ————. "Die Geistige Biographie Teilhard de Chardins." *Zeitwende* (1965): 4, 225-242.
      Also in Item 4316.

966. ————. "L'idée de progrès dans la pensée du Père Teilhard de Chardin." *Actualités et culture vétérinaires* (1959): 20, 13-14.

967. ————. *Introduction à la pensée de Teilhard de Chardin.* Paris: S.P.E.R.A.R., 1964.

968. ————. "Jean Guitton et Teilhard de Chardin." *Revue vue Montalembert* (1963): 4/5, 146-154.

969. ————. "Lettre ouverte au Père Bouyer." *La France catholique* (1958): 628, 3.

970. ————. "Leur pensée maitresse: Teilhard de Chardin." *Plaisir de France* (1963): 291, 1-7.

971. ————. *Lexique Teilhard de Chardin.* Paris: Seuil, 1963. See also Item 978. Contains Item 4469.

972. ————. "Maximum de l'homme, maximum de Dieu, ou la spiritualité de Teilhard de Chardin." *Rencontre* (1963): 3, 13-17; 4, 9-15.

973. ————. "La métamorphose: Pierre Teilhard de Chardin." *La table ronde* (1958): 121, 45-53.

974. ————. "Mise au point à propos d'un article paru dans le nᵒ de mars de la même revue: 'Teilhard de Chardin au grand jour.'" *L'âge nouveau* (1956): 97, 125.

975. ————. "La morale et l'homme selon Pierre Teilhard de Chardin." *Morale chrétienne et morale marxiste.* Paris/Genève: La Palatine, 1960, pp. 117-147.
      "Morala in človek v smilu očeta Pierra Teilharda

de Chardin." *Nova pot* (1961): 13, 185-199.

976. ————. "Myśl Teilharda de Chardin." [The Thought of Teilhard de Chardin.] *Więź* (1963): 2, 57-68; 3, 70-75; 4, 23-26; 5, 66-70; 6, 45-46; 7/8, 172-187.

977. ————. "Notice complémentaire à 'Les débuts de l'oeuvre scientifique du Père Teilhard de Chardin' de J. Piveteau." *Europe* (1965): 431/432, 37-39.

978. ————. *Nouveau lexique Teilhard de Chardin.* Paris: Seuil, 1968. See also Item 971. *Nuevo léxico de Teilhard de Chardin.* Madrid: Taurus, 1970.

979. ————. "Nouvelles lettres de voyage (1939-1945) de Pierre Teilhard de Chardin." *La table ronde* (1958): 151-152.

980. ————. "L'oeuvre du R.P. Teilhard de Chardin et le marxisme." Item 1598, pp. 203-211.

981. ————. "L'originalité philosophique de Pierre Teilhard de Chardin." *Presence* (1956): 2, 46-52.

982. ————. "La pensée teilhardienne est liée à la transformation du monde." *Synthèse* (1960): 172, 195-204.

983. ————. "Le Père Émile Licent SJ, un portrait." *Le ruban rouge* (1963): 19, 36-45.
"Le Père Émile Licent, compagnon et mentor du Père Teilhard." *Ecclesia* (1964): 184, 59-68.

984. ————. "Le Père Teilhard de Chardin et les fouilles de Choukoutien." *Information scientifique* (1958): 5, 159-169.

985. ————. "'Le phénomène humain.'" *L'éducation nationale* (1956): 16, 20-21.

986. ————. "Le phénomène Teilhard." Item 3903, pp. 7-29.

987. ————. "La philosophie du Père Teilhard de Chardin." *Bulletin de l'Union catholique des scientifiques français* (1962): 66, 5-8.

988.   ————. "Pierre Teilhard de Chardin. Bibliographie.
        Sources bibliographiques. Publications posthumes des
        oeuvres. Index alphabétique des oeuvres et opuscules
        publiés. Quelques ouvrages de langue française, por-
        tant en tout ou partie sur Teilhard de Chardin."
        Livres de France (1966): 4, 27-30.

989.   ————. "Pierre Teilhard de Chardin, ébauche d'un
        portrait." *Livres de France* (1966): 4, 2-8.
        "Teilhard de Chardin: Sketch for a Portrait."
        The Teilhard Review (1971): 1, 2-10.

990.   ————. *Pierre Teilhard de Chardin: Les grandes étapes
        de son évolution*. Paris: Plon, 1958. Contains Items
        4396, 4469, 4617, 4680, 4728.
        L'evoluzione di Teilhard de Chardin. Milano: Feltrin-
        elli, 1962.
        Teilhard de Chardin: A Biographical Study. London:
        Burns and Oates, 1965.
        Also Baltimore: Helicon, 1965.
        Pierre Teilhard de Chardin: Leben und Werk. Olten/
        Freiburg-im-Breisgau, 1966.
        Also special edition, 1972.
        *Pierre Teilhard de Chardin: Las grandes etapas de
        su evolución*. Madrid: Taurus, 1967.
        Teilhard de Chardin. [In Arabic.] Jounieh: Im-
        primerie des Paulistes, 1968.
        Aru mirai no zahyô, Teilhard de Chardin. Tokyo:
        Shunjusha, 1970.

991.   ————. "Pierre Teilhard de Chardin: Lettres de voyage
        (1923-1939)." *La table ronde* (1959): 261-262.

992.   ————. "Pierre Teilhard de Chardin. Sa vie mystique
        à Pékin (1939-1946)." *Rencontre Orient-Occident*
        (1957): 2, 3-6.

993.   ————. "Plauderei über Teilhard de Chardin." In Item
        4316.

994.   ————. "Préface." Item 1015, pp. 11-12.

995.   ————. "Présentation de Teilhard de Chardin." Item
        3851, pp. 21-58.

996.   ————. "Une rencontre avec Teilhard de Chardin sous
        le signe de saint Georges." *Rencontre* (1962): 18-28.

997. ———. "Le R.P. Émile Licent SJ." *Bulletin de la Société d'études indochinoises* (1966): 1, 75.

998. ———. "Le R.P. Teilhard de Chardin." *L'éducation nationale* (1955): 17, 12-13.

999. ———. "Le R.P. Teilhard de Chardin entre l'Est et l'Ouest." *France-Asie* (1955): 109-110, 708-711. "Le Père Teilhard de Chardin entre l'Orient et l'Occident." *Le ruban rouge* (1960): 6, 8-14.

1000. ———. "Le R.P. Teilhard de Chardin et la Chine." *Bulletin de la Société d'études indochinoises* (1955): 4, 341-348.

1001. ———. "Der Rolle der Frau in der christlichen Religion. Ein Gespräch mit Teilhard de Chardin." *Perspektiven der Zukunft* (1973): 5, 1-2.

1002. ———. "Science et foi chez Teilhard de Chardin." *Rencontre* (1963): 2, 21-28.

1003. ———. "Science et foi chez Teilhard de Chardin." *Centre de documentation marxiste* (1967): 17, 1-50. Also *Études teilhardienne* (1968): 1, 3-56. *Science and Faith in Teilhard de Chardin.* London: Garnstone, 1967. *Ciencia y fe en Teilhard de Chardin.* Barcelona: Plaza y Janes, 1971.

1004. ———. "Senkinek sem akart tanito mestere leni." [He Didn't Want To Be Anyone's Master.] *Mérleg* (1968): 4, 11-12.

1005. ———. "Situation de Teilhard de Chardin." *Rencontre Orient-Occident* (1961): 5, 16-20. Also *Tendances* (1962): 19, 594-624. Also *Bulletin de la Société industrielle de Mulhouse* (1963): 3, 7-32. "Situación de Teilhard de Chardin." *Orbis Catholicus* (1964): 7, 193-219. "Situacão de Teilhard de Chardin." *Vozes* (1964): 58, 18-26.

1006. ———. "La spiritualité de Teilhard." *Prospective P.U.F.* (1960): 6, 13. Also Item 2744 trans., pp. 17-35. "La spiritualità di Teilhard de Chardin." Item 2744, pp. 17-36.

1007.   ———. "Spirituality on the Frontier." *Frontier*
         (1966/67): 257-259.

1008.   ———. "Teilhard de Chardin." *L'album des lettres*
         (1958): 23, 16-21.

1009.   ———. *Teilhard de Chardin*. Paris: Seuil, 1962.
             Contains Item 4543.
                 Also 1964.
                 Also new edition, 1966.
                 Spanish translation, Barcelona: Labor, 1966.
                 Italian translation, Milano: Il Saggiatore, 1966.
                 Also new edition, 1971.
                 Teilhard de Chardin. Leven, werk, visie. Antwerp-
             en: Spectrum, 1967.

1010.   ———. "Teilhard de Chardin." *Plaisir de France*
         (1963): 1, 2-7. Contains Item 4416.

1011.   ———. "Teilhard de Chardin c'est du Saint Thomas au
         siècle d'évolution." *Arts* (1962): 868, 5.

1012.   ———. "Teilhard de Chardin et la création." *Ren-
         contre* (1963): 1, 18-26.

1013.   ———. "Teilhard de Chardin et les Exercises de Saint
         Ignace." *Rencontre Orient-Occident* (1967): 2, 17-20;
         3, 15-19; 4, 9-16.
             "Teilhard and the Spiritual Exercises of Saint Ig-
         natius." *The Teilhard Review* (1969-70): 1, 50-59.
             "Teilhard de Chardin und die Geistlichen Übungen
         des heiligen Ignatius." *Perspektiven der Zukunft*
         (1971): 5, 2-5; 6, 4-6.

1014.   ———. "Teilhard de Chardin et nous." *Arts* (1962):
         868, 2.
             "I grandi temi di Teilhard de Chardin." *Leggere*
         (1962): 8, 6-8.

1015.   ———. *Teilhard de Chardin et la pensée catholique.*
         Colloque de Venise sous les auspices de Pax Romana
         (9-11 juin 1962). Paris: Seuil, 1965. Contains Items
         925, 961, 994, 1890, 1891, 2531, 3507, 3284.
             Teilhard de Chardin e il pensiero cattolico. Fir-
         enze: Sansoni, 1966.

1016.   ———. "Teilhard de Chardin et les philosophies."
         La table ronde (1955): 80, 36-40.

1017. ———. "Teilhard de Chardin (Pierre) 1881-1955." *Encyclopaedia Universalis* (1973): 15, 844-845.

1018. ———. "Teilhard de Chardin, R. Pierre." *Grande Encyclopédie Larousse* (1964): 10, 210-211.

1019. ———. "Teilhard: Democracy and Dialogue." *Pax Romana Journal* (1967): 2, 13-16.

1020. ———. "Teilhard et le marxisme." *Europe* (1965): 431/432, 164-185.
"Teilhard y el marxismo." *Cuadernos para el dialogo* (1964): 9, 26-29.
Also *Orbis catholicus* (1964): 3, 193-219.
Teilhard de Chardin a marksizm." *Zeszyty Argumentów* (1966): 2, 77-87.

1021. ———. "Teilhard und Deutschland." Item 2902, pp. 9-25.

1022. ———. *Unsere dynamische Welt. Teilhard de Chardin zwischen Dogma und Wissenschaft.* Olten/Freiburg-im-Breisgau; Walter-Verlag, 1968.

1023. ———. "La véritable question entre chrétiens et communistes." *Clarte* (1960): 28, 6-7.

1024. ———. "Vie de Teilhard de Chardin. Esquisse chronologique." *Livres de France* (1966): 4, 25-26.

1025. ———. "Die Weltschau Teilhards de Chardin, dargestellt an den grossen Etappen seines Lebens und Denkens." Item 3924, pp. 13-14.

1026. ———, and Yves Vadé. "Bibliographie Teilhard de Chardin." *Recherches et débats* (1962): 40, 99-148.

1027. Culbertson, Diana. "Teilhard and Unamuno: The Definition of Faith." *Cithara* (1973): 13, 3-15.

1028. Culliton, Joseph Thomas. "The Cosmic Visions of John Dewey and Teilhard de Chardin: A Comparative Study." Doctoral dissertation, Fordham University, 1972.

1029. ———. "Dewey and Teilhard." *The Teilhard Review* (1976): 11, 42-47.

1030.   ————. *A Processive World View for Pragmatic Chris-*
        tians. New York: Philosophical Library, 1975.

1031.   Cuny, Hilaire. "De la bactérie à l'homme." *Diagrammes*
        (1960): 43, 1-82.

1032.   ————. "De P. Teilhard de Chardin au rationalisme."
        Combat, October 12, 1960, p. 8.

1033.   Curtis, Charles J. "Process Theology: Teilhard de Char-
        din." *Contemporary Protestant Thought*. Milwaukee:
        Bruce, 1970.

1034.   Curtis, Jack H. "Consciousness and Alienation in the
        Social Psychology of Teilhard de Chardin." *American
        Catholic Sociological Review* (1962): 4, 324-329.

1035.   Curvers, A. "Algo más sobre Teilhard de Chardin."
        Cuadernos del Sur (1969): 6, 454-465.

1036.   ————. "Gardez-vous des faux prophètes." In Item
        3744.

1037.   ————. "La grande hérésie de Teilhard de Chardin."
        Arts (1964): 968, 5.

1038.   ————. "Teilhard et la subversion dans l'Église."
        Itinéraires (1966): 102, 56-57.

1039.   Curzon, Gordon. "Teilhard and the Apocalyptic Vision."
        The Teilhard Review (1971-72): 2, 69-72.

1040.   Cuttat, Jacques-Albert. "L'expérience chrétienne est-
        elle capable d'assumer la spiritualité orientale?"
        La mystique et les mystiques, ed. by André Ravier.
        Paris: Desclée de Brouwer, 1965, pp. 825-1020. See
        pp. 886-890.

1041.   Cuypers, Hubert. "L'avenir du monde." *Le Phare dimanche*,
        April 2, 1961, p. 6.

1042.   ————. "Comment comprendre le Christ de Teilhard de
        Chardin?" *Cahiers de la Biloque* (1960): 10, 98-111.

1043.   ————. "Convergence de l'évolution vers l'esprit."
        Item 3917, pp. 71-85.
        Also *Revue Teilhard de Chardin* (1964): 20/21, 15-18.

1044. ———. "Echos scientifiques." *Revue Teilhard de Chardin* (1967): 32, 35-36.

1045. ———. "Exposé de la pensée du P. Teilhard de Chardin." Mimeographed. Paris: Fondation Teilhard de Chardin, n.d.

1046. ———. "Hypothèse d'une religion comme à l'humanité." *Revue Teilhard de Chardin* (1962): 13, 11-15.

1047. ———. "L'inconnu aux deux pôles de l'existence. Le monogenisme." *Cahiers de la Biloque* (1958): 2, 49-60.

1048. ———. "Mega-synthèse." *Revue Teilhard de Chardin* (1961): 8/9, 25-27.

1049. ———. "Morale chrétienne et morale marxiste." *Revue Teilhard de Chardin* (1961): 5, 21-22. Also *Cahiers de la Biloque* (1960): 6, 251-253.

1050. ———. "L'origine de la vie." *Revue Teilhard de Chardin* (1971): 47/48, 16-19.

1051. ———. "Où en est le problème Teilhard de Chardin?" *Cahiers de la Biloque* (1964): 4, 153-160.

1052. ———. "Il posto del Milieu divin nel pensiero del Padre Teilhard de Chardin." Item 2744, pp. 85-91. "La place du Milieu divin dans la pensée du Père Teilhard de Chardin." Item 2744 trans., pp. 79-84.

1053. ———. *Pour ou contre Teilhard.* Paris: Éditions Universitaires, 1962. *Voor en tegen Teilhard.* Tielt/Den Haag: Lannoo, 1964. *Teilhard pro o contra?* Petrópolis: Vozes, 1967. *Por y contra Teilhard.* Buenos Aires: Columba, 1968.

1054. ———. "Pour l'unité humaine." *Revue Teilhard de Chardin* (1964): 19, 7-11.

1055. ———. "Le problème de l'homme fossile en Chine. Situation actuelle." *Revue Teilhard de Chardin* (1962): 13, 27.

1056. ———. "Quelques aspects de la pensée religieuse de Pierre Teilhard de Chardin." *Cahiers de la Biloque* (1957): 3, 128-131.

1057.   ———. "Réflexions sur les problèmes de la vie et de
         la mort." *Cahiers de la Biloque* (1958): 3, 109-127.

1058.   ———. "Science et conscience." *Revue Teilhard de
         Chardin* (1967): 31, 38-50.

1059.   ———. "Le sens de la mort." *Revue Teilhard de Chardin* (1963): 15, 17-23.

1060.   ———. "Le sens de la vie d'après Teilhard de Chardin."
         Cahiers de la Biloque (1960): 1, 18-27.

1061.   ———. "La société de demain dans Teilhard de Chardin."
         Balisage (1961): 16/17, 21-24.

1062.   ———. "Teilhard de Chardin et la critique." *Cahiers
         de la Biloque* (1959): 6, 259-268.

1063.   ———. "Teilhard de Chardin philosophe de l'espoir."
         Le Phare dimanche, February 14, 1960, p. 5.

1064.   ———. "Unanimisation selon P. Teilhard de Chardin et
         hypothèse d'une religion commune." *Revue Teilhard de
         Chardin* (1962): 12, 24-28.

1065.   ———. *Vocabulaire Teilhard de Chardin. Lexique,
         citations, références.* Paris: Éditions Universitaires,
         1963.
             Teilhard-lexicon. Tielt/Den Haag: Lannoo, 1967.
             Vocabulário Teilhard. Petrópolis: Vozes, 1967.
             Vocabulário Teilhard. Buenos Aires: Columba, 1968.

1066.   ———. "Vue panoramique sur l'unité de la matière."
         Revue Teilhard de Chardin (1961): 6, 18-22.

1067.   Czarnecki, Jean. "Remarques sur la pensée de Teilhard
         de Chardin." *Christianisme social* (1956): 8/9, 588-
         597.

1068.   Daecke, Sigurd Martin. "Bericht über die Teilhard de
         Chardin Literatur." *Pastoraltheologie* (1966): 6,
         257-269; 7, 312-328.

1069.   ———. "Fortschrittsglaube und Heilserwartung bei
         Pierre Teilhard de Chardin." *Evolution.* Stuttgart:
         E. Klett, 1970, pp. 153-185.

1070. ———. "Der Grössere Christus. Zum 'neuen Glauben' Teilhard de Chardin." *Sonntagsblatt* (1963): 15, 13.

1071. ———. "Das Ja und das Nein des Konzils zu Teilhard." *Die Autorität der Freiheit.* München: Kösel, 1967, pp. 98-112.

1072. ———. "Neues über Teilhard de Chardin." *Sonntagsblatt* (1963): 48, 15.

1073. ———. "Teilhard de Chardin." *Tendenzen der Theologie im 20. Jahrhundert. Eine Geschichte in Portrats*, ed. by Hans Jurgen Schultz. Stuttgart/Berlin: Kreuz Verlag, 1966, pp. 175-180.
Also Olten/Freiburg-im-Breisgau: Walter-Verlag, 1966.
Also *Lessico dei teologi del secolo XX*. Brescia: Queriniana, 1978, pp. 185-191.

1074. ———. "Teilhard de Chardin et la théologie de l'avenir." Item 3851, pp. 269-302.

1075. ———. "Teilhard de Chardin and Protestant Theology." *The Teilhard Review* (1969): 1, 2-15.

1076. ———. *Teilhard de Chardin und die envangelische Theologie.* Göttingen: Vandenhoeck und Ruprecht, 1968.

1077. Dallaire, Jean-Paul. "Teilhard de Chardin et l'évolution. Documents inédits présentés et annotés." *Revue de l'Université de Laval* (1963-64): 18, 406-415.
Also in *Revue Teilhard de Chardin* (1964): 19, 25-34.

1078. Dalle Nogare, Pedro. "Alucinado ou profeta?" *A tarde*, October 21, 1966.

1079. ———. "Humanismo teilhardiano." *A tarde*, November 11, 1966.

1080. ———. *Humanismos e anti-humanismos em conflito. Introdução à antropologia filosófica.* São Paulo: Herder, 1973. See pp. 191-217.

1081. ———. "Maritain e Teilhard." *A tarde*, June 13, 1967.

1082. ———. "A missa sobre o mundo de Teilhard de Chardin." *A tarde*, March 26, 1967.

1083. ———. *Pessõa e amor segundo Teilhard de Chardin*.
       São Paulo: Herder, 1970.

1084. ———. "Teilhard de Chardin homen farol." *A tarde*,
       September 29, 1966.

1085. ———. "Teilhard e Marx." *A tarde*, December 13, 1966.

1086. Dall'Olio, Alessandro. "Mentalità scientifica moderna
       e concettualità filosofico-teologica nel Milieu divin."
       Item 2744, pp. 99-102.
       "Mentalité scientifique moderne et outillage con-
       ceptual philosophico-théologique dans le Milieu divin."
       Item 2744 trans., pp. 90-93.

1086a. ———. "Mentalità teilhardiana e mentalità mariteniana."
       Futuro dell'uomo (1978): 5, 35-36, 51.

1087. ———. "Rassegna di studi teilhardiani." *Civiltà
       cattolica* (1968): 557-562; (1969): 462-470; (1970):
       495-502.

1088. ———. "'Sistema uomo' e fenomenologia teilhardiana."
       *Bolletino informazioni del Centro di studi e di recerca
       Teilhard de Chardin, Istituto Stensen* (1973): 16, 16-
       22.

1089. ———. "Studi recenti su Teilhard de Chardin." *Civiltà
       cattolica* (1973): 4, 504-510.

1090. ———. "Teilhard de Chardin, pensatore sapienziale."
       Gesuiti (1972-73): 81-86.

1090a. ———. "Teilhard de Chardin, Pierre." *Enciclopedia
       biografica degli scienziati e dei tecnologi*. Milan:
       Mondadori, 1975, vol. 3, pp. 55-58.

1091. Dalmais, I.H. "Les 'oeuvres complètes' du P. Teilhard
       de Chardin." *Informations catholiques internationales*,
       October 15, 1976, pp. 57-59.

1092. ———. "Teilhard de Chardin: Un héritage en explora-
       tion." *Livres et lectures*, February, 1962, pp. 73-77.

1093. ———. "Teilhard de Chardin, prophète du 'Grand Christ
       de l'en-avant.'" *Informations catholiques internation-
       ales*, October 1, 1973, pp. 19-21, 25.

1094. Dalmasso di Gazegna, Angelica. "L'azione umana nelle componenti che la costituiscono atto morale secondo Teilhard de Chardin." Typescript. Roma: Istituto di teologia del Centro "Ut sint unum," 1973.

1095. Damante, Hélio. "Introdução a 'O fenômeno humano.'" *Vozes* (1967): 685-695.

1096. Dambriūnas, Leonardas. "Pasaulèziūra, evoliucija ir Teilhard de Chardin." [Ideology, Evolution and Teilhard de Chardin.] *Aidai* (1973): 173-179, 213-221, 266-270.

1097. Danek, Jaromir. "Une tentative humaniste de notre temps." *Laval theologique et philosophique* (1971): 67-79.

1098. Daniel, P.M. "Introduction à la vision cosmique de Teilhard de Chardin." *Lovania* (1965): 62, 37-43.

1099. ———. "Jalons pour une biographie de Pierre Teilhard de Chardin." *Lovania* (1965): 62, 25-36.

1100. Daniélou, Jean. "Les certitudes et les incertitudes du Père Teilhard de Chardin." *Arts*, April, 1955, pp. 1, 6.

1101. ———. "Dos conferencias del cardenal Danielou sobre Teilhard de Chardin." *Principe de Viana* (1972): 33, 169-187. Contains Items 1103 and 1104.

1102. ———. "Esquisse d'un portrait." Item 3903, pp. 81-99.

1103. ———. *El pensamiento religioso de Teilhard--Pensée religieuse de Teilhard.* Pamplona: Editorial Aranzadi, 1972.
Also Item 1101, pp. 178-187.

1104. ———. *La personalidad de Teilhard de Chardin--Portrait de Teilhard de Chardin.* Pamplona: Editorial Aranzadi, 1972.
Also Item 1101, pp. 169-178.

1105. ———. "Signification de Teilhard de Chardin." *Études* (1962): 6, 146-161.
"Gottes Wiederentdeckung. Die Bedeutung Teilhard de Chardins für die Gegenwart." *Wort und Wahrheit* (1962): 17, 517-528.
"Sens i znaczenei Teilharda de Chardin." *Znak* (1962): 14, 732-744.

"The Timeliness of Teilhard de Chardin." *Philosophy Today* (1962): 6, 212-222.

"La 'grand avventura' de Teilhard de Chardin." *Digest cattolico* (1963): 4, 49-56.

1106. ———. "La vision totale chez Teilhard de Chardin." *Revue de Paris*, October, 1968, pp. 1-9.

1107. Daniel-Rops, Henri. "Pour ou contre le Père Teilhard de Chardin." *Ecclesia* (1965): 86, 25-35.

1108. Daniëls, Jos. "Teilhard de Chardin in zijn brieven." *Streven* (1962-63): 16, 360-366.

1109. Dansereau, Pierre. "Teilhard and the Language of Science." Item 3247, pp. 41-56.

1110. Dantine, Wilhelm. "Die Bedeutung Teilhards de Chardin für die Theologie." Item 3299, pp. 17-40.

1111. ———. "Christliche Weltverantwortung." *Perspektiven der Zukunft* (1969): 1, 2-4.

1112. ———. "Zur kosmischer Stellung des Menschen nach Teilhard de Chardin." *Acta teilhardiana* (1968): 16-32.

1113. D'Arcy, Martin C. *Facing God*. London: Burns and Oates, 1966.

1114. ———. *The Meaning and Matter of History*. New York: Farrar, Straus and Cudahy, 1959.

1115. ———. "The Varieties of Human Love." *Saturday Evening Post* (1959): 231, 38ff.
Also *Adventures of the Mind*, ed. by R. Thruelsen and J. Kobler. New York: Knopf, 1959.

1116. Dark, Raymond. "Réponse." *Itinéraires* (1965): 96, 41-44. Reply to questionnaire in Item 3259.

1117. Darms, G. "P. Teilhard de Chardin SJ. Gedanken zu einem römischen Monitum." *Freiburger Zeitschrift für Philosophie und Theologie* (1963): 10, 95-115.

1118. Darms, Louis. "Des techniques pour la convergence." Item 3917, pp. 33-50.
Also *Revue Teilhard de Chardin* (1964): 20/21, 14-15.

1119. ———. "Le phénomène inter-humain." *Univers* (1966): 3, 11-17. Also *Revue Teilhard de Chardin* (1966): 27/28, 11-17.

1120. Number deleted.

1121. Daujat, Jean. "A propos de Teilhard de Chardin." *Doctrine et vie* (1962): 46, 16-22.

1122. David, J. "Fragen, die P. Teilhard de Chardins Werk an Philosophie und Theologie stellt." *Orientierung* (1963): 27, 110.

1123. ———. "Eine grossartige Weltschau. Zum Werk von P. Teilhard SJ." *Der katholische Erzieher* (1963): 16, 490-495.

1124. ———. "Der Mensch und sein Werk in der Weltschau P. Teilhards." *Der katholische Erzieher* (1963): 16, 555-560.

1125. Davison, Donald Arthur. "The Concept of Person in the Evolutionary Process of Pierre Tielhard de Chardin: Some Educational Implications." Doctoral dissertation, Marquette University, 1976.

1126. Davy, Marie Magdeleine. "Dieu et l'homme moderne." *La revue des lettres modernes* (1956): 24, 641-704.

1127. ———. "Le sens de l'absolu chez Teilhard." *Revue Teilhard de Chardin* (1961): 6, 31-32.

1128. ———. "Teilhard homme de l'absolu." *Revue Teilhard de Chardin* (1974): 60, 19-24.

1129. Day, Michael. "Lacuna or Breakthrough? Review Article of 'Psychosexuality: The Teilhardian Lacunae.'" *The Teilhard Review* (1969-70): 2, 93-97. See Item 3825.

1130. ———. "Teilhard's Rediscovery of the Cosmic Christ." *The Teilhard Review* (1976): 11, 109-112.

1131. Debelmas, Jacques, and Anne-Marie Debelmas. "Le travail humain et sa finalité." Item 3041, pp. 99-115.

1132. Debray, Pierre. "Une magie rationelle: le système du
       R.P. Teilhard de Chardin." *Ordre français* (1961):
       11, 7-23.

1133. Dechet, Jacques. "La pensée mystique de Teilhard."
       In Item 3744.

1134. Deckers, M.-C. *Le vocabulaire de Teilhard de Chardin.
       Les éléments grecs.* Gembloux: J. Duculot, 1968.

1135. Declusy, J. "L'homme et le monde chez le P. Teilhard
       de Chardin. Compte rendu d'une réunion du 15 novembre
       1958." Typescript. Paris: Fondation Teilhard de
       Chardin, 1958.

1136. Decourt, P. "La science et la religion." *Archives
       internationales Claude Bernard* (1971): 4, 19-124;
       (1977): 10, 9-109.

1137. Decoux, René. *L'énergie dans la cosmogenèse de Pierre
       Teilhard de Chardin.* Gran/Annecy: Vaccari, 1964.

1138. Dedeban, G.J. "L'esprit et l'activité missionaire du
       Père Teilhard de Chardin." *Cahiers d'éducation mis-
       sionaire* (1967): 18, 5-12.
       Also *Malades et missions* (1967): 131, 6-13.

1139. Dedek, John F. "The Phenomenon of Man: A Review of
       Reviews." *Chicago Studies* (1962): 1, 63-75;

1140. Dederra, Erich. "Teilhard de Chardin, Professor und
       Prophet." *Die Mitarbeit* (1962): 11, 545-549.
       Also *Theologisches Jahrbuch* (1968): 502-512.

1141. Deedy, John. "Teilhard de Chardin: The New York Years."
       Critic (1975): 33, 18-20+.

1142. Deely, John N. "The Vision of Man in Teilhard de Char-
       din." *Listening* (1966): 201-209.

1143. Dégalier, Joël. "Prise de conscience." *Évoluer* (1964):
       20, 4.

1144. Degenaar, Johannes Jacobus. *Evolusie en Christendom:
       'n opstel oor Teilhard de Chardin.* Kaapstad: Simon-
       dium, 1965.

1145. Dehner, Eugene W. "The Phenomenon of Christ and Man."
       St. Louis Book Review Section, March 4, 1960, p. 1.

1146. Deissler, Alfons. "Die biblischen Schöpfungserzählungen
       und das evolutionistische Weltbild." *Perspektiven
       der Zukunft* (1967): 6, 4-6.

1147. De Jong, P. "Teilhard's Vision of Hope." *Conflicting
       Images of Man*, ed. by W.H. Nicholls. New York: Sea-
       bury, 1966, pp. 109-132.

1148. Delacôte, Guy. "Le monde et l'éternité." *L'Alsace*,
       April 14, 1965, pp. 5, 9.

1149. Deladrière, Elisabeth. "L'homme par sa vie." *Balisage*
       (1961): 16/17, 2-4.

1150. ————, and Rodolphe Dirix. "'Le phénomène humain.'"
       Balisage (1961): 16/17, 10-15.

1151. Delattre, A. "La cosmologie du Père Teilhard de Char-
       din." *Saint Luc. Evangile et médecine* (1958): 64,
       160-177.

1152. Delbove, R. *L'humanisme énergetique de Teilhard.*
       Paris: Bloud and Gay, 1966.

1153. Delcourt, Albert. "De la cellule à la pensée." *Revue
       Teilhard de Chardin* (1971): 47/48, 20-27.

1154. ————. "Les deux énergies du Père Teilhard de Char-
       din." *Revue Teilhard de Chardin* (1961): 7, 8-17.

1155. ————. "Energie humaine totale." *Univers* (1965): 2,
       7-15.

1156. ————. "Le faisceau des races ne peut progresser qu'en
       convergeant." *Revue Teilhard de Chardin* (1964): 19,
       15-16.

1157. ————. "Histoire de la vie. Évolution des êtres
       vivants." *Revue Teilhard de Chardin* (1965): 23, 29-
       45; 24/25, 50-54; (1966): 26, 27-31; 29, 30-36.

1158. ————. "Incidences de l'oeuvre du P. Teilhard dans
       l'enseignement." *Humanités chrétiennes* (1958): 5,
       38-39.

1159. ———. "Notions de biosphère et de noosphère." *Revue Teilhard de Chardin* (1961): 8/9, 13-19.

1160. ———. "La vision scientifique du monde. Introduction à la lecture de Teilhard de Chardin." *La revue nouvelle* (1958): 27, 591-610.

1161. Delcourt, M. "Le teilhardisme." *Revue de l'Université de Bruxelles* (1964): 16, 303-330.

1162. Deletie, Henri. "Teilhard de Chardin et la philosophie traditionelle de l'Extrême Orient." *Rencontre Orient-Occident* (1962): 4, 13-18.
      Also *Symbolisme* (1962): 358, 27-36.

1163. Delfgaauw, Bernard. "Evolutie?" *Ter Elfder Ure* (1956): 11, 335-344.

1164. ———. "Histoire et progrès." *Études philosophiques* (1962): 4, 475-486.

1165. ———. "Een kritische waardering van de beteknis van Teilhard de Chardin." *Wending* (1962): 17, 229-238.

1166. ———. "De methode bij Teilhard de Chardin." *Handelingen van het XXVe Vlaams Filologencongres*. Zellik: Secretariaat van de Vlaamse Filologencongressen, 1967, pp. 31-40.

1167. ———. "Pierre Teilhard de Chardin en de ekstase." *Speling* (1972): 24, 41-50.

1168. ———. "Pierre Teilhard de Chardin en het evolutievraagstuk." *Nieuwe Stem* (1961): 16, 728-741.

1169. ———. *Teilhard de Chardin*. Baarn: Het Wereldvenster, 1961.
      Also 12th ed., 1966.
      Evolution: The Theory of Teilhard de Chardin. Kaapstad: Simondium, 1965.
      Also London: Collins, 1969.
      Also New York: Harper and Row, 1969.
      Teilhard de Chardin und das Evolutionsproblem. München: C.H. Beck, 1965.
      Teilhard de Chardin y el problema de la evolución. Buenos Aires: Carlos Lohle, 1966.

1170. ———. "Teilhard de Chardin en de politiek." Item 3724, pp. 108-122.

1171. ———. "Teilhard en het vraagstuk van het kwaad." *Revue Teilhard de Chardin* (1960): 1/2, 27-28.

1172. ———. "De veroordeling van Pierre Teilhard de Chardin." *De Maand* (1963): 1, 17-24.
Also *Te Elfder Ure* (1963): 12-19.

1173. Delorme, Albert. "Le 'phénomène' Teilhard de Chardin." *Revue de synthèse* (1956): 77, 789-794.

1174. Del Portillo, Manuel. *Teilhard de Chardin, un autor discutido.* Madrid: Saéz, 1973.

1175. Del Río, Emilio. "El 'Punto Omega' ye los límites de una teoria." *Sal terrae* (1972): 60, 526-533, 627-637.

1176. ———. "Teilhard de Chardin, cristiano del siglo XX." *Sal terrae* (1969): 57, 659-675, 759-775, 848-864; (1970): 58, 269-279, 323-333, 674-690, 778-786; (1972): 60, 179-192, 265-273.

1177. Delsol, Michel. "Entrevue avec le professeur Delsol." *Sept-Jours* (1966): 2.

1178. ———. "L'évolution biologique. Les faits acquis, les faits discutables, les fausses philosophies." *Itinéraires* (1965): 96, 45-92. Reply to questionnaire in Item 3259.

1179. De Luca, Benedetto. "Considerazioni sul pensiero scientifico et religioso di Pierre Teilhard de Chardin." *Realta nuova* (1964): 29, 588-605.

1180. De Lucchi, Mario Augusto. "L'antropologia del Milieu divin." Item 2744, pp. 267-271.
"L'anthropologie du Milieu divin." Item 2744 trans., pp. 248-252.

1181. ———. "Attualità del pensiero scientifico di Teilhard de Chardin." *Testimonianze* (1965): 8, 761-765.

1182. ———. "Evoluzione e cultura (Meditazione di un biologo)." *Testimonianze* (1965): 8, 169-188.

1183.   ————. "Introduzione al pensiero scientifico di Pierre
         Teilhard de Chardin." *Testimonianze* (1964): 1, 12-30.

1184.   ————. "Il messagio spirituale del Milieu divin."
         Item 2744, pp. 159-164.
         "Le message spirituel du Milieu divin." Item 2744
         trans., pp. 148-153.

1185.   Del Vasto, Lanza. "Teilhard de Chardin o la confusión
         de los planos." *Indice cultural español* (1967): 219/
         220, 13-18.

1186.   De Mari, Vincenzo. "Lineamenti di una antropologia
         cristiana nel Milieu divin." Item 2744, pp. 237-250.
         "Les grandes lignes d'une anthropologie chrétienne
         dans le Milieu divin." Item 2744 trans., pp. 221-233.

1187.   De Medicis, Stelios Castanos. "Actualité de la pensée
         d'Heraclite." *Philosophia* (1974): 137-154.

1188.   Démeron, Pierre. "Deux livres vont révéler la vie pas-
         sionnante du Père Teilhard de Chardin." *Arts* (1958):
         689, 3.

1189.   Demoment, Auguste. *Françoise Teilhard de Chardin, petite
         soeur des pauvres, Soeur Marie Albéric du Sacré-Coeur
         (1879-1911). Lettres et témoignages.* Paris: Beau-
         chesne, 1975.

1190.   ————. "Jeunesse et vocation de Pierre Teilhard de
         Chardin. D'apres des documents inédits." *Ecclesia*
         (1962): 162, 47-63.
             Also *Procès-verbaux et mémoires de l'Académie des
         sciences, belles-lettres et arts de Besançon* (1958/
         59): 173, 215-225.

1191.   ————. "Lettres d'Egypte et d'Angleterre du Père
         Teilhard de Chardin." *Procès-verbaux et mémoires de
         l'Académie des sciences, belles-lettres et arts de
         Besançon* (1966): 176, 57-68.

1192.   ————. "Lettres inédites du Père Teilhard de Chardin.
         Enfance et jeunesse." *Jésuites de l'assistance de
         France* (1962): 3, 15-30.

1193.   ————. "Quand Teilhard était étudiant." *Ecclesia*
         (1966): 207, 103-112.

1194. Demoulin, Jean-Pierre. "Brève étude chronologique à propos de la 'Note sur l'essence du transformisme.'" *Études teilhardiennes* (1969): 20-24.

1195. ————. "L'energie humaine." *L'Utopie* (1963): 11, 1-2.

1196. ————. "Foi au monde et vérité scientifique." *Études teilhardiennes* (1968): 1, 107-142.

1197. ————. "Intégration de l'humain dans l'évolutif." *Études teilhardiennes* (1969): 2, 109-135.

1198. ————. "Oeuvres et lettres de Teilhard parues en 1967." *Études teilhardiennes* (1968): 1, 151-158.

1199. ————. *Teilhard de Chardin.* Bruxelles: Centre Belge Teilhard de Chardin, 1964.
Portuguese translation in *O tempo e o modo* (1966): 407-427.

1200. ————. "Teilhard de Chardin." *L'Utopie* (1960): 9-10.

1201. ————. "Teilhard de Chardin en l'universel dialogue." *Témoignage chrétien*, July 24, 1967, p. 21.

1202. ————. "La verité de l'univers pour l'homme." *Balisage* (1961): 16/17, 6.

1203. Denat, A. "Note sur Bergson, Teilhard et Camus." *Synthèses* (1964): 216, 134-137.

1204. Déponcelle, Maurice. *Teilhard de Chardin au chevet de la souffrance.* Clermont-Ferrand: G. de Boussac, 1968.

1205. Deschoux, Marcel. "La nature et la culture selon Teilhard de Chardin." *Comprendre* (1958): 9, 250-252.

1206. "De spanning tussen 'naar voren' en 'omhoog.'" *De Maand* (1966): 9, 566-574. Contains Items 1605, 3856, 3898, 4006, 4121.

1207. Desreumaux, Eugene. "Le problème de Teilhard de Chardin et le notre. Comment 'relier' la terre et le ciel?" *Catéchistes* (1966): 15, 255-274, 387-399.

1208. Dessart, Charles. "En lisant l'Avenir de l'homme." In Item 3744.

1209. "Des textes attribués à Teilhard." *La revue nouvelle*
       (1967): 4, 376-378.

1210. De Terra, Helmut. *Bibliographie des deutschsprachigen
       Schrifttums von und über Pierre Teilhard de Chardin,
       1955-1964.* Frankfurt-am-Main: Werner Reimers-stiftung
       für anthropogenetische Forschung, 1965.

1211. ————. "En Inde avec le Père Teilhard." *Revue Teilhard
       de Chardin* (1961): 6, 3-6: 7, 4-7.

1212. ————. *Mein Weg mit P. Teilhard de Chardin--Forschungen
       und Erlebnisse.* München: C.H. Beck, 1962.
       Also 2d ed., 1966.
       Teilhard als reisgenoot. Baarn: Het Wereldvenster,
       1963.
       Memories of Teilhard de Chardin. London: Collins,
       1964.
       Also New York: Harper and Row, 1964.
       Mes voyages avec Teilhard. Paris: Seuil, 1965.
       *Mi camino junto a Teilhard de Chardin. Investiga-
       ciones y experiencias.* Madrid: Alfaguara, 1967.

1213. ————. *Perspektiven Teilhard de Chardins.* München:
       C.H. Beck, 1966. Contains Items 209, 309, 1384,
       1753, 2199, 3031, 3302.

1214. ————, and George B. Barbour. "Teilhard--Mensch und
       Forscher--von Freunde gesehen." *Perspektiven der
       Zukunft* (1970): 1, 2-4.

1215. De Tollenaere, M. "De mens in Teilhards wereldvisie."
       Streven (1956): 9, 820-828.

1216. ————. "Weltschöpfung und Entwicklung Teilhard de
       Chardins. Vision und das christliche Dogma." *Wort
       und Wahrheit* (1961): 16, 273-282.

1217. "Devant une émission de télévision sur le P. Teilhard
       de Chardin." *Notes hebdomadaires de la CTIC* (1965):
       371, 1-2.

1218. Devaux, André A. "Bergson et Teilhard de Chardin. Une
       thèse en Sorbonne." *La Croix*, June 30, 1963.

1219. ————. "De l'humain vers l'ultra-humain." *Les études
       philosophiques* (1958): 14, 59-63.

1220. ————. "La décade Teilhard de Chardin." *Les études philosophiques* (1958): 14, 59-63.

1221. ————. "Deux ardents: Péguy et Teilhard face au problème de l'inchristianisation." *Item* 3950, pp. 158-194.

1222. ————. "L'élément féminin dans la phénoménologie teilhardienne." *Revue Teilhard de Chardin* (1963): 14, 8-10.

1223. ————. "Essai sur l'idée de dilation du concept de nature humaine dans la pensée contemporaine." *Revue Teilhard de Chardin* (1961): 8/9, 34-38.

1224. ————. "Une exégèse magistrale de la pensée teilhardienne." *Revue Teilhard de Chardin* (1963): 16, 29-32.

1225. ————. "Le féminin selon Teilhard de Chardin." *Recherches et débats* (1963): 45, 120-138.
       "L'indispensable féminité et le culte de la Vierge Marie selon Teilhard de Chardin." *Ecclesia* (1964): 182, 35-42.

1226. ————. "L'homme de demain selon Pierre Teilhard de Chardin." *La table ronde* (1963): 180, 64-74.
       "El hombre de mañana según Teilhard de Chardin." *Indice* (1963): 171, 16-17.

1227. ————. "Humanisme et christianisme selon Pierre Teilhard de Chardin." *Revue Teilhard de Chardin* (1960): 3/4, 3-7.

1228. ————. "L'idée de nature humaine." *Civiltà delle macchine* (1964): 6, 23-31. Includes Italian version.

1229. ————. "Méthode dialectique et philosophie personaliste chez Teilhard de Chardin." *Science et esprit* (1968): 2, 291-298.

1230. ————. "Notes bibliographiques." *Revue Teilhard de Chardin* (1962): 10, 31-34; 11, 26-31; 12, 31-34; (1963): 14, 36-39; 15, 36-39, 43-44; 16, 33-37; 17, 33-38; (1964): 18, 27-33; 19, 35-41; 20/21, 45-51; (1965): 22, 42-46; 23, 44-49; 24/25, 59-62; (1966): 26, 33-37; 29, 37-41; (1967): 32, 26-34.

1231. ————. "Pierre Teilhard de Chardin d'après ses lettres
       de guerre." *Revue Teilhard de Chardin* (1962): 12, 6-
       12; 13, 16-22.
       Also *Cahiers universitaires catholiques* (1962): 14-32.

1232. ————. "Teilhard de Chardin d'après ses lettres à
       Léontine Zanta." *Revue de Paris* (1966): 7/8, 69-77.

1233. ————. "Teilhard de Chardin en Sorbonne." Item 3041,
       pp. 153-159.

1234. ————. "Teilhard de Chardin et la construction d'une
       morale pour notre temps." *Perspectives* (1965): 23,
       31-38.

1235. ————. "Teilhard de Chardin selon 'l'ordre des raisons.'"
       Revue Teilhard de Chardin (1974): 60, 54-59.

1236. ————. "Teilhard et la reconciliation du ciel et de
       la terre." *Cahiers universitaires catholiques* (1962-
       63): 8, 363-369.

1237. ————. *Teilhard et Saint-Exupéry. Convergences et
       divergences.* Paris: Éditions Universitaires, 1962.
       Teilhard en Saint-Exupéry. Tielt/Den Haag: Lannoo,
       1964.
       Teilhard e Saint-Exupéry. Petrópolis: Vozes, 1967.
       Teilhard y Saint-Exupéry. Buenos Aires: Columba,
       1968.

1238. ————. *Teilhard et la vocation de la femme.* Paris:
       Editions Universitaires, 1964.
       Teilhard e la vocazione della donna. Roma: A.V.E.,
       1966.
       Teilhard e a vocação da mulher. Petrópolis: Vozes,
       1967.
       Teilhard and Womanhood. Glen Rock, N.J.: Paulist
       Press, 1968.
       Teilhard y la vocación de la mujer. Buenos Aires:
       Colomba: 1968.

1239. ————. "Teilhard et la vocation de la femme." *Jeunesse
       nouvelle* (1966): 20, 13-16. Excerpt from Item 1238.

1240. Devine, W.T. "Scientist Missionaries in China." *Irish
       Ecclesiastical Record* (1930): 36, 136-143.

1241. De Vooght, Paul, and Jules Hens. "La signification religieuse de la phénoménologie teilhardienne." *Revue générale belge* (1964): 100, 13-29.

1242. *Dialog i współdzialanie.* [Dialogue in Cooperation.] Warszawa: Pax, 1970.

1243. "Dialogue sur Teilhard." *Itinéraires* (1963): 77, 112-129. Contains Items 2581, 2790, 3563.

1244. Dias, Joseph M. "Priestly Ministry in the Life and Writings of Teilhard de Chardin." *Clergy Monthly* (1974): 38, 60-76.

1245. Díaz Araujo, Enrique. "Evolucionismo: Cuestiones disputadas." *Mikael* (1976): 11, 39-55.

1246. ————. "Paralelo entre Las Casas y Teilhard." *Verbo* (1977): 175, 25-48.

1247. Diaz Corvalán, Eugenio. "La persona en Teilhard de Chardin." *BIDI* (1965): 76, 4-8. Also *Pax Romana Journal* (1965): 4-8.

1248. "Dictionnaire critique." *Écrits de Paris*, September, 1958, pp. 106-111; October, 1958, pp. 60-65.

1249. Didier, Jean C. "La pensée du Père Teilhard de Chardin. Note documentaire." *Bulletin ecclésiastique* (1958): 117-122, 155-160, 177-183.

1250. Dieška, Jozef. "Teilhard de Chardin or Thomas Aquinas?" *Social Justice Review* (1967): 11, 438-451. Also *University of Dayton Review* (1966): 2, 57-76.

1251. ————. "Teilhardovo poňatie ducha a hmoty." [The Teilhardian Concept of Spirit and Matter.] *Echo* (1973): 5, 33-39.

1252. Dietsche, Bernwald. "Grundzüge einer dynamischen Ethik nach Teilhard de Chardin." *Acta teilhardiana* (1972): 1, 3-29.

1253. ————. "Notes on Teilhard de Chardin and the Invisible." *The Teilhard Review* (1970-71): 5, 105.

1254. ————. "L'optimisme chez Teilhard de Chardin." Item 741, pp. 133-144.

1255. ——————. "Optimisme et pessimisme dans la socialisation.
       L'optimisme comme phénomène de structure chez Teilhard
       de Chardin. Version intégrale de la conférence pro-
       noncée au colloque de Nice, mars 1963." Typescript.
       Paris: Fondation Teilhard de Chardin, 1963.

1256. ——————. "Zu einem 'Achsengestez' im Weltbild von Teil-
       hard de Chardin." *Acta teilhardiana* (1967): 4, 35-52.

1257. ——————. "Zum kosmischen Christus nach Teilhard de Char-
       din." *Acta teilhardiana* (1971): 1, 13-31.

1258. Dietz, Margaret Mary C. "The Theology of the Redemption
       of Duns Scotus and Teilhard de Chardin." Doctoral
       dissertation, St. Mary's Seminary and University, Balti-
       more, 1975.

1259. *Le Dieu de l'évolution.* Paris: Seuil, 1968. Contains
       Items 113, 191, 400, 751, 1940, 2349, 2376, 2378, 2379,
       2424, 2610, 2747, 2797, 2806, 3090, 3151, 3647, 3648,
       4548, 4549, 4555.

1260. "Diez años despues." *Cuadernos para el diálogo* (1965):
       19, 22-23.

1261. Díez Ravena, Antolina Violeta. "Determinismo y libertad
       en la obra de Pierre Teilhard de Chardin." Typescript.
       Madrid: Facultad de filosofía y letras, 1965.

1262. ——————. "Entre yo y los otros." *La estafeta literaria*
       (1964): 290, 10-11.

1263. Di Natale, Luigi. "Il biologo dell'evoluzione." *Osserva-
       tore, politico et letterario* (1965): 7, 83-88.

1264. Diop, Thomas. "Problèmes philosophiques et religieux."
       Pensée française (1957): 3, 20-23.

1265. Dirix, Rodolphe. "'Le milieu divin' de Pierre Teilhard
       de Chardin." *Balisage* (1961): 16/17, 33-35.

1266. ——————. "Recherche et adoration." *Balisage* (1961): 16/
       17, 32.

1267. ——————. "'L'unique science.'" *Balisage* (1961): 16/17, 2.

1268. "Discussions About Pierre Teilhard de Chardin." *Tablet*,
       January 27, 1962, p. 93.

1268a. Disertori, Beppino. *Sfida al secolo. La natura, l'uomo, il tessitore.* Padua: Liviana, 1975. Also Trent: Temi, 1975.

1269. Dobzhansky, Theodosius. *The Biology of Ultimate Concern.* New York: New American Library, 1967.

1270. ———. *Dynamik der menschlichen Evolution.* S. Fischer Verlag: Frankfurt-am-Main, 1965.

1271. ———. "Teilhard and Monod: Two Conflicting World Views." *The Teilhard Review* (1973): 2, 36-40.

1272. ———. "Teilhard de Chardin and the Orientation of Evolution." *Zygon* (1968): 3, 242-258.

1273. Dolan, Miguel Eduardo. "Teilhard de Chardin, poeta." *Criterio* (1969): 41, 69-72.

1274. Dolch, Heimo. "Christlicher Schöpfungsglaube und naturwissenschaftliche Entwicklungstheorie. Zur Aussage Teilhard de Chardins." Item 1331, pp. 50-62. Also *Wort und Antwort* (1966): 6, 97-104.

1275. ———. "Einige Bemerkungen zu den neuen Ubersetzungen der Werke Pierre Teilhards de Chardin." *Theologie und Glaube* (1959): 68, 426-429.

1276. ———. "Erwägungen über die Aussage Teilhards de Chardin." *Catholica* (1962): 16, 81-102.

1277. ———. *Der Glaube des Teilhards de Chardin.* Wiesbaden: F. Steiner, 1971.

1278. ———. "Der Punkt 'Omega.' Zur Aussage Teilhards de Chardin." Item 3924, pp. 125-145.

1279. ———. "Sünde in evolutiver Welt." *Concilium* (1967): 3, 465-469.
"El pecado en un mundo en evolución." *Concilium* (1967): 2/3, 415-424.
"Sin in an Evolutive World." *Concilium* (1967): 6, 36-40.
"Le péché dans un monde en évolution." *Concilium* (1967): 26, 71-78.
"Il peccato in un mondo in evoluzione." *Concilium* (1967): 6, 88-98.
"De zonde in een evolutieve wereld." *Concilium* (1967): 6, 70-78.

"Pecado no mundo evolutivo." *COncilium* (1967): 6,
66-74.

1280.   ———. *Teilhard de Chardin im Disput*. Köln: Bachem,
1964.
Teilhard de Chardin en juicio. Buenos Aires: Ediciones Paulinas, 1965.

1281.   ———. "Weltgeschehen in Notwendigkeit und Freiheit."
Philosophia naturalis (1967): 10, 3-22.

1282.   ———. "Zukunftsvision und Parusie (Die Evolution auf
den Punkt omega hin). *Wahrheit und Verkundigung*.
Festschrift M. Schmaus. Paderborn: Schöningh, 1967,
pp. 327-339.
Also Item 2035, pp. 148-173.

1283.   Domenach, Jean-Marie. "Le personnalisme de Teilhard de
Chardin." Item 1284, pp. 337-365.
"El personalismo de Teilhard de Chardin." Item
1284 trans., pp. 9-48.
Also *Sic* (1964): 37, 299-300, 337-348.
"O personalismo de Teilhard de Chardin." *O tempo
e o modo* (1966): 37, 466-484.

1284.   ———. "Teilhard de Chardin et le personnalisme."
Esprit (1963): 31, 337-390; (1964): 32, 354-403.
Contains Items 226, 637, 1283, 2077, 2112, 2879,
3249, 3430, 3755.
Teilhard de Chardin y el personalismo. Barcelona:
Nova Terra, 1969.

1285.   Domenicali, Guido. "Teilhard de Chardin. 1. La vita.
2. L'opera. 3. Apostolato di Cristo nell'universo."
Item 4724 trans., pp. 6-16.

1286.   Domínguez, Ernesto. "El sentido humanístico de las car-
reras técnico-científicas." *Comunidad* (1968): 18,
177-189.

1287.   Donceel, Joseph. F. "Of, By and About Teilhard de Chardin." *The National Catholic Reporter*, June 28, 1967,
p. 9.

1288.   ———. "A Pangalactic Christ?" *Continuum* (1968): 6,
115-119.

1289. ————. *Philosophical Anthropology.* New York: Sheed and Ward, 1967. See pp. 76-80.

1290. ————. "Teilhard de Chardin." *Encyclopedic Dictionary of Christian Doctrine.* Gastonia, N.C.: Goodwill Publishers, 1970, pp. 1066-1076.

1291. ————. "Teilhard de Chardin and the Body-Soul Relation." *Thought* (1965): 158, 371-389.

1292. ————. "Teilhard de Chardin: Scientist or Philosopher?" *International Philosophical Quarterly* (1968): 248-266.

1293. Doncoeur, Paul. "L'Alpha et Oméga. 'L'avenir de l'homme.'" *Cahiers Sainte Jeanne* (1959): 257-259.

1294. Donders, J. "After Ten Years. (A Successful Exponent of the New 'Modern Devotion': Father Pierre Teilhard de Chardin SJ, 1881-1955)." *Afer* (1965): 3, 233-235.

1295. Donnelly, William. "The Thought of Teilhard de Chardin." *The Clergy Review* (1960): 3, 324-349.

1296. Doornink, H.W. "Teilhard de Chardin." *Rekenschap* (1966): 13, 66-71.

1297. Doppelhammer, Stjepan. "Temelj Teilhardovih misli." [The Foundations of Teilhard's System.] *Bogoslovska Smotra* (1965): 35, 103-106.

1298. Dorget, Laure. "1941 à Pékin." *La table ronde* (1955): 90, 76-78.

1299. Dorsey, James M. "The Excellence of Man." Item 1544, pp. 64-76.

1300. "Dossier Teilhard de Chardin." *Riscoperta dell'uomo.* Milano: A. Mondadori, 1967, pp. 183-287. Contains Items 634, 2084, 3503.

1301. Doucette, R. "De Chardin: A Critique." *Priestly Studies* (1964): 30, 2-16.

1302. Downs, Hugh. "Vision of Father Pierre Teilhard de Chardin." *Science Digest* (1965): 57, 85-91.

1303. Doyle, E. "Teilhard and Theology." *Irish Theological Quarterly* (1971): 38, 103-115.

1304. Dozon Daverio, Annette. "Alla luce di Teilhard: l'arte
       nella evoluzione." *Il loggione* (1971): 2, 38-45.

1305. ————. "Teilhard de Chardin amava la Madonna." *Regina
       Martyrum* (1972): 9/10, 8-12; (1973): 1/2, 5-9; 3/4,
       5-11.

1306. Drennan, D.A. "More on Teilhard's Spirituality." *Amer-
       ica*, April 17, 1971, pp. 413-414.

1307. Drexel, Albert. *Teilhard de Chardin. Analyse einer
       Ideologie.* Egg/Zürich: Akademie-Verlag, 1969.
       *Ein neuer Prophet? Teilhard de Chardin. Analyse
       einer Ideologie.* 2d ed.; Stein am Rhein: Christiana
       Verlag, 1971.
       Analisi di una ideologia (Teilhard de Chardin).
       Brescia: Edizioni Civiltà, 1970.

1308. Drouguet, Bruno. "Justice à Teilhard." *Le caducée*
       (1967): 5.

1309. Drova, H. "L'homme comme création de l'homme selon Fried-
       rich Engels et selon Pierre Teilhard de Chardin." *Les
       études philosophiques* (1957): 12, 467-470.

1310. Duarte, Jorge. *O tema da religião dos modernistas a
       Teilhard de Chardin.* Rio de Janeiro: J. Duarte, 1967.

1311. ————. *O tema da religião dos modernistas a Teilhard
       de Chardin. Adendo.* Rio de Janeiro: J. Duarte, 1967.

1312. Dubarle, Dominique. "A propos du 'Phénomène humain' du
       P. Teilhard de Chardin." *La vie intellectuelle* (1956):
       3, 6-25.

1313. ————. "Épistémologie et cosmologie." In *Idée de
       monde et philosophie de la nature.* Paris: Desclée
       de Brouwer, 1966, pp. 127-132.

1314. ————. "Le Père Teilhard de Chardin." *La vie intel-
       lectuelle* (1955): 27, 150-152.

1315. ————. "Teilhard de Chardin Entwurf einer neuen Kos-
       mologie." *Dokumente* (1956): 12, 171-180.

1316. Dubouchet, J. "Sur l'écriture du Père Teilhard de Char-
       din." Typescript. Paris: Fondation Teilhard de Char-
       din, n.d.

1317. Dubuis, Samuel. "Peut-on suivre Teilhard de Chardin?" *La vie protestante*, March 19, 1967, p. 3. See Item 1433.

1318. Ducharme, Léonard. "En abordant Teilhard de Chardin. Propos de méthodologie." *Revue de l'Universite d'Ottawa* (1963): 33, 168-181.

1319. ————. "Les premiers écrits de Teilhard de Chardin." *Église et théologie* (1972): 3, 111-131.

1320. Dufort, Jean-Marc. "Consommation du monde d'après 'Le phénomène humain' et 'L'avenir de l'homme.'" Item 3935, pp. 89-116.

1321. ————. "Sens spirituel de la création d'après 'Le phénomène humain' et 'L'avenir de l'homme.'" Item 3935, pp. 53-87.

1322. Dufosse, Marie-Bruno. "Cosmologie, philosophie et prophétisme chez Teilhard de Chardin." Mimeographed. Master's thesis, University of Lille III, 1972.

1323. Duggan, G.H. "Teilhard de Chardin: A Great Religious Thinker?" *Priest* (1967): 23, 715-719.

1324. ————. "Teilhard: Philosopher." *Priest* (1968): 24, 49-53.

1325. ————. *Teilhardism and Faith*. London: Mercier Press, 1969.

1326. Dumas, André. "Immortalité et évolution." *Spiritualisme moderne* (1958): 15.

1327. Dumoulin, Heinrich. *Christlicher Dialog mit Asien*. München: Max Hueber, 1970. See pp. 28-33.

1328. ————. "Die geistige Vorbereitung des Abendlandes für den Dialog mit Asien." *Stimmen der Zeit* (1966): 177, 275-288.

1329. Dumur, Guy. "Un ordinateur dans une cave gothique." *Le nouvel observateur* (1968): 210, 12-14.

1330. Dunajski, Antoni. "Fenomenologoczny aspekt antropogenezy w ujeciu Piotra Teilharda de Chardin." [The Phenomenological Aspect of Anthropogenesis in the Thought of Pierre Teilhard de Chardin.] *Studia Pelplińskie* (1975): 217-238.

1331. Dungern, Eleonore. *Forschung und Lebensordnung. Mit und ohne Teilhard de Chardin.* München: Reinhardt, 1965. Contains Items 311, 1274, 3159.

1332. Du Passage, Henri. "Le Père Teilhard de Chardin: poète dans la pensée." *Cinquième saison* (1958): 2, 9-12.

1333. Du Plessis, Alberto Luiz. "Influências gnósticas no pensamento do Padre Teilhard de Chardin." *Gil Vicente* (1966): 17, 98-102.

1334. Dupré, Louis. "Themes in Contemporary Philosophy of Religion." *New Scholasticism* (1969): 577-601.

1335. Dupré, Wilhelm. "Anselm and Teilhard de Chardin. Remarks on the Modification of the Ontological Argument in the Thought of Teilhard de Chardin." *Die Wirkungsgeschichte Anselms von Canterbury.* Frankfurt-am-Main: Minerva: 1975, vol. 1, pp. 323-331.

1336. ————. "Die Ehe zwischen Alpha und Omega. Gedanken zum Wesen der Ehe im Weltbild von Pierre Teilhard de Chardin." *Trierer theologische Zeitschrift* (1965): 74, 166-176.

1337. Dupuy, Henri. "La vision teilhardienne du monde et le problème de l'homme." *Revista brasileira de filosofia* (1958): 398, 401-415.

1338. Dupuy, Marthe. "La pensée sociale de Teilhard de Chardin." *Vie judiciaire* (1967): 1084, 6-7; 1085, 8-9; 1087, 8-9.

1339. ————. "Teilhard de Chardin." *L'Auvergnat de Paris* (1965): 15, 16.

1340. Duquaire, Henri. "Le Père de Lubac dénonce une crise spirituelle de l'Eglise." *Le Figaro*, April 4, 1968.

1341. ————. *Si les astres sont habités....* Paris/Genève: La Palatine, 1963. Contains Item 4407.

1342. ————. "Teilhard de Chardin vivant." *Le Figaro*, April 24, 1968.

1343. Durand, Maurice M. "Pierre Teilhard de Chardin." *Bulletin de la Société d'études indochinoises* (1960): 3, 582-587.

1344. Durkin, Joseph T. "Un document inédit: 'Carrel juge de Teilhard.'" *Centre international de réflexion prospective sur la personne et sur la société. Cahier* (1974): 8, 53-66.

1345. ————. *Hope for Our Time.* New York: Harper and Row, 1965.

1346. Duroux, Paul Émile. "Ancêtres de l'homme et hommes fossiles." *Revue Teilhard de Chardin* (1967): 32, 14-20.

1347. ————. "Ancêtres et ancêtres communs de l'humanité." *Univers* (1964): 1, 57-61.

1348. ————. *Contribution à l'étude des pensées de Pierre Teilhard de Chardin. La prévie, la réconciliation de la science et de la foi.* Lyon: Bosc Frères, 1961.

1349. ————. *L'histoire naturelle de l'humanité.* Paris: Éditions Universitaires, 1964.
     História natural da humanidade segundo Teilhard. Petrópolis: Vozes, 1967.
     Historia natural de la humanidad según Teilhard. Buenos Aires: Columba, 1968.

1350. ————. "La philosophie d'évolutionnisme." *Revue Teilhard de Chardin* (1966): 29, 13-18.

1351. ————, and J. Gleize. *L'histoire naturelle de l'humanité vue à travers les pensées du Père Teilhard de Chardin.* Lyon: Imprimerie Générale Lyonnaise, 1960. See Item 1691.

1352. Durtal, Mme. Jean, "L'homme et le monde chez le P. Teilhard de Chardin." Typescript. Paris: Fondation Teilhard de Chardin, 1958.

1353. Dussault, Gabriel. "Le Dieu que notre siècle attend. Essai sur le 'panthéisme' teilhardien." Item 3036, pp. 13-67.
     "El Dios que nuestro siglo aspera. Ensayo sobre el el 'pantéismo' teilhardiano." Item 3036 trans., pp. 11-59.

1354. ————. "Index teilhardien." Item 3036, pp. 197-206.

1355. ———. "Teilhard a-t-il le sens de l'analogie?" *Sciences ecclésiastiques* (1967): 1, 121-127.

1356. ———. "Teilhard, prophète de la terre des hommes." *Relations* (1967): 316, 130-131.

1357. Dussel, Enrique. "En torno a la obra de Teilhard de Chardin." *Ciencia y fe* (1963): 19, 391-400.

1358. ———. "Pierre Teilhard de Chardin, quaestio disputata." *Estudios* (1965): 562, 121-132.

1359. Dutailly, Didier. "Teilhard assassiné...." *Combat*, March 15, 1966.

1360. Duval, Nicole. "De Socrate à Teilhard de Chardin." *Cahiers de Neuilly* (1963): special number, 20-33.

1361. ———. "Humanisme du travail et pensée biblique." *Cahiers de Neuilly* (1963): special number, 3-19.

1362. Duvall, Mary Vera. "Man's Concept of His Religious Fulfillment: A Cross-Cultural Study of Teilhard de Chardin and Classical Buddhist, Hindu and Confucian Thought." Doctoral dissertation, Fordham University, 1966.

1363. Duynstee, W.J. "Teilhard de Chardin's 'Het verschijnsel mens.'" *Nederlandse Katholieke Stemmen* (1963): 59, 134-143.

1364. Duyvené de Wit, J.J. *A New Critique of the Transformist Principle in Evolutionary Biology*. Kampen: J.H. Kok, 1966.

1365. ———. "Pierre Teilhard de Chardin." *Creative Minds in Contemporary Theology*, ed. by Philip E. Hugues. Grand Rapids, Mich.: Eerdmans, 1965, pp. 407-450.

1366. ———. "Pierre Teilhard de Chardin, the Founder of a New Pseudo-Christian Evolutionary Mysticism." *Philosophia Reformata* (1964): 29, 114-149.

1367. Dwyer, John D. "Evolution and Father Teilhard." *Bulletin of the Albertus Magnus Guild* (1967): 3.

1368. "Dyskusja o antropologii filosoficznej Teilharda de Chardin." [Discussions on the Philosophical Anthropology of Teilhard de Chardin.] *Życie i myśl* (1965):

10, 59-94.
Also *Zeszyty Argumentów* (1965): 5, 27-88.

1369. Dyson, Anthony O. "Marxism, Evolution and the Person of Christ." Item 1421, pp. 73-85.

1370. ————. "Polarisation." *The Teilhard Review* (1972): 7, 65.

1371. ————. "Teilhard: Analogy and Dialectic." Item 1919, pp. 33-40.

1372. E.P. "Chardin (Teilhard de)." *Écrits de Paris*, November, 1958, p. 62.

1373. Ebacher, Roger. "Évolution technique et progrès humaine selon Teilhard de Chardin." *Laval théologique et philosophique* (1970): 26, 115-130.

1374. Ebersberger, Ludwig. "Biosphäre, Noosphäre, Punkt Omega: Zur Diskussion um Teilhard de Chardin SJ." *Ärtzliche Mitteilungen* (1963): 9, 468-474. See Item 3259.

1375. ————. "Schlusswort." *Ärtzliche Mitteilungen* (1963): 38, 9-14.

1376. Ebertin, Reinhold. "Teilhard de Chardin, der revolutionärste Denker der europäischen Christenheit des 20. Jahrhunderts." *Kosmobiologie* (1962): 29, 193-199.

1377. Eckhoff, Lorentz. "Pierre Teilhard de Chardin. Perspektiv." *Tidskrift for Kulturdebatt* (1960): 11, 299-301.

1378. Eggers Lahn, Conrado. "Teilhard de Chardin y el historicismo." *Estudios* (1965): 562, 107-112.

1379. Elisabeth de Belgique, Reine. "Message." *Revue Teilhard de Chardin* (1965): 23, 3.

1380. Elliot, Francis G. "The Christology of Pierre Teilhard de Chardin." Item 1421, pp. 86-98.
Also Item 3653, pp. 61-70.

1381. ————. "The Creative Aspect of Evolution." *International Philosophical Quarterly* (1966): 6, 239-247.

1382. ————. "L'origine de la vie et la vision du monde de Teilhard de Chardin ou de l'aspect créatur de l'évolution." *Présence universitaire* (1967): 25/26, 39-59.

"The Origin of Life and the World Vision of Teilhard de Chardin: The Creative Aspect of Evolution." Item 1421, pp. 11-29.

1383.   ————. "Le progrès dans la vision du monde de Pierre Teilhard de Chardin." *Antennes. Chroniques culturelles congolaises* (1962-63): 10, 395-400.

1384.   ————. "The World-Vision of Teilhard de Chardin." *International Philosophical Quarterly* (1961): 4, 620-647.
          Also *The Teilhard Review* (1966): 1, 5-14: (1966/67): 2, 42-49.
          "De wereldbeschouwing van Teilhard de Chardin." Item 3978, pp. 59-94.
          "Pierre Teilhard de Chardins Welt-Anschauung." Item 1213, pp. 66-79.

1385.   Elmgren-Heinonen, Tuomi. "Pierre Teilhard de Chardin hengen esitaistelija." [Pierre Teilhard de Chardin, a Wrestler of the Spirit.] *Takoja* (1962): 2, 6-10.

1386.   Emery, Léon. *De Montaigne à Teilhard de Chardin via Pascal et Rousseau.* Lyon: Cahiers libres, 1965.

1387.   ————. "Karl Marx et Teilhard de Chardin." *Orientierung* (1963): 4e annexe, 17.

1388.   Emminger, E. "Hat die Bibel nicht doch Recht? (Oder Versuch einer Deutung Teilhard de Chardins)." *Arzt und Christ* (1962): 8, 55-57.

1389.   "Encore Teilhard." *Le courrier rationaliste* (1960): 8, 174-188. Contains Items 1916, 2031, 2317.

1390.   Engelson, Suzanne. "A propos du P. Teilhard de Chardin." *Rencontre Orient-Occident* (1956): 1, 17-18.

1391.   ————. "Pierre Teilhard de Chardin: 'Le Milieu divin.'" *Rencontre Orient-Occident* (1959): 6, 22-23.

1392.   ————. "Le R.P. Teilhard de Chardin entre l'Est et l'Ouest." *Rencontre Orient-Occident* (1956): 3, 24.

1393.   Englehardt, Paulus. "Präsenz und Aktion." Item 2902, pp. 27-64.

1394. "En marge de l'Assemblée, la rentrée du Père Teilhard au concile." *Informations catholiques internationales* (1964): 205, 30.

1395. Enriquez, Luis. "Materia-espiritu en la vision antropologica teilhardiana." *Pensamiento* (1970): 26, 199-211.

1396. *En torno a Teilhard*. Madrid: Taurus, 1969. Contains Items 932, 3354, 3418, 3571.

1397. "Entwicklung, Geschichte, Fortschritt." *Kompass* (1960): 7, 94-97.

1398. Erdey, Ferenc. "Teilhard de Chardin miszticus misejc." [The Mystical Mass of Teilhard de Chardin.] *Vigilia* (1963): 28, 414-417.

1399. Ernst, Cornelius. "Another View of Teilhard de Chardin." *The Clergy Review* (1961): 46, 223-234.

1400. ———. "The Cosmological Myth of the Unesco Man." *The Tablet*, May 7, 1960, p. 587.

1401. ———, and J. Todd. "On Reading Teilhard de Chardin." *The Tablet*, June 18, 1960, p. 587.

1402. Ernst, Jerome B. "Teilhard de Chardin's Evolutionary Approach: Man in the Making." *Extension*, June, 1966, pp. 50-51.

1403. *Gli errori di Teilhard de Chardin*. Torino: Edizioni dell'Albero, 1963. Contains Items 579, 1551, 2110.

1404. Escalère, Bernard. "A partir de Teilhard de Chardin." *Vie sociale* (1967): 191-206.

1405. Escribar Wicks, Ana. "El problema del método en la obra de Pierre Teilhard de Chardin." *Teología y vida* (1976): 1/2, 65-86. Also *Cuadernos de filosofía* (1976): 197-224.

1406. Esponera Cerdán, Alfonso. "La concepción de la Iglesia en la visión de Teilhard de Chardin." *Teología espiritual* (1973): 17, 93-114. "The Ecclesiology of Teilhard." *Theology Digest* (1975): 23, 4-7.

1407.   ————. "La revolución científico-técnica y la teología
        según Pierre Teilhard de Chardin." *Escritos del Vedat*
        (1975): 5, 133-182.

1408.   Esteban Romero, Andrés Avelino. "El Padre Teilhard de
        Chardin. Científico optimista y teólogo pesimista?"
        Crisis (1962): 9, 163-180.

1409.   Etô, Tarô. "Ningen jitsuzon no fuan to sentaku--Teil-
        hard de Chardin no genshôgakuteki kôsatsu ni okeru."
        [Anxiety and Choice in Human Existence According to
        the Phenomenological Analysis of Teilhard de Chardin.]
        Ningenron no shomondai. [Problems of Anthropology.]
        Tokyo: Sophia University, 1968, pp. 91-127.

1410.   ————. "Teilhard de Chardin no tetsugaku shisô ni
        tsuite." [Regarding Teilhard de Chardin's Philo-
        sophical Thought.] *Risô* (1969): 7, 9-17.

1411.   ————. "Teilhard wa konnichi nani o wareware ni ut-
        taeru ka?" [What Appeal Has Teilhard for Us?] *Con-
        vergence* (1971): 1, 3-10.

1412.   ————. "Tô-ôen de no Teilhard no eikô." [The Influ-
        ence of Teilhard in Europe and the Far East.] *Con-
        vergence* (1972): 45-52.

1413.   "Études récentes sur le Père Teilhard de Chardin."
        *Union catholique des scientifiques français. Bul-
        letin* (1957): 40, 7-20.

1414.   Evain, François. "Croire et savoir selon le témoign-
        age de Teilhard de Chardin." *Teoresi* (1963): 18,
        136-176.

1415.   ————. "Dieu Point Oméga dans l'apologétique de Teil-
        hard de Chardin." *Rivista rosminiana* (1966): 60,
        276-284.

1416.   ————. "Eminence de la personne dans l'univers selon
        Teilhard de Chardin." *Rivista rosminiana* (1965):
        59, 39-53.

1417.   Evans, John Whitney. "The Phenomenon of Man: Dilemmas
        and Limitations." *Commonweal* (1960): 18, 439-441.

1418.   ————. "Science vs. Teilhard." *Homiletic and Pastoral
        Review* (1961): 426.

1419. *La evolución.* Madrid: Editorial Católica, 1966. Contains Items 792, 3039.

1420. "Evolution and Eschatology: England Establishes Teilhard de Chardin Association." *The Tablet*, April 3, 1965, p. 373.

1421. *Evolution, Marxism and Christianity: Studies in the Teilhardian Synthesis.* London: Garnstone, 1967. Contains Items 1369, 1380, 1382, 1516, 1595, 4005.

1422. *L'Évolution Rédemptrice du P. Teilhard de Chardin.* Paris: Éditions du Cèdre, 1950.

1423. *Evolutive Anthropologie. Das Bild des Menschen in der Sicht moderner Wissenschaften.* Akten des Internationales Kongresses der Gesellschaft Teilhard de Chardin für den Deutschen Sprachraum. München: Sighart, 1971. Contains Items 1854, 3694.

1424. *Evoluzionismo e storia umana. Atti del XXII Convegno del Centro di studi filosofici tra professori universitari, Gallarate 1967.* Brescia: Morcelliana, 1968.

1425. Ewing, J. Franklin. "The Human Phenomenon." *Theological Studies* (1961): 1, 86-102.

1426. Ezcurdia, Alberto de. "La obra de Teilhard de Chardin." *Revista de la Universidad de México* (1966): 6, 17-20.

1427. Facchini, Fiorenzo. "La concezione evoluzionistica di Teilhard de Chardin." *Medicina e società* (1969): 3, 260-266.

1428. ———. "Sur l'apport de Pierre Teilhard de Chardin à la Paléo-anthropologie et à l'étude de l'évolution humaine." *Revue des questions scientifiques* (1968): 139, 167-189.

1429. Faessler, Marc. "L'anthropologie selon Karl Barth et Teilhard de Chardin." Item 3851, pp. 207-267.

1430. ———. "Attualità del messagio spirituale dell'Ambiente divino." Item 2744, pp. 251-266.
    "Actualité du message spirituel du Milieu divin." Item 2744 trans., pp. 234-237.

1431. ———. "La experiencia espiritual del Padre Teilhard
       de Chardin." *Confluencias* (1964-65): 5, 13-17; 6,
       11-17.

1432. ———. "Homme réel et phénomène humain. Essai sur
       les fondements christologique et cosmologique de
       l'anthropologie à partir des oeuvres de Karl Barth
       et de Pierre Teilhard de Chardin." Mimeographed.
       Faculté autonome de théologie protestante de l'Uni-
       versité de Genève, 1968.

1433. ———. "Oui, on peut suivre Teilhard de Chardin."
       La vie protestante (1967). See Item 1317.

1434. ———. "Pour ou contre l'évolution." *Réforme* (1963):
       1082, 6.

1435. Faggiola, Guido della. "Il fenomeno humano." *Il fuoco*
       (1956): 1, 48-49.

1436. Falconi, Carlo. "Niente da fare in Francia per Teil-
       hard de Chardin. Ottaviani insiste contro la nuova
       teologia." *L'Espresso*, July 29, 1962, p. 10.

1437. Falk, Heinrich. "Can Spirit Come from Matter?" *Inter-
       national Philosophical Quarterly* (1967): 7, 541-555.

1438. Fantoni, Annibale. "Teilhard de Chardin no hôhôron
       wo meguru saikin no ronsô." [Recent Discussions on
       the Methodology of Teilhard de Chardin.] *Sophia*
       (1964): 13, 325-444.

1439. Faricy, Robert Leo. "Cosmic Redemption and Church
       Authority." *American Ecclesiastical Review* (1969):
       161, 40-50.

1439a. ———. "The Heart of Jesus in the Eschatology of
       Teilhard." *The Teilhard Review* (1978): 13, 82-89.

1440. ———. "The Image of Man in the Writings of Teilhard."
       Proceedings of the Catholic Theological Society (1968):
       60-68.

1441. ———. "Matter and Holiness: The Spiritual Theology
       of Pierre Teilhard de Chardin." *The Teilhard Review*
       (1975): 2, 34-40.

1442. ————. "La perfection chrétienne selon le Père Teilhard de Chardin." *Gregorianum* (1974): 55, 319-338.

1443. ————. "Religious Education." *The Teilhard Review* (1970): 2, 85-93.

1444. ————. "Teilhard de Chardin: A Critical Survey." *American Ecclesiastical Review* (1968): 159, 261-269.

1445. ————. "Teilhard de Chardin on Creation and the Christian Life." *Theology Today* (1966/67): 23, 505-520.

1446. ————. "Teilhard de Chardin's Spirituality of the Cross." *Horizons* (1976): 3, 1-15. "La croce negli scritti di Teilhard de Chardin." *La sapienza della croce oggi.* Torino: Elle Di Ci Leumann, 1976, vol. 1, pp. 348-355.

1447. ————. *Teilhard de Chardin's Theology of the Christian in the World.* New York: Sheed and Ward, 1967. *Teilhard de Chardin: Teologia del cristiano en el mundo.* Estella: Verbo Divino, 1972.

1448. ————. "Teilhard de Chardin's Theology of Redemption." *Theological Studies* (1966): 27, 553-579.

1449. ————. "A Theology of Human Endeavor." Item 2158, pp. 51-71. "Una teologia della sforzo umano." Item 2158 trans., pp. 76-103.

1450. ————. "The Value of Human Endeavor According to Pierre Teilhard de Chardin." Doctoral dissertation, Catholic University of America, 1966.

1451. Farran, Jean. "Ce jésuite qui inquiète le Vatican." *Paris-Match*, August 11, 1962, pp. 68-70, 72, 74.

1452. Father X. "¿Teilhard de Chardin mos colégios católicos?" *Conferencia dos religiosos do Brazil* (1966): 131, 304-305.

1453. Favaro, Arcangelo. "Significato di un Covegno." Item 2744, pp. 9-12. "Sens d'un colloque." Item 2744 trans., pp. 7-10.

1454. Febas Borra, José Luis. "Les noms du Christ dans les oeuvres de Teilhard de Chardin. Pour une approche

linguistique de la théologie." Mimeographed. Institut
Catholique de Paris, 1976.

1455. Febvre, Lucien. "Pierre Teilhard de Chardin." *Annales:
       économies, sociétés, civilisations* (1956): 1, 194-196.

1456. Fehlner, Peter D. "Pierre Teilhard de Chardin: His Life
       and Spirit." *Homiletic and Pastoral Review* (1959-60):
       60, 1202-1210.

1457. ————. "Teilhard de Chardin: Ambiguity by Design."
       Homiletic and Pastoral Review (1959-60): 60, 709-717.

1458. ————. "Teilhard de Chardin: 'Leading to Confusion.'"
       Homiletic and Pastoral Review (1960-61): 61, 40-47.

1459. Felipe Guerra, L. *La filosofía de la naturaleza en
       Teilhard de Chardin.* Lima: Instituto Riva-Agüero,
       1964.

1460. Fellermeier, Jakob. "Die Einheit des Kosmos. Zum Welt-
       bild Teilhard de Chardins." *Theologie und Glaube*
       (1973): 63, 197-218, 257-279.

1461. Feneberg, Rupert. *Die Phänomenologie bei Teilhard de
       Chardin. Eine Untersuchung der hermeneutischen Vor-
       aussetzungen ihrer Interpretation.* Meisenheim: Hain
       Verlag, 1968.

1462. Ferkiss, Victor C. *Technological Man.* New York: New
       American Library, 1969.

1463. Fernandez, A. "Aspektoj el la monbildo de Teilhard de
       Chardin." *Sennacieca revuo* (1964): 92, 23-29.

1464. Fernández Marcantoni, J.L. *La evolucion según Teilhard
       de Chardin (origen y destino del hombre).* Santa Fé,
       Argentina: Editorial Castellví, 1970.

1465. Feron, Bernard. "Teilhard intrigue les athées soviét-
       iques." *Le Monde,* November 6-7, 1966, p. 3.

1466. Ferrara, Alessandro. *Noi. Precisazione e difesa della
       spiritualità mediterranea.* Roma: Edizioni Abete,
       1972. See pp. 241-283.

1467. Ferreira, Pedro M. Guimarães. "Teilhard missionário."
       Verbum (1972): 29, 199-214.

1468. Ferreira, Vergílio. "Teilhard de Chardin e o humanismo
       contemporâneo." *O tempo e o modo* (1966): 33, 428-455.

1469. Ferrier, François. "La convergence dans le 'Milieu Di-
       vin.'" *Cahiers de vie franciscaine* (1963): 40, 33-49.

1470. ———. "Le dynamisme du Ressuscité dans la pensée du
       Père Teilhard de Chardin." *Parole et pain* (1970): 37,
       30-39.

1471. ———. "L'Euchariste chez Teilhard de Chardin." *Pa-
       role et pain* (1965): 8, 473-491.

1472. ———. "Le Père Chenu: une théologie pour le monde."
       L'union (1966): 14, 3-14.

1473. ———. "Le Père Teilhard de Chardin révélé par ses
       lettres et ses écrits posthumes." *Promesses* (1957):
       28, 17-22.

1474. ———. "'S'immerger pour soulever.'" *Spiritus* (1969):
       37, 3-13.

1475. ———. "Le vrai visage du Père Teilhard de Chardin."
       Ecclesia (1957): 104, 49-58.

1476. Fesquet, Henri. *Le Catholicisme religion de demain?*
       Paris: Grasset, 1962.

1477. ———. "Convergence de l'Église et du monde." *Revue
       Teilhard de Chardin* (1963): 14, 18-19.

1478. ———. "Deux nouvelles conférences sur Teilhard de
       Chardin." *Le Monde*, October 20, 1965, p. 10.

1479. ———. "'Genèse d'un pensée' un nouveau receuil de
       lettres du Père Teilhard de Chardin." *Le Monde*,
       November 11, 1961, pp. 8-9.

1480. ———. "Une pensée hardie et un prestige considér-
       able." *Le Monde*, July 3, 1962, p. 13.

1481. Fessard, Gaston. "La vision religieuse de Teilhard
       de Chardin." *L'homme devant Dieu. Mélanges offert
       au Père de Lubac.* 3 vols.; Paris: Aubier, 1963-64,
       vol. 3, pp. 223-248.

1482. Feuerstein, Jeanne-Noel. "A propos du Père Teilhard de Chardin." *Lotus bleu* (1962): 67, 50-56.

1483. ———. "Aperçus sur l'oeuvre du Père Teilhard de Chardin." *Lotus bleu* (1962): 67, 188-191.

1484. Feuillet, André. *Le Christ sagesse de Dieu. D'après les épitres pauliniennes.* Paris: Gabalda, 1966. See pp. 376-385.

1485. Feys, Jan. *The Philosophy of Evolution in Aurobindo and Teilhard.* Calcutta: K.L. Mukhopadhyay, 1973.

1486. ———. *The Yogi and the Mystic: A Study in the Spirituality of Sri Aurobindo and Teilhard de Chardin.* Calcutta: K.L. Mukhopadhyay, 1977.

1487. Fierro Bardaji, Alfredo. *El proyecto teológico de Teilhard de Chardin.* Salamanca: Sígueme, 1971.

1488. Fiévet, André. "Et si Teilhard n'était qu'un auteur de science-fiction?" *Le monde et la vie* (1963): 120, 65-67.

1489. ———. "Teilhard de Chardin et la science-fiction." In Item 3744.

1490. Figueiredo, Manuel Versos. "Bibliografia teilhardiana." *Revista portuguesa de filosofia. Supplemento bibliográfico* (1967): 6, 334-340; (1968): 7, 95-99.

1491. ———. "Nota bibliográfica sobre Teilhard de Chardin." *Revista portuguesa de filosofia* (1972): 355-369.

1492. Fiolet, H.A.M. "De boodschap van de christen Teilhard de Chardin." *De Protestant* (1965): 5, 3-6.

1493. ———. *Mens-wording en wording van de mens. Geloof en wetenschap in het denken van Teilhard de Chardin.* 's-Hertogenbosch: Geert Groote Genootschap, 1963.

1494. Fiorioli, E. "Un savant au service de la foi." *Culture française* (1965): 12, 249-252, 266.

1495. Fischer, E. "What Do Young Cassidy and Teilhard Share?" *Ave Maria*, June 26, 1965, p. 9.

1496. Fischl, Johannes. "Teilhard de Chardin—der letzte 'Fall Galilei'?" *Theologisch-praktische Quartal-schrift* (1970): 118, 169-176.

1497. Fitzer. Joseph. "Teilhard's Eucharist: A Reflection." *Theological Studies* (1973): 34, 251-264.

1498. Flanagan, John W. "A Periscope on Teilhard de Chardin." *Social Justice Review* (1975): 68, 49-52.

1499. Flavia Maria, Sr. "'Song of Myself': A Presage of Modern Teilhardian Paleontology." *Walt Whitman Review* (1969): 15, 43-49.

1500. Fleming, David L. "'Passion' in the Spiritual Writings of Teilhard de Chardin: A Study of Detachment and Diminishment." Doctoral dissertation, Catholic University of America, 1969.

1501. ————. "Pilgrim of the Future: Teilhard." *America* (1975): 132, 279-282.

1502. Fleming, T.V. "Two Unpublished Letters of Teilhard." *Heythrop Journal* (1965): 1, 36-45.

1503. Flick, Maurizio. "Progresso umano ed edificazione del corpo mistico. (A proposito del sistema di Teilhard de Chardin)." *Stella matutina* (1964): 60, 161-166.

1504. Foley, L. "Cosmos and Ethos." *New Scholasticism* (1967): 41, 141-158.

1505. Forbelsky, Josef. "Teilhard de Chardin en el Este." *El ciervo* (1967): 164, 4-5.

1506. Forceville, P. de. *Une hypothèse. Réflexion sur la conception teilhardienne de l'évolution.* Abbeville: F. Paillard, 1965.

1507. Formi, Guglielmo. "Ipotesi evoluzionista e filosofia della storia in Maritain e Teilhard de Chardin." *Il mulino* (1964): 144, 1056-1074.

1508. Forsthoefel, Paulinus F. "Beneath the Microscope." Item 1544, pp. 98-114.

1509. Fortmann, H.M. "Teilhard de Chardin en het H. Office." *Nederlandse Katholieke Stemmen* (1963): 59, 129-133.

1510.   "For Your Information: Vicariate of Rome Instruction to
        Catholic Bookstores in Rome Not to Sell Certain Books."
        Priest (1963): 19, 988+.

1511.   Forster, Karl. *Schopfungsglaube und biologische Entwick-
        lungslehre.* Würzburg: Echter-Verlag, 1962.

1512.   Foster, K., M. Leigh, E.M. Stewart, and F. Walshe. "On
        Reading Père Teilhard de Chardin." *The Tablet*, May 21,
        1960.

1513.   Fothergill, Philip G. "A Christian Interpretation of
        Evolution." *Proceedings of the University of Durham
        Philosophical Society, 13, Series A (Science)*(1957):
        4, 23-32.

1514.   ————. "Men on Their Nature and Place in Nature."
        The Teilhard Review (1967): 1, 11-22.

1515.   ————. "Pierre Teilhard de Chardin. Some Aspects of
        His Thought." *Proceedings of the University of New-
        castle upon Tyne Philosophical Society* (1964): 3,
        24-34.

1516.   ————. "Teilhard and the Question of Orthogenesis."
        Item 1421, pp. 30-46.

1517.   ————. "Teilhard de Chardin and the Attenuated Con-
        sciousness." *Newman Association, Philosophy of Sci-
        ence Group, Bulletin* (1960): 38, 4-22.

1518.   Fougey-Rolla, Pierre. "La cosmologie comme nostalgie
        et comme prospective." *Arguments* (1961): 4, 57-61.

1519.   Foulquié, P. "Encore le P. Teilhard de Chardin, mais
        par le principal témoin de sa vie." *École des lettres*
        (1971): 11, 33-37.

1520.   Fourez, Gérald. "Teilhard, la mission de l'Église et
        les missions." *Science et esprit* (1969): 21, 357-369.

1521.   Foy, James L. "Man and the Behavioral Sciences." Item
        1544, pp. 115-130.

1522.   ————. "Teilhard de Chardin, Phenomenology and the
        Study of Man." *Bulletin of the Guild of Catholic
        Psychiatrists* (1963): 3, 155-170.

1523. Fraenkel, Fritz. "Teilhard de Chardin. Eine Einfuhrung in seine Gedankenwelt." *Quatember* (1965-66): 30, 146-154.

1524. Fragata, Júlio. "Teilhard de Chardin. Noticia bibligráfica." *Revista portuguesa de filosofia* (1966): 287-300.

1525. Fragueiro, José María. "El panteísmo en Teilhard de Chardin." *IIº Congreso nacional de filosofía. Actas.* Buenos Aires: Sudamericana, 1973, vol. 2, pp. 354-361.

1526. Francia, Ennio. "La caccia alla streghe." *Leggere* (1962): 8/9, 6.

1527. Franck, Richard. "Social Evolution and the Human Species." *American Catholic Sociological Review* (1962): 4, 310-323.

1528. Francoeur, Robert T. "Be an Instant Expert on Teilhard de Chardin." *Critic* (1971): 30, 34-37.

1529. ———. "The Challenge of Teilhard de Chardin." *U.S. Catholic* (1966): 32, 30-36.

1530. ———. *Changing Ideas About Marriage: Thoughts from Teilhard de Chardin.* St. Meinrad, Ind.; Abbey Press, 1966.

1531. ———. "Conflict, Cooperation and the Collectivization of Man." Item 528, pp. 226-244.

1532. ———. "The Cosmic Christianity of Teilhard de Chardin." *The Sign* (1967): 46, 8-13.

1533. ———. "The Cosmic Piety of Teilhard de Chardin." *Catholic Mind* (1964): 62, 5-15.
Also *Catholic Messenger*, October 1, 1964, pp. 5-6.
Also *Cosmic Piety, Modern Man and the Meaning of Universe*, ed. by Christopher Derrick. New York: P.J. Kennedy, 1965, pp. 99-118.

1534. ———. "For Teilhard, No Flight from Time." *The Catholic World* (1961): 1, 367-373.

1535. ———. "Heretical Idol or Prophetic Spirit?" *Marist* (1966): 3, 18-19.

1536. ———. "The Influence of Teilhard de Chardin." *Homiletic and Pastoral Review* (1966-67): 67, 109-116.

1537. ———. "Introduction." Item 1544, pp. 24-34.

1538. ———. "The Nature of Self in a Philosophy of Being
and a Philosophy of Becoming." *Research Journal of
Philosophy and Social Sciences* (1965): 2, 16-29.

1539. ———. "The Phenomenon of Man: A Call to Greatness."
Commonweal (1960): 18, 441-443.

1540. ———. "A Prelude to Further Thought." Item 1544, pp.
186-188.

1541. ———. "The Process of Evolution and 'Panpsychism'
in Teilhard de Chardin." *American Benedectine Review*
(1961): 12, 206-219.

1542. ———. "Teilhard de Chardin: 'Prophet of a New Vision....'" *Homiletic and Pastoral Review* (1960-61):
61, 36-39.

1543. ———. "Teilhard de Chardin: Some Recent Literature."
Jubilee , July, 1965, pp. 36-39.
Also *U.S. Catholic* (1966): 8, 30-38.

1544. ———. *The World of Teilhard.* Baltimore: Helicon,
1961. Contains Items 154, 166, 373, 1299, 1508, 1521,
1537, 1540, 1568, 2197, 2295, 3296, 3794, 4185, 4201.

1545. ———, and Judy Visyak. "A Revised and Annotated Bibliography of Writings About Pierre Teilhard de Chardin."
Mimeographed. Southfield, Mich.: the authors, 1960.

1546. Francotte, Auguste. "Une soirée teilhardienne." In
Item 3744.

1547. Frank, Richard. "Social Evolution and the Human Species.
Teilhard de Chardin and Sociology." *American Catholic
Sociological Review* (1962): 23, 310-323.

1548. Frauchiger, Ernst. *Auf Spuren des Geistes. Ein Neur-
ologe mit Ludwig Klages und Teilhard de Chardin.*
Stuttgart: Huber, 1974.

1549. ———. "Teilhard de Chardin und Ludwig Klages."
Perspektiven der Zukunft (1973): 2, 7-9. Excerpt
from Item 1548.

1550. Freible, Charles W. "Teilhard, Sexual Love, and Celibacy." *Review for Religious* (1967): 26, 282-294.

1551. Frenaud, Georges. *Pensée philosophique et religieuse du Père Teilhard de Chardin.* Le Chesnay: J. de Saint-Chamas, 1963.
    Also 2d ed., 1965.
    Étude critique sur la pensée philosophique et religieuse du Père Teilhard de Chardin." *La cité catholique* (1963).
    Il pensiero filosófico e religioso del Padre Teilhard de Chardin. Item 1403, pp. 9-59.
    Estudio critico sobre el pensamiento filosófico y religioso de Teilhard de Chardin. Buenos Aires: Iction, 1967.
    Also *Verbo* (1963): 58-81
    Also *Colligite* (1963): 3: 83-91.

1552. Frenkel, F.E. "Kerk versus Galilei en Teilhard." *Gids* (1965): 128, 33-41.

1553. Frescaroli, Antonio. "A proposito di Teilhard de Chardin." *Vita e pensiero* (1963): 46, 308-314.

1554. "Fresh Look at the Exile Priest." *Time*, February 28, 1977, pp. 53-54.

1555. Frétigny, Roger. "Place de l'oeuvre teilhardienne dans la pensée philosophique contemporaine." *Revue Teilhard de Chardin* (1962): 10, 4.

1556. Frey, Christopher. *Mysterium der Kirche. Öffnung zur Welt. Zwei Aspekte der Erneuerung französischer katholischer Theologie.* Göttingen: Vandenhoeck und Ruprecht, 1969. See pp. 205-209.

1557. Friedmann, Georges. *La puissance et la sagesse.* Paris: Gallimard, 1970. See pp. 323-342.

    Frisch, Jean. See Kitahara, Takashi.

1558. Fritsch, Vilma. "Welche Zukunft erwartet den Menschen? Einleitung zu einem Dialog zwischen dem Marxismus und der zeitgenossischen Philosophie." *Frankfurter Hefte* (1962): 17, 377-380.

1559. Froese, Leonhard. "Die Lehre vom Menschen im Verständnis heutiger Forschung." *Universitas* (1966): 21, 915-926.

1560. Frys, Joseph. "Recherche scientifique et politique."
      Revue Teilhard de Chardin (1966): 26, 23-26.

1561. Fuchs, Claude. "Les débuts de la 'commission Teilhard.'"
      Responsables (1963): 2, 13-17.

1562. Fuchs, Emil. "Pater Teilhard de Chardin." *Communio*
      Viatorium (1961): 4, 123-138.

1563. ————. "Le phénomène humain. Présentation et critique
      de la pensée du Père Teilhard de Chardin." *Bulletin*
      du Centre protestant d'études (1958): 8, 3-23.

1564. Fujiwara, Naotatsu. "Teilhard de Chardin to Imanishi
      Kinji." [Teilhard de Chardin and Immanuel Kant.]
      Convergence (1977): 5, 5-27.

1565. ————. "Teilhard ni okeru kaishû no imi." [The Idea
      of Convergence in Teilhard.] *Convergence* (1972): 2,
      23-29.

1566. ————. "Teilhard no tôyôkan." [How Teilhard Saw the
      Orient.] *Convergence* (1975): 4, 25-37.

1567. Fullat, Octavi. "Teilhard de Chardin y Santo Tomás
      frente al problema de la evolución." *Crisis* (1959):
      6, 61-76.

1568. Fullman, Christopher E., and Henry J.J. D'Aoust. "The
      Energetics of Love." Item 1544, pp. 146-155.

1569. Fumer, Stanislas. "'Le paysan de la Garonne' de Jacques
      Maritain. Controverse autour d'un livre." *Le Monde*
      (1966): 6823, 1, 8.

1570. Furlong, Guillermo. "Carlos Darwin y Teilhard de Char-
      din." *Anales de la Academia Argentina de geografia*
      (1959): 3, 15-19.

1571. Fuss, Albert. *Bemerkungen zur Symbolik und Metaphorik*
      bei Teilhard de Chardin. Würzburg: Julius-Maximilian-
      Universitat Würzburg, 1969.

1572. ————. "Quelques remarques concernant l'emploi de la
      majuscule chez Teilhard de Chardin." *Français moderne*
      (1969): 37, 336-345; (1970): 38, 35-43, 105-130.

1573. ————. "Zum Stande der Teilhardforschung (1967-1969)." *Romantisches Jahrbuch* (1969): 20, 130-160.

1574. Gaba, Charles Raymond. "The Christian Apologetic of Pierre Teilhard de Chardin." Doctoral dissertation, Southern Baptist Theological Seminary, Louisville, Ky., 1968.

1575. Gable, Mariella. "The Concept of Fame in Teilhard de Chardin and Dante." *American Benedictine Review* (1965): 16, 341-358. "Teilhard and Dante." Item 607, pp. 10-30.

1576. Gaboriau, F. *Les grandes étapes de la pensée. Décision 2.* Paris: Castermann, 1965. See pp. 180-191, 231-233, 314-325.

1577. Gabriel, Leo. "Evolution und Zeitbegriff, von H. Bergson zu Teilhard de Chardin." *Wissenschaft und Weltbild* (1962): 15, 31-36.

1578. Gaete, Arturo. "Introducción al 'Fenómeno humano.'" *Mensaje* (1965): 14, 687-692; (1966): 15, 102-106; (1967): 16, 415-421, 664-670.

1579. ————. "Teilhard de Chardin, entusiasmo o reserva?" *Mensaje* (1963): 12, 82-89.

1580. ————. "Teilhard de Chardin, una nueva noción de ciencia." *Mensaje* (1963): 12, 359-364.

1581. Gaffney, James. "The Teilhardian Invitation—Respectfully Declined." *America*, April 12, 1975, pp. 282-285.

1582. Gagnon, Jean-Claude. "Une théorie de l'éducation chez Teilhard de Chardin." *Prospectives* (1966): 4, 76-83.

1583. Gál, Ferenc. "Der Betrag Teilhards zum Dialog." *Acta teilhardiana* (1970): 1, 5-18.

1584. Galeano, Adolfo. "El sentido de la acción en Teilhard de Chardin." *Franciscanum* (1967): 9, 3-37, 99-120.

1584a. Gallagher, Blanche Marie. "A Teilhardian Aesthetic." *The Teilhard Review* (1978): 13, 127-128.

1585. Galli, Mario Von. "Teilhard de Chardin kein authen-
       tischer Zeuge Christi?" *Neue zürcher Nachrichten*,
       July 5, 1962, p. 1.

1586. ————. "Teilhard de Chardin: Theologe und Forscher."
       Der christliche Sonntag (1960): 1, 5-7; 2, 2-14.
       "Pierre Teilhard de Chardin, el hombre y el pensa-
       dor." *Orbis catholicus* (1960): 4, 300-314.

1587. Galot, J. "Le 'Phénomène humain.' A propos d'un livre
       récent." *Nouvelle revue théolgique* (1956): 2, 177-
       182.

1587a. Galy, Monique. "Pour le R.P. Teilhard de Chardin la
       doctrine de Saint Paul s'applique à l'ère atomique."
       Samedi-Soir, April 21, 1955, p. 2.

1588. Gandillac, Maurice de. "Pourquoi cette mise en garde
       du Saint Office contre le 'teilhardisme'?" *Le Figaro
       littéraire*, July 7, 1962, p. 2.

1589. Garaudy, Henriette. "Le temps chez Gaston Berger."
       Les Livres (1965): 6.

1590. Garaudy, Roger. "Une apologétique qui part de l'homme."
       Cahiers littéraires (1965): 13, 19-25.

1591. ————. "Dans le sens ascendant de la vie." *Le Figaro
       littéraire*, September 17, 1960, p. 10.

1592. ————. *De l'anathème au dialogue--Un marxiste s'adresse
       au concile*. Paris: Plon, 1965. See pp. 32-41.

1593. ————. "Freedom and Creativity: Marxist and Christian."
       The Teilhard Review (1968-69): 2, 42-49. See Item
       3412.

1594. ————. "Les marxistes: nous concédons un côté positif
       à la religion." *Réalités* (1966): 244, 99-101.

1595. ————. "The Meaning of Life and History in Marx and
       Teilhard de Chardin: Teilhard's Contribution to the
       Dialogue Between Christians and Marxists." Item
       1421, pp. 58-72.
       "Teilhard de Chardin en Marx. Zin van leven en
       geschiednis." *Streven* (1966-67): 889-900.

1596. ————. "Le pensée de Teilhard et le marxisme." Item 3903, pp. 215-235.

1597. ————. "Le Père Teilhard, le Concile et les marxistes." *Europe* (1965): 431/432, 185-208.

1598. ————. *Perspectives de l'homme. Existentialisme. Pensée catholique. Marxisme. 1929-1959.* Paris: Presses Universitaires de France, 1959. Contains Item 980.
Also 4th ed., incl. structuralism, 1969.
Perspektivy človĕka. Prague: Nakladatelství politiké literatury, 1965.
Perspektywy czlowieka. Warszawa: Ksiązka i Wiedza, 1968.
Prospettive dell'uomo. Esistenzialismo, cattolicismo, strutturalismo, marxismo. Turin: Borla, 1972.

1599. ————. "La phénoménologie de la nature et le R.P. Teilhard de Chardin." Item 1598, pp. 170-203.
"Fenomenologie přírody a Pierre Teilhard de Chardin." Item 1598 trans., pp. 182-232.
"Fenomenologia natury ojca Piotra Teilharda de Chardin." Item 1598 trans., pp. 186-242.

1600. ————. "Un pionnier du dialogue." *Le Monde*, April 11-12, 1965, p. 13.

1601. ————. "Réponse à E. Borne." *Le Monde*, May 10, 1960, p. 9.

1602. ————. "Socialization and Human Fulfillment." *Pax Romana Journal* (1967): 2, 9-12.

1603. ————. "Teilhard de Chardin." *Zeszyty Argumentów* (1962): 4, 7-29.

1603a. ————. "Teilhard de Chardin och människans framtid." Item 1944, pp. 68-88.

1604. ————. "Teilhard de Chardin: prophète d'un monde nouveau." *Paris-Match*, April 12, 1975.
"Teilhard de Chardin: Prophet of a New World." *Cross Currents* (1975): 25, 287-288.

1605. ————. "... van allen die in de menselijke vooruitgang geloven." Item 1206, pp. 568-569.

1606. García Abril, Gaspar. "Bibliografía sobre Teilhard de
       Chardin." *Orbis catholicus* (1964): 7, 238-250.

1607. ———. "Evolución y conciencia en Pierre Teilhard de
       Chardin." Typescript. Universidad de Barcelona,
       Facultad de filosofía y letras, Sección filosofía
       1962.

1608. ———. "Teilhard de Chardin." *Abside* (1963): 41,
       10-11.

1609. García Álvarez, Jesus. "La nueva visión del universo
       de Teilhard de Chardin." *Estudios filosóficos* (1964):
       253-270.

1610. García Rodríguez de Quesada, Luis. "Sociología política
       de Teilhard de Chardin." *Proyeccion* (1971): 18, 165-
       171.

1611. Gargan, Edward T. "Teilhard's Letters." *Cross Currents*
       (1963): 3, 383-385.

1612. Garkowski, John Joseph. "The Problem of Human Action in
       the Mature Period of Pierre Teilhard de Chardin (1930-
       1955)." Doctoral dissertation, Fordham University,
       1977.

1613. Garnysz, Maria. "Przejrzystść rzeczy." [Transparency
       of Things.]. *Znak* (1960): 12, 293-309.

1614. Garric, Robert. "Le Père Teilhard et Mademoiselle
       Zanta." Item 4569, pp. 11-20.

1615. Garrigan, Owen W. "Chemical Evolution." Item 3247,
       pp. 23-39.

1616. Garrigou-Lagrange, Madeleine. "Teilhard et le féminin."
       Témoignage chrétien (1963): 1213, 18-19.

1617. Garrod, D.A.E. "Pierre Teilhard de Chardin SJ: 1881-
       1955." *Man* (1955): 78.

1617a. Gaudefroy, Christophe. *Les missions géologiques du
       Père Teilhard de Chardin*. Semur: H. Canat, 1926.
       Contains Item 4568.

1618. Gauthier, Joseph D. *Douze voix françaises, 1900-1960*.
       Englewood Cliffs, N.J.: Prentice-Hall, 1969. See
       pp. 225-242.

1619. Gavalda, Berthe. "La Bible est-elle d'accord avec Teilhard et la nouvelle religion?" *Le monde et la vie* (1966): 159, 15-17.

1620. ————. "La Bible, Teilhard et le retour du Christ." *Le monde et la vie* (1966): 161.

1621. ————. "Le sens du péché et la doctrine teilhardienne." *Le monde et la vie* (1966): 160, 26-77.

1622. Gavran, Ignacije. "Vizija svemira O. Teilharda de Chardin." [Teilhard de Chardin's Vision of the Universe.] *Dobri pastir* (1962): 11/12, 229-240.

1623. Gawecki, Boleslaw J. "Dwie współczesne filozofie rozwoju." [Two Contemporary Philosophies of Evolution.] *Życie i myśl* (1967): 2, 1-18. Also Item 3888, pp. 114-135.

1624. Gawronski, J. *Wzdluż mojej drogi.* [The Length of My Road.] Warszawa: Pánstwowy Instytut Wydawniczy, 1968.

1625. Geerts, G., and A. Hulsbosch. "De kosmogenese van Teilhard de Chardin." *Annalen van het Tijdgenootschap* (1959): 47, 307-323.

1626. Gehring, H. *Evolution und christliches Weltbild.* Karlsruhe: Badenia Verlag, 1966.

1627. Geiger, Max. "Zukunft und Geschichte in der Weltschau Teilhard de Chardins." *Geschichte und Zukunft,* ed. by Jürgen Fangmeier. Zürich: EVG Verlag, 1967, pp. 29-60.

1628. Gemeslay, E.H. "Sur la philosophie spiritualiste du P. Teilhard de Chardin." *Le lotus bleu* (1960): 5, 151-159.

1628a. Gemmingen, Eberhard von. *Gott in der Welt entdecken. Glaubens--und Lebenshilfe durch Teilhard de Chardin.* München/Luzern: Rex, 1978.

1629. Gendreau, Bernard A. "The Person in Teilhard de Chardin." Typescript. Paris: Fondation Teilhard de Chardin, n.d.

1630. Gendron, Louis. "Le problème de l'action humaine chez
       Teilhard de Chardin." Item 3036, pp. 69-136.
       "El problema de la acción humana segun Teilhard de
       Chardin." Item 3036 trans., 61-124.

1631. Genest, Raymond. *Introduction à la pensée de Teilhard
       de Chardin.* Montréal: R. Genest, 1970.

1632. Gent, W. "Biosphäre, Noosphäre, Punkt Omega. Zu dem
       Aufsatz von Dr. Ludwig Ebersberger." *Ärtzliche Mit-
       teilungen* (1963): 38, 1920-1924. See Item 1374.

1633. Gentili, Elio. "Pierre Teilhard de Chardin in Italia.
       Bibliografia." *Scuola cattolica* (1965): suppl. bib-
       liogr., 1, 247-334; (1967): suppl. bibliogr. 2, 138-
       181.

1634. Gentili, Marcello. "Note su Teilhard de Chardin e sul
       nuovo umanesimo cattolico." *Nuova presenza* (1963):
       10, 47-50.

1635. ————. "La realtà terrestre in Teilhard de Chardin e
       nel nuovo cattolicismo." *Momento* (1965): 1, 3-15.

1636. Gentner, D.R. "The Scientific Basis of Some Concepts of
       Pierre Teilhard de Chardin." *Zygon* (1968): 3, 432-
       441.

1637. George, André. "L'apparition de l'homme." *Revue Teil-
       hard de Chardin* (1960): 3/4, 8-9.

1638. ————. "Hommage au Père Teilhard de Chardin." *Re-
       cherches et débats* (1955): 12, 149-173.

1639. ————. "Mais il a tout enflammé." *Le Figaro*, July
       7, 1966.

1640. ————. "Le 'pélerin de l'avenir.'" *Le Figaro*, April
       7, 1965, p. 1.

1641. ————. "Pour le Père Teilhard de Chardin." Item 3292,
       pp. 49-52.

1642. ————. "Les reliques scientifiques." *Plaisir de
       France* (1965): special number, 25-29.

1643. ————. "Témoignage sur le Père Teilhard de Chardin."
       Les nouvelles littéraires (1956): 1508, 1, 4.

1644. George, Nicholas. *D'Einstein à Teilhard*. Paris: Éditions Universitaires, 1964. *De Einstein a Teilhard*. Barcelona: Betis, 1966.

1645. Gérard, Fr. "L'optimisme de Teilhard de Chardin." *Les cahiers Albert le Grand* (1964): 70, 17-18.

1646. Gerats, A. "Ler over de ascese of ascese van Teilhard zelf?" *Ons Geestelijk Leven* (1964-65): 41, 342-348.

1647. Gerber, Uwe. *Katholischer Glaubensbegriff. Die Frage nach den Glaubenbegriff in der katholischen Theologie vom I. Vatikanum bis zur Gegenwart*. Gütersloh: G. Mohn, 1966. See pp. 188-208.

1648. Germain, Gabriel. "En lisant 'Comment je crois.'" Item 3653, pp. 103-118.

1649. ————. "Le place et le sens de la vie intérieure dans l'évolution selon le Père Teilhard et Sri Aurobindo." Item 3653, pp. 171-188.

1650. ————. "Rencontre avec le Père Teilhard de Chardin." *Cahiers du Sud* (1956): 335, 96-98.

1651. Gerstner, F.X. "Der 'totale Christus' des Teilhard de Chardin." *Klerusblatt* (1964): 44, 134-135.

1652. Gesche, A. "Comment aborder l'oeuvre de Pierre Teilhard de Chardin? In leiding tot de lezing van Teilhard de Chardin." *Collectanea mechliniensia* (1964): 49, 492-498.

1653. Gesquière, Jacqueline. "Jean Rostand et Pierre Teilhard de Chardin." *Revue Teilhard de Chardin* (1963): 15, 24-33.

1654. Gex, Maurice. "Les évolutionnismes contemporains de Gustave Mercier et du Père Teilhard de Chardin." *Dialectica* (1954): 4, 322-346.

1655. ————. "L'homme et l'univers selon le P. Teilhard de Chardin." *Connaissance de l'homme* (1955): 14, 7-19.

1656. ————. "Où va l'univers? (L'évolutionnisme integral du P. Teilhard de Chardin)." *Les cahiers protestants* (1953): 6, 338-355.

1657. ———. "La philosophie d'inspiration scientifique."
       Dialectica (1959): 2, 160-184.

1658. ———. "Philosophie et parapsychologie." *Rivista
       parapsycologia* (1955): 2, 1-19.

1659. ———. "Le problème des rapports du devenir et l'in-
       telligibilité dans l'évolutionnisme de Teilhard de
       Chardin." *Studia philosophica* (1959): 19, 119-129.

1660. ———. "La synthèse de Teilhard de Chardin." *Le rotar-
       ien suisse* (1968): 3, 1-6.
       Also *Alpina* (1968): 321-324.

1661. ———. "Vers un humanisme cosmologique. La synthèse
       de Teilhard de Chardin." *Revue de théologie et de
       philosophie* (1957): 7, 186-205.
       Also *Évoluer* (1961): 7.

1662. Ghent, Ralph. L. "Dr. Thompson's Statements." *Michael
       de la Bedoyere's Search* (1962): 1, 313-314. See Item
       3970.

1663. Gherman, Pierre. "Teilhard de Chardin. Sa conception
       de l'univers, de l'homme et du Christ." *Les dossiers
       de l'action sociale catholique* (1963): 40, 161-178.

1664. Ghyka, Matila. "A Talk with Teilhard de Chardin." *The
       Tablet* (1962): 6348, 57.

1665. Giacon, Carlo. "L'evoluzione integrale del P. Teilhard
       de Chardin." *Vichiana* (1966): 2, 182-193.

1666. ———. "Teilhard de Chardin." *Enciclopedia filosofica*,
       2d ed.; Firenze: G.C. Sansoni, 1967-69, vol. 4, pp.
       349-353.

1667. Gibellini, Rosino. *La discussione su Teilhard de Char-
       din.* Brescia: Queriniana, 1968.

1668. Giblet, Jean. "La vision chrétienne de l'univers."
       La revue nouvelle (1958): 27, 611-622.

1669. Gier, G. de. "Het goddelijk milieu." *Ons Geestelijk
       Leven* (1964-65): 41, 349-360.

1670. Giersch, M. "Biologische Theologie. Teilhard de Char-
       din 'Der Mensch im Kosmos.'" *Zeichen der Zeit* (1965):
       19, 293-298.

1671. Gilch, Gerhard. *Evolution des Lebens und Wandel des Glaubens bei Teilhard de Chardin.* Stuttgart: Calwer Verlag, 1969.

1672. ————. *Das Weltbild Teilhard de Chardins.* Stuttgart: Calwer Verlag, 1970.

1673. Gil Cremades, Juan José. "La visión del mundo de Pierre Teilhard de Chardin." *Nuestro tiempo* (1959): 61, 21-36.

1674. Gilka-Bötzow, Eberhard. "Jakob Böhme und Teilhard de Chardin." *Perspektiven der Zukunft* (1970): 6, 5-7.

1675. ————. "Lorber, Böhme, Swedenborg und Teilhard, Vertreter einer universlen christlichen Mystik." *Perspektiven der Zukunft* (1972): 2, 9-11.

1676. ————. "Lorber, Böhme, Swedenborg und Teilhard. Das Weltbild Teilhard de Chardins." *Perspektiven der Zukunft* (1972): 3, 5-8.

1677. Gill, John G. "Teilhard and Religious Humanism." *Religious Humanism* (1969): 3, 169-172.

1678. Gilles, A. "Teilhard and the Maharishi: The Thought of Teilhard and the Teachings of the Maharishi." *The Teilhard Review* (1977): 12, 10-14.

1679. Gillet, Edmond. "Du transformisme et du rôle de l'hypothèse dans la science." *Bulletin de la Société royale belge d'études géologiques et archéologiques* (1961): 17, 221-236.

1680. Gilot, F.R. dos S. "Do panteismo em Teilhard de Chardin." *Palestra* (1968): 33, 35-44.

1681. Gilson, Etienne. "Amende honorable au Père Teilhard de Chardin." *La France catholique*, June 30, 1967.

1682. ————. "Le cas Teilhard de Chardin." *Seminarium* (1965): 17, 720-737.
Also *Nouvelles de chrétienté* (1966): 502, 17-25.
Also Item 1684, pp. 73-99.
"Il caso Teilhard de Chardin." In his *Problemi d'oggi*, pp. 83-118. Torino: Borla, 1967.
"El caso Teilhard de Chardin." *Christiandad* (1966): 23, 31-38.
Also *Finis terrae* (1966): 57, 3-20.

1683. ———. "Le dialogue difficile." *Seminarium* (1966): 18, 968-990.

1684. ———. *Les tribulations de Sophie.* Paris: J. Vrin, 1967. Contains Item 1682.

1685. Giovannoni, Héctor. "La 'meditatio mortis' en Teilhard de Chardin." *Criterio* (1968/69): 605-606.

1686. Giralt Bermúdez, Maria de los Ángeles. "El diálogo: Zubiri-Aristóteles, Zubiri-Teilhard." *Revista de filosofía de la Universidad de Costa Rica* (1971): 9, 223-242.

1687. ———. "Jacques Monod y Teilhard de Chardin." *Revista de filosofía de la Universidad de Costa Rica* (1974): 12, 211-215.

1688. Gispert-Sauch, G. "Aurobindo, Teilhard and Theology." *Clergy Monthly* (1972): 36, 471-476.

1689. Glässer, Alfred. *Konvergenz. Die Struktur der Weltsumme Pierre Teilhards de Chardin.* Kevelaer: Butzon und Bercker, 1970.

1690. ———. "Teilhard de Chardin und die geistesgeschichtliche Tradition." *Theologie und Glaube* (1971): 61, 276-286.

1691. Gleize, Jean. "L'histoire naturelle d'humanité vue à travers les pensées du Père Teilhard de Chardin." Mimeographed thesis, Lyon, 1959. See Item 1351.

1692. "Glosy o Teilhardzie de Chardin." [Opinions on Teilhard.] *Znak* (1962): 14, 224-250.

1693. Glotin, E. "Coeur de Jésus et mystique cosmique." *Priere et vie* (1963): 323-340.

1694. Glowienka, Emerine. "Notes on Consciousness in Matter." *New Scholasticism* (1969): 63, 602-613.

1695. Godard, Henri. "Un gesuita allarma il Vaticano." *Epoca* (1962): 625, 38-39, 41.

1696. Godel, Roger. "Évolution et révolution de la conscience humaine." *Revue Teilhard de Chardin* (1965): 24/25, 10-19.

1697. Goergen, Donald. "The Eucharistic Presence: A Process Perspective." *The Teilhard Review* (1974): 1, 16-23.

1698. ————. "Personality-in-Process and Teilhard de Chardin." Doctoral dissertation, Aquinas Institute of Theology, 1972.

1699. Goertmann, Alphonse. *L'Évangile de la miséricorde.* Paris: Cerf, 1965.

1700. Goessman, Elisabet. "Teilhard to chûsei." [Teilhard and the Middle Ages.] *Convergence* (1975): 4, 17-24.

1701. Gomez Bosque, Pedro. "Las concepciones metafísicas del Padre Teilhard de Chardin." Item 745, pp. 265-313.

1702. Gomez Caffarena, Jose. "Teilhard y el marxismo." *Hechos y dichos* (1966): 288-294.

1703. Gómez-Pallette, Manuel. "Senghor, Teilhard y el socialismo senegales." *Africa* (1970): 342, 14-16.

1704. Gomis, Joan. "Teilhard de Chardin." *El ciervo* (1957): 57, 8.

1705. Gondra, José Maria. "El 'Fenómeno' de Pierre Teilhard de Chardin." *Ensayos* (1964): 38, 10-13.

1706. Gora, Stanislaw Josef. "Entretien avec Teilhard de Chardin, soit avec un métaphysicien et un naturaliste, au sujet de l'évolution." *Bulletin du SIQS* (1961): 26. Summary of Item 1707.

1707. ————. "Spotkanie z Teilhardem de Chardin czyli rozmowa metafizyka z przyrodnikiem o ewolucji." [Conversation with Teilhard de Chardin, i.e. with a Metaphysician and Naturalist, on the Subject of Evolution.] *Znak* (1960): 12, 445-471. See Item 1706.

1708. Gorce, Maxime. *Le Concile et Teilhard. L'éternel et l'humain.* Neuchâtel: H. Messeiller, 1963. Contains Item 4551.

1709. ————. "Un grand disparu. Le Père Teilhard de Chardin ou le Galilée de notre génération." *Le protestant* (1955): 6, 4.

1710. Gorgulho, P. "Bultman, Teilhard y el Cristo Histórico
       (Entrevista)." *Víspera* (1968); 4, 45-49.

1711. Gormley, John. "A Man for All Faiths." *The Tablet*,
       October 23, 1965, p. 1182.

1712. ————. "Pilgrim's Progress: Reflections on Vézelay
       1966." *The Tablet*, September 24, 1966, pp. 1068-
       1069.

1713. Görres, Ida Friederike. "Biographie in Bildern. Ein-
       fuhrung in den schönen Bildband: 'Pierre Teilhard de
       Chardin.'" *Perspektiven der Zukunft* (1967): 6, 2-4.

1714. ————. "Die Frau in der Sicht Teilhard de Chardins."
       Perspektiven der Zukunft (1968): 1, 1-5.

1715. ————. *Sohn der Erde: Der Mensch Teilhard de Chardin.*
       Drei Versuche. 3d ed.; Frankfurt: J. Knecht, 1971.
       Teilhard de Chardin hijo de la tierra. Buenos
       Aires: Guadeloupe, 1974.

1716. ————. *Teilhard de Chardin als Christ und als Mensch.*
       Wiesbaden: F. Steiner, 1971.

1717. ————. "Teilhard de Chardin, Glaubender and Beter."
       Perspektiven der Zukunft (1970): 5, 4-6.

1718. ————. "Teilhard de Chardin: Der Mystiker. Notizen
       aus Anlass eines Buches." *Hochland* (1969): 61, 497-
       509.

1719. ————. "Teilhard de Chardins erste und zweite Person.
       Notizen aus Anlass eines Buches." *Hochland* (1969):
       61, 385-402.

1720. ————. "Unter den Augen einer Frau. Dritter Versuch
       über Teilhard de Chardin." *Hochland* (1970): 62,
       496-508.

1721. ————. "Die Zweite Entdeckung der Feuers." *Perspek-
       tiven der Zukunft* (1969): 3, 2-4.

1722. Gorrissen, Norbert. "Le Christ, témoin du Père dans
       la vie et l'oeuvre de Teilhard." *Revue diocésaine
       de Tournai* (1966): 2, 11-32, 124-166.

1723. ———. "L'évolution spiritualisante du P. Teilhard et l'eschatologie biblique." *Parole et pain* (1967): 371-391.

1724. ———. "Le Père Teilhard de Chardin: le chrétien." *Revue diocésaine de Tournai* (1963): 9, 341-351.

1725. ———. "Le Père Teilhard de Chardin d'après ses lettres." *Revue diocésaine de Tournai* (1963): 7, 429-438.

1726. ———. "Le Père Teilhard de Chardin: le prophète." *Revue diocésaine de Tournai* (1963): 9, 329-340.

1727. ———. "Le Père Teilhard de Chardin: le savant." *Revue diocésaine de Tournai* (1963): 8, 445-463.

1728. ———. *Le Père Teilhard de Chardin témoin du Christ.* Bruxelles: Pensée catholique, 1966. Also Paris: Office général du livre, 1966.

1729. ———. "Unité et liberté spirituelle chez le P. Teilhard de Chardin." *Revue diocésaine de Tournai* (1967): 22, 260-278.

1730. Gosztonyi, Alexander. "Bergson und Teilhard." *Perspektiven der Zukunft* (1972): 2, 7-9.

1731. ———. "Einheit von Materie und Geist. Problem oder Tatsache?" *Perspektiven der Zukunft* (1967): 6, 7-8.

1732. ———. "Der Fall Davis und der Fall Teilhard." *Neue Zürcher Zeitung* (1968): 50, 13-14.

1733. ———. "Gott, die Evolution, und die Erbsünde: Zum 10. Band von Teilhards Werken." *Perspektiven der Zukunft* (1970): 6, 8-10.

1734. ———. "Grundsätzliches zur Teilhard-Kritik." *Perspektiven der Zukunft* (1967): 1, 6.

1735. ———. "Kernprobleme des Denkens von Teilhard de Chardin." *Orientierung* (1968): 32, 198-202.

1736. ———. *Der Mensch und die Evolution. Teilhard de Chardins philosophische Anthropologie.* München: C.H. Beck, 1968. See Item 4281. *El hombre y la evolución. La antropología*

filosófica de Teilhard de Chardin. Madrid: Difusora
del libro, 1970.
Teilhard de Chardin. Cristianesimo e evoluzione.
Firenze: Sansoni, 1970.

1737. ————. "Philosophische Probleme bei Teilhard de Chardin." *Schweizer Monatshefte* (1964): 44, 725-747.

1738. ————. "Das Problem des Bösen." *Perspektiven der
Zukunft* (1968): 3, 7-9.

1739. ————. "Teilhard de Chardin und das praktische
Christentum." *Zeitschrift für Religions- und Geistesgeschichte* (1967): 19, 153-166.
Also *Orientierung* (1965): 29, 73-75.
"Teilhard de Chardin e cristianesimo practico."
Digest religioso (1965): 3, 29-34.

1740. ————. "Teilhard de Chardins Begriff der Sozialisation." *Perspektiven der Zukunft* (1967): 2, 2-3.

1741. ————. "Teilhard de Chardins Begriff der Zeit."
Perspektiven der Zukunft (1967): 5, 3-4.

1742. ————. "Teilhard in evangelischer Sicht." *Orientierung* (1968): 32, 145-147.

1743. ————. "Teilhard und die Reinkarnation, Anthroposophie
und Evolution." *Perspektiven der Zukunft* (1969): 1, 7.

1744. ————. "Teilhard und die Weltverantwortung der Christen." *Perspektiven der Zukunft* (1968): 4, 5-7.

1745. ————. "Zum zehnten Todestag von Teilhard de Chardin."
Schweizer Monatshefte (1965): 1, 91-95.

1746. ————. "Zur Frage der kosmischen Natur Christi."
Perspektiven der Zukunft (1967): 4, 7.

1747. Gott, Maria von. "Gedanken zu Pierre Teilhard de
Chardins 'Der göttliche Bereich.'" *Klerusblatt*
(1965): 2, 29-31.

1748. Gotto, Antonio M. "Uncertainty of Survival: Cradle of
Consciousness?" *Thought* (1976): 51, 378-392.

1749. Götz, L. "The Prophet and the Pentagon: Mumford's
Criticism of Teilhard de Chardin." *The Teilhard Review* (1976): 11, 82-87.

1750. Goudge, T.A. "The Evolutionary Vision of Teilhard de Chardin." *University of Toronto Quarterly* (1962): 1, 70-80.

1751. ————. "Salvaging the 'Noosphere.'" *Mind* (1962): 284.

1752. ————. "Teilhard de Chardin, Pierre." *Encyclopedia of Philosophy*. New York: Macmillan, 1967, vol. 8, pp. 83-84.

1752a. Gould, Stephen Jay. "The Piltdown Conspiracy." *Natural History*, August, 1980, p. 8.

1753. Govinda, Lama Anagarika. "Die Weltanschauung Teilhard de Chardins im Spiegel östlichen Denkens." Item 1213, pp. 124-153.

1754. Gozzini, Mario. "Ascesa di Teilhard de Chardin." *Nuovo osservatore* (1962): 3, 392-395.

1755. ————. "Il nuovo Galileo." *Leggere* (1962): 2, 4-5.

1756. ————. "Teilhard de Chardin in Italiano a novembre." *La fiera letteraria* (1964): 35, 1-2.

1757. Graef, Hilda. *Mystics of Our Times*. London: Burns and Oates, 1962.
Mystiker unserer Zeit. Luzern: Rex, 1964.
Mystieken van onze tijd. Haarlem: De Spaarnestad, 1963.

1758. Graef, Richard. "An Encounter with the Numinous in the Life and Thought of Teilhard de Chardin." Doctoral dissertation, Lutheran School of Theology at Chicago, 1971.

1759. Graf, Gerhard. "Emmanuel Mounier, ein Geistes- und Zeitgenosse Teilhard de Chardins." *Perspektiven der Zukunft* (1973): 2, 9-10.

1760. Graham, R. "Jacques Maritain on Aggiornamento." *America*, March 11, 1967, pp. 348-349.

1761. Grall, Xavier. "Les grands chemins du P. Teilhard." *La vie catholique illustrée*, May 19-25, 1965, pp. 21-23; May 26-June 1, pp. 36-37; June 2-8, pp. 23-25; June 9-15, pp. 22-23.

1762. Gramigna, Giuliano. "La creazione continua." *La Domenica del corriere* (1965): 24, 38, 96.

1763. Grand, Jean. "Teilhard de Chardin et l'avenir de l'humanité." *Responsables* (1964): 5, 49-57; 6, 64-72; 8, 9-17.

1764. "La grande illusion de Teilhard de Chardin." *Amitiés françaises universitaires* (1965): 100, 9.

1765. Grandi, Nine. "De la pensée théosophique à la pensée de Teilhard de Chardin." *Lotus bleu* (1970): 75, 204-213.

1766. Grand'Maison, Jacques. *Le monde et le sacré. I: Le sacré.* Paris: Éditions ouvrières, 1966. See pp. 71-78.

1767. Grandpré, Pierre de. *Dix ans de vie littéraire au Canada français.* Montréal: Beauchemin, 1966.

1768. ————. "Le phénomène humain." Item 3292, pp. 103-109.

1769. Grau, Joseph August. *Morality and the Human Future in the Thought of Teilhard de Chardin: A Critical Study.* Rutherford, N.J.: Fairleigh Dickinson University Press, 1976.
      Also London: Associated University Press, 1976.

1770. ————. "Social Process and Human Moral Energy in Teilhard de Chardin." Doctoral dissertation, Catholic University of America, 1973.

1771. Gray, Donald P. "The Cosmic Christ and the New Consciousness." *The Teilhard Review* (1972): 1, 8-12.

1772. ————. "Creative Union in Christ in the Thought of Teilhard de Chardin." Doctoral dissertation, Fordham University, 1968.

1773. ————. *The One and the Many: Teilhard de Chardin's Vision of Unity.* London: Burns and Oates, 1969.
      Also New York: Herder and Herder, 1969.

1774. ————. "The Phenomenon of Teilhard." *Theological Studies* (1975): 36, 19-51.

1775. ———. "Teilhard de Chardin's Vision of Love."
Thought (1967): 167, 519-542.
Also Item 2158, pp. 73-98.
"La concezione dell'amore in Teilhard." Item 2158
trans., pp. 104-140.

1776. Gray, Wallace. "Oomoto and Teilhard de Chardin: Two
Case Studies in Revitalization." *Japanese Religions*
(1974): 19-29.

1777. Grech, F. "Pierre Teilhard de Chardin." *Problemi
ta'llum* (1965): 5, 165-169.

1778. Greco, A. "Teilhard et le droit d'être heureux." *Revue Teilhard de Chardin* (1962): 11, 19-20.

1779. Greenson, Ralph R. "The Personal Meaning of Perfection."
Item 528, pp. 180-194.

1780. Gregorio de Jesus, Fr. "San Juan de la Cruz y Teilhard
de Chardin." *Ephemerides carmeliticae* (1967): 18,
362-367.

1781. Grenet, Paul Bernard. "Controverse sur Teilhard de Char-
din." *Bulletin du Cercle thomiste Saint-Nicolas de
Caen* (1965): 32, 9-21.
Also *L'homme nouveau* (1965): 401, 7-12, 15.

1782. ———. "Une étape decisive dans la critique de Teil-
hard." *Bulletin du Cercle thomiste Saint-Nicholas de
Caen* (1965): 31, 14-22.
Also *L'homme nouveau* (1961): 401, 4-5.

1783. ———. "Grandeur et faiblesse de la cosmologie du Père
Teilhard de Chardin." *Vie diocésaine de Rouen* (1957):
28-29, 426-428, 443-446.

1784. ———. "... huit questions sur Teilhard de Chardin."
L'homme nouveau, January 6, 1963.

1785. ———. "Littérature récente sur Teilhard de Chardin."
L'ami du clergé (1965): 618-623, 696-701; (1966): 439-
441.

1786. ———. "L'oeuvre de Teilhard de Chardin, ses grandeurs
et ses faiblesses. Discutable: le préexistence larvée."
L'homme nouveau (1957): 220, 10; 222, 5.

1787. ———. "La pensée de Teilhard devant le Tribunal su-
       prême de l'Église catholique." *L'homme nouveau*, Au-
       gust 5, 1962, p. 17.

1788. ———. "La pensée scientifique de Teilhard de Chardin."
       L'ami du clergé (1966): 76, 433-439.

1789. ———. "Le Père Teilhard de Chardin ou l'histoire."
       Bulletin du Cercle thomiste Saint-Nicolas de Caen
       (1959): 12, 43-48.

1790. ———. "La personne et le dessein du Père Teilhard de
       Chardin. D'après sa correspondance 1914-1919." *L'ami
       du clergé* (1962): 72, 673-683.

1791. ———. "Un philosophe sans instruments: Teilhard de
       Chardin." *Bulletin du Cercle thomiste Saint-Nicolas
       de Caen* (1956): 6, 35-42.

1792. ———. *Pierre Teilhard de Chardin ou le philosophe
       malgré lui*. Paris: Beauchesne, 1960.
       Teilhard de Chardin. The Man and His Theories.
       London: Souvenir, 1965.
       Also New York: P.S. Erikson, 1966.
       Teilhard de Chardin, filósofo a pesar suvo. Buenos
       Aires: Paulinas, 1965.

1793. ———. "Le R.P. Teilhard de Chardin." *Bulletin histor-
       ique et scientifique de l'Auvergne* (1956): 570, 20-30.

1794. ———. "Réponse de l'Abbé P. Grenet." *Bulletin du
       Cercle thomiste Saint-Nicolas de Caen* (1965): 32,
       10-21.

1795. ———. "Services et dangers des écrits du R.P. Teil-
       hard de Chardin." *L'ami du clergé* (1958): 68, 600-
       610; (1959): 69, 51-58, 65-75, 438-444, 745-755.

1796. ———. "Teilhard de Chardin: A propos de quelques
       publications récentes." *Esprit et vie* (1970): 80,
       247-253.

1797. ———. "Teilhard de Chardin et l'existentialisme."
       Revue thomiste (1969): 69, 412-433.

1798. ———. "Teilhard de Chardin et le positivisme." *Re-
       vue thomiste* (1970): 70, 604-628.

1799. ———. "Teilhard de Chardin et marxisme." *Revue thom-
       iste* (1972): 72, 588-617.

1800. ———. *Teilhard de Chardin, un évolutionnisme chrétien.*
       Paris: Seghers, 1961. Contains Items 4371a, 4423,
       4557, 4562, 4591, 4812.
       Teilhard de Chardin. Madrid: Halar, 1962.
       *Un cristianismo fedele alla terra: Teilhard de Char-
       din.* Firenze: Vallechi, 1963.

1801. ———. "Teilhard de Chardin. La faiblesse congénitale
       d'une synthèse des sciences par la biologie."
       L'homme nouveau (1957): 222, 3.

1802. ———. "Teilhard de Chardin: Une philosophie du tout
       sans la notion d'être, une philosophie du devenir sans
       les notions d'acte et du puissance, l'analogie des
       êtres sans l'analogie de l'être." *Bulletin du Cercle
       thomiste Saint-Nicolas de Caen* (1957): 7, 23-25;
       (1958): 8, 27-42; 9, 33-46.

1803. ———. "Teilhard de Chardin, Pierre." *Dictionnaire
       de théologie catholique* (1971): vol. 16, fasc. 17,
       cc. 4119-4135.

1804. ———. "Teilhard malgré le teilhardisme ou: les dif-
       ficultés d'une saisie totale du réel." *La France
       catholique*, December 16, 1966, p. 16.

1805. ———. "La vision de Teilhard de Chardin selon le
       Père Pierre Smulders." *Bulletin du Cercle thomiste
       Saint-Nicolas de Caen* (1965): 32, 22-43.

1806. Grenier de Ruère, J. "Le R.P. Teilhard de Chardin."
       Bulletin historique et scientifique de l'Auvergne
       (1956): 76, 22-30.

1807. Grinevald, Theó. "A propos de Teilhard de Chardin."
       Syndicalisme (1967): 1, 2.

1808. ———. "Un nouveau sens du travail." *Revue Teilhard
       de Chardin* (1968): 36, 57-66.

1809. ———. "Teilhard de Chardin a-t-il un message pour
       les travailleurs de la terre?" *Syndicalisme* (1969):
       18, 7.

1810.   Grison, Michel. "La pensée du Père Teilhard de Chardin
        (1881-1955) et la théologie naturelle." *Théologie
        naturelle ou théodicée.* Paris: Beauchesne, 1965,
        pp. 187-192.

1811.   ————. *Problèmes d'origines: l'univers, les vivants et
        l'homme.* Paris: Letouzey et Ane, 1959.

1812.   Groot, Sybren R. De. "Marihuana voor de intelectuelen."
        Hollande Maandblad (1963): 4, 1-7.

1813.   Grootaers, Willem A. "Bibliographie de Teilhard en
        japonais." *Acta teilhardiana* (1970): 2, 129-133;
        (1971): 2, 107-112.

1814.   ————. "Chûkaku de no Teilhard de Chardin no omoide."
        [Memories of Teilhard in China.] *Convergence* (1971):
        1, 11-32.

1815.   ————. "Hommage à Teilhard de Chardin." *La relève*
        (1955): 25, 8-9.
            Also in *Rencontre Orient-Occident* (1958): 5, 3-7.
        "In Memory of Teilhard de Chardin." *Sophia* (1955):
        3, 55-59.
        "Teiyâru do Shardan tsuitô." *Sophia* (1955): 4,
        327-331.
        "Teiyâru do Shardan." *Apollo* (1959): 3, 45-58.

1816.   ————. "Pas de nouvelle affaire Galilée!" *La relève*
        (1963): 10, 8-9.

1817.   ————. "Shinyaku 'Sekai no ue de sasageru Misa' ni
        tsuite." [Regarding a New Translation of "The Mass
        on the World."] *Convergence* (1977): 5, 40-44.

1818.   ————. "Teilhard in China." *Cross Currents* (1976):
        26, 67-68.

1819.   ————. "Teilhard no shisô to Roma no kanryôshugi."
        [Teilhard de Chardin and the Roman Bureaucracy.]
        Misuzu (1964): 61, 30-39.

1820.   ————. "Teilhard o do no yô ni yomu ka?" [How to
        Read Teilhard.] *Convergence* (1972): 2, 33-41.

1821.   ————.   "Teilhard's Synthesis of Science and Religion."
        Japan Missionary Bulletin (1963): 17, 102-109.

1822. ————. "When and Where Was 'The Mass on the World' Written?" *The Teilhard Review* (1977): 12, 91-94.

1823. ————, and Yurie Iso. "'Sekai no ue de sasageru Misa' (Shinyaku)." ["The Mass on the World" (Translation).] *Convergence* (1977): 5, 27-40.

1824. Gross, Julius. "Der Mensch im Kosmos. Zu dem gleichnamigen Werk von Pierre Teilhard de Chardin." *Zeitschrift für Religions- und Geistesgeschichte* (1961): 35, 267-271.

1825. Grozinger, Wolfgang. "Teilhard de Chardin: Leben und Werk." *Politische Studien* (1962): 13, 645-649.

1826. ————, and Alois Guggenberger. "Der Entwicklung der Kosmos. Die Erkenntnisse und das Weltbild Teilhard de Chardins." *Universitas* (1963): 18, 1311-1326.

1827. Guardamonte, Simon. "Inquisition pas morte!" *La sentinelle—Le peuple*, June 17, 1966.

1828. Gubern Salisachs, L. "Prematuriedad zoológica del recién nacido. Deducciones prácticas." *Anales de medicina y cirurgia* (1965): 7/8, 223-253.

1829. Guelluy, Robert. *La création.* Tournai: Desclée de Brouwer, 1963. See pp. 142-145.

1830. ————. "Dzielo stworenia." [The Work of Creation.] *Tajemnica Boga.* [The Mystery of God.] Warszawa: Księgarnia św. Wojciecha, 1967, pp. 325-422.

1831. Guérard des Lauriers, M.L. "La démarche du Père Teilhard de Chardin. Réflexions d'ordre épistemologique." *Divinitas* (1959): 3, 221-268.
    Also *Ordre français* (1963): 65, 45-66; 66, 54-67.
    Also *Pensée catholique* (1959): 63, 8-25.

1832. ————. "Finalité et animisme." *Aquinas* (1963): 6, 224-238.
    Also *Pensée catholique* (1963): 87, 61-75.
    Also *Ordre français* (1963): 1, 68-80; 9, 48-64.

1833. ————. "Le 'Phénomène humain' du Père Teilhard de Chardin." *Revue thomiste* (1956): 56, 518-527.

1834. Guérin, Maurice. "La paix selon Pierre Teilhard de
       Chardin." *La Corse nouvelle*, September 9, 1959.

1835. Guerin, W.L. "Browning's Cleon: A Teilhardian View."
       Victorian Poetry (1974): 12, 13-23.

1836. ————. "Dynamo, Virgin, and Cyclotron: Henry Adams and
       Teilhard de Chardin on Pilgrimage." *Renascence* (1976):
       28, 139-146.

1837. Guerini, Edmund W. *Evolution in the Afterlife: The
       Extended Concepts of Pierre Teilhard de Chardin.*
       New York: Exposition, 1967.

1838. Guerra, Jose. "El evolucionismo de Teilhard de Chardin."
       Compostellanum (1957): 2, 501-520.

1839. Guerra, Luis Felipe. *La filosofía de la naturaleza
       en Teilhard de Chardin.* Lima: Instituto Riva-Aguero,
       1964.

1840. Guerrero López, Eustaquio. *Teilhard de Chardin. As-
       pectos fundamentales de su obra. Exposición y valor-
       ación.* Madrid: Studium, 1969.

1841. Guggenberger, Alois von. "Christus und das Selbstver-
       standnis des heutigen Menschen nach Teilhard de Char-
       din." Items 3924, pp. 89-124.

1842. ————. "Christus und die Welt nach Teilhard de Char-
       din." *Theologie der Gegenwart in Auswahl* (1965): 8,
       9-19.

1843. ————. "Cur Deus homo? Das Interesse Gottes an der
       Welt nach Teilhard de Chardin." *Theologie der Gegen-
       wart* (1970): 13, 1-9.

1844. ————. "Die Diskussion um Pierre Teilhard de Chardin.
       Ende oder Anfang?" *Theologie der Gegenwart* (1963):
       1, 1-12.
       "Teilhard de Chardin: End or Beginning?" *Philo-
       sophy Today* (1964): 1, 101-109.

1845. Number deleted.

1846. ————. "Einleitung." Item 3299, pp. 9-16.

1847. ————. "Entwicklung und Weltende." *Theologie der
       Gegenwart* (1960): 2/3, 69-79, 144-155.

1848. ———. "Der Mensch als Person und Persönlichkeit aus philosophischer Sicht." *Arzt und Christ* (1964): 3, 130-143.

1849. ———. "Mensch und Welt: Personalisation. Teilhards psychische Weltformel." *Acta teilhardiana* (1974): 11, 77-78.

1850. ———. "Die Menschheit hat schon begonnen. Sozialisation, das Wegziel der Geschichte nach Teilhard de Chardin." *Theologie der Gegenwart* (1974): 17, 129-138.

1851. ———. "Neues und Altes, oder Theologie im Wandel bei Teilhard de Chardin." *Theologie im Wandel*. Freiburg-im-Breisgau: Erich Wewel, 1967, pp. 291-306.

1852. ———. "Nimmt das Gute in der Welt zu? Zur Auseinandersetzung mit der Eschatologie und Ethik Teilhard de Chardins." *Zeitwende* (1965): 6, 243-251, 310-318. Also in Item 4316.

1853. ———. "Person." Mimeographed. Paris: Fondation Teilhard de Chardin, n.d.

1854. ———. "Die personierende Welt Teilhards de Chardin." Item 1423, pp. 77-78.

1855. ———. "Personierende Welt und Inkarnation. Zur Theologie Teilhards de Chardin." *Hochland* (1961): 53, 318-322.

1855a. ———. *Eine Realutopie. Sozialisation in Werk Teilhards de Chardin*. Bergen/Enkheim: G. Kaffke, 1974.

1856. ———. "Teilhard contra Teilhard?" *Theologie der Gegenwart* (1969): 12, 46-49.

1857. ———. "Teilhard de Chardin, Biograph der Weltentwicklung." *Schöpfungsglaube und biologische Entwicklungslehre*. Würzburg: Echter, 1962, pp. 97-132.

1858. ———. "Teilhard de Chardin in der Konzilsaula." *Theologie der Gegenwart* (1977): 20, 31-39.

1859. ———. "Teilhard de Chardin. Der Umstrittene. Der Unentbehrliche." *Der christliche Sonntag*, April 19, 1965, pp. 133-134.

1860.   ———. *Teilhard de Chardin. Versuch einer Weltsumme.*
        München: Matthias-Grunewald, 1963.
        Also 2d ed., 1964.

1861.   ———. "Teilhard de Chardin: Werke, Briefe, Kommentaire.
        Eine Übersicht." *Religion und Theologia* (1964): 19,
        2-4.

1862.   ———. "Das Verhältnis von Materie und Geist." *Münch-
        ener theologische Zeitschrift* (1965): 16, 277-282.

1863.   ———. "Wissenschaftliches Weltverständnis und christ-
        licher Glaube nach Pierre Teilhard de Chardin." *Gott,
        Mensch, Universum*. Köln/Graz: Styria-Verlag, 1963.
        pp. 452-499.

1864.   ———. "Zur Diskussion zu Teilhard de Chardin." *The-
        ologisch-praktische Quartalschrift* (1964): 3, 214-217.

1865.   Guichard, Marie-Thérèse. "Science et religion d'après
        Teilhard de Chardin." Typescript. Faculté des let-
        tres de Nanterre, 1969.

1866.   Guillaume, Michel. "Pierre Teilhard de Chardin." *Oméga*
        (1960): 11, 2-3.

1867.   Guillén Soto, César Edmundo. "Presupuestos éticos del
        'universo personal' de Pierre Teilhard de Chardin."
        Typescript. Faculdad de filosofía, Universidad de
        Madrid, 1965.

1868.   ———. "Presupuestos éticos del 'universo personal'
        de Pierre Teilhard de Chardin." *Revista de la Uni-
        versidad de Madrid* (1965): 14, 182-183. Summary of
        Item 1867.

1869.   Guillon, Clément. "Hérétique? ... ou précurseur?"
        Rencontre (1965): 2, 12-19.

1870.   ———. "Qui est Teilhard de Chardin?" *Notre vie
        eudiste* (1964-65): 104, 193-203.

1871.   Guissard, Lucien. "Dix ouvrages sur Teilhard de Chardin."
        La Croix, March 14-15, 1965, p. 5.

1872.   ———. "Il y a dix ans. Teilhard de Chardin." *La
        Croix*, April 9, 1965.

1873. Guitton, Jean. "Bergson et Teilhard de Chardin." *Tre saggi*. Brescia: Morcelliana, 1966, pp. 65-91.

1874. ———. "Le phénomène Teilhard." *Informations catholiques internationales*, January 1, 1960, pp. 28-29.

1875. ———. "Pouget et Teilhard." *Renaissance Fleury* (1971): 3, 6-14.

1876. ———. "Réflexions sur l'oeuvre d'un pionnier: le Père Teilhard de Chardin." *Journal. Études et rencontres (1952-1955)*. Paris: Plon, 1959, pp. 229-237. Also 1968 ed., pp. 235-251.
    "Refleksje nad dzielem pioniera, Ojca Teilharda de Chardin." *Dziennik. Rozwazania i spotkania, 1952-1955*. Warszawa: Pax, 1965, pp. 314-323.

1877. ———. "Réflexions sur l'oeuvre du Père Teilhard de Chardin." *La table ronde* (1955): 91, 179-183.

1878. ———. "Teilhard et Bergson." *Profils parallèles*. Paris: Fayard, 1970, pp. 401-457.
    "Teilhard i Bergson." *Profile*. Warszawa: Pax, 1973, pp. 393-449.

1879. Günther, Joachim von. "Die Schwierigkeiten mit Teilhard de Chardin." *Frankfurter allgemeine Zeitung* (1962): 187, 24.

1880. Günzl, H. Christof. "Teilhard de Chardin--Prophet der 'Einen Welt.' Die Zukunft des Geistes." *Österreichische Monatshefte* (1965): 12, 59-63; 1, 24-26.

1881. Guske, Hubertus. "Bibliographie der in der DDR erschienenen Teilhard-Literatur." *Mitteilungen der Gesellschaft Teilhard de Chardin für den deutschen Sprachraum* (1968): 1, 16-18.

1882. ———. "Einheit von Wissenschaft und Glauben. Eine Skizze über Leben und Werk Teilhard de Chardins." *Begegnung* (1965): 7, 12-17.

1883. Gustafsson, Ake, and Erik. H. Lindner. "Den medvetna atomen. Ett nytt perspektiv pa männskan utvecklingen?" [The Sentient Atom. A New Perspective for Human Evolution?] *Arsbok för kristen humanism* (1961): 23, 53-70.

1884. Gutiérrez, Gustavo. *A Theology of Liberation.* Mary-
       knoll, N.Y.: Orbis Books, 1973.

1885. Gutiérrez Semprún, Manuel. "La vida del Padre Teilhard
       de Chardin." Item 745, pp. 5-22.

1886. Gyssling, W. "Glanz und Elend Teilhard de Chardins."
       Freidenker (1961): 44, 9-10.

1887. Haag, H., Adolf Haas and J. Hurzeler. *Evolution und*
       Bibel. Luzern/München: Rex-Verlag, 1962.

1888. Haas, Adolf. "La conscience qui change et son action
       sur les valeurs établies." *Le lotus bleu* (1963):
       1-8.

1889. ————. "Elementare Anthropologie. Das Verhältnis
       Mensch-Natur, beleuchtet durch den Teilhardschen
       Person- und Elementenbegriff." *Acta teilhardiana*
       (1974): 11, 113-121.

1890. ————. "Essai de représentation schématique du spec-
       tacle global de la création et de l'évolution." Item
       1015, pp. 162-167.

1891. ————. "L'être et le devenir. Création et évolution
       dans la conception du monde de Teilhard de Chardin."
       Item 1015, pp. 125-132.

1892. ————. "Der Schöpfungsgedanke bei Teilhard de Chardin
       nach der unveröffentlichen Schrift 'Comment je vois.'"
       Item 3924, pp. 27-51.

1893. ————. "Schöpfungslehre als 'Physik' un 'Metaphysik'
       des Einen und Vielen bei Teilhard de Chardin. Nach
       der unveröffentlichen Schrift 'Comment je vois.'"
       Scholastik (1964): 3, 312-342, 510-527.

1894. ————. "Die 'Stilänlichkeit' christlicher Glauben-
       statsachen mit den beiden Lebensakten der Entwick-
       lung." *Festgabe für Karl Rahner zum 60. Geburtstag.*
       Freiburg/Basel/Wien: Herder, 1964, pp. 756-778.

1895. ————. "Tagebücher von Teilhard de Chardin." *Stimmen*
       der Zeit (1975): 193, 397-408.

1896. ————. "Teilhard de Chardin." *Staatslexikon* (1970):
       11, 473-478.

1897. ———. *Teilhard de Chardin--Lexikon. Grundsbegriffe, Erläuterungen, Texte.* 2 vols.; Freiburg/Basel/Wien: Herder, 1971. Also *Acta teilhardiana* (1967): 4, 53-59; (1968): 5, 33-44; (1969): 6, 27-50; (1970): 7, 49-62; (1971): 8, 37-45.

1898. ———. "Teilhard de Chardin. Der Mensch im Kosmos." *Scholastik* (1961): 36, 246-249.

1899. ———. "Teilhard de Chardin. Persönlichkeit und Werk." *Wissen und Gewissen in der Technik.* Graz: Styria-Verlag, 1964, pp. 116-136. Also *Theologische Akademie II.* Frankfurt-am-Main: Knecht, 1965, pp. 79-99.

1900. ———. "Welt in Christus--Christus in Welt. Darstellung und Deutung der geistlichen Welt bei Teilhard de Chardin." *Geist und Leben* (1964): 37, 98-109, 184-201, 272-279, 358-375, 441-459.

1901. Habachi, René. "Teilhard de Chardin et le drame du XXe siècle." *Les conférences du Cénacle* (1956): 6, 254-299.

1902. Habermehl, Lawrence LeRoy. "Value in the Evolutionary World. Views of Samuel Alexander, C. Lloyd Morgan, and Pierre Teilhard de Chardin." Doctoral dissertation, Boston University, 1967.

1903. Hacker, Frieder. "Teilhard und der Priesterzölibat. Zu dem Artikel von Waldemar Kurtz." *Perspektiven der Zukunft* (1973): 7, 7-9. See Item 2251.

1904. Haguette, Andre. "Le point Oméga et la révélation. Essai sur les rapports entre Oméga et la révélation chez Teilhard de Chardin." Item 3036, pp. 137-195. "El punto Omega y la revelación." Item 3036 trans., pp. 125-176.

1905. Hajdok, Zsolt. "Teilhard de Chardin hüperfizikájának értéke." [The Value of Teilhard's Hyperphysical.] *Teológia* (1969): 3, 225-231.

1906. ———. "Teilhard de Chardin szeretettana." [The Idea of Love in Teilhard de Chardin.] Typescript. Budapest: Hittudományi Akadémia, 1969.

1907. Hale, Paul. "The Earthly Dimensions of the Church Ac-
       cording to Teilhard de Chardin." *American Benedictine
       Review* (1967): 18, 443-455.

1908. Hale, Robert William. *Christ and the Universe: Teilhard
       de Chardin and the Cosmos.* Chicago: Franciscan Herald
       Press, 1973.
       Il cosmo e Cristo. Basi di una ecologia secondo
       Teilhard de Chardin. Camaldoli/Arezzo; Camaldoli
       Edizioni, 1974.
       Also Firenze: Istituto Stensen, 1974.

1909. ————. "The Cosmic Body of the Christ: Teilhard and
       the Christic Nature of the Universe." Doctoral dis-
       sertation, Fordham University, 1972.

1910. ————. "Il metodo teologico di Teilhard de Chardin."
       Aquinas (1975): 18, 358-384.

1911. Haley, Martin. "Evolution." *The Advocate* (1960): 5492,
       20.

1912. ————. "Sintesi di studi sulla evoluzione." *Osserva-
       tore romano*, September 8, 1961, p. 3.

1913. Halle, Louis J. "Ariadne's Threat." *The New Republic*
       (1962): 25, 17-22.

1914. Hammelrath, Willi. "Wissenschaft und Religion. (Zum
       Phänomen Teilhard de Chardin.)" *Natur und Kultur*
       (1962): 54, 178-183.

1915. Hampl, Franz. "Teilhard de Chardin als Geschichtsdenk-
       er." Item 3299, pp. 41-63.

1915a. Hampson, Peter John. "Reflections on Reflection: Cog-
       nitive Psychology and the Teilhardian Synthesis."
       The Teilhard Review (1978): 13, 128-131.

1916. Hannoun, Hubert. "Encore Teilhard!" *Le courrier ration-
       aliste* (1960): 8, 174-176.

1917. Hanson, Anthony T. "Ecclesia Quaerens: The Future of
       Christian Doctrine." Item 1919, pp. 157-178.

1918. ————. "Teilhard de Chardin and the Priesthood."
       Expository Times (1968): 79, 308-310.

1919. ————. *Teilhard Reassessed. A Symposium of Critical Studies on the Thought of Père Teilhard de Chardin, Attempting an Evaluation of his Place in Contemporary Christian Thinking.* London: Darton, Longman and Todd, 1970. Contains Items 376, 377, 477, 1371, 1917, 3708, 3710, 4067.

1920. Hanson, James E. "Evil and Optimism in the Thought of Teilhard de Chardin." Doctoral dissertation, Fordham University, 1975.

1921. Harel, Claude. "Teilhard de Chardin a prophétisé à l'homme un avenir grandiose: Vie collective et convergence vers la conscience suprême." *La vie collective* (1956): 2, 12-14.

1922. Harman, Paul Frederick. "Education and the Human Hope: The Contribution of Pierre Teilhard de Chardin." Doctoral dissertation, Columbia University, 1971.

1923. Haroun-Tazieff, J. "L'humanité à la vielle d'un essor nouveau." Item 3292, pp. 109-112.

1924. Harrie, Ivar. "Teilhard de Chardin och kyrkan." [Teilhard de Chardin and the Church.] *Var Lösen* (1961): 52, 47-49.

1925. Harrington, Donald Szantho. "Science, Theology and Human Values." *Zygon* (1971): 6, 271-284.

1926. Hasenfuss, Josef. "Entwicklung des Universums und Zukunft der Religion. Gedanken aus dem Weltbild Teilhards de Chardin." *Die Seele* (1959): 35, 177-181.

1927. Hassenforder, J. *Étude de la diffusion d'un succès de librairie.* Paris: Centre d'études économiques, 1957.

1928. Haynes, Renee. "Teilhard's Tidings of Gladness." *The Catholic Herald* (1965): 4, 6.

1929. Head, D. "The Mass on the World and the Masses on the World." *The Teilhard Review* (1972): 7, 77-80+.

1930. Heagle, John L. "Conflict Resolution and the Future of Man: The Perspective of Teilhard de Chardin." *American Benedictine Review* (1973): 24, 46-58.

1931. Heckenroth, Jean. *Un prophète de notre temps, Teilhard de Chardin.* Paris: SEPT, 1969.

1932. Heer, Friedrich. "'Secte des catholiques.'" *Die Furche,* July 14, 1962.

1933. ———. "Teilhard de Chardin." *Offener Humanismus.* Bern/Stuttgart/Wien: Scherz, 1962, pp. 161-195.

1934. ———, Adolf Köberle, Josef Vital Kopp, and Walter Weymann-Weyhe. *Ein neues Menschenbild? Rundfunkstimmen zur Weltschau von Pierre Teilhard de Chardin.* Luzern/München: Rex, 1963.
       La nueva imagen del hombre en Teilhard de Chardin. Buenos Aires: Guadeloupe, 1967.

1935. Hefling, Charles Clifford. "The Whole Phenomenon: Scientific Methodology in the Work of Teilhard de Chardin." Honors thesis, Harvard University, 1971.

1936. Hefner, P.J. *The Promise of Teilhard: The Meaning of the Twentieth Century in Christian Perspective.* Philadelphia: Lippincott, 1970.

1937. ———. "Die Zukunft als unsere Zukunft. Eine Teilhardische Perspektive." *Evangelische Theologie* (1972): 32, 353-371.
       "The Future as Our Future: A Teilhardian Perspective." *Hope and the Future of Man.* London: Garnstone Press, 1973, pp. 15-29.

1938. Hegarty, Charles M. "Bonhoeffer and Teilhard: Christian Prophets of Secular Sanctity." *Catholic World* (1968-69): 207, 31-34.
       Also Item 607, pp. 111-117.

1939. ———. "Bonhoeffer and Teilhard on Worldly Christianity." *Science et esprit* (1969): 21, 35-70.

1940. Heim, Roger. "Discours à l'occasion de l'inauguration officielle de la Fondation Teilhard de Chardin." Item 1305, pp. 36-43.

1941. Hejdanek, Ladislav. "Vira a veda v dile Pierra Teilharda de Chardin." [Faith and Science in the Work of Teilhard de Chardin.] *Teologická priloha krestanské revue* (1965): 2, 31-36.

1942. Helein, S. "Teilhard de Chardin face à Pascal." *French Review* (1965): 39, 250-257.

1943. Helena. "The Optimism of Fr. Teilhard de Chardin." *The Southern Cross*, April 20, 1966, pp. 9, 189.

1944. Hemberg, Jarl. *Teilhard de Chardin.* Stockholm: Verbum, 1975. Contains Items 69a, 1603a, 3615a, 4051.

1945. Hemleben, Johannes. *Pierre Teilhard de Chardin in Selbstzeugnissen und Bilddokumenten.* Reinbek bei Hamburg: Rowohlt Taschenbusch-Verlag, 1966. *Teilhard de Chardin. Zijn leven in brieven en documenten.* Rotterdam: Lemniscat, 1966.

1946. Hemmings, F.W.J. "Holy Innocents." *New Statesman*, August 20, 1965, p. 258.

1947. Hengstenberg, Hans-Eduard. *Evolution und Schöpfung. Eine Antwort auf den Evolutionismus Teilhard de Chardins.* München: Pustet, 1964.

1948. ————. *Mensch und Materie. Zur Problematik Teilhard de Chardin.* Stuttgart: Kohlhammer, 1965.

1949. ————. "Der moderne Evolutionismus bei Teilhard de Chardin." *Die Kirche in der Welt* (1960): 5, 25-34.

1950. ————. "Der Personalismus bei Teilhard de Chardin und seine Folgen für die Ethik." *Vierteljahrsschrift für wissenschaftliche Pädagogik* (1963): 39, 77-102.

1951. ————. "Philosophie und Naturwissenschaft." *Die Kirche in der Welt* (1960): 27, 159-164; 44, 281-288.

1952. ————. "Die Religion auf dem Kampffeld der Schöpfungs- und Evolutionslehre." *Lebendiges Zeugnis* (1966): 3/4, 57-74.

1953. ————. "Untersuchungen zur Christologie Teilhards de Chardin." *Wissenschaft und Wahrheit* (1963): 26, 165-179.

1954. Henrici, J. "Blondel und Teilhard de Chardin." *Orientierung*, August 31, 1962, p. 179.

1955. Hens, J. "La recherche dans l'optique de Teilhard de Chardin." *Perspectives* (1965): 22, 47-49.

1956. Herbst, Walter. "Begegnung der Naturwissenschaften mit
       Teilhard de Chardin." *Perspektiven der Zukunft* (1967):
       1, 5.

1957. ———. "Faszination des Naturwissenschaftlers durch
       Teilhard de Chardin." *Perspektiven der Zukunft* (1968):
       4, 4-5.

1958. Herrmann, Alfred. "Teilhard de Chardin, Melvin Calvin
       et l'origine de la vie." *Revue Teilhard de Chardin*
       (1963): 16, 20-25. Excerpt from Item 1959.

1959. ———. *Teilhard, Melvin Calvin et l'origine de la vie
       sur notre terre et dans le cosmos.* Paris: Editions
       Universitaires, 1964.
       *Teilhard, Melvin Calvin e a origen de vida sobre
       nossa terra e no cosmo.* Petrópolis: Vozes, 1968.

1960. Hertz, Georges. "Le 'Dieu des Juifs' et notre temps."
       L'arche (1961): 54, 50-89, 93.

1961. Hess, M.W. "Two Evolutionists: Teilhard and Browning."
       Contemporary Review (1965): 207, 261-264.

1962. Hiernaux, Jean. "L'avenir biologique de l'homme." Item
       4060, pp. 111-120.

1963. ———. "Convergence des sciences de l'homme." *Univers*
       (1964): 1, 43-48.

1964. ———. "De la montée de la conscience à la montée des
       consciences." *Revue Teilhard de Chardin* (1971): 47/
       48, 24-27.

1965. ———. "Évolution humaine et progrès." *Univers*
       (1966): 3, 78-83.

1966. ———. "L'homme, axe et flèche de l'évolution." *Re-
       vue Teilhard de Chardin* (1964): 20/21, 20-23.

1967. ———. "Le racisme: Une malade sociale." *Revue Teil-
       hard de Chardin* (1964): 19, 17-18.

1968. Hildebrand, Dietrich von. "Teilhard de Chardin, un faux
       prophète." *Pensée catholique* (1972): 139, 14-36.
       "Teilhard de Chardin: A False Prophet." *Catholic
       Positon Papers*, July, 1973.
       Also *Overseas Review*, August 2, 1973.
       Also in Item 1969.

"Teilhard de Chardin: Towards a New Religion." *Triumph*, May, 1967, pp. 13-16+.

1969. ————. *Trojan Horse in the City of God*. Chicago: Franciscan Herald Press, 1967. Contains Item 1968.
Das trojanische Pferd in der Stadt Gottes. Regensburg: J. Habbel, 1968.
El caballo de Troya an la Ciudad de Dios. Madrid: Fax, 1969.
Il cavallo di Troia nella città di Dio. Roma: G. Volpe, 1969.
Le cheval de Troie dans la cité de Dieu. Paris: Beauchesne, 1970.

1970. Hill, Ronald. "The Alpha and Omega of Dialogue." *The Tablet*, November 4, 1967, pp. 1145-1146.

1971. ————. "Teilhard und Marx." *Frankfurter allgemeine Zeitung*, October 20, 1966.

1972. Himmelsbach, Arthur Conrad. "Teresa und Teilhard. Untersuchung einer bemerkenswerten Übereinstimmung." *Geist und Leben* (1967): 40, 323-339; (1968): 41, 122-141.

1973. Hinojosa Berrones, José Antonio. "Teilhard de Chardin y Maritain, y la filosofía de la naturaleza." *Humanismo en las ciencias puras*. México: Jus, 1972, pp. 83-90.

1974. Hinske, Norbert. "Der Mensch als Achse und Spitze der Entwicklung. Ein Bericht über Pierre Teilhard de Chardin." *Monatschrift für Pastoraltheologie* (1961): 50, 137-144.
Also *Kommunität* (1961): 5, 171-177.

1975. ————. "Pierre Teilhard de Chardin und die Lage des Menschen. Zu den geschichtlichen Voraussetzungen seines Denkens." *Neues deutsche Hefte* (1962): 86, 21-38.

1976. Hock, Wilhelm. "Eine missglückte Versöhnung. Über Teilhard de Chardins wissenschaftlich-religiöse Weltschau." *Deutsche Rundschau* (1963): 12, 54-59.

1977. Hodgkin, Robin A. "Christ in the Universe." *Friends' Quarterly* (1968): 16, 70-79.

1978.   Hoffmann-Axthelm, Dieter. "Glaube oder Theologie? Pi-
        erre Teilhard de Chardin. Eine kritische Besinnung."
        Deutsches Pfarrerblatt (1965): 65, 667-671.

1979.   Hohoff, Kurt. "Teilhard de Chardin." *Merkur* (1964):
        18, 275-283.

1980.   Hollis, Christopher. "Man or Superman?" *The Tablet*,
        February 20, 1960, p. 177.

1981.   ————. *The Mind of Chesterton.* London: Hollis and
        Carter, 1970. See pp. 277-288.
        Also Coral Gables, Fla.: University of Miami Press,
        1970.

1982.   Hollitzscher, W. "Az eretnek. Teilhard de Chardin
        kisérlete a tudomány és a vallás összhangjának a
        bizonitására." [The Heretic. Teilhard de Chardin's
        Attempt to Demonstrate the Agreement Between Science
        and Religion.] *Világosság* (1961): 6, 29-31.

1983.   Homlish, John Stephen. "The Cosmos and God According
        to Pierre Teilhard de Chardin and Alfred North White-
        head." Doctoral dissertation, McMaster University,
        1974.

1984.   "Hommage à Pierre Teilhard de Chardin." *Cahiers littér-
        aires* (1965): 13, 1-41. Contains Items 286, 403, 1590,
        2368, 2578, 3431, 3652.

1985.   Hopps, Donald Wallace. "Teilhard de Chardin and the
        Vision of the Scientific State: A Critical Evalua-
        tion." Doctoral dissertation, University of Wash-
        ington, 1969.

1986.   Hoskins, Hubert. *L'homme devant Dieu. Mélanges offerts
        au Père Henri de Lubac. III. Perspectives à aujourd-
        'hui.* Paris: Aubier-Montaigne, 1964. See pp. 125-
        132, 223-248, 331-346.

1987.   ————. "Makers of Modern Theology. 2. Teilhard de
        Chardin." *London Times*, October 14, 1967.

1988.   Hospital, Jean d'. "'L'Osservatore romano' publie un
        commentaire sévère sur la pensée du jésuite P. Teil-
        hard de Chardin." *Le Monde*, July 1, 1962, p. 13.

1989. Hottenroth, Mary. "The Eucharist as Matrix in the System of Thought of Teilhard de Chardin." *American Benedictine Review* (1970): 21, 98-121.

1990. Houde, Roland. "Essai de bibliographie méthodique." *Dialogue* (1964-65): 3, 368-381.

1991. Hourdin, Georges. "L'homme est toujours dans l'Homme." *Le Monde*, November 17, 1966.

1992. ————. "Les intuitions du P. Teilhard de Chardin." *Informations catholiques internationales* (1962): 172, 1-2.

1993. ————. "Un prophète et un pionnier: Teilhard de Chardin." *Cri du monde* (1971): 42-43.

1994. ————. "Savoir lire Teilhard." *Informations catholiques internationales* (1962): 172, 7-9.

1995. ————. "Teilhard de Chardin, la foi et le mouvement du monde." *Informations catholiques internationales* (1968): 324, 23-24.

1996. Hourton, Jorge. "Las condiciones de posibilidad de la filosofía cristiana. Irradiación de la posición blondeliana." *Anales de la Facultad de filosofía y ciencias de la educación* (1965): 11-36.

1997. ————. "Teilhard de Chardin: ¿ciencia o filosofía?" *Mapocho* (1965): 2, 25-36.

1998. ————. "Teilhard de Chardin y la educación." *Anales de la Facultad de filosofía y ciencias de la educación* (1966): 1-34.

1999. Hovald, Patrice. "La vie." *L'Alsace*, April 14, 1965, pp. 5, 9.

2000. Howlett, Jacques. "'Genèse d'un pensée' par le P. Teilhard de Chardin." *L'Express*, March 12, 1962, pp. 34-35.

2001. Hoyos Vasquez, Jaime. "La fenomenologia teilhardiana y la filosofía." *Revista javeriana* (1965): 64, 568-580.

2002.   ————. "El método del Padre Teilhard de Chardin."
        Revista javeriana (1965): 64, 471-483.

2003.   Hrachovec, Herbert. "Teilhard de Chardin und die The-
        ologie der Zukunft. Ein Kapitel im Streit um die
        Ontologie in der Theologie." Wort und Wahrheit (1972):
        27, 273-284.

2004.   Hromádka, J.L. "The Second Vatican Council." Communio
        viatorum (1966): 1/2, 5-24.

2005.   Huant, Ernest. Les pressions du nouveau temporel. Élé-
        ments d'une étude socio-religieuse d'actualité. Paris:
        Éditions du Cèdre, 1968. See pp. 151-156.

2006.   Huber, Georges. "Paul VI: Le Christ est l'Alpha et
        l'Omega de l'univers." La Croix, May 29, 1965.

2007.   Hübner, Jürgen. Teilhard de Chardin in Antwort und
        Kritik. Ein Querschnitt durch die wissenschaftliche
        Diskussion. Hamburg: Furche, 1968.

2008.   ————. Theologie und biologische Entwicklungslehre.
        Ein Beitrag zum Gespräch zwischen Theologie und Natur-
        wissenschaft. München: C.H. Beck, 1966.

2009.   Huchingson, James Edward. "A General Systems Approach
        to Theology, with Special Reference to Teilhard de
        Chardin." Doctoral dissertation, Emory University,
        1977.

2010.   Huelsman, Richard Joseph. "Implications in the Work of
        Teilhard de Chardin for a Philosophy of Guidance."
        Doctoral dissertation, Ohio State University, 1972.

2011.   Hug, Herbert. "Fortschritt? Gedanken zu Teilhards
        Buch 'Die Zukunft des Menschen.'" Kirchenblatt für
        die reformierte Schweiz (1964): 120, 50-53.

2012.   Hugedé, Norbert. Le cas Teilhard de Chardin. Paris:
        Fischbacher, 1966.

2013.   Hugron, A. "Place et rôle de l'homme dans la création."
        Isen (1966): 19-22.

2014.   Hugues, Philip E. "Review of Current Religious Thought."
        Christianity Today, March 27, 1961, p. 576.

2015. Hulsbosch, A. "De kosmogenese van Teilhard de Chardin." *Annalen van het Tijdgenootschap* (1959): 47, 1-317. *God in Creation and Evolution.* London: Sheed, 1966.

2016. Hurley, Denis E. "Amour, loi et Christ dans la création." *Pax Romana Journal* (1965): 4, 3-6.

2017. ————. "Gehoorzamen in het mystieke milieu: Teilhard de Chardin." *Carmel* (1966): 18, 350-361.

2018. Hutten, E.H. "The Errors of Teilhard de Chardin." *Humanist* (1971): 86, 115-116.

2019. Huxley, Julian. "L'avenir de l'humanité par la convergence des races humaines." *Univers* (1964): 1, 99-104.

2020. ————. "Une aventure spirituelle." *Revue Teilhard de Chardin* (1960): 1/2, 23-25. Also *Planète*, October/November, 1961.

2021. ————. "Glosy o Teilhardzie de Chardin." [Views on Teilhard de Chardin.] *Znak* (1962): 92/93, 229-234.

2022. ————. "The Human Phenomenon." *Encounter* (1956): g, 84-86. Also Item 3292, pp. 97-102.

2023. ————. "Introduction." Item 4702 trans., pp. 11-28. In Chinese in *Universitas* (1967): 6, 215-221.

2024. ————. "Message." *Europe* (1965): 431/432, 12-13.

2025. ————. "Une pensée vivante." *Les nouvelles littéraires* (1960): 1693, 1, 4.

2026. ————. "Teilhard de Chardin." *Essays of a Humanist.* London: Chatto and Windus, 1964, pp. 202-217. Also *Ich sehe den kunftigen Menschen. Natur und neuer Humanismus.* München: List-Verlag, 1965, pp. 203-218.

2027. ————. "Het verschijnsel Mens." Item 3978, pp. 115-120.

2028. Huybens, Maurits. "Ébauche d'une christologie teilhard-
      ienne." *Revue du clergé africain* (1966): 21, 129-146.

2029. Idatte, Paul. *Clefs pour la cybérnetique.* Paris:
      Seghers, 1969.

2030. ———. "L'idéologie technocratique et le teilhardisme."
      Temps modernes (1966-67): 22, 254-295.

2031. Imbert-Nergal, R. "Encore Teilhard!" *Le courrier
      rationaliste* (1960): 8, 185-188.

2031a. ———. "L'inspiration scientifique dans la philosophie
       de Teilhard de Chardin." *Cahiers rationalistes* (1960):
       187, 129-152.

2032. Imbrighi, Gaston. *La paleografia in Teilhard de Chardin.*
      L'Aquila: L.U. Japadre, 1967.

2033. Inglott, Serracino. "Teilhard de Chardin." *Problemi
      ta'llum* (1965): 201-204.

2034. Innocenti, Ennio. *Il ripensamento cattolico dell'evol-
      uzione.* Roma: Innocenti, 1961. See pp. 12-18.

2035. Institut der Görres Gesellschaft für die Begegnung von
      Naturwissenschaft und Theologie. *Teilhard de Char-
      din und das Problem des Weltbildenkens.* München:
      Karl Alber, 1968. Contains Items 1282, 2538, 2749,
      3169.

2036. "Introduction à la pensée de Teilhard de Chardin." *Le
      Bulletin. Documentes et recherches* (1956): 5, 25-29.

2037. Ipser, Karl. *Michelangelo, der Künstler-Prophet der
      Kirche.* Augsburg: A. Kraft, 1963. See pp. 78-81.

2038. Iriarte, Joaquin. "Al dimidiar este gran siglo nuestro:
      Lombardi, Przywara, Teilhard de Chardin." *Razón y fe*
      (1956): 154, 77-91.

2039. Iriarte, Raúl R. "Hipótesis sobre analogías y difer-
      encias entre los modelos del universo dados por Anax-
      ágoras y por Teilhard de Chardin." *IIº Congreso na-
      cional de filosofía. Actas.* Buenos Aires: Sudamer-
      icana, 1973, vol. 2, pp. 368-373.

2040.   Isaye, Gaston. "Avertissement du 30 juin 1962 concernant
        les oeuvres du Père Teilhard de Chardin." *Nouvelle
        revue théologique* (1962): 84, 866-869.

2041.   ———. "Bergson et Teilhard de Chardin." *Bulletin de
        la Société française de philosophie* (1959): 53, 167-
        169.

2042.   ———. "La cybernétique et Teilhard de Chardin." *Cy-
        bernetica* (1962): 5, 25-37.
        Also *3e Congrès international de cybernétique 1961*.
        Namur: Association internationale de cybernétique,
        1961, pp. 168-181.

2043.   ———. "The Method of Teilhard de Chardin: A Critical
        Study." *New Scholasticism* (1967): 1, 31-57.

2044.   ———. "Philippe de la Trinité, Rome et Teilhard de
        Chardin." *Nouvelle revue théologique* (1967): 438-439.

2045.   Ito, Sachiko. "'Kami no ba' ni yoru uchû to ningen no
        kansei." [Perfection of the Universe and Man According
        to "The Divine Milieu."] *Convergence* (1975): 4, 38-43.

2046.   ———. "Teilhard de Chardin no reisei." [The Spiri-
        tuality of Teilhard de Chardin.] *Convergence* (1972):
        2, 29-33.

2047.   ———. "Teilhard ni okeru ningen to uchû no kansei."
        [The Perfection of Man and the Universe According to
        Teilhard.] *Convergence* (1973): 3, 19-23.

2048.   J.C. "Science et synthèse. Au colloque de l'UNESCO."
        Le Monde, December 17, 1965, p. 13.

2049.   Jabouin, Louis. "Teilhard à la recherche du point vi-
        vant." *Revue de Paris* (1968): 6/7, 73-76.

2050.   Jacob, A. "Ein neuer Fall Galilei?" *Frankreich Geist-
        iges* (1963): 7, 1-4.

2051.   Jacob, Charles. "Notice nécrologique sur Pierre Teil-
        hard de Chardin." *Comptes rendus de l'Academie des
        sciences* (1955): 240, 1673-1677.

2052.   ———. "Notice sur la vie et l'oeuvre scientifique
        du Père Teilhard de Chardin." *La table ronde* (1955):
        90, 15-18.

2053.   Jacques, Leon. "The Challenge of Father Teilhard de
         Chardin." *Journal of the Indian Academy of Philosophy*
         (1964): 3, 58-71.

2054.   Jadot, Claude, and Guy Jadot. "Journées de Saint-Jean
         de Luz 1964." *Revue Teilhard de Chardin* (1964): 20/21,
         27-29.

2055.   Jakubowska, Janina. "Teilhard de Chardin e il pensiero
         protestante contemporaneo." *Futuro dell'uomo* (1977):
         1, 33-39.

2056.   Jamison, Timothy. "Teilhard de Chardin, the Personal-
         ized Universe." *Cord* (1966): 16, 324-332.
         "Chardin's Personalized Universe." *Insight* (1966-
         67): 5, 23-28.

2056a.   Janeira, Ana Luisa. "Crítica espistmológica de 'Le
         groupe zoologique humain' de Teilhard de Chardin."
         Revista portuguesa de filosofia (1978): 34, 376-396.

2057.   ————. "A dialectica energetica em Teilhard de Char-
         din." *Revista portuguesa de filosofia* (1972): 28, 284-
         298.

2058.   ————. "Do planeta a planetizacão: Explorando pistas
         abertas por Teilhard de Chardin." *Revista portuguesa
         de filosofia* (1972): 28, 17-34.

2059.   ————. "Fenómeno humano, energética e analogia evo-
         lutiva, em Teilhard de Chardin." *Brotéria* (1977):
         105, 21-34.

2060.   ————. "Réflexion philosophique sur l'énergétique
         dans la pensée de Pierre Teilhard de Chardin." Mimeo-
         graphed. Université de Paris I, 1972.

2061.   Jánosi, Gyula. "Teilhard és Giesswein." [Teilhard and
         Giesswein.] *Vigilia* (1974): 39, 486-489.

2062.   Jans, Henk. "De historische geologie als fundament an
         Teilhard's denken." *Streven* (1962-63): 16, 840-848.
         Also *Handelingen van het XXVᵉ Vlaams Filologen-
         congres*. Zellik: Secretariaat van de Vlaamse Filo-
         logencongressen, 1967, pp. 61-77.

2063.   Jansohn, H. "Anthropologie als aktivistische Utopie.
         Zum Menschenbild Teilhard de Chardins." *Trierer the-
         ologische Zeitschrift* (1973): 82, 1-28.

2064. Jaramillo, Rodolfo. "Molina, cientiffco y patriota de ayer y de hoy." *Mensaje* (1965): 563-566.

2065. Jaroszewski, Tadeusz M. "Koncepcja czlowieka i spoleczeństwa Pierre Teilharda de Chardin." [Teilhard de Chardin's Conception of Man and Society.] *Filozoficzne problemy współczesnego chrzescijaństwa.* [Philosophical Problems of Contemporary Christianity.] Warszawa: Pañstwowe Wydawnictwo Naukowe, 1973, pp. 51-98.

2066. ———. "Plaszczyzny dyskusji." [Basis for Discussion.] *Życie i myśl* (1965): 10, 60-62.

2067. Jarque i Jutglar, Joan E. *L'apologétique dans la pensée et dans l'oeuvre du Père Teilhard de Chardin.* Paris: Desclée, 1969.
Foi en l'homme. L'apologétique de Teilhard de Chardin. Paris: Desclée, 1970.
La fe de l'home d'avui? La reposta de Teilhard de Chardin. Barcelona: Laia, 1972.

2068. ———. *Bibliographie générale des oeuvres et articles sur Pierre Teilhard de Chardin parus jusqu'à fin décembre 1969.* Fribourg: Editions Universitaires, 1970.

2069. ———. "Per a un debat teològic sobre injusticia social i ètica de la revolució." *Qüestions de vida cristiana* (1969): 47, 100-106.

2070. Jean, F. "Teilhard de Chardin et la guerre." *Nouvelle revue pédagogique* (1966-67): 8, 473-487.

2071. Jeanniere, Abel. "Approches christologiques." Item 1015, pp. 223-238.

2072. ———. "L'avenir de l'esprit." *La table ronde* (1962): 117, 137-149.

2073. ———. "L'avenir de l'humanité d'après Teilhard de Chardin." *Reuve de l'action populaire* (1962): 154, 5-12.
Also *Revue Teilhard de Chardin* (1962): 12, 13-18; 13, 3-10.
"L'avenir de l'espèce humaine, d'après Teilhard de Chardin." *Orient littéraire* (1962): 4-5.

2074. ———. "Il cristocentrismo del Milieu divin." Item
2744, pp. 205-220.
"Le Christo-centrisme du 'Milieu divin.'" Item
2744 trans., pp. 192-205.
Also *Lettre* (1965): 83/84, 34-42.

2075. ———. "L'homme, peut-il modifier l'homme?" *Revue
d'action populaire* (1962): 162, 1053-1063.

2076. ———. "Socialisation et christogénèse." Item 741,
pp. 34-56.

2077. ———. "Sur le mal, l'union et le point Omega." Item
1284, pp. 360-366.
"Acerca del mal, la unión y el punto omega." Item
1284 trans., pp. 99-107.
"Sul male, l'unione e il punto Omega." *Nuovo Osservatore* (1965): 6, 380-385.

2078. ———. "Teilhard dix ans après." *Cahiers d'action
religieuse et sociale* (1965): 407, 225-236.

2079. ———. Jelsma, S. "Heilzame op leven en dood." *Ons
Geestelijk Leven* (1964-65): 41, 334-341.

2080. Jerkovic, Jerônimo. *Teilhard de Chardin e S. Bonaven-
tura: Itinérario do Cosmos ao Omega.* Petrópolis:
Vozes, 1968.

2081. ———. "Teilhard de Chardin: O Evangelho do Cristo
Cósmico." *Vozes* (1968): 62, 223-256, 306-320.

2082. Jiménez Duque, Baldomero. "Dios, cosmos, historia."
Arbor (1961): 184, 397-420.

2083. Jeurissen, Nico. "Aux alentours de Teilhard." *Le Vaillant* (1965): 44, 6.

2084. Joannes, Fernando Vittorino. "Teilhard de Chardin o
della fede nell'uomo." Item 1300, pp. 185-197.

2085. Johann, Robert O. "Teilhard's Personalized Universe."
Item 3247, pp. 93-100.

2086. Johnston, William. *The Still Point: Reflections on Zen
and Christian Mysticism.* New York: Harper and Row,
1971.

2087. Jones, David Gareth. "The Phenomenon of Teilhard de Chardin." *Faith and Thought* (1967): 96, 55-74.

2088. ———. *Teilhard de Chardin: An Analysis and Assessment.* London: Tyndale Press, 1969. Also Grand Rapids, Mich.: Eerdmans, 1970.

2089. Jonker, W.D. "Teilhard de Chardin en de theologie van ons tyd." *Nederlandse Gereformeerde Teologiese Tydskrift* (1972): 13, 20-25.

2090. Joublin, Jean. "L'évolutionnisme soi-disant 'chrétien.' L'Évangile sur mesure des 'Progressistes' plus ou moins grimés sous un voile transparent de science et de foi." *Pensée catholique* (1962): 78/79, 86-138.

2091. ———. "Examen de l'alibi 'scientifique' du teilhardisme." *Pensée catholique* (1962): 81, 59-97; (1963): 84, 83-122; 85/86, 101-108.

2092. Jourdan, J.M. "'Une figure moderne de l'anté-Christ.'" *Permanences* (1965): 24, 25-50.

2093. Journet, Charles. "Au R.P. Henri de Lubac." *Nova et vetera*, July-September, 1962, pp. 224-228.

2094. ———. "L'effort théologique du P. Teilhard de Chardin." *Nova et vetera* (1964): 3, 305-310. "Il tentativo teologico del P. Teilhard de Chardin." *Studi cattolici* (1965): 47, 7-9. "El intento teológico de Teilhard de Chardin." *Arco* (1965): 7, 439-442.

2095. ———. "L'explication du monde selon Pierre Teilhard de Chardin." *Nova et vetera* (1956): 31, 210-224.

2096. ———. "Note sur Teilhard de Chardin." *Nova et vetera* (1958): 3, 223-230.

2097. ———. "Pierre Teilhard de Chardin de l'Académie des Sciences. 'Le groupe zoologique humain, structures et directions évolutives.'" *Nova et vetera* (1956): 3, 225-228.

2098. ———. "Pierre Teilhard de Chardin ou Bergson? Hérédité ou non hérédité de la culture?" *Nova et vetera* (1956): 3, 229-239.

2099.   ————. "Pierre Teilhard de Chardin, penseur religieux.
        De quelques jugements récents." *Nova et vetera* (1962):
        4, 284-313.

2100.   ————. "La synthèse du Père Teilhard est-elle dissoci-
        able?" *Nova et vetera* (1966): 41, 144-151.

2101.   ————. "La vision teilhardienne du monde." *Divinitas*
        (1959): 3, 330-344.
        "Wizja świata Teilharda de Chardin." *Znak* (1960):
        12, 269-280.

2102.   Journoud, Robert. "Les grandes lignes de la pensée sci-
        entifique du P. Teilhard de Chardin." *Le courrier
        de l'Ouest*, March 7, 14, 21, 28, 1961.

2103.   Joussain, André. "Teilhard de Chardin et le marxisme."
        Écrits de Paris (1963): 9, 80-83.

2104.   Joyce, Mary Rosera. "The Evolution of Love--Chardin."
        Insight (1967-68): 6, 11-14.

2105.   ————. "Towards Virginal Marriage?" *Cross Currents*
        (1967): 3, 368-370.

2106.   Juan, R. "El nuevo humanismo del P. Teilhard de Char-
        din." *Sic* (1963): 254, 170-173.

2107.   Jugnet, Louis. "Claudel, saint Thomas et Teilhard."
        Itinéraires (1967): 115, 102-106.

2108.   ————. "Les erreurs de Teilhard de Chardin." *Aujourd-
        'hui-Québec*, February, 1966, pp. 35-38.

2109.   ————. *Le monitum du Saint Office sur les ouvrages du
        P. Teilhard de Chardin.* Angers: Supplément à Revue
        des cercles d'études d'Angers, 1963.

2110.   ————. "Réflexions sur le teilhardisme." *Ordre fran-
        çais* (1963): 5, 37-56.
        Also *Revue des cercles d'études d'Angers* (1962-63):
        5, 113-120.
        "Riflessioni sul teilhardismo." Item 1403, pp. 61-
        88.

2111.   ————. *Teilhard y los no creyentes.* Madrid: Speiro,
        1967.

2112. Jussieu, Marc. "Discussion." Item 1284, pp. 366-368. "Fragmento de una carta." Item 1284 trans., pp. 51-54.

2113. Juste, André. "L'hyperphysique teilhardienne devant la science." *Perspectives* (1965): 24/25, 55-58.

2114. Kachama-Nkoy, Stéphane. "De Karl Marx à Pierre Teilhard de Chardin dans la pensée de L.S. Senghor et Mamadou Dia." *Journées africaines--Louvain 1963. Voies africaines du socialisme.* Leopoldville: Bibliothèque de l'Étoile, 1963, pp. 63-83. Also *Dia* (1964-65): 4, 135-158.

2115. ————. "Débat sur Teilhard de Chardin." *Documents pour l'action* (1963): 18, 364-369.

2116. Kadowaki, Kakichi. "Shakai henkaku to uchû kaihatsu ni kansuru shingakuteki kôsatsu, Teilhard de Chardin no shisô." [Teilhard's Theological Consideration of the Changing of Society and Building the Earth.] *Atarashii shakai to uchûkan wo motomete* [Researching a New Conception of the Universe and Society.] Tokyo: Chûô Shuppansha, 1970, pp. 85-109.

2117. Kahane, Ernest. "Analyses bibliographiques." *Le courrier rationaliste* (1960): 8, 189, 191.

2118. ————. "L'apport de Teilhard de Chardin à la pensée rationelle." *Europe* (1965): 431-432, 88-96.

2119. ————. "L'inépuisable realité." *Le courrier rationaliste* (1961): 8, 160-164.

2120. ————. "P. Teilhard de Chardin, ou le philosophe malgré lui." *Pensée* (1960): 94, 116-121.

2121. ————. "Présentation de Teilhard de Chardin." *Chemia* (1963): 20, 8-9.

2122. ————. "Progrès et finalité d'après Teilhard de Chardin et dans la perspective materialiste." *Revue Teilhard de Chardin* (1962): 10, 14-15.

2123. ————. "La religion change de visage." *Le courrier rationaliste* (1961): 8, 165-173.

2124. ———. *Teilhard de Chardin.* Paris: Union Rationaliste, 1960.
Teilhard de Chardin, ciência o fe. Buenos Aires: Tekne, 1967.

2125. ———. "Teilhard de Chardin." *Le courrier rationaliste* (1960): 187, 109-113.

2126. ———. "Teilhard de Chardin anti-raciste." *Droit et liberté,* December, 1963, p. 11.

2127. ———. "Teilhard de Chardin devant la pensée catholique." *Le courrier rationaliste* (1966): 1, 34-35.

2128. ———. "Teilhard de Chardin et le materialisme." *Planète* (1962): 5, 140-141.

2129. ———. "Teilhard de Chardin vu par un teilhardien." *Pensée* (1962): 106, 109-119.

2130. ———. "Le teilhardisme, une pensée en évolution." *L'action laïque* (1963): 242.

2131. ———. "Vers la convergence des croyants et des incroyants." *Actuelles* (1963): 2.

2132. ———, and Roger Garaudy. *Teilhard de Chardin.* Budapest: Kossuth Könyvkiadó, 1967.

2133. Kainz, Howard. "Teilhard de Chardin's Evolutionary Perspective." *Way,* December, 1972, pp.22-31.

2134. Kakei, Setsuko. "Teilhard hôbun bunken mokuroku." [Lists of Works in Japanese on Teilhard.] *Convergence* (1971): 1, 45-49.

2135. Kaneko, Yoshiyuki. "Teilhard de Chardin kankei hôbun bunken mokuroku (1973-1977 sen o chûshin to shite)." [Publications in Japanese on Teilhard de Chardin, 1973-1977.] *Convergence* (1977): 5, 44-48.

2136. Kaplan, Lester. "Teilhard and Alfred Adler." *The Teilhard Review* (1974): 2, 44-55.

2137. Kappes, Heinz. "Sri Aurobindo und Teilhard de Chardin." *Perspektiven der Zukunft* (1970): 5, 7-10.

2138. Karisch, Rudolf. *Teilhard de Chardin. Anliegen und Aussagen seiner Entwicklungslehre.* Essen: Fredebeul und Koinen, 1962.

2139. Kasprzyk, L., and A. Węgrecki. "Koncepcja Teilharda de Chardin." [Teilhard's Conception.] *Wprowadzenie do filozofii.* [Introduction to Philosophy.] Warszawa: Państwowe Wydawnictwo Naukowe, 1970, pp. 231-237.

2140. Katayama, Toshhito. "Simone Weil to Teilhard de Chardin." [Simone Weil and Teilhard de Chardin.] *Bulletin franco-japonais d'informations culturelles et techniques* (1960): 48, 3-8.

2141. Katô, Chûichi. "Teilhard de Chardin no shisô." [Teilhard de Chardin's Thought.] *Futatsu no kyoku no aida de.* [Between Two Poles.] Tokyo: Kobundo, 1960, pp. 92-96.

2142. Katona, Adam. "A Teilhard-jelenség." [The Teilhard Phenomenon.] *Korunk* (1967): 21, 28-33.

2143. Kay, William, and Jane Mathison. "Ontology and Values. A Teilhardian Resolution of the Naturalistic Fallacy." *The Teilhard Review* (1970): 1, 22-35; 2, 71-84.

2144. Keating, Maurice, and H.R.F. Keating. *Understanding Pierre Teilhard de Chardin: A Guide to the Phenomenon of Man.* London: Lutterworth Press, 1969.

2145. Kecskes, Pal. "Teilhard de Chardin világszemlélete." [Teilhard de Chardin's Theory of the World.] *Vigilia* (1963): 28, 137-146.

2146. Kehnscherper, G. "Wissenschaft und Glaube. Eine Einführung in das Werk von Pierre Teilhard de Chardin 'Der Mensch im Kosmos.'" *Glaube und Gewissen* (1965): 3, 43-45.

2147. Kelber, Wilhelm. "Pierre Teilhard de Chardin." *Die Christengemeinschaft* (1962): 34, 371-375.

2148. Kelleher, Derry. *An Alien Ideology?: Republicanism, Christianity, Marxism.* Dublin: Sinn Fein, n.d.

2149. Kelly, Paul J. "Empedocles and Teilhard." *The Teilhard Review* (1971-72): 2, 76-83.

2150. Kenny, J. Peter. "Teilhard de Chardin and Twentieth
       Century Theology of the Supernatural." *Australasian
       Catholic Record* (1971): 48, 334-339; (1972): 49, 108-
       112.

2151. Kenny, Tony. "Father Kenny's Reply." *Bulletin of the
       Newman Association, Philosophy of Science Group* (1960):
       38, 13-22; 39, 3-6. See Item 2837.

2152. ————. "Thoughts on 'The Phenomenon of Man.'" *Bul-
       letin of the Newman Association Philosophy of Science
       Group* (1960): 37, 4-9. See Item 2837.

2153. Kenny, W. Henry. *A Path Through Teilhard's Phenomenon.*
       Dayton: Pflaum, 1970.
       *El fenómeno humano de Teilhard de Chardin. Guía
       para el lector.* Santander: Sal Terrae, 1973.

2154. ————. "Teilhard de Chardin: His Theory of Evolution."
       Mimeographed. Faculty Colloquium, Xavier University,
       Cincinnati, Ohio, March 2, 1960.

2155. Keon, Ellen. "A Note on Teilhard as a Creative Writer."
       The Teilhard Review (1969): 1, 24-27.

2156. ————. "Two Poems Characteristic of Teilhard's Thought,
       by Alice Meynell and Joseph Plunkett." *The Teilhard
       Review* (1976): 11, 98-100.

2157. Kerer, Rupert. "Hoffnungen und Provokationen." Item
       3299, pp. 112-119.

2158. Kessler, Marvin, and Bernard Brown. *Dimensions of
       the Future. The Spirituality of Teilhard de Chardin.*
       Cleveland: Corpus Books, 1968. Contains Items 363,
       1449, 1775, 2819, 2941, 2956, 3667, 4167.
       La spiritualità di Teilhard de Chardin. Assisi:
       Cittadella Editrice, 1972.

2159. Ketele, Georges. "Avant-propos." *Isen* (1966): 9.

2160. Ketman, Georges. "Teilhard de Chardin, nouveau Darwin."
       Science et vie (1960): 514, 76-80.

2161. Number deleted.

2162. Khalifé, Abdo. "Teilhard et Vatican II." *Revue Teil-
       hard de Chardin* (1974): 58/59, 5-11.

2163. Kim, D.S. "Irenaeus of Lyons and Teilhard de Chardin: A Comparative Study of Recapitulation and Omega." *Journal of Ecumenical Studies* (1976): 13, 69-93.

2164. King, Ursula. "The One and the Many: The Individual and the Community from the Religious Perspective." *The Teilhard Review* (1976): 11, 9-15.

2165. ————. "The Phenomenology of Teilhard de Chardin." *The Teilhard Review* (1971): 1, 33-45.

2166. ————. "Religion and the Future: Teilhard de Chardin's Analysis of Religion as a Contribution to Inter-religious Dialogue." *Religious Studies* (1971): 7, 307-323.

2167. ————. "Socialization and Mankind's Future According to Teilhard de Chardin." *Social Action* (1970): 20, 134-146.

2168. ————. "Sri Aurobindo's and Teilhard's Vision of the Future of Man." *The Teilhard Review* (1974): 1, 2-5.

2169. ————. "Teilhard and the World Congress of Faiths." *The Teilhard Review* (1976): 11, 48-52.

2170. ————. "Il confronto tra mistica occidentale e mistica orientale secondo Teilhard de Chardin." *Il futuro dell'uomo* (1974): 2, 3-19.
"Teilhard's Comparison of Western and Eastern Mysticism." *The Teilhard Review* (1975): 1, 9-16.

2170a. Kirschke, S. "Zur Einschätzung der Differenzierung im Katholizismus der Gegenwart. Enzyklika Humani generis und die Forschungen Teilhards." *Biologie in der Schule* (1964): 13, 268-272.

2171. Kishi, Eishi. "Religious Aspects of Cosmic Consciousness: A Comparison of Teilhard de Chardin and Toyohiko Kagawa." *Christian Century*, December 23, 1970, pp. 1533-1536.
"Uchū ishiki no shūkyōsei Pierre Teilhard de Chardin to Kagawa Toyohiko." *Koe* (1970): 40-47.

2172. Kitahara, Takashi [pseud. Jean Frisch]. "Hashi wo kakeru ningen." [The Man Who Built a Bridge.] *Misuzu* (1964): 61, 27-30.

2173. ————. "Teilhard de Chardin no chosaku o yomu tebiki." [Guide for Reading "The Hymn of the Universe."] *Convergence* (1975): 4, 10-16.

2174. ———. "Teilhard no shisô e mihi annai." [Itinerary
        for Exploring the Thought of Teilhard.] *Convergence*
        (1972): 2, 42-44.

2175. Kittler, Glenn D. "Father Teilhard de Chardin." *Cath-
        olic Digest*, September, 1966, pp. 80-86. Excerpt from
        Item 2176.

2176. ———. *The Wings of Eagles*. New York: Doubleday, 1966.
        See pp. 85-112.

2177. Klauder, Francis J. *Aspects of the Thought of Teilhard
        de Chardin*. No. Quincy, Mass.: Christopher, 1971.

2178. ———. "The Challenge of the Thought of Pierre Teil-
        hard de Chardin." *Chicago Studies* (1968): 7, 101-108.

2179. Klein, Wolfgang. *Teilhard de Chardin und das Zweite
        Vatikanische Konzil: Ein Vergleich der Pastoral-Kon-
        stitution über die Kirche in der Welt von Heute mit
        Aspekten der Weltschau Pierre Teilhards de Chardin*.
        Paderborn: F. Schöningh, 1975.

2180. Kleipool, R.J.C. *De "Font" van Teilhard de Chardin.
        Een constructieve uitbouw van ons mensbeeld, gefund-
        eerd in geloof en wetenschap*. Mimeographed. Amers-
        foort: Kleipool, 1964.

2181. Klever, W.N.A. "De 'hyperfysica' van Teilhard de Char-
        din en de traditionele 'metafysica' met betrekking
        tot de intersubjectiviteit als zedelijk ideaal."
        *Algemeen Nederlands Tijdschrift voor Wijsbegeerte
        en Psychologie* (1962-63): 55, 179-189.

2182. Klinger, Jerzy. "O Teilhard de Chardin a tradycja
        kosciola wschodniego." [Teilhard de Chardin and
        the Tradition of the Eastern Church.] *Życie i myśl*
        (1968): 6/7, 154-167.
        Also Item 3888, pp. 267-289.

2183. Klohr, Olof, and Herbert Trebs. *Beiträge zur Deutung
        von Teilhard de Chardin. Der Mensch im Kosmos*. Ber-
        lin: Union-Verlag, 1966.

2184. Klósak, Kazimierz. "Antropogeneza no empiriologicznym
        ujęciuks Piotra-Teilhard de Chardin." [Anthropo-
        genesis in the Empiriological Perspective of Pierre
        Tielhard de Chardin.] *Zeszyty Naukowe Katholickiego
        Uniwersytetu Lubelskiego* (1963): 4, 3-18.

2184a. ———. "Z antropologii Ks. Teilhard de Chardin."
[Father Teilhard de Chardin's Anthropology.] *Znak*
(1960): 77.

2185. ———. "Fenomenologia O. Teilharda de Chardin ramowej.
Analizie epistemologicznej i metodologicznej." [Father Teilhard de Chardin's Phenomenology. Epistemological and Methodological Analysis.] *Roczniki Filozoficzne Katholickiego Uniwersytetu Lubelskiego* (1964):
12, 93-105.

2186. ———. "Ks. Piotra de Chardin a zagadnienia monogenistycznych poczatkow ludzkosci." [Father Pierre
Teilhard de Chardin and the Problem of Monogenism.]
Studia Theologica Varsaviensis (1964): 83-113.

2187. ———. "Natura czlowieka w fenomenologicznym ujęciu
Ks. Teilhard de Chardin." [The Nature of Man in
Father Teilhard de Chardin's Phenomenological Perspective.] *Znak* (1960): 77, 1464-1483.

2188. ———. "La nature de l'homme dans la perspective
phénoménologique du Père Teilhard de Chardin." *Bulletin du SIQS*. *Pax Romana* (1961): 26, 3-4. Digest
of Item 2187.

2189. ———. "O wlásciwa interpretacje i krytyke dziela
Ks. Teilharda de Chardin." [Toward a Proper Interpretation and Critique of the Work of Father Teilhard de Chardin.] *Znak* (1960): 72, 823-841.

2190. ———. "Poczatk duszy ludkiej." [The Origin of the
Human Soul.] *Znak* (1961): 87-88, 5-9.

2191. ———. "Pour une juste interprétation et critique
de l'oeuvre de Teilhard de Chardin." *Bulletin du
SIQS*. *Pax Romana* (1961): 26, 2-3. Digest of Item
2189.

2192. ———. "Spór o Orygenesa naszych csasów." [The Dispute About the Origin of Our Times.] *Znak* (1960):
2/3, 253-268.

2193. Number deleted.

2194. ———. "Z zagadnien filozofii przyrody Ks. P. Teilhard de Chardin." [Problems of Father Pierre Teilhard de Chardin's Philosophy of Nature.] *Zeszyty
Naukowe Katholickiego Uniwersytetu Lubelskiego* (1960):
3, 3-10.

2195. ————. "Zagadnienie stworzenia wszechświata w ujęciu
       Ks. P. Teilharda de Chardin." [The Question of the
       Creation of the Universe in the Thought of Father
       Pierre Teilhard de Chardin.] *Studia philosophiae
       christianae* (1965): 2, 276-293.

2196. Knight, Alice Vallé. *The Meaning of Teilhard de Char-
       din: A Primer.* Old Greenwich, Conn.: Devin-Adair,
       1974. Contains Item 46.

2197. Knodel, Arthur J. "A 'Gentile's' View." Item 1544,
       pp. 77-91.

2198. ————. "An Introduction to the Integral Evolutionism
       of Teilhard de Chardin." *Personalist* (1957): 38,
       347-355.

2199. Knoll, Max. "Bemerkungen zu Pierre Teilhard de Char-
       dins Schrift 'La mystique de la science.'" Item
       1213, pp. 176-180.

2200. ————. "Teilhard de Chardin in evangelischer Sicht."
       Lutherische Monatshefte (1968): 7, 357-362.

2201. ————. "Die Zukunftserwartung bei Teilhard de Char-
       din. Zeitwende." *Die neue Furche* (1963): 34, 455-
       461.
       Also *Reformatio* (1963): 12, 131-137.

2202. Knudsen, Lillian Catherine. "The Problem of God in
       the Early Writings of Pierre Teilhard de Chardin."
       Doctoral dissertation, Graduate Theological Union,
       Berkeley, Cal., 1973.

2203. Köberle, Adolf. "Mundum amare in Deo." *Acta teilhard-
       iana* (1971): 1, 32-36.

2204. Kobler, John. "The Priest Who Haunts the Catholic
       World." *Saturday Evening Post,* October, 1963.
       "Teilhard sera excomungado?" *A turbina* (1964):
       8, 3-4.

2205. Koenig, Franz. "Les tâches de l'intellectuel catho-
       lique dans le monde d'aujourd'hui." *Union catho-
       lique des scientifiques français* (1961): 63, 17-18.

2206. Koenigswald, G.H.R. "De visie van Teilhard de Chardin op de evolutie van het leven." Typescript. Paris: Fondation Teilhard de Chardin, 1961.

2207. Kolakowski, Leszek. "Szanse Teilharda--szanse chrzescijaństwa." *Argumenty* (1965): 10.
"Chances de Teilhard--chances du christianisme." *Perspectives polonaises* (1965): 6, 29-32
"Teilhard--A Chance for Christianity." *Polish Perspectives* (1965): 6, 27-30.

2208. Kopp, Josef Vital. "Entstehung und Zukunft des Menschen. Pierre Teilhard de Chardin und sein Weltbild." *Arzt und Christ* (1961): 7, 19-29. Summary of Item 2211.

2209. ————. "Pierre Teilhard de Chardin--Naturwissenschaftler und Theologe." *Der Pflug* (1966): 15, 14-17.

2210. ————. "Der Streit um Teilhard de Chardin." *Civitas* (1961-62): 17.

2211. ————. *Teilhard de Chardin.* Tielt: Lannoo, 1961. Also 6th ed., 1966.
Entstehung und Zukunft des Menschen. Pierre Teilhard de Chardin und sein Weltbild. Luzern-München: Rex-Verlag, 1961.
Origen y futuro del hombre. Pierre Tielhard de Chardin y su concepción del mundo. Barcelona: Herder, 1964.
Teilhard de Chardin Explained. Glen Rock, N.J.: Paulist Press, 1964.
Also Cork: Mercier Press, 1965.

2212. ————. "Teilhard de Chardin: Eine Übersicht." *Civitas* (1964-65): 20, 526-529.

2213. Kornacki, Jerzy. "Orfeusz." *Znak* (1960): 2/3, 281-292.

2214. Korvin-Krasinski, Cyrill von. "Rehabilitation der Materie. Ein fernöstlicher Beitrag zur Teilhardschen 'Religion der Zukunft.'" *Perspektiven der Zukunft* (1971): 3, 5-8; 4, 2-5.

2215. Kosa, J. "The Phenomenon of Teilhard de Chardin." *Humanist* (1967): 27, 16-18.

2216. Kościuch, Jan. "Sympozjum teilhardowskie." *Życie i myśl* (1967): 2, 27-46; 11/12, 163-169; (1968): 6/7, 176-182; 9, 113-117.

2217. Kovalevsky, Eugraphe. "L'oeuvre de Teilhard de Chardin et la pensée orthodoxe." *Revue Teilhard de Chardin* (1962): 10, 16-18.

2218. Kowalski, Jerzy. "Antropologia Ks. Piotra Teilharda de Chardin." [Father Teilhard de Chardin's Anthropology.] *Zeszyty Naukowe Katholickiego Uniwersytetu Lubelskiego* (1967): 3, 82-84.

2219. Kozlowski, Jan. "Kosmologia Teilharda de Chardin. Próba krytycznej rekonstrukcji." [Teilhard de Chardin's Cosmology. Attempt at a Critical Reconstruction.] *Czlowiek i Światopoglad* (1971): 12, 76-99.

2220. ――――. "Teilhard de Chardin--poglądy na fizyke i kosmologia (Próba krytycznej rekonstrukcji)." [Teilhard de Chardin: Viewpoints on Physics and Cosmology. Attempt at a Critical Reconstriction.] *Filozoficzne problemy wspólczesnego chrześijaństwa*. [Philosophical Problems of Contemporary Christianity.] Warszawa: Państwowe Wydawnictwo Naukowe, 1973, pp. 99-134.

2221. Kraft, R. Wayne. *The Relevance of Teilhard*. Notre Dame, Ind.: Fides, 1968.

2222. ――――. *Symbols, Systems, Science, and Survival: A Presentation of the Systems Approach from a Teilhardian Perspective*. New York: Vantage, 1975.

2223. ――――. "The World's Energy and Teilhard's Vision." *America*, December 15, 1973, pp. 457-460.

2224. Kramlinger, T. "The Salvation of the Natural World in the Thought of Teilhard de Chardin." *Michigan Academician* (1974): 6, 313-320.

2225. Krariec, Mieczslaw Albert. "Aspekty filozoficzne teorii ewolucji." [Philosophical Aspects of the Theory of Evolution.] *Znak* (1960): 72, 776-801.

2226. Krasinski, Andrzej. "W poszukiwaniu senu ewolucji świata." [Regarding Research on the Understanding of Cosmic Evolution.] *Kierunki*, September 23, 1956.

2226a. Krekhovetsky, Yakiv. "The Concept of Divinization: Theological Usage Before Teilhard de Chardin." *The Teilhard Review* (1978): 13, 112-119. Excerpt from Item 2227.

2227. ————. "Evolution and Divinization: The Orientation of Man to Perfection and His Divinization in the Thought of Pierre Teilhard de Chardin." Doctoral Dissertation, Institute of Christian Thought, St. Michael's College, University of Toronto, 1973.

2228. Kremmeter, Anton-Franz. "Evolution-Faktizität und historischer Ablauf." *Acta teilhardiana* (1967): 4, 16-34.

2229. ————. "Der Mensch im Kosmos. Rekonstruktion des Teilhardschen Werkes." *Philosophia naturalis* (1969): 11, 454-473.

2230. ————. "Teilhard de Chardin und die moderne Biologie." *Forschungen und Fortschritte* (1967): 41, 1-3.

2231. Kristof, L.K.D. "Teilhard de Chardin and the Communist Quest for a Space Age World View." *Russian Review* (1969): 28, 277-288.

2232. Kroeger, Heinrich. "Teilhard de Chardin en de natuurwetenschap." *Rekenschap* (1962): 9, 162-167.

2233. Krone, Sebald. "Zu Teilhard de Chardins Weltbild." *Wissenschaft und Weisheit* (1965): 28, 132-135.

2234. Kropf, Richard W. "Christogenesis. A Study of Teilhard de Chardin's Reinterpretation of Pauline Themes." Doctoral dissertation, St. Paul University, Ottawa, 1972.

2235. ————. "Ecumenism and Convergence: Teilhard de Chardin's Plan for Christian Reunion." *Journal of Ecumenical Studies* (1975): 12, 69-77.

2236. ————. "Teilhard, Pacifism and Gandhi." *The Teilhard Review* (1976): 11, 23-26.

2237. Krutch, Joseph Wood. "A Beggar in the Past, a Pilgrim of the Future." *New York Times*, July 8, 1962.

182   Works About Teilhard de Chardin

2238. Kubeck, John C. "Teilhard de Chardin Revisited." *Homiletic and Pastoral Review* (1969): 69, 370-376.

2239. Kubilius, Jonas. "Teilhard de Chardin." *Laiskai Lietuviams* (1965); 16, 364-371.

2240. Kuhn, Wolfgang. "Teilhard de Chardin und die Biologie." *Stimmen der Zeit* (1963): 172, 346-363.

2241. ————. "Teilhard de Chardin y el materialismo dialectico. ¿Ciencia o metafísica?" *Estudios Centroamericanos* (1964): 19, 4-8.

2241a. Kulisz, Jozef. "Eucharystia sakramentem wcielenia w ujęciu Teilharda de Chardin." [The Eucharist as the Sacrament of Incarnation in Teilhard de Chardin's Vision.] *Collectanea theologica* (1978): 48, 69-77.

2242. ————. "Kościół jako konsekwencja wcielenia wedlug Teilharda de Chardin." [The Church as a Consequence of the Incarnation According to Teilhard de Chardin.] *Collectanea theologica* (1977): 1, 5-16.

2243. Kunz, Wilhelm. "Christlicher Glaube und chinesisches Denken in der Sicht von Liebnitz, veglichen mit Teilhard de Chardin." *Perspektiven der Zukunft* (1971): 4, 5-7.

2244. ————. "Das Denken des Fernen Ostens in der Sicht Teilhard de Chardins." *Perspektiven der Zukunft* (1967): 3, 4-8.

2245. ————. "Jenseit des Positivismus. Heisenberg und Teilhard de Chardin." *Perspektiven der Zukunft* (1970): 3, 6-7.

2246. ————. "Ein Marxist sieht Teilhard de Chardin." *Der christliche Sonntag* (1965): 18, 376+.

2247. ————. "Persons und Gemeinschaft bei Teilhard de Chardin." *Evolution*. Stuttgart: E. Klett, 1970, pp. 186-205.

2248. ————. "Teilhard und die Sowjetphilosophie." *Perspektiven der Zukunft* (1971): 2, 2-3.

2249. ————. "Vom Göttlichen Bereich zum christlichen.
Züge des Teilhardschen Christusbildes." *Perspektiven
der Zukunft* (1969): 2, 2-3.

2250. Kurth, G. "Evolutionstheorie, Abstammungsgeschichte,
Anthropologie. Neues Schriftum." *Münchener medizinische Wochenschrift* (1965): 107, 2140+.

2251. Kurtz, Waldemar. "Teilhard und die Begründung des
Priesterzölibats." *Perspektiven der Zukunft* (1972):
6, 3-5. See Item 1903.

2252. Kuruthukulangara, Peter. "Teilhard's Urge for Unity."
Caritas (1971-72): 39, 48-51.

2253. Kurylas, B. "Le Père Teilhard de Chardin." *Lohos* 1961,
12, 48-61.

2254. Kushner, Eva. "Tresmontant on Teilhard de Chardin."
Revue de l'Université d'Ottawa (1965): 35, 100-106.

2255. Kusíc, Ante. "Suvremeni kršćanin u viziji Teilharda de
Chardina." [The Contemporary Christian in Teilhard
de Chardin's Vision.] *Crkva u svijetu* (1966): 3,
31-45; 4, 21-31.

2256. Kuzmickas, B.P. "Tejardizmas ir mėginimai atnaujinti
katalikybe." [Teilhardism and Attempts to Renew
Catholicism.] *Komunistas* (1971): 1, 69-72.

2257. ————. "Tejaro de Šardeno krikcioniskasis evoliu-
cionizmas." [The Christian Evolutionism of Teilhard
de Chardin.] *Problemos* (1971): 1, 60-69.

2258. Laberge, Jacques. *Pierre Teilhard de Chardin et Ignace
de Loyala. Les notes de retraite (1919-1955)*. Paris:
Desclée de Brouwer, 1973.
*Da angústia à visão (Oração inaciana de Teilhard
de Chardin)*. São Paulo: Loyola, 1975.

2259. ————. "Teilhard de Chardin et les Exercises spir-
ituels de saint Ignace." Doctoral thesis, Institut
Catholique de Paris, 1971.

2260. Laborit, H. *Du soleil à l'homme. L'organisation
énergétique des structures vivantes*. Paris: Masson,
1963.

2261. Labourdette, Michel. "L'oeuvre du Père Teilhard de
       Chardin." *Revue thomiste* (1964): 403-436; (1967):
       263-290.

2262. Lachance, L. "Teilhard de Chardin e as grandes correntes
       do pensamento contemporâneo." *Symposium* (1968): 8,
       7-18.

2263. Lachenmann, Hans. "Der Griff in den Kosmos." *Christ
       und Welt* (1965): 18, 12+.

2264. ———. *Hoffnung oder Illusion? Die Frage nach der
       Zukunft im Werk Teilhard de Chardins.* Konstanz:
       Bahn, 1965.

2265. ———. "Die innerkatholische Kontroverse um das Werk
       Pierre Teilhard de Chardins." *Materialdienst des
       Konfessionkundlichens Instituts* (1965): 16, 21-29.

2266. ———. "Von Alpha bis Omega. Teilhard de Chardin."
       Deutsches Pfarrerblatt (1963): 63, 129-133.

2267. Lacocque, Jean. "Réflexions d'un pasteur." *Revue Teil-
       hard de Chardin* (1963): 16, 7-16.

2268. Lacout, Pierre. "The Religious Experience of Teilhard
       de Chardin." *Friends' Quarterly* (1967): 15, 486-496,
       545-551.

2269. Lacroix, Jean. *L'échec.* Paris: Presses Universitaires
       de France, 1964. See pp. 70-74.

2270. ———. "La philosophie. Teilhard et le drame humain."
       Le Monde, May 7-8, 1967, p. 17.

2271. ———. *Le sens de l'athéisme moderne.* Liège: CCIB,
       1956.

2272. Ladrière, J. "Teilhard de Chardin." *Le Vaillant* (1965):
       44, 3.

2273. Ladrille, G. "Le R.P. Teilhard de Chardin et l'énergie
       spirituelle de la matière." *Salesianum* (1966): 28,
       383-411.

2274. La Farge, John. "The Divine Milieu." *America*, November
       12, 1960, pp. 224-227.

2275. ———. "Preface." Item 1544, pp. 3-6.

2276. Lafargue, F. "La phenomenologie du P. Teilhard de Chardin: Quelques précisions sur un des aspects de sa pensée, à propos de 'Un sommaire de ma perspective phénomenologique du monde.'" *Les études philosophiques* (1955): 4, 582-591.

2277. La Fay, Georges. *La montée de conscience. Essai de synthèse de la pensée de Teilhard de Chardin.* Paris: Éditions ouvrières, 1964. *Teilhard de Chardin. Síntesis de su pensamiento.* Salamanca: Sígueme, 1967.

2278. Lafitte, Jacques. "Construire une terre vivante." *Revue Teilhard de Chardin* (1962): 11, 10-16. Also *Industrie* (1960): 3, 150-154.

2279. ———. "Teilhard de Chardin et le machinisme." Item 741, pp. 145-157.

2280. Lainey, Y. "Teilhard de Chardin as Witness of His Age." *Theoria* (1965): 25, 33-40.

2281. La Maya, Jacques. "Os grandes temas teilhardianos e alegria criadora do artista." *A tarde*, January 25 and February 4, 1967.

2282. Lambert, Jean. "La liberté: dilemme et option." Item 741, pp. 121-132.

2283. ———. "La socialisation dans l'oeuvre de Pierre Teilhard de Chardin." Typescript. Faculté des lettres et sciences humaines de l'Université de Paris, 1964.

2284. Lambilliotte, Maurice. "Désaliénation de la conscience." *Revue Teilhard de Chardin* (1967): 30, 40-44.

2285. ———. "D'où venons-nous? Où allons-nous?" *Revue Teilhard de Chardin* (1971): 47/48, 14-15.

2286. ———. "Du sens du divin." *Revue Teilhard de Chardin* (1961): 5, 15-19.

2287. ———. "Une étape de haute libération." *Synthèses* (1955): 305-318.

2288. ────. "Évolution et création." *Synthèses* (1955): 345-
354.

2289. ────. "La fonction de la conscience." *Univers* (1965):
2, 17-22.

2290. ────. "L'homme en déséquilibre." *Synthèses* (1957):
134, 133-138.

2291. ────. "Le Père Teilhard de Chardin, prophète de l'évolution." *Synthèses* (1955): 108/109, 5-17.

2292. ────. "Se garder à tout prix du racisme." *Revue
Teilhard de Chardin* (1964): 19, 24-26.

2293. ────. "Teilhard de Chardin, l'ardent...." *Revue
Teilhard de Chardin* (1961): 8/9, 5-7.

2294. ────. "Teilhard figure de proue de notre temps."
Revue Teilhard de Chardin (1962): 10, 21-22.

2295. Lamouche, André. *Rhythmologie universelle et métaphys-
ique de l'harmonie. I. De la science à la métaphys-
ique.* Paris: Dunod, 1966. See pp. 292-305.

2296. Lanceau, Geneviève. "Une vue chrétienne des fins de
l'éducation." *Cahiers de Neuilly*, October, 1962.
pp. 3-11.

2297. Land, Philip. "What is Development? Questions Raised
for Theological Reflection." *Gregorianum* (1969): 1,
33-62.

2298. Landucci, Pier Carlo. "Pierre Teilhard de Chardin."
Miti e realtà. Roma: La Roccia, 1968, pp. 7-118.
Contains Items 2299-2303.

2299. ────. "Pierre Teilhard de Chardin: Aberrazioni te-
ologiche." *Palestra del clero* (1964): 43, 1193-1214.
Also in Item 2298.

2300. ────. "Pierre Teilhard de Chardin: Fantasie offensive
della società scientifica." *Palestra del clero* (1964):
43, 605-621.
Also in Item 2298.

2301. ────. "S. Paolo e Teilhard de Chardin." *Palestra
del clero* (1967): 46, 411-415.
Also in Item 2298.

2302. ———. "Teilhard de Chardin: Un santo! Il sesso in Teilhard de Chardin." *Palestra del clero* (1967): 46, 673-679.
Also in Item 2298.

2303. ———. "Teilhardiana." *Palestra del clero* (1967): 46, 339-343.
Also in Item 2298.

2303a. ———. "La verità sul 'sinantropo.'" *Palestra del clero* (1978): 57, 1008-1014.

2304. Lange, Daniel de. "De Gedachtenwereld van Teilhard de Chardin." *Wijsgerig perspectief op maatschappij en wetenschap* (1960-61): 1, 179-191.

2305. Langer, Roger. "Das religiöse Christusbild bei Teilhard de Chardin." *Vom Berge unserer lieben frau* (1966): 29, 99-122.

2306. Langer, Wolfgang. "Pierre Teilhard de Chardin. Vertrauen zum Kosmos." *Das Wagnis mit der Welt*, ed. by Otto Betz. München: Pfeiffer, 1965, pp. 25-37.

2306a. Langlois, Jean. "Teilhard de Chardin et Ignace de Loyola. La spiritualité de Teilhard dans les dernières années de sa vie." *Cahiers de spiritualité ignatienne* (1978): 2, 76-86.

2307. ———. "Teilhard et la cosmologie." *Sciences ecclesiastiques* (1964): 2, 321-349.

2308. ———. "Teilhard et la philosophie." *Dialogue* (1964-65): 3, 341-352.

2309. ———. "La terre 'village global' d'après Pierre Teilhard de Chardin et Marshall McLuhan." *La communication*. Montréal: Montmorency: 1971, pp. 332-339.

2310. Lanning, Bill Lester. "Man in Progress: The Religious and Political-Social Future of Man According to the Thoughts of Sri Aurobindo Ghose and Pierre Teilhard de Chardin, a Comparative Analysis." Doctoral dissertation, Baylor University, 1976.

2311. Lapparent, Fr. "Hommage au Père Teilhard de Chardin." *Recherches et débats* (1955): 12, 149-173.

2312.   Lara Guittard, A.   "En torno a Teilhard de Chardin."
        Arbor (1962): 53, 86-87.

2312a. L'Archevêque, Paul.   "Index nominum pour l'ensemble des
        oeuvres publiées."   Item 4385, pp. 247 ff.

2313.   ———. *Teilhard de Chardin. Index anayltique.*   Québec:
        Presses de l'Université Laval, 1967.

2314.   ———. *Teilhard de Chardin. Nouvel index
        analytique.*   Québec: Presses de l'Université
        Laval, 1972.

2315.   ———. "Vertige de l'humain."   In *L'éducation dans
        Québec en évolution.*   Québec: Presses de l'Université
        Laval, 1966, pp. 49-73.

2316.   L'Arco, Adolfo. *Messaggio di Teilhard de Chardin. Intu-
        izioni e idee madri.*   Torino: Elle di Ci Leumann, 1964.

2317.   Las Vergnas, Georges.   "Encore Teilhard!"   *Le courrier
        rationaliste* (1960): 8, 177-185.

2318.   Latour, Hans.   "Evolution, göttliche Dimension und per-
        sonale Sozialisation im Denken Teilhards de Chardin
        und ihre Bedeutung für die pädagogische Praxis."
        Photocopy. Dissertation in the Pädagogischen Hoch-
        schule Rheinland, 1976.
        Das pädagogische Denken Teilhards de Chardin.
        Frankfurt-am-Main: P. Lang, 1977.

2319.   Laudadio, Leonard.   "Teilhard de Chardin on Technolog-
        ical Progress."   *Review of Social Economy* (1973):
        31, 167-178.

2320.   Lauff, John G.   "Teilhard de Chardin and Freedom."
        Existential Psychiatry (1969): 7, 122-124.

2321.   Laurendeau, Louis.   "L'ottimismo di Teilhard davanti
        al mondo moderno."   *Bolletino informazioni del Centro
        di studi e di recerca Teilhard de Chardin, Istituto
        Stensen* (1972): 10, 1-10.
        "L'ottimismo di Teilhard di fronte al mondo moderno."
        Incontri (1972): 2, 5-9.

2322.   Laurette, P.   "Paul Valéry et Teilhard de Chardin."
        Revue des sciences humaines (1968): 33, 41-58.

2323. Lavallard, J.L. "L'hybridation de l'ADN aidera-t-elle à comprendre l'évolution." *Le Monde*, June 11, 1964, p. 11.

2324. Lawler, Justus G. "Chardin and Human Knowledge." *Commonweal* (1958): 68, 40-49.

2325. Lay, Rupert. "Komplexität und Bewusstsein." *Acta teilhardiana* (1969): 6, 64-68.

2326. ————. *Der neue Glaube an die Schöpfung.* Olten/Freiburg-im-Breisgau: Walter-Verlag, 1971. See pp. 59-87, 134-175.

2327. Lazard, Didier. "La convergence actuelle des civilisations." Item 3917, pp. 1-11.

2328. ————. "Energie universelle et action humaine." *Univers* (1965): 2, 23-31.

2329. ————. "Plénitude de l'homme et pluralité des civilisations." *Revue Teilhard de Chardin* (1963): 15, 5-6.

2330. ————. "Un seul esprit, un seul amour." *Univers* (1966): 3, 25-31.

2331. ————. "Supériorité de certaines races?" *Revue Teilhard de Chardin* (1964): 19, 19-20.

2332. ————. "Vers la convergence des civilisations." *Univers* (1964): 1, 49-56.

2333. Lazo de Conover, Luz. *El universo de Teilhard de Chardin.* México: Citlaltépetl, 1968.

2334. Lazzarini, Renato. "L'apriori gnoseologico e la noogenesi teilhardiana." *Evoluzionismo e storia umana.* Brescia: Morcelliana, 1968, pp. 131-150.

2335. ————. "Lo status transnaturale dell'umanità e l'evoluzionismo convergente." *Accademia delle scienze dell-'Istituto di Bologna, Memorie* (1963): ser. 5; 11, 161-197.

2336. ————. "Tre osservazioni sulla cristologia di Teilhard." *Bolletino informazioni del Centro di studi e di recerca Teilhard de Chardin* (1973): 15, 2-8;

2337. Leahy, Louis J. "Présentation." Item 3036, pp. 1-13.

2338. Leal, José Tarcisio. "Uma via para a comprensão de Teil-
       hard." *Convivium* (1965): 3, 55-65.

2339. Leary, Daniel J. *Voices of Convergence*. Milwaukee:
       Bruce, 1969.

2340. ――――. "Voices of Convergence: Teilhard, McLuhan and
       Brown." *Catholic World* (1966-67): 1222, 206-211.
       Also Item 607, pp. 118-127.

2341. Le Blond, Jean Marie. "Consacrer l'effort humain."
       Études (1958): 296, 58-68.
       Also *Civitas* (1958): 13, 427-435.

2342. ――――. "Mise en garde contre le P. Teilhard de Char-
       din." *Études* (1962).

2343. ――――. "Le sens religieux de l'oeuvre du P. Teilhard
       de Chardin." *Études* (1962): 7/8, 122-124.

2344. ――――. "Veillées sur la vue du monde selon le P. Teil-
       hard de Chardin." Typescript. Paris: Fondation Teil-
       hard de Chardin, 1955.

2345. Leclerc, Thomas. "Comparative Religion." *Cross Cur-
       rents* (1963): 4, 495-496.

2346. ――――. "The Future of Man." *Cross Currents* (1964):
       4, 475-477.

2347. ――――. "Marriage in Evolution." *Marriage* (1965):
       47, 7-14.

2348. ――――. "Teilhard de Chardin Today." *Twentieth Cen-
       tury* (1963-64): 5, 217-223.

2349. Lecomte du Noüy, Mary. "Lettre au P. Teilhard de Char-
       din, New York, 9 septembre 1947." Item 1259, p. 22.
       See Item 4549.

2350. Lecourt, J. *Carl Gustav Jung et Pierre Teilhard de
       Chardin. Leur combat pour la sante de l'âme*. Dam-
       martin-en-Goële: Institut Coué, 1970.

2351. Lee, Bernard. *Becoming of the Chruch: A Process The-
       ology of the Structure of Christian Experience*. New
       York: Paulist Press, 1974.

2352. Leenhardt, J. "Défense de Teilhard de Chardin." *Reforme*, December 11, 1965, p. 6.

2353. Lefebvre, Marcel. "Le 'Christ universel' d'après Teilhard." *Revue Teilhard de Chardin* (1971): 47/48, 31-43.

2354. ————. "Existence chrétienne d'après 'Le milieu divin.'" Item 3935, pp. 33-51.

2355. ————. "Incidences religieuses de la synthèse teilhardienne." Item 3935, pp. 13-31.

2356. ————. "Une mystique de la science et du progrès selon Teilhard." *Culture* (1969): 30, 27-44.

2357. ————. "Le vouloir de participation dans la construction du monde." *Dialogue* (1969-70): 8, 195-214.

2358. Lefevre, Charles. "Sur la méthode de Teilhard." *Revue nouvelle* (1967): 45, 184-202.

2359. ————. "Teilhard aujourd'hui et demain." *Revue nouvelle* (1965): 42, 446-467.

2360. ————. "Teilhard et notre dialogue avec le monde." *Revue diocésaine de Tournai* (1965): 20, 219-235.

2361. ————. "Thèmes philosophiques dans les études teilhardiennes." *Revue philosophique de Louvain* (1975): 73, 368-389.

2362. Le Fevre, Georges. *Le Crosière Jaune*. Paris: Plon, 1952.

2363. Lefevre, Luc J. "La cosmologie du 'Phénomène humain' et les sciences." *Pensée catholique* (1957): 52, 23-31.

2364. ————. "Jean Rostand et Teilhard de Chardin." *Pensée catholique* (1965): 98, 62-67.

2365. ————. "Personne humaine et teilhardienne." *Pensée catholique* (1963): 87, 76-95.

2366. Lefevre, Perry. "Teilhard's Vision of Man." *Chicago Theological Seminary Register* (1964): 4, 1-9.

2367.   Légaut, Marcel. "L'itinéraire spirituel du Père Teil-
        hard de Chardin." *Cahiers universitaires catholiques*
        (1966): 1, 36-43.

2368.   ————. "La spiritualité de Teilhard." *Cahiers littér-
        aires* (1965): 13, 8-10.

2369.   Léger, Bernard. "L'avenir de l'homme et du monde." In
        Item 3237.

2370.   ————. "Nos raisons de vivre et d'espérer, ou essai
        de résumé de la doctrine du P. Teilhard de Chardin."
        Bâtir la République, November, 1959.

2371.   ————. "Teilhard face aux problemes essentiels." *Re-
        vue Teilhard de Chardin* (1963): 15, 13-16.

2372.   Léger, Paul-Émile. *Les origines de l'homme.* Montréal:
        Fides, 1961.

2373.   Legros, Clark. "The Reverend Pierre Teilhard de Char-
        din." *Nature* (1955): 4462, 795.

2374.   Le Guillou, M.-J. "Comment redécouvrir le mystère du
        Christ." *La Croix*, February 18, 1967, p. 7.

2375.   ————. "Une étude d'A. Feuillet. Teilhard et l'exé-
        gèse paulinienne." *Le Monde*, February 11, 1967, p. 11.

2376.   Lehman, Jean-Pierre. "Allocution." Item 1257, pp.
        48-52.

2377.   Lehmann, Eduard. "Pierre Teilhard de Chardin." *Die
        Schulwarte* (1965): 18, 290-297.

2378.   Le Lionnais, François. "La révolution relativiste."
        Item 1259, pp. 77-83.

2379.   ————. "Vers l'unité dans les sciences physiques?"
        Item 1259, pp. 83-85.

2380.   Lemaître, Solange. "Deux lettres de Teilhard de Char-
        din." *Revue de Paris*, December, 1964, pp. 149-150.

2381.   ————. "In Memoriam." Item 3292, pp. 151-158.

2382.   ————. "Louis Massignon." *Ecclesia* (1965): 200, 37-
        48.

2383. Le Morvan, Michael. *Pierre Teilhard de Chardin: Priest and Evolutionist*. London: Catholic Truth Society, 1965.

2384. ————. "Teilhard the Man." *Catholic Herald*, December 1, 1969, p. 9.

2385. Le Moyne, Jean. "Message du Canada." Item 3292, pp. 129-136.

2386. ————. "Teilhard ou la réconciliation." *Convergences*. Montréal: Éditions HMH, 1961, pp. 187-194.

2387. Lenicque, Pierre. "Kristus Pantokrator enligt Teilhard de Chardin." [Christ Pantokrator According to Teilhard de Chardin.] *Lumen*. *Katolsk teologisk tidskrift* (1961-62): 5, 48-66.

2388. ————. "Pierre Teilhard de Chardin och Sven Silén." [Pierre Teilhard de Chardin and Sven Silen.] *Var Lösen* (1961): 52, 218-225.

2389. Léon-Dufour, Michel. "Fiche sur les théories du Père Teilhard de Chardin et conclusions personnelles sur une idéologie possible comme base de l'action psychologique." *Contacts* (1959): 7, 133-141.

2390. ————. "Remerciement de M. Léon-Dufour, élu mainteneur, prononcé en séance publique le 13 janvier 1974." *Receuil de l'Académie des jeux floraux* (1974): 127-140.

2391. ————. *Teilhard de Chardin et le problème de l'avenir humain. Essai de vulgarisation des idées du Père Teilhard de Chardin*. Toulouse: Imprimerie des Capitouls, 1966.
    Also 1968.
    Teilhard de Chardin e o problema do futuro humano. Ensaio de vulgarização das ideias do Padre Teilhard de Chardin. Lisboa: Livraria Morais, 1966.
    Teilhard de Chardin y el problema del porvenir humano. Madrid: Taurus, 1968.

2392. Le Page, Jacques. "Regards sur l'oeuvre du Père Teilhard de Chardin." *Le Bayou* (1959): 77, 303-305.

2393. Lepargneur, Francisco H. "A ética de Teilhard de Chardin." *Convivium* (1965): 3, 39-54.

2394. ————. "Místico e sábio P. Teilhard de Chardin, 1881-
       1955." *Revista ecclesiastica brasiliera* (1964): 24,
       606-638.

2395. Lepp, Ignace. "L'amour construit l'humanité." *Revue
       Teilhard de Chardin* (1967): 30, 6-15.

2396. ————. "Lobpreis des Weltalls." *Orientierung* (1961):
       25, 189-191.

2397. ————. "Nature de l'homme et morale naturelle." *Uni-
       vers* (1965): 2, 70-77.

2398. ————. *Die neue Erde, Teilhard de Chardin und das
       Christentum in der modernen Welt.* Olten/Freiburg-
       im-Breisgau: Walter-Verlag, 1962.
       Also Würzburg: Arena, 1968.
       *Teilhard de Chardin en het christendom in de moderne
       wereld.* Utrecht/Antwerpen: Spectrum, 1963.
       Teilhard et la foi des hommes. Paris: Éditions
       universitaires, 1963.
       *Shinseikai. Shi Teilhard de Chardin to waga kokoro
       no henreki.* Tokyo: Katsura Shobô, 1967.
       *The Faith of Men. Meditations Inspired by Teilhard
       de Chardin.* New York: Macmillan, 1967.

2399. ————. "Obstacles psychologiques à l'unification."
       Univers (1966): 3, 32-42.

2400. ————. "Qu'est-ce que l'athéisme de Jean Rostand?"
       Ecclesia, February, 1962, pp. 16-18.

2401. Leroi-Gourhan, J. "L'apparition de l'homme." Item
       3292, pp. 113-116.

2402. Le Roy, Édouard. *L'exigence idéaliste et le fait de
       l'évolution. Essai d'un philosophie première.* Paris:
       Presses universitaires de France, 1956.

2403. Leroy, Pierre. "Arriver au bout de lui-même." *Le
       Figaro littéraire*, September 17, 1960, p. 10.

2404. ————. "Le dimanche de Pâques 1955." *Revue Teilhard
       de Chardin* (1967): 33/34, 73-77.

2405. ————. "Hommage au Père Teilhard de Chardin." *Radio-
       Télévision catholique belge* (1965): 92, 2-3.

2406. ———. "L'Institut de géobiologie à Pékin, 1940-1946. Les dernières années du Père Teilhard de Chardin en Chine." *Anthropologie* (1965): 3/4, 360-367.

2407. ———. "Le message du Père Teilhard à la jeunesse." *Citadelle* (1963): 4, 5-7.

2408. ———. "Modifications biologiques imposées." *Revue Teilhard de Chardin* (1964): 18, 1-10.

2409. ———. "Le Père Licent." *Jésuites de l'assistance de France* (1956): 4, 11-16.

2410. ———. "Le Père Teilhard de Chardin." *Jésuites de l'assistance de France* (1955): 4, 20-27.

2411. ———. "Le Père Teilhard de Chardin. Aspects de sa vie intérieure." Typescript. Paris: Fondation Teilhard de Chardin, n.d.

2412. ———. "Pierre Teilhard de Chardin, homme de science." *Les cahiers Albert le Grand* (1964): 70, 51-64.

2413. ———. *Pierre Teilhard de Chardin tel que je l'ai connu.* Paris: Plon, 1958. Contains Item 4562.
Also *Revue Teilhard de Chardin* (1962): 11, 33-34.
Das Ja zur Erde. Pierre Teilhard de Chardin, Priester und Forscher. Wien/München: Herold, 1960.
Also 1962.
English version in Item 4603 trans., pp. 13-42.
Teilhard de Chardin nel ricordo di un amico. Brescia: Morcelliana, 1964.
"Pierre Teilhard de Chardin SJ zo als ik hem gekend heb." Item 3978, pp. 9-42.

2414. ———. "Teilhard de Chardin, mon ami." *Panorama chrétien* (1962): 60, 10-11.

2415. ———. "Vues d'un biologiste." *Revue Teilhard de Chardin* (1964): 19, 3.

2416. ———, and Louis Barjon. *La carrière scientifique de Pierre Teilhard de Chardin.* Monaco: Rocher, 1964.

2417. Leroy, Yveline. "Teilhard de Chardin." *Le trèfle. Revue de la Federation française des éclaireuses.* April, 1961, pp. 1-6.

2418. Lertora Mendoza, Celina Ana. "Persona y evolución. El
       desarrollo del ser personal en el pensamiento de Teil-
       hard de Chardin." *Arbor* (1975): 90, 457-460.

2419. Lescaze, Edmond. *De l'étoile à l'homme. Introduction
       à la pensée de Pierre Teilhard de Chardin.* Genève:
       Labor et Fides, 1959.

2420. Lessa, Almerino. "Uma visão espiritualista do fenómeno
       humano." Item 3917, pp. 87-110.
       "Une vision spiritualiste du phénomène humain."
       Revue Teilhard de Chardin (1964): 20/21, 20-23.

2421. Lessertisseur, J. "Réflexions sur l'évolutionisme de
       Pierre Teilhard de Chardin." *Bulletin trimestriel du
       service d'information géologique du bureau de recher-
       ches géologiques, géophysiques et minières* (1958):
       38, 6-10.

2422. Lestavel, Jean. "Teilhard de Chardin, les pierres et
       la terre." *Vie spirituelle* (1972): 126, 853-860.

2423. Levada, Iouri A. "'Fenomen Teilharda' i spory vokrug
       nego." [Discussions Concerning the Teilhard Phenom-
       enon.] *Voprosy filosofii* (1962): 153-155.
       "Vitak a 'Teilhardjelenseg' Izörül." *Világosság*
       (1962): 6, 38-40.

2424. ———. "Vera v človeka." *Nauka i Religija* (1966):
       10, 26-28.
       "Teilhard de Chardin en U.R.S.S.: Foi en l'homme."
       In Item 1259, pp. 132-140.
       "Der Glaube an der Menschen." *Perspektiven der
       Zukunft* (1968): 2, 4-6.

2425. Lévy, Louis. "'Le phénomène humain' de Pierre Teilhard
       de Chardin." *Les cahiers français* (1960), 49, 17-20.

2426. Lévy, Roger. "Hommage au Père Teilhard de Chardin."
       Politique étrangère (1955): 4, 389-392.

2427. Leys, Roger. "Convergences." *Univers* (1964): 1, 9-13.

2428. ———. "Un peu de science mène au racisme, beaucoup
       de science en éloigne." *Revue Teilhard de Chardin*
       (1964): 19, 24.

2429. ————. "Le point Omega." *Balisage* (1961): 16/17, 29-31.

2430. ————. "Questions et réponses au sujet de Teilhard de Chardin." *Revue Teilhard de Chardin* (1963): 16, 1-6.

2431. ————. "Une seule espèce biologique." *Revue Teilhard de Chardin* (1964): 19, 2.

2432. ————. "Teilhard dangereux?" *Bijdragen* (1963): 23, 1-20. Also in *Revue Teilhard de Chardin* (1963): 14, 20-35. "Is Teilhard Dangerous?" *Theology Digest* (1966): 1, 36-40.

2433. ————. "Teilhard de Chardin et le péché originel." Item 3851, pp. 175-205.

2434. ————. "Vers le point Omega." *Revue Teilhard de Chardin* (1971): 47/48, 28-30.

2435. L'Heritier, P. "Liberté et conditionnement biologique et génétique." *Union catholique des scientifiques français. Bulletin* (1966): 93, 29-40.

2436. Liam, Sr. "The Relevance of Teilhard de Chardin for Modern Man." *Dominicana* (1966): 51, 338-349.

2437. Liauzu-Bontemps, J. "La naissance de la civilisation d'après Platon et le Père Teilhard de Chardin." *Bulletin de l'Association Guillaume Budé* (1967): 2, 212-220.

2438. Number deleted.

2439. Ligneul, André. "De la mort de Dieu à la mort de l'homme." *Revue Teilhard de Chardin* (1969): 39, 14-30.

2440. "De la vision à l'action." *Revue Teilhard de Chardin* (1967): 27-39.

2441. ————. "Dialectique et convergence chez Teilhard de Chardin et Marx." *Univers* (1964): 1, 29-42.

2442. ————. "La dialectique spirituelle chez Teilhard." *Revue Teilhard de Chardin* (1971): 47/48, 1-12.

2443.   ————. "L'essentiel et le quotidien." *Revue Teilhard de Chardin* (1970): 44/45, 14-26.

2444.   ————. "La fin de l'histoire." *Revue Teilhard de Chardin* (1964): 20/21, 33-40.

2445.   ————. "L'idée d'évolution et la philosophie." *Perspectives* (1965): 24/25, 26-33.

2446.   ————. "Perspective christocentrique de Teilhard." *Perspectives* (1965): 22, 5-16.

2447.   ————. "Réflexions sur le sens de la temporalité chez Teilhard." *Revue Teilhard de Chardin* (1962): 13, 23-26.

2448.   ————. "Simples réflexions sur l'action." *Perspectives* (1965): 26, 7-13.

2449.   ————. *Teilhard de Chardin et l'unité du genre humain.* Lisboa: Instituto Superior de Ciencias Sociais e Política Ultramarina, 1965.

2450.   ————. "Teilhard éducateur de l'homme nouveau." *Univers* (1965): 2, 33-47.

2451.   ————. *Teilhard et le personnalisme.* Paris: Éditions Universitaires, 1964.
          Teilhard and Personalism. Glen Rock, N.J.: Paulist Press, 1968.
          Teilhard e o personalismo. Petrópolis: Vozes, 1968.
          Teilhard y el personalismo. Buenos Aires: Columba, 1968.

2452.   ————. "Teilhard l'inclassable?" *Revue Teilhard de Chardin* (1963): 17, 19-22.

2453.   ————. "Vouloir une terre totale." *Univers* (1966): 3, 43-54.

2454.   Linnerz, Heinz. "Denker an der Gefahrgrenze. Zum Werk von Pierre Teilhard de Chardin." *Natur und Geist* (1964): 17-28.

2455.   ————. "Grundlagen fur die Diskussion." *Echo der Zeit* (1961): 14, 14.

2456. Linssen, Robert. "Mystères atomiques et spiritualité de la matière." *Univers* (1964): 1, 15-27.

2457. ———. "La pensée de Teilhard de Chardin en Inde." *Rhythmes du monde* (1964): 12, 35-37.

2458. Lionel, Wilfred. "The Vision of Teilhard de Chardin." *Quest* (1966): 8, 230-235.

2459. Lischer, Richard. "From Earth to Heaven: Teilhard's Politics and Eschatology." *Christian Century*, April 9, 1975, pp. 352-357.

2459a. ———. *Marx and Teilhard: Two Ways to a New Humanity.* Maryknoll, N.Y.: Orbis, 1979.

2460. Livi, Antonio. "Étienne Gilson et Teilhard de Chardin." *Rumo* (1968): 12, 176-183.
"Étienne Gilson y Teilhard de Chardin." *Arco* (1968): 10, 176-183.
Also *Nuestro tiempo* (1969): 31, 129-136.

2461. Llano, Alonso. "Preámbulos para entender a Pierre Teilhard de Chardin SJ. El fenómeno humano en Teilhard de Chardin SJ." *Universitas* (1965): 29, 34-57.

2462. Llanos, José María de. "Teilhard y libertad de espíritu." *Hechos y dichos*, August/September, 1973, p. 43.

2463. Lobut, Paul. "Teilhard de Chardin kaj ties kosma vizio." *Monda kulturo* (1963-64): 6, 169-171.

2464. Locas, Clément. "Fondements teilhardiens d'une anthropologie chrétienne." Item 3935, pp. 117-154.

2465. Locatelli, Aldo. "Dio e il miracolo conoscibile al di là della scienza." *La scuola cattolica* (1963): 121.

2466. ———. "La mistica del Milieu divin nel quadro della sintesi teilhardiana e la fondazione scientifica." Item 2744, pp. 103-107.
"La mystique du Milieu divin dans le cadre de la synthèse teilhardienne et ses fondements scientifiques." Item 2744 trans., pp. 94-98.

2467. ———. "Il punto Omega di Teilhard de Chardin." *La scuola cattolica* (1962): 90, 99-114.

2468. ———. "Singularità di Cristo e cristologie evoluzioniste." *La scuola cattolica* (1975): 778-796.

2469. Locchi, Giorgio. "Con il crisma dottrinario di Teilhard
       de Chardin. Senza veli a Parigi il flirt tra i 'neo-
       cristiani' e i marxisti." *Il Tempo*, March 31, 1965,
       p. 3.

2470. Lochet, Louis. "L'optimisme chrétien du Père Teilhard
       de Chardin." *Fils de Dieu*. Paris: Cerf, 1963, pp.
       358-368.

2471. Lombardo Radice, Lucio. "L'uomo responsable dell'evo-
       luzione nel pensiero di Teilhard de Chardin." *Il di-
       alogo alla prova*. Firenze: Vallecchi, 1964, pp. 101-
       104.

2472. Londoño Ramos, C. Alonso. "La ley de la complejidad--
       conciencia en Teilhard de Chardin." *Franciscanum*
       (1970): 12, 281-332; (1971): 13, 3-33.

2473. ————. "¿Quién era Teilhard de Chardin?" *Revista
       javeriana* (1965): 63, 83-93.
       Also *Mensaje* (1965): 14, 90-98.
       Also *Estudios centroamericanos* (1965): 20, 194-201.

2474. Lönnqvist, Conrad. "Var kristna livssyn och etiken.
       Tillika nagra ord om Teilhard de Chardins bok 'Fenom-
       enet Människan.'" [Our Christian Life and Morality.
       Some Words About Teilhard de Chardin's Book, "The
       Phenomenon of Man."] *Religion och kultur* (1962):
       33, 33-43.

2475. López del Castillo, Manuel Carlos. *Del ateísmo a la
       fe*. Madrid: I.C.A.I., 1972.

2476. López-Méndez, Antonio. *Die Hoffnung im theologischen
       Denken Teilhard de Chardins. Hoffnung als Synthese:
       Versuch einer systematischen Darstellung*. Frankfurt-
       am-Main/Bern: Lang, 1976.

2477. López Sáez, Jesus. "El concepto evolutivo de la muerte
       en Teilhard de Chardin." *Verdad y vida* (1968): 26,
       475-506.

2478. López Salgado, Cesáreo. "Metafísica y creación en
       Teilhard de Chardin." *Sapienta* (1965): 275-289.

2479. López-Silva, Luis. "Contribution à l'étude de l'inter-
       prétation biologique du phénomène social humain selon
       Teilhard de Chardin." Mimeographed. Thesis, Univers-
       ity of Paris I, 1972.

2480. Lorés, Jaume. "El cas 'Teilhard.'" *Qüestions de vida cristiana* (1962): 13, 90-95.

2481. Losada, Joaquin. "El sentido teológico de la figura y de la obra de Pierre Teilhard de Chardin." Item 745, pp. 59-88.

2482. Loudot, P. "Teilhardisme et structuralisme." *Nouvelle revue théologique* (1970): 92, 1076-1085.

2483. Louis, Eugène. "'Pacem in terris.' Teilhard et l'évolution des principes." *Itinéraires* (1964): 79, 223-226.

2484. Louvet, Françoise. "L'avenir de la pensée de Teilhard." *Revue Teilhard de Chardin* (1963): 16, 27-28.

2485. ————. "La machine et l'enfant." *Revue Teilhard de Chardin* (1965): 22, 35-37.

2486. Lowith, Karl. "Pierre Teilhard de Chardin." *Philosophische Rundschau* (1962): 10, 187-208. Also *Der Aquädukt*, pp. 323-354. München: Beck, 1963.

2487. ————. "Teilhard de Chardin: Evolution, Fortschritt und Eschatologie." *Zur Kritik der christlichen Überlieferung*. Stuttgart: Kohlhammer, 1966, pp. 323-354.

2488. Lubac, Henri de. "L'apport de Teilhard à la connaissance de Dieu." Item 3903, pp. 193-214.

2489. ————. *Athéisme et sens de l'homme*. Paris: Cerf, 1968. See pp. 130-141.

2490. ————. "Autour de 'teilhardogenèse'?" *Pensée catholique* (1964): 89, 49-61.

2491. ————. "Defense d'un mort et de la verité. A propos de l'article de Ch. Journet." *Nova et vetera* (1958): 3, 223-230.

2492. ————. "Defense d'un mort et de la verité. A propos de l'article de L. Salleron." *Centre d'études politiques et civiques, dossier*, March 13, 1958, pp. 5-23.

2493. ————. "'Descente' et 'montée' dans l'oeuvre du Père Teilhard de Chardin." Item 4883, pp. 127-153. "'Absteigende Bewegung' und 'Aufsteigende Bewegung' im Werke von P. Teilhard de Chardin." *Theologisches Jahrbuch* (1969): 503-520.

2494. ———. "Du bon usage du 'Milieu divin.'" Mimeographed.
Paris: Fondation Teilhard de Chardin, n.d.

2495. ———. "Du monde à Dieu et au Christ dans l'oeuvre du
Père Teilhard de Chardin." *De Deo in philosophia S.
Thomae et in hodierna philosophia. VI Congressus
Thomisticus Internationalis, Acta.* Roma: Officium
libri catholici, 1966, vol. 7.
Also in Item 2514.
Also *Prière et vie* (1966): 141, 385-396.

2496. ———. "Envergure et limites du Père Teilhard de Chardin." *Choisir* (1965): 66, 19-20.

2497. ———. "Envergure et limites de l'oeuvre teilhardienne."
Item 4883, pp. 107-126.

2498. ———. "L'épreuve de la foi." Item 4569, pp. 33-47.
Also *Revue générale belge* (1965): 11, 1-18.

2499. ———. *L'eternel féminin. Étude sur un texte du Père
Teilhard de Chardin.* Paris: Aubier-Montaigne, 1968.
Bound with an edition of Item 2513.
Hymne an das Ewig Weibliche. Einsielden: Johannes-
Verlag, 1968.
El eterno femenino. Salamanca: Sígueme, 1969. Con-
tains translation of Item 2513.
L'eterno femminino. Da Teilhard de Chardin. Torino:
Marietti, 1969. Contains translation of Item 2513.
*The Eternal Feminine. A Study on the Poem by Teil-
hard de Chardin.* London: Collins, 1971. Contains
translation of Item 2513.
Also New York: Harper & Row, 1971.

2500. ———. *Images de l'Abbé Monchanin.* Paris: Aubier-
Montaigne, 1967.

2501. ———. "Maurice Blondel et le P. Teilhard de Chardin.
Mémoires échanges en décembre 1919." *Archives de
philosophie* (1961): 24, 123-156.

2502. ———. "'La mort en Dieu' de Teilhard de Chardin."
Ecclesia (1966): 212, 199-206.

2503. ———. "Note sur l'apologétique teilhardienne." Item
2507, pp. 143-222.

2504. ————. *La pensée religieuse du Père Teilhard de Chardin*. Paris: Aubier-Montaigne, 1962. Contains Items 4571, 4577.
Il pensiero religioso del Pierre Teilhard de Chardin. Brescia: Morcelliana, 1965.
Also 2d ed., 1967.
El pensamiento religioso de Teilhard de Chardin. Madrid: Taurus, 1967.
The Religion of Teilhard de Chardin. Paris: Desclée de Brouwer, 1967.
Also London: Collins, 1967.
Also New York: Harper & Row, 1967.
Also Garden City, N.Y.: Doubleday, 1968.
El pensament religiós de Teilhard de Chardin. Barcelona: Estela, 1968.
Teilhard de Chardins religiöse Welt. Freiburg: Herder, 1969.

2505. ————. "Le Père Teilhard de Chardin missionaire et disciple de saint Paul." *Spiritus* (1966): 26, 31-48.
Also in Item 2514.
"El Padre Teilhard de Chardin, misionero y discipulo de S. Pablo." *Hechos y dichos* (1966): 257-273.

2506. ————. "Le personnalisme du Père Teilhard de Chardin." *Bulletin de l'Union catholique des scientifiques français* (1961): 64, 3-11.

2507. ————. *La prière du Père Teilhard de Chardin*. Paris: Fayard, 1964. Contains Item 4558.
Also 2d ed., 1968.
La preghiera di padre Teilhard de Chardin. Brescia: Morcelliana, 1965.
Also 2d ed., 1966.
Also 3d ed., 1968.
The Faith of Teilhard de Chardin. London: Burns and Oates, 1965.
Teilhard de Chardin: The Man and His Meaning. New York: Hawthorn Books, 1965.
Le pregària de Teilhard de Chardin. Barcelona: Estela, 1965.
A oração de Teilhard de Chardin. Lisbon: Livraria Morais, 1965.
Der Glaube des Teilhards de Chardin. München: Herold, 1968.

2508. ————. "La prière du Père Teilhard de Chardin." *Ecclesia* (1963): 166, 27-37.

2509. ————. "Teilhard de Chardin credeva alla creazione?"
       Digest cattolico (1963): 4, 545-550.

2510. ————. "Teilhard de Chardin dans le contexte de re-
       nouveau." *Théologie de renouveau*. Paris: Cerf, 1968,
       vol. 2, pp. 165-187.
       "Teilhard de Chardin in the Context of Renewal."
       Theology of Renewal. New York: Herder and Herder,
       1968, vol. 1, pp. 208-235.
       "Teilhard de Chardin nel contesto del rinnovamento."
       Teologia del rinnovamento. Assisi: Cittadella, 1969,
       pp. 215-238.

2511. ————. "Teilhard de Chardin et Saint Paul." *Spiritus*
       (1966): 16, 31-48.
       "Teilhard de Chardin, misionár a učeník svätého
       Pavla." *Echo* (1973): 5, 14-31.

2512. ————. "Teilhard de Chardins Sicht des Todes." *Doku-
       mente* (1962): 18, 255-263.

2513. ————. *Teilhard et notre temps*. Paris: Aubier, 1971.
       For earlier edition and translations, see Item 2499.

2514. ————. *Teilhard missionaire et apologiste*. Toulouse:
       Prière et vie, 1966.
       Teilhard de Chardin missionario del nostro tempo.
       Brescia: Morcelliana, 1967.
       Teilhard en diálogo con el hombre de hoy. Zaragoza:
       Hechos y dichos, 1968.
       Teilhard Explained. New York: Paulist Press, 1968.
       *Teilhard de Chardin, Misionar und Wegbereiter des
       Glaubens*. Kevelaer: Butzon und Bercker, 1969.

2515. ————. *Teilhard posthume. Réflexions et souvenirs*.
       Paris: Fayard, 1977.

2516. ————. "Tradition et nouveauté dans la position du
       problème de Dieu chez le Père Teilhard de Chardin."
       *De Deo in philosophia S. Thomae et in hodierna philo-
       sophia. VI Congressus Thomisticus Internationalis,
       Acta*. Roma: Officium libri catholici, 1966, vol. 2,
       pp. 212-220.

2517. Lubnicki, Narcyz. "Czy metoda naukowa da sie pogodzić
       ze spekulacja mistyczna? Rzut oka na filosofie Teil-
       harda de Chardin." *Zagadnienia Naukoznastwa* (1969):
       4, 53-59.
       "Science et mystique sont-elles conciliables? (Le

cas Teilhard de Chardin)." *Akten des XIV. Internationalen Kongresses für Philosophie*. Wien: Herder, 1969, vol. 3, pp. 377-382.

2518. ⸺. "'Filozofia uniwersalna' Teilharda de Chardin." *Studia filosoficzne* (1969): 6, 3-54.
"'Universal Philosophy' of Teilhard de Chardin." *Dialectics and Humanism* (1973): 115-130.

2519. Lucchi, M.A. de. "Introduzione al pensiero scientifico di Pierre Teilhard de Chardin." *Questitalia* (1964): 70, 12-30.

2520. Luce, Henry R. "A Great Thinker's Joyful Vision: The Spiritual Perfection of Mankind." *Life*, October 16, 1964, p. 12.
Also *Catholic Digest*, February, 1965, pp. 32-34.

2521. Luckesi, C.C. "Teilhard de Chardin, sua interpretação da historia." *Revista brasiliera de filosofia* (1971): 21, 396-409.

2522. Lugosfalvi, Ervin. "A bün evolúciója--az evolíció büne. Teilhard de Chardin bünfogalmähoz." [The Evolution of Sin--The Sin of Evolution. Regarding the Concept of Sin in Teilhard de Chardin.] *Világosság* (1971): 12, 587-595.

2523. Luján, Nestor. "La obra de Teilhard de Chardin." *Glosa* (1960): 69, 23-24, 124.

2524. ⸺. "Le semana Teilhard." *Tele-exprés*, January 18, 1968.

2525. Lukács, József. "'Teremtö egyesüles.' A teilhardi 'union créatrice' és a történelem tendenciája." ["Creative Union." The "Creative Union" of Teilhard and the Tendency of History.] *Vigilia* (1973): 38, 583-585.
Also *Igent mondani az emberre*. [Saying Yes to Man.] Budapest: Magveto, 1973, pp. 351-358.

2526. Lukas, Mary. "Teilhard de Chardin: A Cathedral for the Wasteland." *Show* (1963): 12, 100-101, 162-163.

2527. ⸺, and Ellen Lukas. *Teilhard: The Man, the Priest, the Scientist. A Biography*. London: Collins, 1977.
Also New York: Doubleday, 1977.

2528.   Lupo, Valeria. "A colloquio con i lettori di Teilhard
        de Chardin." *Humanitas* (1967): 22, 440-474, 639-668,
        978-1013.

2529.   ————. "Alcune pubblicazioni intorno a Teilhard de
        Chardin." *Humanitas* (1964): 19, 710-722.

2530.   ————. "Continua la pubblicazione dei carteggi di
        Teilhard de Chardin." *Humanitas* (1970): 24, 1064-
        1073.

2531.   ————. "Dall'atomo all'avvenire dell'uomo. La visione
        mistica di Teilhard de Chardin." *Humanitas* (1973):
        28, 605-622.

2532.   ————. "Leggendo Teilhard de Chardin." *Rivista di
        pedagogia e di scienze religiose* (1970): 8, 43-69,
        289-307.

2533.   ————. "La mistica dell'incarnazione in Pierre Teil-
        hard de Chardin." *Humanitas* (1964): 19, 293-314.

2534.   ————. "Mistica ed esperienza in Teilhard de Chardin."
        Nuova antologia di lettre, arti e scienze (1963): 98,
        379-388.

2535.   ————. "La pubblicazione in Italia delle opere di Teil-
        hard de Chardin." *Humanitas* (1969): 24, 473-479.

2536.   Luyten, Norbert A. "Die Botschaft Teilhards an unsere
        Zeit." *Civitas* (1972-73): 28, 437-445.

2537.   ————. "Materie, Bewusstsein, Geist, in der Sicht
        Teilhard de Chardins." Item 3924, pp. 53-78.
        Also Item 2546, pp. 211-233.
        "Matière et esprit dans la pensée de Teilhard de
        Chardin." *Revue thomiste* (1967): 67, 226-247.

2538.   ————. "Die Materie, Quelle des Geistes? Das Entstehen
        des Geistes in der Evolution." Item 2035, pp. 117-140.

2539.   ————. "La méthode du Père Teilhard." Item 1015, pp.
        19-27.

2540.   ————. "Eine neue Synthese des Wissens? Teilhard de
        Chardin." *Heilpädagogische Werkblatter* (1963): 32,
        55-66.
        Also *Oberrheinisches pastoralblatt* (1964): 65, 321-330.
        Also Item 2546, pp. 178-190.

2541. ————. "Neuere Aspekte in der Anthropologie." *Menschenbild und Menschenführung* (1967): 15-34.

2542. ————. "Le Père Teilhard de Chardin (1881-1955)." *La Liberté*, April 17-18, 1965, pp. 19-20.
Also *Pax Romana Journal* (1965): 5, 14-16.

2543. ————. "Pierre Teilhard de Chardin vernieuwer van de wetenschap." *Sint Lucas tijdschrift* (1964): 2/4.

2544. ————. "Réflexions sur le méthode de Teilhard de Chardin." *Contributions to Logic and Methodology in Honor of I.M. Bochenski*, ed. by Anna Teresa Tumieniecka. Amsterdam: North Holland, 1965, pp. 290-314.
Also *Spectrum* (1968): 3, 2.
Also Item 2546, pp. 191-210.

2545. ————. *Schriften zur Naturphilosophie*. Freiburg: Universitätsverlag, 1969.

2546. ————. "Teilhard de Chardin." In his *Ordo rerum*, pp. 178-233. Freiburg: Universitätsverlag, 1969. Contains Items 2537, 2540, 2544.

2547. ————. "Teilhard de Chardin." *Pax Romana Journal* (1962): 4, 3-6.

2548. ————. *Teilhard de Chardin. Een neuwe weg van het weten?* Louvain: Nauwelerts, 1965.
Teilhard de Chardin. Nouvelles perspectives du savoir? Fribourg: Éditions Universitaires, 1965.
Teilhard de Chardin. Eine neue Wissenschaft. Freiburg-im-Breisgau/München: Karl Alber, 1966.

2549. ————. "Teilhard 1881-1955. Pour le dixième anniversaire de sa mort." *Spectrum* (1965): 2, 53-59.

2550. Luzzi, Jacinto. "El fenómeno del ateísmo moderno. Análisis en Teilhard de Chardin." *Stromata* (1976): 32, 289-381.

2551. ————. "La percepción del tiempo en Teilhard de Chardin." *Criterion* (1968): 41, 334-340.

2552. ————. "Teilhard de Chardin." *Estudios*, July, 1968, pp. 29-35.

2553. ———. "Teilhard de Chardin y el malestar de los teológicos." *Estudios* (1965): 92-98.

2554. ———. "Teilhard: Ser puente entre dos mundos."
Estudios, October, 1968, pp. 37-43.

2555. ———. "Teilhard y el fenómeno del ateísmo moderno."
Estudios, August, 1968, pp. 35-40.

2556. Lynch, William F. "In Admiration of Teilhard." *America*,
April 12, 1975, pp. 274-276.

2557. M.J.L. "Le cas de Teilhard de Chardin." *Le monde et
la vie* (1966): 162, 54.

2558. MacCormac, Earl. "Metaphysics and Metaphor." *Teilhard
Review* (1969): 1, 28-30.

2559. MacDonald, Sr. Matthew Anita. "Epistemological Dimensions of Process Philosophy in John Dewey and Pierre
Teilhard de Chardin: Implications for Education."
Doctoral dissertation, University of Pennsylvania,
1973.

2560. Maceina, Antanas. "Religija ir evoliucija. Kritinēs
pastabos Teilhard de Chardino pasaulēžiūrai."[Reli-
gion and Evolution. Critical Notes About Teilhard
de Chardin's Vision of the World.] *Aidai* (1968):
337-347, 406-410, 450-456. See Item 3047.

2561. MacGrath, Georges. "Pierre Teilhard de Chardin." *Précis analytique des travaux de l'Académie des sciences,
belles-lettres et arts de Rouen* (1971-1972): 27-56.

2562. Mache, Régis. "Science, culture et eschatologie: Ré-
flexions d'un scientifique sur Teilhard de Chardin."
Concilium (1968): 39, 101-108.
"Wissenschaft, Bildung und Eschatologie: Gedanken
eines Wissenschaftlers über Teilhard de Chardin."
Concilium (1968): 4, 694-699.
"Science, Culture and Eschatology: A Scientist's
Reflections on Teilhard de Chardin." *Concilium*
(1968): 9, 56-60.
"Ciencia, cultura y escatología: Reflexión de un
científico sobre Teilhard de Chardin." *Concilium*
(1968): 3, 457-466.
"Scienza, cultura ed escatologia: riflessione di
uno scienziato su Teilhard de Chardin." *Concilium*

(1968): 4, 1708-1717.
"Wetenschap, cultuur en eschatologie: Gedachten van een wetenschapmens over Teilhard de Chardin." *Concilium* (1968): 9, 105-113.
"Ciência, cultura e escatologia: Reflexões de um cientista sobre Teilhard de Chardin." *Concilium* (1968): 9, 101-109.

2563. Mackenzie, L. "Teilhard and Catholic Indifference." *Michael de la Bedoyere's Search* (1962): 1, 315-316.

2564. Mackey, J.P. "Teilhard de Chardin and Evolution." *Furrow* (1967): 18, 619-627.

2565. Mackinnon, D.M. "Teilhard de Chardin: A Comment on His Context and Significance." *Modern Churchman* (1962): 5, 195-199, 255-260.

2566. ———. "Teilhard's Achievement." Item 501, pp. 60-66. Also Item 497, pp. 60-66.

2567. ———. "Teilhard's Vision." *Frontier* (1965): 3, 169-171.

2568. Macquarrie, John. "The Natural Theology of Teilhard de Chardin." *The Expository Times* (1961): 71, 335-338. Also *Studies in Christian Existentialism*. London: SCM Press, 1966, pp. 182-193.

2569. Madaule, Jacques. "A propos de Teilhard. Batailles perdues?" *Le Monde*, July 12, 1962, p. 91.

2570. ———. "Claudel et Teilhard de Chardin." *Revue de Paris* (1962): 2, 85-95.

2571. ———. "Une existence parfaitement remplie." Item 3903, pp. 57-80.

2572. ———. "L'histoire de l'avenir." *Janus* (1964-65): 4, 11-17.

2573. ———. *Initiation à Teilhard de Chardin*. Paris: Cerf, 1963.
Teilhard de Chardin. Een eenste kennismaking met zijn leven en denken. Turnhout/Brussel: Brepols, 1964.
Teilhard de Chardin. Einführung in sein Leben und Denken. Osnabrück: Fromm, 1968.

2574. ———. "La pensée politique de Teilhard de Chardin." *France-forum* (1958): 11, 16-20.

2575. ———. "Réflexions sur la méthode et la perspective teilhardienne." *Les études philosophiques* (1966): 21, 510-532.

2576. ———. "La saisie de l'univers chez Teilhard de Chardin et Claudel." *Cahiers de vie franciscaine* (1963): 40, 51-57.

2577. ———. "Le sens d'une vie." *Europe* (1965): 431/432, 13-25.

2578. ———. "Teilhard de Chardin écrivain." *Cahiers littéraires* (1965): 13, 36-38.

2579. ———. "Teilhard de Chardin und das zeitgenössische französische Denken." *Perspektiven der Zukunft* (1967): 1, 2.

2580. ———. "Teilhard s'explique." *Témoignage chrétien* (1964): 23.

2581. Madiran, Jean. "Introduction." Item 1243, pp. 112-119.

2582. Magalhães, Vasco Pinto de. "A coerência dos fenómenos convergentes em Teilhard de Chardin." *Revista portuguesa de filosofia* (1972): 28, 241-283.

2583. Maggioni, Ernesto. "Fede e scienza per Teilhard de Chardin." *Protestantesimo* (1964): 19, 157-163.

2584. Magloire, Georges [pseud. of Dominique de Wespin]. *Album Teilhard*. Paris: Editions universitaires, 1962. *Klein Teilhard Album*. Tielt/Den Haag, 1963.

2585. ———. "Les amis de Pierre Teilhard de Chardin." *Synthèses* (1959): 159, 105-108.

2586. ———. "'L'avenir de l'homme,' témoignage capital de Pierre Teilhard de Chardin." *Synthèses* (1959): 158/159, 448-491.

2587. ———. "La cité dans la vision de Teilhard de Chardin." *Revue Teilhard de Chardin* (1961): 5, 20.

2588. ————. "Le colloque Teilhard de Chardin à Nice."
Synthèses (1962): 471-478.

2589. ————. "Convergence des civilisations. Colloque de
Lisbonne." *Revue Teilhard de Chardin* (1964): 20/21,
23-26.

2590. ————. "Dixième symposium international Pierre Teilhard de Chardin: Les âges de l'homme." *Revue Teilhard
de Chardin* (1970): 44/45, 3-13.

2591. ————. "Le génie que j'ai vu vivre en liberté." *Planète* (1962): 3, 23-33.

2592. ————. "Le Père Teilhard m'a dit...." *Le Phare
dimanche*, April 2, 1961, p. 5.

2593. ————. "Pierre Teilhard de Chardin tel qu'en lui-même."
Synthèses (1959): 14, 199-201.

2594. ————. "Pour comprendre Teilhard." *Synthèses* (1962):
191/193, 179-183.

2595. ————. "Présence du Père Teilhard." *Revue Teilhard
de Chardin* (1962): 10, 19-26.

2596. ————. "Quelque chose d'essentiel." *Revue Teilhard
de Chardin* (1967): 32, 21-25.

2597. ————. "Le rayonnement de la pensée de Pierre Teilhard dans le monde." *Perspectives* (1966): 29, 23-26.

2598. ————. "Sarcenat, berceau de Teilhard de Chardin."
Synthèses (1959): 160, 74-78. Contains Item 4564.

2599. ————. "Septième symposium international." *Revue
Teilhard de Chardin* (1967): 32, 10-13.

2600. ————. "Teilhard de Chardin, tel que je l'ai connu."
Synthèses (1957): 132, 422-429; 134, 193-200; 137,
77-83; 138, 274-282; 139, 449-455. Contains Item
4448.
Also Bruxelles: Éditions Synthèses, 1958.

2601. ————. "Teilhard de Chardin, tel que je l'ai connu."
Revue Teilhard de Chardin (1961): 6, 9-14. Extract
from Item 2600.

2602.   ————. *Teilhard et le sinanthrope*. Paris: Éditions
        Universitaires, 1964.
        Teilhard e o sinantropo. Petrópolis: Vozes, 1967.

2603.   ————. "La vida de Pierre Teilhard de Chardin." *Polit-
        ica y espíritu* (1963): 280, 24-29.

2604.   ————, and Hubert Cuypers. *Presence de Pierre Teilhard
        de Chardin. L'homme et sa pensée*. Paris: Éditions
        Universitaires, 1961. Contains Item 4585.
        Teilhard de Chardin. L'homme et l'oeuvre. Paris:
        Nouvel Office d'Édition, 1964.
        *Pierre Teilhard de Chardin. Leven en levensbesch-
        owing*. Kasterlee: De Vroente, 1962.
        Also Utrecht: Desclée de Brouwer, 1962.
        Teilhard de Chardin, l'uomo e il pensiero. Torino:
        Borla, 1963.
        Leben und Denken Pierre Teilhard de Chardins. Olten:
        Roven, 1964.
        Also Frankfurt-am-Main/Berlin: Ullstein, 1967.
        *Presencia de Teilhard de Chardin. El hombre. El
        pensamiento*. Barcelona: Betis, 1967.

2605.   ————, and Dominique de Wespin. "Pierre Teilhard de
        Chardin et l'homme de Pékin." *Synthèses* (1955): 115,
        489-492.

2606.   Magnarelli, Giovanni. "Il 'caso' Teilhard de Chardin."
        Cultura (1964): 2, 248-258.

2607.   Maguire, Marjorie Reilley. "The Implications of the
        Thought of Teilhard de Chardin for Contemporary Ethical
        Methodology." Doctoral dissertation, Catholic Univer-
        sity of America, 1976.

2608.   Mahan, Mary. "Symposium on Chardin's Thought." *The
        Catholic Voice*, February, 1967, 5.

2609.   Maheu, René. "Incarnations de l'humain: Einstein et
        Teilhard de Chardin." *Civilisation de l'universel*.
        Paris: Laffont-Gonthier, 1966, pp. 249-255.

2610.   ————. "Science et synthèse. Allocution à l'ouver-
        ture du collouqe organisé à l'occasion du dixième an-
        niversaire de la mort d'Albert Einstein et de Pierre
        Teilhard de Chardin." Item 1259, pp. 52-60.
        Also in Item 3635.

2611. Number deleted.

2612. Mainx, Felix. "Réponse." *Itinéraires* (1965): 96, 93-96. Reply to questionnaire in Item 3259, pp. 93-96.

2613. Mairet, P. "Evolution and Prophecy." *Frontier* (1960): 3, 55-58.

2614. Maissel, René. "Teilhard de Chardin et les apologies de la confusion." *Rencontres* (1964): 48, 14-19.

2615. Maitland, B. "The Phenomenon of Man." *Downside Review* (1960): 78, 227-229.

2616. Malczewski, Jeremi, and Ewa Gierat. "Sapere auso." *Kontynenty* (1963): 55/56, 7-14.

2617. Malevez, Louis. "Deux théologiens catholiques de l'histoire." *Bijdragen* (1949): 225-240.

2618. ———. "Les dimensions de l'histoire de salut." *Nouvelle revue théologique* (1964): 8, 561-579.

2619. ———. "La méthode du P. Teilhard de Chardin et la phénoménologie." *Nouvelle revue théologique* (1957): 5, 579-599.
   "The Method of Teilhard and Phenomenology." *Theology Digest* (1960): 3, 137-142.

2620. Malinow, Carlos A. "Finalidad y determinismo en los sistemas evolutivos de Pierre Teilhard de Chardin y Henri Bergson." *Diálogos* (1965): 2, 111-131.

2621. Mallemann, René de. *Notice sur la vie et les travaux de Pierre Teilhard de Chardin (1881-1955).* Paris: Institut de France, 1963.

2621a. Maloney, George A. *The Cosmic Christ from Paul to Teilhard.* New York: Sheed and Ward, 1968.
   El Cristo cósmico de San Pablo a Teilhard. Santander: Sal Terrae, 1969.

2622. Malusa, Luciano. "Caratteristiche del discorso metafisico in Teilhard de Chardin." *Senso e valore del discorso metafisico.* Padova: Gregoriana, 1966, pp. 70-87.

2623. ————. "Note sul metodo fenomenologico di Pierre Teil-
       hard de Chardin." *Posizione e criterio del discorso
       filosofico.* Bologna: Patrón, 1967, pp. 99–114.

2624. ————. "L'ultimo Maritain e Pierre Teilhard de Chardin."
       Humanitas (1972): 2, 661–693.

2625. Manacorda, Guido. "Teilhard de Chardin poeta." *Lettura
       del medico* (1963): 15, 265–268.

2626. Mansion, Françoise. "'La planétisation' ou la notion de
       communauté internationale dans la pensée de Teilhard
       de Chardin." Mimeographed. Institut des Hautes Études
       Internationales de la Faculté de droit de Paris, 1969.

2627. Mansuy, Michel. "Pierre Teilhard de Chardin." *Études
       sur l'imagination de la vie.* Paris: José Corti, 1970,
       pp. 175–209.

2628. Manten, A.A. *Vraagtekens rondom ... Teilhard de Chardin.*
       Amsterdam: Stiching IVIO, 1966.

2629. Marasigan, Vicente. "Dark Night of Christogenesis: St.
       John of the Cross and Teilhard de Chardin." *The Teil-
       hard Review* (1976): 11, 88–89.

2630. ————. "Planetization Problems." *Philippine Studies*
       (1973): 21.
       Also *The Teilhard Review* (1976): 11, 27–30.

2631. ————. "Teilhard on Alienation." *Philippine Studies*
       (1971): 19, 450–509.
       Also *The Teilhard Review* (1975): 2, 46–53.

2632. ————. "Teilhard's 'Phenomenon': Its Three Aims."
       Philippine Studies (1968): 3, 487–500.

2633. Marcel, Gabriel. "La sagesse à l'âge technique."
       *Revue des travaux de l'Académie des sciences morales
       politiques* (1964): 1, 19–20, 28–29.

2634. ————. "Vers une conscience planétaire?" *La France
       catholique,* June 28, 1964, pp. 1–2.

2635. Marcellien, F. "Le problème des races chez Teilhard de
       Chardin." *Nouvelle revue pédagogique* (1963–64): 9,
       561–570.

2636. ———. "Teilhard de Chardin et la découverte du passé" *Nouvelle revue pédagogique* (1963-64): 4, 202-206.

2637. ———. "Teilhard de Chardin et l'histoire." *Nouvelle revue pédagogique* (1963): 19, 21-30.

2638. ———. "Teilhard de Chardin et sa vision du monde." *Nouvelle revue pédagogique* (1963): 2, 78-88.

2639. Marchal, Jean. "'Science et Christ' du P. Teilhard de Chardin." *Le Monde*, July 2, 1965.

2640. Marchese, Angelo. "La cristianità e il mondo attuale." *Il gallo* (1963): 17, 106-107, 127-128, 183-185, 203-204; (1964): 18, 5-6, 27-28, 44-45, 68-69, 83-85, 107-108, 154-155, 175-176, 198-200.

2641. ———. "Il monitum del sant'uffizio." *Leggere* (1962): 8/8, 3-6.

2642. Marciano, Gelsomina. "La formazione dell'uomo in Pierre Teilhard de Chardin." Typescript. Istituto Maria Assunta, Roma, 1973.

2643. Marcotte, Gilles. "Le 'monde ouvert' de Teilhard de Chardin." *La Presse*, June 2, 1961, p. 8.

2644. Marcozzi, Vittorio. "Due commentatori del Padre Teilhard de Chardin." *La civiltà cattolica* (1968): 2, 165-168.

2645. Margerie, Bertrand de. *Le Christ pour le monde. Le Coeur de l'Agneau*. Paris: Beauchesne, 1971. See pp. 69-111.
   Cristo para o mundo. O Coração do Cordeiro. São Paulo: Herder, 1972. See pp. 69-118.
   Christ for the World. The Heart of the Lamb. A Treatise on Christology. Chicago: Franciscan Herald Press, 1974. See pp. 68-120.
   Cristo, vida del mundo. Madrid: Editorial Católica, 1974. See pp. 61-98.

2646. Maritain, Jacques. "Dieu et la science." *La table ronde* (1962): 179, 25.

2647. ———. "Teilhard de Chardin et le teilhardisme." *Le paysan de la Garonne*. Paris: Desclée de Brouwer, 1966, pp. 173-187.
   "Teilhard de Chardin y el teilhardismo." *El campesino del Garona*. Bilbao: Desclée de Brouwer, 1967, pp.

163-175.
"Teilhard de Chardin and Teilhardism." *The Peasant of the Garonne*. London: Geoffrey Chapman, 1968, pp. 116-126. Also New York: Holt, Rinehart & Winston, 1968. Also *U.S. Catholic* (1967): 7, 6-10.
"Teilhard de Chardin e il teilhardismo." *Il contadino della Garonna*. Brescia: Morcelliana, 1969, pp. 177-192.
"Teilhard de Chardin und der Teilhardismus." *Der Bauer von der Garonne*. München: Kösel-Verlag, 1969, pp. 124-133.

2648. ———. *Teilhard, oui ou non?* Paris: Fayard, 1961.

2649. ———. "Über zwei Untersuchungen zur Theologie Teilhards." *Der Bauer von der Garonne*. München: Kösel-Verlag, 1969, pp. 259-263.

2650. ———. "Vers une idée thomiste de l'évolution. Première approche." *Nova et vetera* (1967): 2, 87-136.

2651. ———. "Wie ich Teilhard sehe." *Dokumente* (1967): 23, 46-52.

2652. Markus, György, and Zador Tordai. *Irányzatok a mai polgári filozofiában*. [Currents in Contemporary Bourgeois Philosophy.] Budapest: Gondolat, 1964. See pp. 225-269.

2563. Maroky, Paul. "The Teilhardian Ideal of Spirituality." *Vidyajyoti* (1977): 41, 59-67.

2654. Marquès, Andreu. "Estructuralisme i mentalitat evolucionista." *Qüestions de vida cristiana* (1969): 47, 47-56.

2655. Marquínez Argote, Germán. "A qué nel nivel discurre el pensamiento de Teilhard de Chardin?" *Revista javeriana* (1967): 68, 373-380.

2656. ———. "La metafísica que Teilhard rechaza." *Revista javeriana* (1966): 66, 386-394.

2657. ———. "Naturaleza y método de la hiperfísica teilhardiana." *Universidad de Santo Tomas* (1969): 195-203.

2658. Marranzini, Alfredo. "Le Milieu divin e la Chiesa nel mondo d'oggi." Item 2744, pp. 221-228. "Le Milieu divin et l'église dans le monde d'aujourd'hui." Item 2744 trans., pp. 206-213.

2659. Marrou, Henri-Irénée. "Le Père Teilhard de Chardin." *Témoignage chrétien*, April 22, 1955, p. 7.

2660. ————. "Un savant chrétien. A propos du 'Phénomène humain' de Pierre Teilhard de Chardin." *Témoignage chrétien*, December 23, 1955, p. 7.

2661. Marsch, Wolf-Dieter. "Idealismus, Materialismus, Schöpfungsglaube." *Kommunität* (1961): 5, 164-171.

2662. ————. "Jesus Christ: Hoffnung auf die Welt der Menschen. Herrschaft Christi und Schöpferglaube in der Mystik Pierre Teilhard de Chardins." *Horen und Handeln. Festschrift für Ernst Wolf zum 60. Geburtstag*. München: Kaiser, 1962, pp. 272-300.

2663. ————. "Schöpfungsglaube und Evolutionstheorie." *Mitteilungen der Gesellschaft Teilhard de Chardin für den deutschen Sprachraum* (1968): 1, 3-14.

2664. Martelet, Gustave. "Le Christ universel d'après les écrits de la première période de l'union créatrice." *Études teilhardiennes* (1970): 3, 51-62.

2665. ————. "La creazione: Teologia e visione cosmica delle origini." *Bolletino informazioni del Centro di studi e di recerca Teilhard de Chardin, Istituto Stensen* (1973): 14, 1-12; 18, 9-17.

2666. ————. "Teilhard et le mystère de Dieu." Item 3653, pp. 77-102.

2667. Martim-Branco, A. "A mensagem do P. Teilhard de Chardin." *Estudios* (1966): 44, 480-489.

2668. Martin, Charles-Marie. "Les implications politiques de la pensée de Pierre Teilhard de Chardin." Typescript. University of Nice, 1962.

2669. ————. "Portrait politique de Pierre Teilhard de Chardin." Mimeographed. Faculté de droit et des sciences économiques de l'Université de Nice, 1968.

2670. ———. "L'univers a-t-il éclaté ou est-il éternel?"
Le Figaro littéraire, May 6, 1961, p. 13.

2671. Martin, Jacques. "Le Christ universel dans l'oeuvre de
Pierre Teilhard de Chardin." Typescript. University
of Toulouse, 1967.

2672. Martin, Maria Gratia. The Spirituality of Teilhard de
Chardin. Westminster, Md.: Newman Press, 1968.
La espiritualidad de Teilhard de Chardin. Madrid:
Perpetuo Socorro, 1969.

2673. Martin, Paulette. "Teilhard May Become a Prophet in
his Homeland Yet." The National Catholic Reporter,
July 20, 1966, p. 9.

2674. Number deleted.

2675. Martinazzo, Eusebio. "Cristo na visão de Teilhard de
Chardin." Veritas (1970): 15, 101-110.

2676. ———. Teilhard de Chardin. Conamen lecturae cri-
ticae. Roma: Herder, 1965.
Teilhard de Chardin, ensaio de leitura crítica.
Petrópolis: Vozes, 1968.

2677. ———. "Visio critica in synthesi Teilhard de Chardin."
Typescript. Pontificium Athenaeum Antonianum Facultas
Philosophiae, Roma, 1962.

2678. Martindale, C.C. "Letter." The Tablet (1955): 205, 460.

2679. ———. "Theology and Science: What Teilhard Was."
Month, February, 1961, pp. 118-120.

2680. ———. "Thy Labor Under the Sun." Item 501, pp. 92-
95.
Also Item 497, pp. 92-95.

2680a. Martin-Deslias, Noël. Un aventurier de l'esprit, Pierre
Teilhard de Chardin. Paris: Nagel, 1963.
Also Genève: Nagel, 1964.
Aventureiro do espirito. Lisboa: Livraria Morais,
1965.

2681. Martinez-Gomez, Luis. "Teilhard de Chardin entre dos
siglos." Pensamiento (1970): 26, 255-275.

2682. Martínez-Sáez, Santiago. "Lo inadmisibile en el pensamiento teólogico de Teilhard de Chardin." *Istmo* (1966):
43, 8-17.

2683. ———. "Teilhard de Chardin." *Istmo* (1965): 41, 27-32.

2684. ———. "Teilhard de Chardin. Presupuestos filosóficos
en el pensamiento teológico de Teilhard de Chardin."
Istmo (1966): 43, 23-32.

2685. Martinez Torrero, José. "Teilhard de Chardin, evolución
y espiritualidad." *Sic* (1964): 27, 306-309.

2686. Martini, Costanzo. "Teilhard de Chardin scienziato.
Cosí le pietre cantano la storia dell'uomo." *Pagine
aperte* (1977): 6, 15-21.

2687. Martini, Paul. "Die geistige Evolution des Menschen-
geschlechts. Zur umstrittenen These Teilhard de Chardins." *Hochland* (1962): 54, 312-321.

2688. Mascall, Eric. "Perspective scientifique et message
chrétien." *Concilium* (1967): 26, 115-121.

2689. Masi, Roberto. "A dieci anni dalla morte. Il contrasto
Teilhard." *La rocca* (1965): 27, 31-33.

2690. ———. "Il 'fenomeno umano' di Teilhard de Chardin.
Il metodo ed i principi cosmologici." *Divinitas*
(1959): 3, 269-284.

2691. Massis, Henri. *Visages des idées.* Paris: Grasset, 1958.
See pp. 259-290.

2692. Masui, J. "In memoriam: Teilhard de Chardin." *Synthèses*
(1955): 108-109, 28-33.

2693. ———. "Mon ami Pierre Teilhard de Chardin." *Revue
Teilhard de Chardin* (1961): 7, 20-22.

2694. ———. "Où en sommes-nous?" *Synthèses* (1958): 219-234.

2695. Mathew, Gervase. "The Religion of Teilhard de Chardin."
New Blackfriars (1968): 49, 320-323.

2696. Mathieu, Pierre-Louis. *La pensée politique et economique
de Teilhard de Chardin.* Paris: Seuil, 1969.
*El pensamiento político y económico de Teilhard de
Chardin.* Madrid: Taurus, 1970.

2697. Mathison, J.A.M., and William Kay. "The Evolution of Consciousness." *The Teilhard Review* (1968-69): 2, 62-75.

2698. Matthews, W.R. "New Theological Understanding." *Daily Telegraph*, June 23, 1966.

2699. Mattson, Alvin D., Jr. "Teilhard and Tillich: An Attempt to Demonstrate Their Use of a Common Method." Doctoral dissertation, The Hartford Seminary Foundation, 1971.

2700. Mauge, Roger. "Teilhard: la matière devient la vie, la vie devient pensée." *Jésus*. Paris: R. Laffont, 1972, pp. 320-360.

2701. Mauriac, François. "Le Bloc-Notes de François Mauriac." *L'Express* (1961): 512, 40.

2702. ⸺. "Bloc-Notes. La pensée religieuse du Père Teilhard de Chardin par le Père de Lubac." *Le Figaro littéraire*, September 2, 1965, p. 14.

2703. ⸺. *Ce que je crois*. Paris: Grasset, 1962.

2704. Maurina, Zenta. "Teilhard de Chardin und Dostojewskij." *Perspektiven der Zukunft* (1972): 2, 2-7.

2705. McCafferty, Richard Basil. "The Influence of Teilhard de Chardin on Marshall McLuhan." Doctoral dissertation, Northwestern University, 1969.

2706. McCarthy, Maureen. "Community from the Perspective of Confucius and Teilhard." *Second Order* (1974): 1, 92-94.

2707. ⸺. "Teilhardian Ethics." *The Teilhard Review* (1973): 1, 11-14.

2708. McCarthy, V. "Maturity: Pierre Teilhard de Chardin and Gordon W. Allport." *Journal of Religion and Health* (1968): 7, 141-150.

2709. McCarty, Doran. *Teilhard de Chardin*. Waco, Tex.: Word Books, 1976.

2710. McCullough, Michael. "Teilhard and the Information Revolution." *The Teilhard Review* (1977): 12, 6-10.

2711. McDermott, Brian O. "Teilhard de Chardin: A Survey of the Recent Literature." *Woodstock Letters* (1968): 97, 134-143.

2712. McHale, John. "Towards the Future." *The Teilhard Review* (1968): 1, 29-35.

2713. McLuhan, Marshall. *The Gutenberg Galaxy: The Making of Typographic Man*. Toronto: University of Toronto Press, 1962. Also New York: New American Library, 1969. *La galaxie Gutenberg*. Paris: Mame, 1967. Also Montréal: Éditions HMH, 1967.

2714. McMahon, John J. "What Does Christianity Add to Atheistic Humanism?" *Cross Currents* (1968): 2, 129-150.

2715. McMullin, Ernan. "Teilhard as Philosopher." *Chicago Theological Seminary Register* (1964): 4, 15-28.

2716. ———. "Teilhard, China and Neo-Marxism." *The Month* (1969): 1221, 274-285. Also *China and the West: Mankind Evolving*. London: Garnstone Press, 1970, pp. 82-102.

2717. McNaspy, C.J. "A Theology of History." *Worship* (1958): 32, 464-469.

2718. Medawar, P.B. *The Art of the Soluble*. London: Methuen, 1965.

2719. ———. "Un fastidieux fatras." *La quinzaine littéraire* (1966): 13, 16-18.

2720. ———. "Teilhard de Chardin. 'The Phenomenon of Man.'" *Mind* (1961): 277, 99-106.

2721. ———. "Über Teilhard de Chardin." *Jahrbuch für kritische Aufklärung* (1963): 1, 31-39.

2722. Megino, Crispín, and Francisco Javier Pineda. "Teilhard de Chardin, ¿profeta de una nueva vivencia de Cristo?" *Revista de espiritualidad* (1971): 30, 236-246.

2723. Meilach, Michael D. *There Shall Be One Christ*. St. Bonaventure, N.Y.: Franciscan Institute of St. Bonaventure University, 1968.

2724.   Meinvielle, Julio. "Le conseguenze del progressismo
        cristiano." *Relazioni* (1965): 7, 19-32.

2725.   ————. "La cosmovisión de Teilhard de Chardin: Una
        metafisica del unir." *Estudios teológicos y filo-
        sóficos* (1960); 2, 107-133.

2726.   ————. "El marxismo en Teilhard de Chardin." *El
        cruzado espanol* (1960): 65, 3-4.

2727.   ————. *P. Teilhard de Chardin o la religión de la
        evolución.* Buenos Aires: Editorial Theoria, 1965.

2728.   Melady, Thomas Patrick. "Teilhard y el despertar del
        nacionalismo africano." *Razón y fe* (1967): 838, 347-
        360.
        "Teilhard and the Emergence of African Nationalism."
        World Justice (1968): 9, 425-446.
        "Teilhard et la montée du nationalisme africain."
        Justice dans le monde (1968): 4, 435-445.

2729.   ————, and Margaret Badum Melady. "Teilhard de Chardin
        and the Afro-Asian World." *Bulletin Africa Service of
        New York*, November, 1965, pp. 102-106.
        Also *Catholic World* (1965-66): 202, 102-116.

2730.   Melchiorre, Virgilio. "L'intelligenza del male come
        ambito de possibilità." Item 2744, pp. 197-201.
        "La compréhension du mal comme domain des possibili-
        tés." Item 2744 trans., pp. 186-191.

2731.   ————. "Riflessioni sul significato del male in Teil-
        hard de Chardin." *Testimonianze* (1965): 8, 756-760.

2732.   Melo, Gilson Garcia de. "Reflexões sobre Jesus Cristo,
        no pensamento do Padre Pierre Teilhard de Chardin."
        *Revista de Pontifícia Universidade Católica de São
        Paolo* (1973): 43, 59-77.

2733.   Melo, Romeu de. "A pessõa como momento de evolução."
        Revista portuguesa de filosofia (1969): 25, 202-209.

2734.   Ménager, Pierre. "Un chercheur optimiste." *L'appel
        des cloches* (1966): 19, 1.
        "Teilhard de Chardin, ce chercheur optimiste." *Le
        pélerin de vingtième siècle*, May 1, 1966, pp. 22-24.

2735. Meneses, Daniel. "Teilhard de Chardin y la acción humana." *Mysterium* (1971): 30, 49-70.

2736. Mercer, Marilyn. "The Vision of Teilhard de Chardin." *Glamour*, December, 1967, pp. 83-89, 167.

2737. Merino, Pedro. "El hombre y la evolución." *Crisis* (1972): 19, 424-428.

2738. Mermod, Denis. *La morale chez Teilhard.* Paris: Éditions Universitaires, 1968.
A moral em Teilhard de Chardin. Petrópolis: Vozes, 1969.

2739. ————. "La pensée morale de Teilhard de Chardin. I. La morale naturelle." Typescript. Faculté autonome de théologie protestante de Genève, 1965.

2740. Merode, François de. "La destinée sait attendre." In Item 3744.

2741. Merton, Thomas. "Teilhard's Gamble: Betting on the Whole Human Race." *Commonweal* (1967-68): 87, 109-111.

2742. Mesa, Carlos E. "Divagaciones en torno al Padre Teilhard." *Universidad de Antioquia* (1971): 47, 503-519.

2743. ————. *Hombres en torno a Cristo.* Medellín: Ediciones Mysterium, 1972. See pp. 236-248.

2744. *Il messagio spiritual di Teilhard de Chardin.* Milano/Torino/Firenze: Centro Italiano di Studi Teilhardiani, 1965. Contains Items 64, 105, 202, 283, 351, 602, 782, 853, 1006, 1052, 1086, 1180, 1184, 1186, 1430, 1453, 2074, 2466, 2658, 2730, 3003, 3005, 3447, 3495b, 4068, 4247.
Le message spirituel de Teilhard de Chardin. Paris: Seuil, 1969.

2745. Metra, Félix. *Un homme à la recherche de son âme.* Lyon: Bosc, 1964. See pp. 57-59.

2746. Mettra, Jacques. "Le Père Teilhard de Chardin." *Travaux et jours* (1961): 2, 9-27.

2747. Metz, André. "Quelques souvenirs sur le Père Teilhard de Chardin." Item 1259, pp. 122-128.

2748. Metz, J.B. "Problèmes frontières." *Concilium* (1967):
       26, 7-9.

2749. Meurers, Joseph. "Der Erkenntnis des Weltganzen und die
       Wissenschaft." Item 2035, pp. 40-76.

2750. ————. "Grenzen der Wissenschaft. Der Welt-Entwurf
       des Teilhard de Chardin." *Rheinischer Merkur*, Janu-
       ary 19, 1962, p. 7.

2751. ————. *Die Sehnsucht nach dem verlorenen Weltbild.*
       Verlockung und Gefahr der Thesen Teilhard de Chardins.
       München: Pustet, 1962.

2752. ————. "Der Weltentwurf Teilhard de Chardins." *Wis-*
       senschaft und Weltbild (1963): 16, 183-194.

2753. Meyer, François. "L'évolution se dirige-t-elle vers un
       terme défini dans le temps?" Item 3041, pp. 90-98.

2754. ————. "Les obstacles à la convergence." *Univers*
       (1964): 1, 75-83.

2755. ————. *Teilhard et les grandes dérives du monde vivant.*
       Paris: Éditions Universitaires, 1963.
          Teilhard en de grote expansie van de levende wereld.
       Tielt/Den Haag: Lannoo, 1965.
          Teilhard e as grandes rotas do mundo vivo. Petró-
       polis: Vozes, 1967.
          Teilhard y las grandes derivas del mundo viviente.
       Buenos Aires: Columba, 1968.

2756. Meyer, Gerbert. "Teilhard de Chardin. Fragen und Prob-
       leme. Wurde er bisher richtig verstanden?" *Die neue*
       Ordnung (1964): 18, 350-359.

2757. ————. "Teilhard de Chardin und seine Interpreten."
       Die neue Ordnung (1961): 15, 361-369.

2758. ————. "Teilhard de Chardin. Zum Verständnis seiner
       Schriften." *Wort und Wahrheit* (1966): 7, 54-59.

2759. Micent, Paul. "Le Coeur du Christ selon Teilhard de
       Chardin et selon saint Jean Eudes." *Notre vie eu-*
       diste, April, 1965, pp. 204-209.

2760. Migoya, Francisco. "El neohumanismo evolutivo de Teil-
       hard de Chardin." *Abside* (1963): 27, 339-345.

2761. Mihelics, Vid. "Az 'elidegenedés' kérdése és Teilhard de Chardin tanitása." [The Problem of Estrangement and the Doctrine of Teilhard de Chardin.] *Vigilia* (1965): 30, 353-357.

2762. ————. "Az erdölsci megítélés elvei Teilhard de Chardin tanitásaban." [The Principles of Moral Judgement in the Thought of Teilhard de Chardin.] *Vigilia* (1962): 27, 291-294.

2763. ————. "Teilhard de Chardin jelentősége a metafizikában es teőlogiában." [Teilhard de Chardin's Importance in Philosophy and Theology.] *Vigilia* (1962): 27, 291-294.

2764. ————. "Teilhard de Chardin tanúsága hitünk erősségerol." [Teilhard de Chardin's Witness on the Solidity of Our Faith.] *Vigilia* (1965): 30, 290-296.

2765. Mikumo, Natsuo. "Gendai do Teilhard de Chardin." [Present Times and Teilhard.] *Risô* (1969): 7, 1-8.

2766. ————. "Teilhard de Chardin." *Seiki* (1961): 132, 10-17.

2767. ————. "Teilhard de Chardin ni okeru Kirisutokyô dôtoku." [Christian Morality According to Teilhard.] *Kirisuto Ron.* [Christology.] Tokyo: Rosôsha, 1968, pp. 193-212.

2768. ————. "Teilhard de Chardin no ningenzô." [The Image of Man in Teilhard de Chardin.] *Gijutsu jidai no ingenzô.* [The Image of Man in the Age of Technology.] Tokyo: Chûô Shuppansha, 1965, pp. 193-210.

2769. ————. "Teilhard de Chardin no shisô." [Teilhard de Chardin's Thought.] *Seiki* (1962): 149, 30-38.

2770. Miros, Lubomira, "Trasaturi ale personalismului Teilhard de Chardin." [Elements of Teilhard de Chardin's Personalism.] *Revista de filozofia* (1966): 663-669.

2771. Miskotte, H. "Teilhard de Chardin als baanbreker naar een verniuwde catholiciteit." *Hervorming en catholiciteit* (1964): 3, 7-15; 5, 3-12.

2772. Mislin, Hans. "Pierre Teilhard de Chardin und die Evolutionslehre." *Kommunitat* (1961): 5, 157-164.

2773. Misraki, Paul. "Divergences." In Item 3237.

2774. ————. "La pensée de Teilhard." In Item 3237.

2775. Mita, Minoru. "Teilhard de Chardin shôden." [Short
       Biography of Teilhard de Chardin.] Item 4036 trans.,
       pp. 151-264.

2776. Mladenio, Monique. "Un humanisme scientifique et chré-
       tien." *L'étudiant catholique* (1955): 3, 2.

2777. Mohr, H. "Erkenntnis theoretische und ethische Aspekte
       der Naturwissenschaften." *Mitteilungen der Verbanden
       deutscher Biologen* (1965): 113, 525+.

2778. Milinaro, Felice. "La rivoluzione copernica di Teil-
       hard." *Città di vita* (1973): 28, 299-312.

2779. Molitor, A. "Bibliographie sommaire." *La revue nou-
       velle* (1958): 14, 623-624.

2780. Molnar, Thomas. "L'aggiornamento chez Teilhard et Rob-
       inson." *Ecrits de Paris*, January, 1965, pp. 38-46.

2781. ————. "The Cult of Teilhard." *Triumph* (1967): 2,
       22-24.

2782. ————. "Teilhard's Collectivist Salvation." *National
       Review*, June, 1963.

2783. ————. *Utopia: The Perennial Heresy.* New York: Sheed
       and Ward, 1967.

2784. Mondin, Battista. *Le cristologie moderne. Un panorama.*
       Roma: Apes Editrice, 1973. See pp. 87-91.

2785. "La prova dell'esistenza di Dio in Teilhard de Chardin."
       Rivista di filosofia neo-scolastica (1965): 57, 1-21.

2786. Monestier, André. "De la querelle sur le teilhardisme."
       Perspectives (1965): 22, 39-41.

2787. ————. "Introduction." In Item 3237.

2788. ————. "Une morale des nations." *Revue Teilhard de
       Chardin* (1962): 12, 19-23.

2789. ———. *Pour Teilhard de Chardin*. Nancy: Berger-Levrault, 1967. Bound with Item 3554.
Teilhard. Torino: Borla, 1967. Bound with Item 3554 trans.
A favor de Teilhard de Chardin. Barcelona: Pomaire, 1967. Bound with Item 3554 trans.
Also Santiago de Chile: Pomaire, 1967.
Teilhard de Chardin. Prô. Lisboa: Livros do Brasil, 1969. Bound with Item 3554 trans.

2790. "Réflexions d'un laïc à propos de la querelle sur le teilhardisme." *Synthèses* (1963): 208, 206-211.
Also Item 1243, pp. 120-126.

2791. ———. "Teilhard et Aurobindo." *Revue Teilhard de Chardin* (1963): 14, 11-13. Excerpt from Item 2792.

2792. ———. *Teilhard et Sri Aurobindo*. Paris: Éditions Universitaires, 1963.
Teilhard e Sri Aurobindo. Petrópolis: Vozes, 1967.

2793. ———. *Teilhard ou Marx? Essai sur la socialisation*. Paris: Minard, 1965.
Also Paris: Lettres modernes, 1965.

2794. ———. "L'unité economique condition préalable à l'unité spirituelle." *Univers* (1966): 3, 18-24.

2795. ———. "Vers un renouveau chrétien." In Item 3237.

2796. Monfried, Henri de. *La cargaison enchantée*. Paris: Grasset, 1947.
Also 1962.

2797. ———. "1922. En mer rouge." *La table ronde*, June, 1955, pp. 68-69.

2798. ———. "Souvenirs." Item 1259, pp. 129-131.

2799. ———. "Témoignage. Mon ami Pierre Teilhard de Chardin." *Revue Teilhard de Chardin* (1963): 16, 37.

2800. "Un monito del Sant'Offizio." *Civiltà cattolica* (1962): 113, 191-193.

2801. "Un 'Monitum' a propósito de la obra de Teilhard de Chardin." *Orbis catholicus* (1962): 2, 415-418.

2802. "The Monitum on Teilhard." *Commonweal*, July 27, 1962, pp. 412–413.

2803. Monkmeyer, Heinrich. "Teilhard de Chardin und die Natur-wissenschaften." *Schulverwaltungsblatt für Nieder-sachsen* (1964): 16, 174–176.

2804. Monnot, Jeanne. "Portrait graphologique." *Revue Teil-hard de Chardin* (1964): 18, 22–24.

2805. Monod, Jacques. "De la biologie à l'ethique: l'aliena-tion de l'homme moderne à l'égard de la culture sci-entifique." *Le Monde*, September 30, 1967, pp. 10–11.

2806. Monod, Théodore. "Allocution." Item 1259, pp. 45–48.

2807. ————."L'energie humaine. Autour d'un livre récent." *Christianisme social* (1963): 71, 307–340.

2808. ————. "Pierre Teilhard de Chardin (1881–1955)." *Christianisme social* (1955): 5/6, 274–276.

2809. ————. "Prespectives et perspective, en écoutant Teil-hard et Gaston Berger." Item 3041, pp. 72–83.

2810. Montgomery, Marion. "O'Connor and Teilhard de Chardin: The Problem of Evil." *Renascence* (1969–70): 22, 34–42.

2811. Moody, Msgr. "The Phenomenal Teilhard." *National Cath-olic Reporter* (1960): 35.

2812. Mooney, Christopher F. "Anxiety and Faith in Teilhard de Chardin." *Thought* (1964): 155, 510–530.

2813. ————. "Blondel and Teilhard de Chardin: An Exchange of Letters." *Thought* (1962): 147, 543–562.

2814. ————. "The Body of Christ in the Writings of Teil-hard de Chardin." *Theological Studies* (1964): 4, 576–610.

2815. ————. "Christianity and the Change in Human Conscious-ness." Item 528, pp. 143–161.

2816. ————. *La christologie de Teilhard de Chardin*. Paris: Aubier-Montaigne, 1966.

2817. ————. "Death and the Phenomenon of Life." *America*, April 12, 1975, pp. 276-279.

2818. ————. "A Fresh Look at Man." *Saturday Review*, February, 1966, pp. 21-24.

2819. ————. "A Modern Spirituality." Item 2158, pp. 1-21. "Una moderna spiritualità cristiana." Item 2158 trans., pp. 7-36.

2820. ————. "Optimism and Christian Hope." *Pax Romana Journal* (1967): 2, 23-24. Also *The Teilhard Review* (1967-68): 2, 54-57.

2821. ————. "Risk in Teilhard de Chardin." *Christianity and Crisis* (1965): 25, 172-175. "The Risk in Teilhard's Thought." *Catholic Mind* (1966): 64, 34-39.

2822. ————. "Teilhard de Chardin and Christian Spirituality." *Thought* (1967): 42, 383-402.

2823. ————. "Teilhard de Chardin and Modern Philosophy." *Social Research* (1967): 34, 67-85.

2824. ————. "Teilhard de Chardin and the Christological Problem." *Harvard Theological Review* (1965): 58, 91-126. Also in Item 2825. "Teilhard's Approach to Christology." *Theology Digest* (1967): 7, 18-25.

2825. ————. *Teilhard de Chardin and the Mystery of Christ.* London: Collins, 1966. Contains Item 2824. Also New York: Harper & Row, 1966. Also Garden City, N.Y.: Doubleday, 1968. *Teilhard de Chardin et la mystère du Christ.* Paris: Aubier-Montaigne, 1968. *Teilhard de Chardin y el misterio de Cristo.* Salamanca: Sígueme, 1968.

2826. ————. "Teilhard de Chardin on Belief in God." In *The Presence and Absence of God.* New York: Fordham University Press, 1969, pp. 31-49.

2827. ————. "Teilhard de Chardin on Freedom and Risk in Evolution." *Freedom and Man.* New York: P.J. Kenedy, 1965, pp. 87-104.

2828. ———. "Teilhard de Chardin on Man's Search for God."
       Continuum (1968): 4, 643-654.

2829. ———. "Teilhard de Chardin on Suffering and Death."
       Journal of Religion and Health (1965): 5, 429-440.

2830. Morawska, Anna. "O chrześcijaúską wizje świata." [For
       a Christian Vision of the World.] Znak (1962): 376-
       399.

2831. ———. "Rozmowa o Teilhardzie." [Essay on Teilhard.]
       Znak (1963): 873-881.
       Also Kontynenty (1963): 55/56, 15-25.

2832. Mordini, Attilio. "Teilhard de Chardin il teologo del
       progressismo." Adveniat (1963): 1, 4-30.

2833. Moreau, Leão José. "Reflexões sobre o teilhardismo."
       A ordem (1960): 40, 7-19.

2834. Morel, Georges. "Karl Marx et le Père Teilhard de
       Chardin." Études (1960): 304, 80-87.

2835. Morfín L., Luis. "Reflexiones de Teilhard de Chardin
       acerca de la felicidad." Christus, September, 1971,
       pp. 10-11.

2836. Morgan, J. "Ethnicity and the Future of Man." The
       Teilhard Review (1976): 11, 16-21.

2837. Morgan, W.J. "Methods of Philosophy and Fr. Kenny's
       Review." Newman Association. Philosophy of Science
       Group. Bulletin (1960): 38, 8-13. See Items 2151,
       2152.

2838. Morgione, Luigi. Teilhard de Chardin. Alba: Edizione
       Paoline, 1977.

2839. Morren, Lucien. "La constitution pastorale 'L'Église
       dans le monde de ce temps' et la science." Nouvelle
       revue théologique (1966): 8.

2840. ———. "Réflexion d'un scientifique croyant." Re-
       cherches et débats (1962): 41, 168-176.

2841. ———. "Une vue anglicane sur Teilhard de Chardin.
       Réflexions oecuméniques." Revue nouvelle (1964):
       2, 123-139.
       "An Anglican View of Teilhard de Chardin. Ecumenical

Reflections." *Eastern Churches Quarterly* (1964): 1,
27-39.

2842. Mortier, Jeanne-Marie. "Fidelité à Teilhard." *Europe*
(1965): 431/432, 25-28.

2843. ————. "Saint-Exupéry d'une certaine manière prépar-
ait Teilhard de Chardin." *Isen* (1965): 5.

2844. ————. "Souvenirs et réflexions." Item 3851, pp. 59-
81.

2845. ————. "Teilhard de Chardin et la fidelité à l'Église."
Documentation catholique, February, 1975, p. 148.

2846. ————. "The Testament of a Friend of Father Teilhard."
Item 528, pp. 42-52.

2847. ————. *Vues ardentes. Une étude suivie de textes
relatifs aux sujets traités.* Paris: Seuil, 1968.

2848. Mouroux, Jean. "Sacrifice de la raison dans la foi."
Recherches et débats (1967): 129-154.

2849. Movius, Hallam L., Jr. "Pierre Teilhard de Chardin,
Paleoanthropologist." *Science* (1956): 3186, 92.

2850. ————. "Pierre Teilhard de Chardin, SJ (1881-1955)."
American Anthropologist (1956): 1, 147-150.

2851. Müller, Armin. *Das naturphilosophische Werk Teilhard
de Chardins. Seine naturwissenschaftlichen Grundlagen und seine Bedeutung für eine natürliche Offen-
barung.* Frankfurt: Alber, 1964.

2852. ————. *Das Schopfungswunder und das Werk von Teilhard
de Chardin.* Berlin/Brandenburg: Berliner, 1964.

2853. ————. "Die Sinnfrage des Lebens und ihre Beantwor-
tung durch Albert Schweitzer und Teilhard de Chardin."
Perspektiven der Zukunft (1969): 4, 5-6.

2853a. Müller, Heinrich. "Uchû ni okeru ningen. Teilhard no
shinkaron." [Man in the Cosmos. Teilhard's Idea of
Evolution.] *Sophia* (1960): 81-95, 227-241.

2854. Müller-Gangloff, Erich. "Literature über Teilhard de
Chardin." *Kommunität* (1961): 20, 201-203.

2855. ———. "Teilhard de Chardin--Prähistorie und Prophetie."
      Kommunität (1961): 5, 44-45.

2856. ———."Wo die Brucke einstürzt, eile hin." Kommunität
      (1961): 20, 2-4.

2857. Mulligan, J.E. "Teilhard and Buber." Religion in Life
      (1969): 38, 362-382.

2858. ———. "Teilhard Speaks to the 1966 Man of the Year."
      Ave Maria, April 8, 1967, pp. 6-9.

2859. Munier, Roger. "P. Teilhard de Chardin et l'avenir de
      l'homme." Cahiers du Sud (1955): 331, 449-452.

2860. Muñoz Alonso, Adolfo. "Entre la ciencia y la fe." La
      estafeta literaria (1964): 290, 6-7.

2861. ———. "Evolución e historia en Teilhard de Chardin."
      Evoluzionismo e storia umana. Brescia: Morcelliana,
      1968, pp. 246-252.

2862. ———. "Los preliminares teilhardianos de la vida."
      Humanitas (1967): 8, 173-195.

2863. ———. "El teilhardismo en la critica marxista."
      Diário de Cuenca, March 26, 1967.

2864. Murray, G.G. "Teilhard and Orthogenetic Evolution."
      Harvard Theological Review (1967): 60, 281-295.

2865. Murray, Michael H. "Soul, Individual and Collective."
      The Teilhard Review (1968-69): 2, 80-84.

2866. ———. The Thought of Teilhard de Chardin. An Intro-
      duction. New York: Seabury Press, 1966.

2867. Mury, Gilbert. "Un jésuite partisan du progrès: le
      Révérend Père Teilhard de Chardin." L'Humanité,
      September 19, 1965.

2868. ———. "La morale et le sens de l'histoire." Cahiers
      internationaux, March/April, 1960, pp. 77-88.

2869. ———. "Science et religion." Les cahiers rational-
      istes (1963): 215, 214-235.

2870. Musurillo, Herbert. "Phenomenon of Man." *Thought* (1960): 35, 450-454.

2871. Mutkoski, Barbara Eileen. "The Teilhard Milieu: Pierre Teilhard de Chardin's Influence on Flannery O'Connor's Fiction." Doctoral dissertation: Fordham University, 1973.

2872. Mynarek, Hubertus. *Der Mensch: Sinnziel der Weltentwicklung. Entwurf eines christlichen Menschenbildes auf dem Hintergrund eines dynamisch-evolutionären Kosmos unter besonderer Berücksichtigung von Ideen H. Schells und Teilhard de Chardins.* Paderborn: F. Schöningh, 1967.

2873. "Mystic and Man of Science." *Times Literary Supplement*, May 25, 1962, pp. 365-366.

2874. *La mystique et les mystiques.* Paris: Desclée de Brouwer, 1965.

2875. Naher, Émile. "Teilhard de Chardin." *Revue philosophique* (1971): 518-521.

2876. Nahon, Alfred. "Signification de l'amour de l'humanité." *Revue Teilhard de Chardin* (1963): 14, 4.

2877. Narbaitz, Pierre. "Faut-il croire au progrès?" *Revue Teilhard de Chardin* (1967): 31, 3-26.

2878. Narr, K.J. "Das kulturelle Phänomen und die Noogenese zum werke Teilhard de Chardins." *Acta praehistorica* (1965): 5/7, 209+.

2879. Natanson, Jacques. "Philosophe ou mystique?" Item 1284, pp. 369-374.
"¿Filósofo o místico?" Item 1284 trans., pp. 55-63.

2880. ————. "Un point de vue protestant sur Teilhard de Chardin." *Esprit* (1962): 31, 135-146.

2881. "Naturalisme et spiritualité." *Les études philosophiques* (1965): 20, 407-511. Contains Items 249, 530, 811. 4109.

2882. Nedeljkovic, Dušan. "Pierre Teilhard de Chardin." *Politika*, October 7, 1962, p. 18.

2883. Nedon, Jacques. "Une amitié chinoise." *La revue nou-velle* (1953): 17, 150-155, 240-250, 390-397, 599-606.

2884. Nédoncelle, Maurice. "Un prophète des convergences hu-maines." *Revue des sciences religieuses* (1957): 31, 293-298.

2884a. Needham, Joseph. "Cosmologist of the Future." *New Statesman*, November 7, 1960.

2885. Neil, Stephen. "Utopia or Ant Heap?" *Christian Cen-tury*, April, 1960, pp. 415-416.

2886. Neilson, F. "The Phenomenon of Man." *American Journal of Economics* (1960): 20, 101-106.

2887. Neira, Enrique. "Amor, sexo y feminismo en Teilhard de Chardin." *Theologica xaveriana* (1975): 25, 69-76.

2888. ———. *Del átomo a Omega: Teilhard de Chardin.* Bogotá: Universidad Javeriana, 1976.

2889. ———. "Una interpretación de Cristo a la luz de la evolución." *Theologica xaveriana* (1975): 3, 77-89.

2890. ———. "El problema de Dios en Teilhard de Chardin." *Revista javeriana* (1966): 65, 235-247. Also *Estudios* (1966): 276-285.

2891. ———. "Problemas teilhardianos (Presentación y dis-cusión)." *Revista javeriana* (1971): 75, 46-60, 169-181.

2892. ———. "La respuesta de Teilhard de Chardin al mundo de hoy." *Revista javeriana* (1965): 63, 466-477.

2893. ———. "Teilhard de Chardin: Signo de nuestro tiempo." *Revista javeriana* (1975): 84, 462-467.

2894. ———. "Teilhard y Marx." *Tierra nueva* (1975): 6, 41-52. Also Item 2888, pp. 217-229.

2895. Nemeck, Francis Kelly. *Teilhard de Chardin et Jean de la Croix.* Tournai: Desclée de Brouwer, 1975. Also Montréal: Bellarmin, 1975.

2896. Nemeshegyi, P. "Teilhard de Chardin no shingaku." [Teilhard de Chardin's Theology.] *Risô* (1969): 7, 25-36.

2897. Nemesszeghy, Ervin, and John Russell. "The Evolutionary Vision of Teilhard." *Theology of Evolution.* Cork: Mercier Press, 1972, pp. 72-91.

2898. Nemo, Maxime. "Présence de Teilhard de Chardin." *Europe* (1965): 431/432, 63-70.

2899. Néran, G. *Kami no ba. Teilhard de Chardin no Kirisutokyokan.* [The Divine Milieu. Teilhard de Chardin's Vision of Christianity.] Tokyo: Shinkyô Shuppansha, 1972.

2900. Neuenschwander, Ulrich. "Mensch und Kosmos bei Teilhard de Chardin." *Alpina* (1970): 139-142, 245-251.

2901. ———. "Pierre Teilhard de Chardin (1881-1955)." *Denker des Glaubens.* Gütersloh: G. Mohn, 1974, vol. 2, pp. 89-116.

2902. *1919-1969. Frankreich und Deutschland in einer evolutiven Welt.* Akten des deutsch-französischen Kongresses, München, 2-4 Mai, 1969. München: Sighart, 1969. Contains Items 1021, 1393.

2903. Neuwirth, Karl. "Zur Bildsprache des 'Milieu divin.'" *Rundbrief der Gesellschaft Teilhard de Chardin* (1966): 6, 1-14.

2904. Nevers, Emmanuelle, "Autour de la communication de M. Madaule." *Revue Teilhard de Chardin* (1962): 10, 8.

2905. Newson, J. "Intimations of Omega." *The Teilhard Review* (1974): 9, 1.

2906. ———. "A Request." *The Teilhard Review* (1973): 8, 65.

2907. ———. "Resonsible Relevance." *The Teilhard Review* (1972): 7, 66.

2908. Nguyen, Duc Xuan. "The Concept of Love in the Thought of Teilhard de Chardin." Doctoral dissertation, Drew University, 1978.

2909. Niaussat, Pierre. "Réponse." *Itinéraires* (1965): 96,
       97-101. Reply to questionnaire in Item 3259.

2910. Nickel, Erwin. "Teilhard de Chardin und die Philosophie
       in der Perspektive des Naturforschers." *Schweizer
       Rundschau* (1964): 63, 640-647.

2911. Nicolas, Marie-Joseph. "Le Christ selon Pascal et Teil-
       hard de Chardin." *Revue thomiste* (1971): 71, 381-403.

2912. ————. *Évolution et christianisme. De Teilhard de
       Chardin à saint Thomas d'Aquin.* Paris: Fayard, 1973.
       *Evoluzione e Cristianesimo. Da Teilhard de Chardin
       a san Tommaso d'Aquino.* Milano: Massimo, 1978.

2913. Nicollier, Jean. "Teilhard de Chardin: 'Le Milieu divin.'"
       La Gazette de Lausanne, January 20, 1958.

2914. Niederworlfsgruber, Franz. "Pierre Teilhard de Chardin.
       Leben und Werk." *Die Pyramide. Naturwissenschaft-
       liche Zeitschrift* (1962): 10, 2, 84-88.

2915. Niel, André. "La bio-métaphysique du P. Teilhard de
       Chardin." *Critique* (1955): 11, 718-723.

2916. ————. "Évolution et religion." *L'âge nouveau* (1959):
       106, 5-6.

2917. ————. "Le moi et l'amour." *Critique* (1958): 14,
       976-987.

2918. ————. "Teilhard de Chardin et la crise contemporaine."
       Preuves (1957): 71, 44-49.

2919. ————. "Vers un humanisme cosmologique." *Critique*
       (1956): 12, 220-229.

2920. ————. "Vers un humanisme de libération." *L'âge nou-
       veau* (1959): 106, 50-62.

2921. ————. "Les vues cosmologiques du P. Teilhard de Char-
       din et la métaphysique indienne." *France-Inde* (1956):
       21, 8-9.

2922. Nielsen, Ellen. "Fanamenet meneske." [The Phenomenon
       of Man.] *Aktuelt*, April 13, 1965, p. 11.

2923.   ———. "Teilhard på Dansk." [Teilhard in Danish.]
        Kristelight dagblad, January 21, 1967, p. 7.

2924.   Nimier, Roger. "Tu aimes Teilhard de Chardin?" *Nou-
        velle revue française* (1973): 250, 272-283.

2925.   Nioac de Salles, Lilia. "Teilhard de Chardin e a con-
        strução do mundo." *Estrutura* (1967): 4.

2926.   ———. "Testemunho de Teilhard de Chardin." *O Globo*,
        January 20, 1965.

2927.   Nobert, A. "De Freud à Teilhard de Chardin." *Laval
        médical* (1967): 38, 868-874.

2928.   Nobile, Philip. "Chardin: The Applause Grows." *Today
        Magazine*, May, 1966, pp. 20-23.

2929.   ———. "A Look at the Native Milieu of Pierre Teilhard
        de Chardin." *The Critic* (1966-67): 2, 66-69.

2930.   Nogar, Raymond. "Le monde étrange du Père Teilhard."
        Le Seigneur de l'absurde. Paris: Cerf, 1969, pp. 125-
        142.

2931.   ———."The Phenomenon of Man." *Dominicana* (1960): 3,
        244-249.

2932.   Noir, Pierre. "La femme et notre destin d'après Pierre
        Teilhard de Chardin." *Étudiants catholiques de Nancy*
        (1966): 27-38.

2933.   Noirot, Luce. "L'apport de Teilhard à l'évolution de
        la femme dans le monde." *Synthèses* (1968): 270, 63-
        70.

2934.   "Noosphere Revisited." *Time*, October 16, 1964, pp. 91-
        92.

2935.   Nordmeyer, Barbara. "Teilhard de Chardin." *Die Christ-
        engemeinschaft* (1967): 39, 339-341.

2936.   Noronha, C. "Um profeta contemporaneo: Teilhard de
        Chardin o padre jesuíta." *Boletim do Instituto de
        Angola* (1968): 30/32, 40-56.

2937.   North, Robert. *Teilhard and the Creation of the Soul.*
        Milwaukee: Bruce, 1967.

2938. ———. "Teilhard and Genesis." *Catholic Biblical Review* (1962): 24, 426.

2939. ———. "Teilhard and Many Adams." *Continuum* (1963-64): 1, 329-342.

2940. ———. "Teilhard and the Problem of Creation." *Theological Studies* (1963): 24, 577-601.

2941. ———. "Tradition in Spirituality." Item 2158, pp. 23-50.
       "La tradizione nella spiritualità." Item 2158 trans., pp. 37-75.

2942. Nosbüsch, Johannes. "Das Leib-Geistproblem bei Max Scheler und Teilhard de Chardin." *Katholische Frauenbildung* (1968): 69, 450-463.

2943. Novella, Vittorio. "Essai de representation du monde psychique." *Synthèses* (1961): 183-199.

2944. Nowell, R. "What Is the World? Schema 13." *Tablet*, October 31, 1964, pp. 1221-1222.

2945. "Numero dedicato al decimo anniversario della morte del Padre Pierre Teilhard de Chardin SJ." *ANAS*, April 17, 1965.

2946. Nunes, José Paulo. "Saint Thomas et Teilhard de Chardin. Parallélisme philosophico-théologique. Convergences et divergences." Mimeographed. Faculté de théologie de l'Institut Catholique de Paris, 1967.

2947. ———. "O sentido da mensagem de Teilhard de Chardin." *Christo ou Marx?* Lisboa: União Grafica, 1965, pp. 122-131.

2948. ———. "Teilhard de Chardin, S. Tomás do século XX." *Encontro. Jornal Universitário* (1968): 13, 17-20.

2949. Nunez, Jacques. "Teilhard de Chardin." *Nouvelle critique* (1960): 114, 120-134.

2950. Nuyens, J. "De person van Teilhard de Chardin." *Adelbert*, November, 1963, pp. 132-134.

2951. Obligado, Alberto. "La antropología de Teilhard de Chardin." *Estudios* (1965): 54, 113-120.

2952. O'Brien, Frances. "Teilhard and 'Prismatic' Painting." *Jesuit Bulletin* (1969): 4, 10-11.

2953. O'Brien, James F. "Teilhard and Aristotle: What is Radial and What is Tangential?" *New Scholasticism* (1975): 49, 486-491.

2954. O'Byrne, M.M., and W.P. Angers. "Jung's Concept of Self-Actualization and Teilhard de Chardin's Philosophy." *Journal of Religion and Health* (1972): 11, 241-251.

2955. O'Connell, Patrick. "The Sinanthropus or Peking Man." *Science of Today and the Problems of Genesis*. St. Paul, Minn.: Radio Replies Press, 1959, pp. 108-138.

2956. O'Connell, Robert J. "The Sacramental Eye." Item 2158, pp. 169-187.
"L'occhio sacramentale." Item 2158 trans., pp. 233-259.

2957. ————. "Teilhard at Fordham, 1963-1964." *Dialogue* (1965): 4, 382-384.

2958. ————. "Teilhard's Synthesis: Some Criteria for Criticism." Item 3247, pp. 1-22.

2959. O'Connor, Catherine Regina. "Woman and Cosmos: The Feminine in the Thought of Pierre Teilhard de Chardin." Doctoral dissertation, Fordham University, 1970. Also Englewood Cliffs, N.J.: Prentice-Hall, 1974.

2960. O'Doherty, E.F. "The Phenomenon of Man." *Philosophical Studies* (1959): 162-165.

2961. O'Donnell, John Philip. "A Philosophy of Education According to Teilhard de Chardin." Doctoral dissertation, Loyola University of Chicago, 1967.

2962. "L'oeuvre du Père Teilhard de Chardin." *Union catholique des scientifiques français. Bulletin* (1957): 9-12.

2963. O'Hea, Regis. "Glosy o Teilhardzie de Chardin." [Views on Teilhard de Chardin.] *Znak* (1962): 92/93, 245-247.

2964. Okumara, Kazushige. "Teilhard no shizenkan kara mita nihonjin (Sono konnichi shakai to mono no kangaekata)." [Teilhard's Sense of Nature as Seen by the Japanese

(Modern Society and His Thought).] *Convergence* (1977):
5, 1-5.

2965. Olarte, Teodoro. "El mensaje de Teilhard de Chardin."
       Diálogos (1965): 4, 73-85.

2966. ———. "El universo según Pierre Teilhard de Chardin."
       Revista de filosofia de la Universidad de Costa Rica
       (1957): 1, 137-148.

2967. Olcoz, Iñigo. "La actitud de y ante Teilhard de Char-
       din." *Sic* (1969): 32, 211-213.

2968. Oliveira, Zacarias de. "Dois autores: Teilhard de Char-
       din e Heinrich Böll." *Lumen* (1966): 30, 254-258.

2969. Olivier, Georges. "La conception de Teilhard de Chardin."
       L'évolution et l'homme. Paris: Fayard, 1965, pp.
       95-101.

2970. ———. "Teilhard de Chardin et le transformisme."
       Actualités et culture vétérinaires (1967): 66, 11-14.
       Also *Annales de l'Université de Paris* (1967): 37,
       358-365.

2971. Olmi, Massimo. "Testimonianze inedite per la biografia
       spirituale del gesuita più discusso. Il mio amico
       Teilhard." *Europeo* (1963): 60-65.

2972. O'Loane, J.K. "Reply to Karl Stern's 'Great and Con-
       troversial Priest and Scientist.'" *Commonweal*, April
       1, 1960, pp. 17-19. See Item 3792.

2973. Olphe-Gaillard, Michel. "Travail et vie spirituelle."
       Revue d'ascétique et de mystique (1961): 147, 382-397.

2974. O'Manique, John T. *Energy in Evolution*. London: Garn-
       stone Press, 1969.
       Also New York: Humanities Press, 1969.
       Energía en evolución. Barcelona: Esplugas de Llobre-
       gat, 1973.

2975. ———. "Teilhard's Lamarckism." *The Teilhard Review*
       (1966-67): 2, 34-41.

2976. Oncieu, J. "Le phénomène humain." *Action catholique
       étudiante* (1957): 829, 4-6.

2977. Ong, Walter J. *American Catholic Crossroads: Religious-Secular Encounters in the Modern World.* New York: Macmillan, 1959.

2978. ————. "Comments on Dr. James L. Foy's Paper." *The Bulletin of the Guild of Catholic Psychiatrists* (1963): 3, 171-175.

2979. ————. *Darwin's Vision and Christian Perspectives.* New York: Macmillan, 1961.

2980. ————. "Evolution and Cyclism in Our Time." *Thought* (1959-60): 547-568.

2981. ————. "Evolution, Myth and Poetic Vision." *Comparative Literature Studies* (1966): 1.

2982. ————. *In the Human Grain.* New York: Macmillan, 1967.

2983. ————. "I Remember Père Teilhard." *Jesuit Bulletin* (1967): 1, 6-7, 17-18.
"Il mio ricordo di Padre Teilhard de Chardin." *Ai nostri amici* (1967): 38, 270-272.

2984. ————. "Macrocosme et microcosme: L'homme religieux et l'effort intellectuel contemporain." *Chroniques* (1963): 43, 125-144.
Also *Recherches et débats* (1963): 43, 125-144.

2985. ————. "The Mechanical Bride." *Social Order* (1962): 2, 79-85.

2986. ————. "Personalism and the Wilderness." *Kenyon Review* (1959): 2, 297-304.

2987. ————. "Secular Knowledge, Revealed Religion and History." *Religious Education* (1957): 5, 341-349.

2988. Onimus, Jean. "En relisant 'Comment je crois' de Teilhard de Chardin." *Cahiers universitaires catholiques* (1970): 13-14.

2989. ————. "La foi et les perspectives philosophiques du Père Teilhard de Chardin." *Cahiers universitaires catholiques* (1957): 4, 145-154.

2990. ————. "Jaurès et Teilhard." *Cahiers universitaires catholiques*, April, 1962.

2991. ———. "L'optimisme conquérant du P. Teilhard de Chardin." *Cahiers du Sud* (1956): 43, 83–95.

2992. ———. *Pierre Teilhard de Chardin ou la foi au monde.* Paris: Plon, 1963. Also Paris/Bruges: Desclée de Brouwer, 1968. *Teilhard de Chardin en zijn geloof in het leven.* Antwerpen/Utrecht: Spectrum, 1965. *Teilhard de Chardin.* Wien/München: Herold, 1966.

2993. ———. "La reconquête du néant. A propos de la conférence de Jacques Monod au College de France." *Choisir* (1968): 102, 19–22.

2994. ———. "Teilhard de Chardin et le renouvellement du christianisme." *Les amitiés philosophiques internationales* (1968): 6.

2995. ———. "Teilhard de Chardin et l'espoir du monde." *Janus* (1964–65): 4, 17–32.

2996. ———. "Teilhardisme et confort moral." *Foi vivante* (1965): 6, 182–187.

2997. ———, and Marie Antoinette Viguier. "Autour du Père Teilhard de Chardin." *Cahiers universitaires catholiques* (1959): 222–230.

2998. Oosthuizen, Jacobus Stefanus. *Van Plotinus tot Teilhard de Chardin. 'n Studie oor de metamorphose van de westerse werklikheidsbeeld.* Amsterdam: Rodopi, 1974.

2999. "Optimism or Pessimism in our Brave New World--Teilhardian Perspectives." *Pax Romana Journal* (1967): 2, 4–24. Contains Items 1019, 1602, 2820, 3033, 3497, 3715, 4014.

3000. Orellana, Mario. "El método crítico de Teilhard." *Boletin de la Universidad de Chile* (1965): 55, 57–60.

3001. Oresme, Nicolás de. "Darwin y Teilhard de Chardin." *Ábside* (1965): 29, 336–341.

3002. Ormea, Ferdinando. "Del mito di 'Dio che muore' al 'Christo universale' di Teilhard de Chardin." *Cronache dell'Instituto Dermopatico Immacolata* (1965): 20, 63–95.

3003. ———. "L'eroica obbedienza di Pierre Teilhard de Chardin." Item 2744, pp. 121-127.
"L'héroique obéissance du Père Teilhard de Chardin." Item 2744 trans., pp. 114-118.

3004. ———. *Pierre Teilhard de Chardin. Il pensiero l'originalità, il messagio.* Torino: Giacomo Contessa, 1963.

3005. ———. "Il problema del male in Teilhard de Chardin." Item 2744, pp. 165-180.
"Le problème du mal chez Teilhard de Chardin." Item 2744 trans., pp. 157-172.

3006. ———. *Teilhard de Chardin. Guida al pensiero scientifico e religioso.* 2 vols., Firenze: Valecchi, 1968.

3007. ———. "Uomo e società nella fase critica dell'evoluzione cosciente." *Futuro dell'uomo* (1975): 4, 7-27.

3008. O'Rorke, Anne. "Teilhard de Chardin and Christ-Omega." *Insight* (1967): 5, 24-48.

3009. Os, C.H. van. *Aspecten der evolutie in het bijzonder aan de hand van de denkbeelden van Teilhard de Chardin en A.N. Whitehead.* Amsterdam: Theosofische Vereeniging, Nederlandse Afdeling, 1965.

3010. Osborn, Henry Fairfield. "Explorations, Researches and Publications of Pierre Teilhard de Chardin, 1911-1931." *American Museum Novitiates* (1931): 485, 1-13. Contains Items 4594, 4865.
Also Item 4669, vol. 4, pp. 1618-1630.

3011. Osborne, William Audley. "The Evolutionary Humanism of Teilhard de Chardin." Doctoral dissertation, New School for Social Research, 1965.

3012. "L'Osservatore Romano's Criticisms." *Tablet*, July 14, 1962, p. 676.

3013. Ott, Heinrich. "Der universale Christus bei Dietrich Bonhoeffer und P. Teilhard de Chardin." *Wirklichkeit und Glaube. I. Zum theologischen Erbe Dietrich Bonhoeffers.* Zürich: Vandenhoeck und Ruprecht, 1966, pp. 328-329.

3014. Ott, Jean. "L'évolution biologique convergente de l'univers vue par Teilhard de Chardin (1881-1955)." *Cahiers des ingénieurs agronomes* (1963): 179, 9-15.

3015. Oudin, J. "Historicisme et materialisme." *Pensée*
       catholique (1969): 119, 76-86.

3016. ⸻. "Teilhard de Chardin et l'hyperphysique."
       Pensée catholique (1955): 192, 61-71.
       Also *Ordre français* (1966): 107, 24-35.

3017. ⸻. "Teilhardisme et marxisme." *Ordre français*
       (1963): 6, 62-63.

3018. ⸻, and J. Boislevant. "Teilhard ou le triomphe
       du verbiage." *Ordre français* (1963): 20, 35-43.

3019. Ouince, Rene d'. "Allocution au service de P. Teilhard
       de Chardin." Item 3041, pp. 30-34.

3020. ⸻. "L'épreuve de l'obéissance dans la vie du Père
       Teilhard de Chardin." *L'homme devant Dieu. Mélanges*
       H. de Lubac. Paris: Aubier, 1964, pp. 331-346. Con-
       tains Items 4560, 4561.
       "Der Gehorsam im Leben des Paters Teilhard de Char-
       din." *Orientierung* (1964): 28, 138-144.
       Also *Perspektiven der Zukunft* (1968): 3, 5-6.
       "La obediencia en la vida del Padre Teilhard de
       Chardin." *Estudios centroamericanos* (1964): 19, 300-
       307.
       "De gehoorzaamheid in het leven van Pater Teilhard
       de Chardin." *De heraut van het H. Hart* (1964): 95,
       269-282.

3021. ⸻. "La pensée religieuse du Père Teilhard de Char-
       din." *Vie chrétienne* (1962): 47, 17-21.

3022. ⸻. *Un prophète en procès. I. Teilhard de Chardin*
       dans l'église de son temps. II. Teilhard de Chardin
       et l'avenir de la pensée chrétienne. Paris: Aubier-
       Montaigne, 1970.

3023. ⸻. "Teilhard e la crisi che noi viviamo." *In-*
       formazioni del Centro di studi e di recerca Teilhard
       de Chardin, Istituto Stensen (1972): 8, 1-15.

3024. ⸻. "Vivre dans la plénitude du Christ." *Christus*
       (1962): 34, 239-247.
       Also Item 3041, pp. 35-45.

3025. Overhage, P. *Die Evolution des Lebendigen. Das Phä-*
       nomen. Freiburg/Basel/Wien: Herder, 1964.

3026. ——. *Um die ursächliche Erklärung der Hominisation.* Leiden: Brill, 1959.

3027. Overloop, Jean. "Considérations sur une convergence religieuse." Item 3917, pp. 51-70.

3028. Overman, R.H. *Evolution and the Christian Doctrine of Creation.* London: Westminster Press, 1968.

3029. Pacula, Stanislaw. "Sympozjum teilhardowskie." *Życie i myśl* (1965): 9, 135-141.

3030. Paepcke, Fritz. "Pierre Teilhard de Chardin--Weltbild und Begriffswelt." *Forum academicum und Mitteilungsblatt der Universität Heidelburg und der Wirtschaftshochschule Mannheim* (1963): 6, 15-18.

3031. ——. "Zur Sprache und Begriffswelt von Pierre Teilhard de Chardin--Ein terminologisches Experiment auf dem Wege zu einer neuen Sprache vom Menschen." *Acta teilhardiana* (1967): 4, 3-15. Also Item 1213, pp. 154-175.

3032. Page, John E. "The Phenomenon of Urbanization and Teilhard." Item 3247, pp. 71-75.

3033. Panikkar, Raymond. "Technique et temps: La technochronie." *Atti del colloquo internzionale su "Tecnica e casistica."* Roma: Istituto di studi filosofici, 1964, pp. 195-229. "Technology and Time: Technochrony." *Pax Romana Journal* (1967): 2, 3-6.

3034. Pannenberg, Wolfhart. "Future and Unity." *Hope and the Future of Man.* London: Garnstone Press, 1973, pp. 60-78.

3035. ——. "Geist und Energie. Zur Phänomenologie Teilhards de Chardin." *Acta teilhardiana* (1971): 1, 5-12.

3036. *Panthéisme, Action, Oméga chez Teilhard de Chardin.* Bruges/Paris: Desclée de Brouwer, 1967. Contains Items 1353, 1354, 1630, 1904, 2337. *Panteísmo, acción, omega, según Teilhard de Chardin.* Marfil: Alcoy, 1969.

3037. Paris, Carlos. "Los aspectos cosmologicos en la obra de Teilhard de Chardin." *Pensamiento* (1970): 26, 181-198.

3038. ———. *Filosofía, ciencia, sociedad*. Madrid: Siglo Vientiuno de España Editores, 1972.

3039. ———. "Ser y evolución." Item 1419, pp. 782-787.

3040. ———. "Unamuno y Teilhard de Chardin." *Cuadernos para el diálogo* (1965): 16, 13-14.

3041. *La parole attendue*. Paris: Seuil, 1963. Contains Items 205, 288, 293, 733, 953, 1131, 1233, 2753, 2809, 3024, 3949, 4628, 4690.

3042. Pascual Marina, Antonia. "Teilhard de Chardin y su visión del mundo." *Eidos* (1961): 7, 175-200.

3043. Pasika, V.M. "Teilhard in a Soviet Encyclopedia." *The Teilhard Review* (1973): 8, 59-60.

3044. ———. "Teologija i nauka v interpretacii teilhard-izma." [Theology and Science in the Interpretation of Teilhardism.] *Nauka i teologija v XX veke*. [Science and Theology in the Twentieth Century.] Moskva: Mysl, 1972, pp. 114-137.

3045. Paskai, László. "Weltbild und Teleologie bei Teilhard. Zur Rolle der Teleologie in einer konvergierenden Evolution." *Acta teilhardiana* (1970): 1, 24-31. "Teilhard világképe és teológiája." *Vigilia* (1973): 38, 573-582.

3046. Paškus, Antanas. "Dūmus apie Teilharda besklaidant. Teilhardas--dvasios o ne medžiagos mistikas." [Clarification: Teilhard, Mystic of the Spirit, Not of Matter.] *Laiškai Lietuviams* (1974): 35, 296-304.

3047. ———. "Teilhard'o Dievas. Keletas pastabų A. Maceinos 'Religijos evoliucijos' klausimu." [Teilhard's God. Some Remarks About "The Evolution of Religion" by A. Maceina.] *Aidai* (1969): 193-206.

3048. ———. "Teilhard'o krikščionybė. Didysis dabarties klausimas ar atsakymas?" [Teilhard's Christianity. The Great Question or the Answer to Today's Problem?] *Aidai* (1973): 13-19, 67-73, 97-102.

3049. Pasolini, Piero. "L'Omega di Teilhard de Chardin."
Città nuova (1970): 17, 21-23.
"La visione di Teilhard de Chardin." *Notizie agli
amici dei gesuiti lombardo-veneto-emiliani* (1971): 1,
17-19.

3050. Passage, Henri du. "Le Père Teilhard de Chardin, poète
dans la pensée." *Cinquième saison* (1958): 2, 9-12.

3051. Passet, R. "Convergences teilhardiennes, convergences
économiques." *Economie et humanisme* (1967): 173, 2-13.

3052. Patry, M. "Pierre Teilhard de Chardin et les communications sociales." *Nouvelle revue théologique* (1976):
98, 447-455.

3053. Paupert, Jean-Marie. *Peut-on être chrétien aujourd'hui?*
Paris: Grasset, 1967.
¿Es todavía posible la fe? Madrid: Peninsula, 1967.

3054. Pauwels, Louis, and Jacques Bergier. "L'homme au-delà
de lui-même." *Revue Teilhard de Chardin* (1961): 5,
7-9.

3055. Pauwels, Luc. "La monde et la vie selon Pierre Teilhard
de Chardin." *Documents pour l'action* (1962): 2, 270-
279.

3056. Pawlov, Dejan. "Filosofskite i sociologickite idei na
Teilhard de Chardin." [Teilhard de Chardin's Philosophical and Sociological Ideas.] *Filosofska misul*
(1966): 6, 84-96.

3057. ————. "Teilhard de Chardin, die Natur des Menschen
und das Problem des Friedens (Beitrag zum christlich-
marxistischen Dialog)." *Akten des XIV. Internationalen Kongresses für Philosophie.* Wien: Herder, 1968,
vol. 2, pp. 656-662.

3058. Pecorini, Giorgio. "L'evoluzione dell'eretico." *L'Europeo* (1965): 18, 78-81.

3059. "Pedagogie teilhardienne." *Revue Teilhard de Chardin*
(1968): 36, 15-21.

3060. Peidró Pastor, Ismael. "Los temas de la filosofía del
derecho en el pensamiento de Pierre Teilhard de Chardin." *Anuario de filosofía des derecho* (1975): 18,
109-152.

3061. Pemán, José Maria de. "Evolución." *Destino* (1958):
       1066, 37.

3062. Penn Anthony, G.F. "Whither Evolution? Some Questions
       to Teilhard de Chardin." *International Philosophical
       Quarterly* (1975): 15, 71-82.

3063. Penning de Vries, Piet. *Aan de bronnen.* Nijmegen: B.
       Gottmer, 1971. See pp. 161-172.

3064. ————. "De geestelijke achtergrond van het werk van
       Teilhard de Chardin." *Streven* (1963-64): 17, 117-128.

3065. ————. *Geestelijk leven vandaag.* Nijmegen: B. Gott-
       mer, 1973. See pp. 176-192.

3066. "O Pensamento de Teilhard de Chardin." *Convivium* (1965):
       3, 3-96. Contains Items 20, 48, 904, 2338, 2393.

3067. "El pensamiento oculto del P. Teilhard de Chardin."
       Cristiandad (1967): 440, 188-198.

3068. Pepper, G. "Le phénomène Teilhard." *Cross Currents*
       (1960): 10, 289-293.

3069. Perazzi, Gianna. "L'eternel feminin teilhardiano nell-
       'interpretazione di P. de Lubac." *Ricerche religiose*
       (1968): 2, 51-57.

3070. "Le Père Teilhard de Chardin neveu de Voltaire." *Cherch-
       eurs et curieux* (1967): 17, 1123-1128; (1968): 18, 75-
       76, 155.

3071. "Le Père Teilhard de Chardin: Rien ne peut arrêter la
       naissance d'une Chine nouvelle." *Croissance des jeunes
       nations* (1968): 82, 16-17.

3072. Peretti, André de. "L'apport du Père Teilhard de Char-
       din à la pensée contemporaine." *Amis du Bec-Hellouin*
       (1963): 7, 17-23.

3073. Peretti, M. de. "Témoignage." *Recherches et débats*
       (1955): 12, 165.

3074. Perez Arbelaez, Enrique. "Desde el átomo al noon. Una
       critica al P. Pierre Teilhard de Chardin." *Revista
       javeriana* (1959): 51, 58-67.

3075. Perez del Viso, Ignacio. "Teilhard: Sacerdote del Cristo cósmico." *Estudios* (1965): 54, 99-106.

3076. Perier, Philippe. "L'Abbé de Tourville inspirateur du P. Teilhard." *Revue Teilhard de Chardin* (1962): 11, 6-9.

3077. ———. "Henri de Tourville et le P. Teilhard de Chardin." *Études sociales* (1957): 39, 45-55.

3078. Périgord, Monique. "De la part maudite à l'énergie humaine. Destination de l'énergie humaine chez Georges Bataille et Teilhard de Chardin." *Revue Teilhard de Chardin* (1970): 43, 16-21; 44/45, 27-34; (1971): 46, 26-37.

3079. ———. *L'esthétique de Teilhard.* Paris: Éditions Universitaires, 1965.

3080. ———. *Évolution et temporalité chez Teilhard.* Paris: Éditions Universitaires, 1963.
Evolucão e temporalidade em Teilhard. Petrópolis: Vozes, 1967.
Evolución y temporalidad segun Teilhard. Buenos Aires: Columba, 1968.

3081. ———. "Y-a-t-il une esthétique teilhardienne? ou les conséquences esthétiques d'un ultra-humain." *Actes du 5e Congrès international d'esthétique.* Amsterdam: Congrès, 1968, pp. 851-854.

3082. Perini, G. "Studio e polemica su Teilhard de Chardin." *Divus Thomas* (1966): 69, 248-273.

3083. Perlinski, Jerome. "Resources for the New Theology." *The Teilhard Review* (1968): 1.

3084. ———. "A Stem of Man: Theory of History in Teilhard de Chardin." Doctoral dissertation, St. Louis University, 1968.

3085. ———. "Teilhard and the Counter-Culture." *The Teilhard Review* (1971): 1, 11-17.

3086. ———. "Teilhard and the Mystical Life." *The Teilhard Review* (1972): 3, 86-91.

3087. ———. "Teilhard and the New Theology." *The Teilhard
       Review* (1968): 1, 21-28.
       Also *Theoria to Theory* (1968-69): 1, 19-30.

3088. ———. "Teilhard's Vision of Peace and War." *Catholic
       Worker* (1968): 3, 4-5.
       Also *The Teilhard Review* (1968-69): 2, 52-61.

3089. ———. "The Unpublished Works of Teilhard de Chardin."
       Theoria to Theory (1968-69): 4, 62-66; (1969-70): 1,
       63-68.

3090. Perrenoud-Theis, William. "L'évolutionnisme renversé
       par Norbert Hugedé." Item 1259, pp. 141-173.

3091. ———. "Kvar figuroj de l'plej vivanta Katolikismo."
       Espero Katolika (1964): 546, 62-64; 547, 74-76.

3092. Pessac, J. "Le R.P. Teilhard de Chardin." *Psyché* (1955):
       10, 2-5.

3093. Pessenesse, Pierre. "Teilhard de Chardin, remarcas d'una
       filosofía nova." *Vida nova* (1961): 22, 25-33.

3094. Peter, V. "Will the Real Teilhard Please Stand Up?"
       Communio (1977): 4, 283-284.

3095. "Petit lexique." In Item 3237.

3096. Petruzzelis, Nicola. "L'avvenire dell'uomo secondo
       Teilhard de Chardin." *Rassegna de scienze filosofiche*
       (1963): 16, 209-230.

3097. ———. "Discorrendo di metafisica, di teilhardismo
       et di scientismo." *Sapienza* (1978): 31, 227-229.

3098. Pfleger, Karl. *Christusfreude. Auf den Wegen Teilhards
       de Chardin.* Frankfurt-am-Main: J. Knecht, 1973.

3099. ———. "Erwacht zum universalen Christus." *Perspek-
       tiven der Zukunft* (1972): 6, 2-3.

3100. ———. "'Im Dienst der Freimaurer?' Teilhard de Char-
       din als Christozentriker und seine Kritiker." *Wort
       und Wahrheit* (1963): 18, 134-137.

3101. ———. "In der Werkstatt des Teilhard de Chardins."
       Acta teilhardiana (1969): 6, 51-53.

3102. ———. *Lebensausklang.* Frankfurt-am-Main: J. Knecht, 1975.

3103. ———. "Teilhard de Chardin auf dem Schlachtfeld des Zeitgeistes." *Perspektiven der Zukunft* (1969): 6, 2-3.

3104. ———. "Teilhardiana. Zu Büchern von und über Teilhard de Chardin." *Wort und Wahrheit* (1961): 16, 301-305.

3105. ———. "Versenkt im Geist. Pfingstliches Bekenntnis." *Seele* (1962): 38, 125-129.

3106. ———. *Die verwegenen Christozentriker.* Freiburg: Herder, 1964. See pp. 129-135, 143-174.

3107. ———. "Warum ich Teilhard de Chardin liebe." *Perspektiven der Zukunft* (1970): 6, 2-4.

3108. ———. "Die Wunder der Evolution, ein Blick in Teilhard de Chardins Weltbild." *Der christliche Sonntag* (1961): 11, 85-86.

3109. "Le 'phénomène Teilhard.'" *Informations catholiques internationales* (1965): 237, 19-29.

3110. "The Phenomenon of Man. Two Views of the Meaning and Importance of Père Teilhard de Chardin's Controversial Work." *Commonweal* (1960): 72, 439-443. Contains Items 1418, 1539.

3111. Philippe de la Trinité, Fr. "Un bulletin bibliographique du P. Labourdette sur Teilhard de Chardin." *Ephemerides carmeliticae* (1969): 20, 403-432.

3112. ———. *Dialogue avec le marxisme?* "Ecclesiam suam" *et Vatican II.* Paris: Cèdre, 1966. See pp. 73-96.

3113. ———. "Europa." *Cristiandad* (1967): 440, 193.

3113a. ———. "Un hommage en collaboration à Teilhard de Chardin." *Pensée catholique* (1970): 125, 32-50.

3114. ———. "Il modernismo teilhardiano." *Relazioni* (1965): 12, 23-31.

3115. ———. *Pour et contre Teilhard de Chardin, penseur religieux.* Saint-Céneré: Éditions Saint-Michel, 1970. See Item 4081.

3116. ———. "Rome et Teilhard." *Seminarium* (1964): 16, 79-121. Excerpt from Item 3117.

3117. ———. *Rome et Teilhard de Chardin.* Paris: Fayard, 1964.

3118. ———. *Teilhard de Chardin: Étude critique.* 2 vols.; Paris: La Table Ronde, 1968. See Item 4081.

3119. ———. "Teilhard de Chardin. Étude critique." *Pensée catholique* (1968): 116, 16-34. Excerpt from Item 3118. "Teilhard de Chardin." *Renovatio* (1968): 3, 175-193. "Teilhard de Chardin." *El cruzado español* (1968): 11, 61-68.

3120. Number deleted.

3121. ———. "Teilhard de Chardin: Synthèse ou confusion? 1e partie." *Divinitas* (1959): 1, 285-329.

3122. ———. "Teilhard de Chardin: Synthèse ou confusion? 2e partie." *Pensée catholique* (1959): 63, 26-40.

3123. ———. *Teilhard et le teilhardisme.* Roma: Libraria Editrice della Pontificia Università Lateranense, 1962. Also *Divinitas* (1963): 7, 126-197.

3124. ———. "Vatican II, 'Philosophia perennis' et Teilhard de Chardin." *Divinitas* (1968): 12, 251-278. Also *Miscellanea André Combes.* Roma: Libraria Editrice della Pontificia Università Lateranense, 1968, vol. 3, pp. 397-424.

3125. "O phylogênese do homem e Padre Teilhard de Chardin." *Catolicismo* (1963): 151. "Phylogenesis of Man and Father Teilhard de Chardin." *Social Justice Review* (1964): 57, 196-199. Also *Rally*, April, 1964.

3126. Pichette, Henri. "Poème offert." Item 3292, pp. 13-14.

3127. Picot, M. "Pierre Teilhard de Chardin et l'heure du protestantisme." *Christianisme social* (1960): 68, 34-47.

3128. Pieper, J. "Der Mensch im Kosmos. Darstellung und Kritik des Werkes von Pierre Teilhard de Chardin." *Hippokrates* (1961): 32, 541-546.

3129. Pierrat, Bernard. *Réflexions d'un teilhardien*. Paris: Le Hameau, 1974. Also 2d ed., 1975.

3130. "Pierre Teilhard de Chardin." *Les cahiers rationalistes* (1960): 106-152.

3131. "Pierre Teilhard de Chardin." *Convivium* (1965): 3, 3-6.

3132. "Pierre Teilhard de Chardin." *Kontynenty* (1963): 55/56, 7-25. Contains Items 2616, 2831.

3133. "Pierre Teilhard de Chardin." *Livres de France* (1966): 4, 27-30.

3134. "Pierre Teilhard de Chardin." *Psyché* (1955): 99/100.

3135. "Pierre Teilhard de Chardin." *La table ronde* (1955): 90, 13-86.

3136. "Pierre Teilhard de Chardin et sa pensée philosophique et religieuse." *L'Osservatore romano*, July 1, 1962. Also issued as *A propos de l'oeuvre du Père Teilhard de Chardin*. Roma: Osservatore Romano, 1962.

3137. "Pierre Teilhard de Chardin. Il gesuita proibito." *L'Europa letteraria* (1960): 2, 11-15.

3138. "Pierre Teilhard de Chardin: 'Lettere di viaggio.'" *Questitalia* (1963): 58, 54-56.

3139. Pimstein Lamm, Abraham. *Teilhard de Chardin, la evolución desfigurada*. Santiago de Chile: Talleres de Arancibia Hermanos, 1967.

3140. Pintacuda, Ennio. *Introduzione alla lettura delle opere di Teilhard de Chardin*. Palermo: E.S.D., 1966.

3141. Piovene, Guido. "L'evoluzione dell'uomo delle molecule a Dio." *La Stampa* (1968): 223, 3.

3142. ———. "Il pensiero di Teilhard de Chardin. Scienziato e mistico." *La Stampa* (1968): 237, 3.

3143. ———. "Teilhard supera la vechie barriere fra scienza
       e religione, materia e spirito." *La Stampa*, March 6,
       1963, p. 9.

3144. Piron, J.O. "Qu'est-ce que le teilhardisme?" *La pensée
       et les hommes* (1964): 7, 197-204, 221-225.

3145. ———. "Teilhard de Chardin ou 'beaucoup de bruit pour
       rien.'" *Le pensée et les hommes* (1962): 12, 211-216.

3146. Piront, Andre. "Réflexion sur la finalité dans la na-
       ture." *Études teilhardiennes* (1969): 2, 39-80.

3147. Piveteau, Jean. "Aspects de la pensée scientifique du
       Père Teilhard de Chardin." *Société des ingénieurs
       civils de France. Mémoires O.C.F.* (1965): 9/10,
       49-57.

3148. ———. "Les conditions organiques du phénomène humain."
       L'anthropologie (1948): 52.

3149. ———. "Conférence." Item 3292, pp. 86-96.

3150. ———. "Les débuts de l'oeuvre scientifique du Père
       Teilhard de Chardin." *Europe* (1965): 431/432, 34-39.

3151. ———. "Discours." Item 1259, pp. 43-45.

3152. ———. "D'où vient l'homme?" *Les nouvelles littér-
       aires* (1964): 1947, 1-2.

3153. ———. "L'histoire de la vie et l'origine des espèces."
       La table ronde (1955): 90, 31-35.

3154. ———. "Hommage au Père Teilhard de Chardin." *Re-
       cherches et débats* (1955): 12, 149-173.

3155. ———. "L'homme de science." Item 3903, pp. 133-154.

3156. ———. "L'oeuvre paléontologique du Père Teilhard de
       Chardin." *Quaternaria. Storia naturale e culturale
       del Quaternario* (1955): 2, 1-3.

3157. ———. *L'origine de l'homme.* Paris: Hachette, 1962.

3158. ———. *Le Père Teilhard de Chardin, savant.* Paris:
       Fayard, 1964.
           Il Padre Teilhard de Chardin scienziato. Modena:
       Edizioni Paoline, 1967.

3159. ———. "Das Phänomen Mensch in der Deutung Teilhards."
Item 1331, pp. 92-107.

3160. ———. "Pierre Teilhard de Chardin." *Bulletin de la
Société géologique de France* (1957): 7, 787-809.

3161. ———. "Pierre Teilhard de Chardin, 1881-1955." Item
3978, pp. 43-57.

3162. ———. "Positions de Jean Piveteau." *Itinéraires*
(1965): 96, 127-140. Reply to questionnaire in Item
3259.

3163. ———. "Quelques aspects de la paléontologie humaine
depuis la mort du P. Teilhard." Item 1259, pp. 68-76.

3164. ———. "Qu'est-ce que l'hominisation?" *Paraboles*,
May 8-9, 1965, p. 5.

3165. ———. "Rapport sur l'attribution du Prix Garaudy
au R.P. Pierre Teilhard de Chardin." *Comptes rendus
sommaires de la société géologique de France*, séance
du 9 juin 1952, pp. 198-201.
Also Item 4669, vol. 10, pp. 4595-4598.

3166. ———. "Teilhard de Chardin et le problème de l'évolution." *Les nouvelles littéraires* (1965): 1993, 1, 11.

3167. ———. "Teilhard de Chardin et la science." *Livres
de France* (1966): 4, 12-15.

3168. ———. "Teilhard et l'hominisation." Item 3653, pp.
119-143.

3169. ———. "Teilhard, tel que je l'ai connu." Item 2035,
pp. 29-39.
Also *Union catholique des scientifiques français*
(1968): 106, 8-15.

3170. Pivot, Bernard. "Pan sur Teilhard!" *Le Figaro littéraire* (1965): 1020, 2.

3171. Plater-Syberg, Alexandre. "Le chanoine Plater-Syberg,
curé de Verneuil, s'interroge sur le message de Teilhard de Chardin." *La Montagne*, February, 1969, p. 5.

3172. ———. *Comment je comprends le message du Père Teilhard de Chardin. (Essai théologique: Un nouveau*

point de vue sur le système teilhardien. Moulins:
Imprimeries réunis, 1968.

3173. ————. Teilhard de Chardin: Sa méthode et synthèse
de son oeuvre. Essai critique. Moulins: Imprimeries
réunies, 1971.

3174. Ploegmakers, Erich. "De totale liefde van een maag-
delijk mens. Een ervaring van Teilhard de Chardin."
Carmel (1965): 17, 350-368.

3175. Plużański, Tadeusz. "Alcune osservazioni sulla dialettica di Teilhard de Chardin e di Marx." Bollettino informazioni del Centro di studi e di ricerca
Teilhard de Chardin, Istituto Stensen (1973): 16, 1-
13.

3176. ————. "Czlowiek w perspektywie Teilharda i Marksa."
Czlowiek i Światopogląd (1970): 3, 76-86.
"L'homme dans la perspective de Teilhard et de Marx."
Europe (1970): 495, 162-171.
"Der Mensch in der Philosophie von Teilhard und
Marx." Acta teilhardiana (1972): 2, 61-68.

3177. ————. "Czlowiek w perspektywie teilhardowskiej."
[Man in the Teilhardian Perspective.] Miesięcznik
Literacki (1967): 6, 79-87.

3178. ————. "Duch Teilharda na Soborze." [The Spirit of
Teilhard at the Council.] Zeszyty Argumentów (1964):
1, 128-131.

3179. ————. "Egzystencjalne aspekty teilhardyzmu." [Ex-
istential Aspects of Teilhardism.] Euhemer (1970):
1, 91-102.

3180. ————. Marksizm a fenomen Teilharda. [Marxism and the
Teilhardian Phenomenon.] Warszawa: Ksiąska i Wiedza,
1967.

3181. ————. "Marksizm e teilhardyzm." [Marxism and Teilhardism.] Studia Filozoficzne (1966): 3, 101-134;
(1970): 4, 159-176.

3182. ————. "Moment-czas-nieskończoność (w ujęciu Pascala,
Teilharda i Marksa)." [Moment, Time and Infinity in
the Concepts of Pascal, Teilhard and Marx.] Życie i
myśl (1971): 3, 86-98.
Also Item 3888, pp. 170-191.

3183. ———. "Nekotorye čerty vozzrenij Teilharda de Chardina." [Some Aspects of Teilhard de Chardin's Vision of the World.] *Ot Erazma Rotterdamskogo do Bertranda Russella*. [From Erasmus of Rotterdam to Bertrand Russell.] Moskva: Myśl, 1919, pp. 158-216.

3184. ———. "Niektóre aspekty antropologii filozoficz ej Piotra Teilharda de Chardin." [Some Aspects of Pierre Teilhard de Chardin's Philosophical Anthropology.] *Życie i myśl* (1965): 10, 63-70. Also *Zeszyty Argumentów* (1965): 5, 34-46. Also Item 3888, pp. 347-359.

3185. ———. "Perchè Teilhard? Riflessioni di un marxista davanti a Teilhard." *Futuro dell'uomo* (1976): 3, 13-20.

3186. ———. "Pierre Teilhard de Chardin." *Euhemer* (1965): 2, 25-40.

3187. ———. "Piotr Teilhard de Chardin w świetle ineditów." [Teilhard in the Light of Unpublished Writings.] *Zeszyty Argumentów* (1967): 1, 71-83.

3188. ———. "Problematika moralna teilhardyzmu." [The Moral Problem of Teilhardism.] *Zeszyty Argumentów* (1964): 5, 25-44.

3189. ———. *Teilhard de Chardin*. Warszawa: Wiedza Powszedura, 1963.

3190. ———. "Teilhard de Chardin i niektóre kontrowersje wspólczesnego humanizmu." [Teilhard de Chardin and Certain Controversies of Contemporary Humanism.] *Filozoficzne problemy wspólczesnego chrześcijaństwa*. [Philosophical Problems of Contemporary Christianity.] Warszawa: Państwowe Wydawnictwo Naukowe, 1973, pp. 7-49.

3191. ———. "Teilhard w Vézelay." [Teilhard at Vézelay.] *Zeszyty Argumentów* (1966): 6, 71-84.

3192. ———. "Teilhardowski paradoks ukryty i przekroczony." [The Teilhardian Paradox Hidden and Drawn Out.] *Paradoks w nowożytnej filozofii chrześcijanskiej*. [Paradoxes in Contemporary Christian Philosophy.] Warszawa: Państwowe Wydawnictwo Naukowe, 1970, pp. 270-322.

3193. ————. "Teilhardyzm jako ruch intelektualny i spo-
leczny." *Studia Filozoficne* (1969): 2, 99-109.
Also Item 3888, pp. 299-316.
"Le teilhardisme en tant que mouvement intellectuel
et social." *Vie catholique en Pologne* (1969): 57-60.

3194. ————. "Teilhardyzm między Pascalem a Heglem." [Teil-
hardism Between Pascal and Hegel.] *Euhemer* (1969): 4,
107-113.

3195. ————. "O Teilhardzie, marksizmie i filozoficznej
antropologii. Dwa humanizmy-jedna ludzkość." [Teil-
hard, Marxism and Philosophical Anthropology: Two Hu-
manisms, One Humanity.] *Zeszyty Argumentów* (1966):
2, 88-89.

3196. ————. "Wikól 'Sporu o Teilharda.'" [Contribution to
the Discussion on Teilhard.] *Zeszyty Argumentów* (1962):
4, 30-54.

3197. Podeur, Lucien. *Image moderne du monde et foi chrétienne.* Paris: Le Centurion, 1976.

3198. Podsian, Antoni. "Droga twórczosci Teilharda de Chardin." [The Direction of Teilhard de Chardin's Activity.] *Życie i myśl* (1963): 910, 171-179.

3199. Poersch, J.L. *Evolucão e antropologia no espaço e no
tempo: Síntese da cosmovisão de Teilhard de Chardin.*
São Paulo: Herder, 1972.

3200. Poggi, Vincenzo. "Teilhard de Chardin e la civiltà
dell'universale secondo L.S. Senghor." *Umanesimo ed
evangelizzazione.* Milano: Vita e Pensiero, 1969, pp.
32-38.

3201. Polanyi, Michael. "An Epic Theory of Evolution." *Saturday Review,* January 31, 1960, p. 20.

3202. Polato, Franco. *Blondel e Teilhard de Chardin. Con-
vergenze et divergenze.* Bologna: Zanichelli, 1967.

3203. Polgar, Ladislas. *Internationale Teilhard-Bibliographie,
1955-1965.* Freiburg/München: Alber, 1965.

3204. ————. "A nem-francia nyelvü Teilhard-irodalom."
[Non-French Literature on Teilhard.] *Katolikus
Szemle* (1965): 3, 261-264.

3205. ————. "Teilhard de Chardin, Pierre." In "Biblio-
graphia de historia Societatis Iesu." *Archivum Historicum Societatis Iesu* (1953): 22, 753; (1955): 24,
321; (1956): 25, 720; (1957): 26, 401; (1958): 27,
462-466; (1959): 28, 458-462; (1960): 29, 503-509;
(1961): 30, 473-476; (1962): 31, 463-470; (1963):
32, 397-405; (1964): 33, 425-439; (1965): 34, 403-
420; (1966): 35, 467-477; (1967): 36, 426-450; (1968):
37, 537-550; (1969): 38, 591-601; (1970): 39, 442-
450; (1971): 40, 558-565; (1972): 41, 421-435; (1973):
42, 428-435; (1974): 43, 457-466; (1975): 44, 397-
404; (1976): 45, 509-515; (1977): 46, 517-522; (1978):
47, 475-479; (1979): 48, 408-410.

3206. Polkowski, Andrzej. "Bibliografia polska." Item 3888,
pp. 419-440.

3207. ————. "Bibliografia teilhardowska." *Życie i myśl*
(1970): 20, 7-8, 165-177.

3208. ————. "Świadectwo Teilharda. [Teilhard's Witness.]
Warszawa: Pax, 1974.

3209. ————. "Teilhard de Chardin w Polsce." *Życie i myśl*
(1971): 3, 99-113.
Also Item 3888, pp. 317-341.
"Teilhard de Chardin in Polonia." *La vita cattolica
in Polonia* (1971): 6, 47-58.

3210. ————. "Teilhard i problem hominizacji." [Teilhard
and the Problem of Hominization.] Item 3888, pp. 93-
113.

3211. Ponce de Leon, Luis. "Problema del hombre: ¿es un ser
'Originario' o es un ser 'Destinado'?" *La estafeta
litteraria* (1964): 290, 3.

3212. Pongs, Hermann. *Symbolik bei Teilhard de Chardin.* Mar-
burg: Elwert, 1974.

3213. Ponnuthurai, C.S. "Teilhard de Chardin and 'Traditional
Catholicism.'" *Quest* (1966): 8, 236-241.

3214. Ponschab, August. *Die Revolution unseres Weltbildes.*
Tübingen: Niemeyer, 1973.

3215. ————. *Teilhard de Chardin. Lehre, Leben und Werk.*
Imst/Tirol: Egger, 1965.

3216. Pontet, Maurice. "Evolution According to Teilhard de
       Chardin." *Thought* (1961): 36, 167-189.

3217. ———. "L'homme et sa religion selon Pascal et Teil-
       hard." *Revue générale belge* (1968): 3, 27-42.

3218. ———. *Pascal et Teilhard, témoins de Jesus-Christ.*
       Paris: Desclée de Brouwer, 1968.

3219. Porte, Guy. "Science et religion chez Teilhard de Char-
       din." *Nice-matin*, April 11, 1967.

3220. Portillo Valcarcel, M. *Teilhard de Chardin un autor
       discutido.* Santander: Portillo, 1973.

3221. Portmann, Adolf. "Das Bild der Natur und der christliche
       Glauben. Zum Werk Teilhard de Chardins." *Universitas*
       (1961): 16, 639-645.

3222. ———. *Der Pfeil des Humanen-über P. Teilhard de Char-
       din.* Freiburg/München: Alber, 1960.

3223. ———. "Pierre Teilhard de Chardin." *Merkur* (1959):
       13, 1020-1033.

3224. ———. "Teilhard de Chardin: Forscher und Seher."
       Perspektiven der Zukunft (1972): 4, 2-5.

3225. ———. *Het wereldbeeld van Pierre Teilhard de Chardin.*
       Antwerpen/Amsterdam: Standaard Boekhandel, 1961.

3226. "Portrait graphologique." *Revue Teilhard de Chardin*
       (1964): 18, 22-24.

3227. Potter, V.R. "Teilhard de Chardin and the Concept of
       Purpose." *Zygon* 3 (1968): 367-376.

3228. Potvin, Raymond. "Introduction. Teilhard de Chardin."
       American Catholic Sociological Review (1962): 4,
       251-293.

3229. Poulain, Dorothy. "Christ and the Universe. The Vision
       of the Great Jesuit Paleontologist, Pierre Teilhard
       de Chardin." *Commonweal* (1959): 69, 460-464.

3230. ———. "The First Teilhard Symposium." Item 497, pp.
       102-107.

3231.   ————. "Le phénomène humain en Amérique." *Revue Teil-hard de Chardin* (1960): 3/4, 21-22.

3232.   ————. "Teilhard de Chardin and the Monitum." *Twenti-eth Century* (1963-64): 18, 139-147.

3233.   ————. "Teilhardians at Vézelay." *Twentieth Century* (1966): 4, 293-299.

3234.   Poulin, Daniel. "Teilhard de Chardin?" *Enseignement* (1968): 3, 15-18.

3235.   ————. "Teilhard de Chardin." *Action pédagogique* (1970): 12/13, 171-184.

3236.   ————. *Teilhard de Chardin. Essai de bibliographie (1955-1965).* Québec: Presses de l'Univeristé Laval, 1966.

3237.   *Pour comprendre Teilhard.* Paris: Lettres modernes, 1962. Contains Items 2369, 2773, 2774, 2787, 2795, 3095, 3254.

3238.   "Pour le nouveau générale des Jésuites: Le Père Teil-hard excusable, c'était un savant, non un théologien." *L'Aurore,* June 15, 1965, p. 11.

3239.   "Pour ou contre Teilhard." *Ecclesia* (1964): 188, 15-26.

3240.   "Pourquoi Teilhard?" *Frères du monde* (1963): 21, 5.

3241.   Prat, Henri. *Métamorphose explosive de l'humanité.* 2 vols.; Paris: Sedes, 1961.

3242.   ————. "L'unité de l'homme et du cosmos." *Univers* (1966): 3, 66-77.

3243.   Prat, O. "Science, God and the Nature of Man." *New-man Association, Philosophy of Science Group. Bul-letin* (1960): 39, 7-8.

3244.   Pratt, Grace K. "Teilhard de Chardin's Theory of the Noosphere: Some Questions and Some Educational Con-cerns." *Proceedings of the Philosophy of Education Society* (1969): 25, 215-223.

3245.   Prentice, Robert. "Piani de coordinamento di Aris-totele G. Duns Scoto e Teilhard de Chardin sul prob-lema di Dio." *Antonianum* (1970): 45, 44-51.

3246. Presicci, Felice. *Il nuovo umanesimo in Teilhard de Chardin.* Taranto: Acta medica tarantina, 1975.

3247. *Proceedings of the Teilhard Conference, 1964.* New York: Fordham University, 1965. Contains Items 337, 352, 1109, 1615, 2085, 2958, 3032, 3784.

3248. Progoff, Ira. "Jung, Synchronicity, and Human Destiny." *Main Currents in Modern Thought: The Journal of Integrative Education* (1974): 30, 94-98.

3249. Pucheu, René. "Teilhard et le pari." Item 1284, pp. 381-390.
    "Teilhard y la apuesta." Item 1284 trans., pp. 75-88.

3250. Quadrio, Giuseppe. "Teilhard de Chardin, Pietro." *Dizionario ecclesiastico* (1958): 3, 1056-1057.

3251. Quagliani, Antonio. "Teilhard de Chardin: La crisi dell' idea di natura." *Il mulino* (1971): 20, 834-855.

3252. Quéant, Olivier. "Il faut de tout pour faire un monde. Biologie et religion." *Plaisir de France*, January, 1963.

3253. Quénétain, Tanneguy de. "Comment le Français voient Dieu." *Réalités* (1964): 219, 76-81.

3254. ————. "L'évolution et la genèse du monde." In Item 3237.

3255. ————. "Un livre qui boulverse notre vision du monde." *Réalités* (1956): 128, 40-44.

3256. ————. "La mission que m'a confiée le Pape." *Réalités* (1965): 239, 73-79.

3257. ————. "Teilhard, une marée montante." *Réalités* (1964): 227, 86-93.

3258. Querol, Antonio de. "Teilhard sigue señalando el punto Omega. Catorce años después de su muerte." *El ciervo* (1969): 182, 17.

3259. "Questionnaire: Teilhard et la science." *Itinéraires* (1965): 96, 5-6.

3260. "Qui est Teilhard de Chardin?" *Le monde et la vie* (1962): 115, 65-66.

3261. Quiles, Ismael. "Evolución y religión en Teilhard y Aurobindo." *Stromata* (1974): 30, 419-436.

3262. ———. *El hombre y la evolución según Aurobindo y Teilhard.* Buenos Aires: Ediciones Depalma, 1976. Contains Item 3266.

3263. ———. *Introducción a Teilhard de Chardin. El cosmos, el hombre y Dios.* Buenos Aires: Tipográfica Editora Argentina, 1975.

3264. ———. "La persona según Sri Aurobindo y Teilhard de Chardin." *Convivium* (1975): 18, 3-12.

3265. ———. "El personalismo, clave dela cosmogénesis, según Teilhard de Chardin." *Stromata* (1973): 29, 259-277.

3266. ———. "El superhombre según Aurobindo Ghose y Teilhard de Chardin." *Stromata* (1976): 32, 151-170. Also Item 3262, pp. 75-103.

3267. Quin, James. "The Teilhardian Visionary Synthesis." *Christian Order* (1964): 5, 459-476.

3268. Quinzio, Sergio. *Che cosa ha veramente detto Teilhard de Chardin?* Roma: Ubaldini, 1967.

3269. ———. "Darwin e Sant'Ignazio. La grande 'sintesi' di Teilhard de Chardin." *Tempo presente* (1963): 3/4, 20-26.

3270. Rabut, Olivier. *Dialogue avec Teilhard de Chardin.* Paris: Cerf, 1958.
Also 2d ed., Paris: Aubier-Montaigne, Cerf, Desclée de Brouwer, Éditions ouvrières, 1968.
Le problème de Dieu inscrit dans l'évolution. Paris: Cerf, 1963.
Teilhard de Chardin: Critical Study. New York: Sheed and Ward, 1961.
Incontro con Teilhard de Chardin. Torino: Borla, 1962.
Gespräch mit Teilhard de Chardin. Naturwissenschaftliche, philosophische und theologische Diskussion seines Werkes. Freiburg/Basel/Wien: Herder,

1963.
   Dialogo con Teilhard de Chardin. Barcelona: Estela,
   1966.
   Diálogo com Teilhard de Chardin. São Paulo: Livraria Duas Cidades, 1967.

3271. ————. "Dialogue with Teilhard de Chardin." *Catholic
       World* (1961): 194, 21-27. Excerpt from Item 3270.

3272. Rada García, Eloy. "Sobre la idea de persona en el P.
       Teilhard de Chardin." *Revista de filosofía* (1967):
       26, 231-246.

3273. Rahmé, Georges. "Teilhard le mystique." *Revue Teilhard
       de Chardin* (1974): 58/59, 30-38.

3274. Rajan, Sundara. "The Concept of Person in de Chardin."
       Darshana International (1970): 10, 34-40.

3275. Rambaud, Henri. "Dans le guêpier teilhardien. Le grand
       virage des jésuites." *Le monde et le vie* (1965): 148,
       39-43.

3276. ————. "L'étrange foi du Père Teilhard de Chardin."
       Itinéraires (1965): 91, 114-143; (1967): 114, 110-
       246.

3277. ————. "Les tricheries du P. de Lubac dans les 'Let-
       tres intimes' de Teilhard de Chardin." *Itinéraires*
       (1972): 168, 69-109.

3278. Ramírez Alvarado, Javier. "La fe y la felicidad."
       Christus, September, 1974, pp. 28-35.

3279. Raulin, Albert. "Teilhard de Chardin. Foredrag
       holdt i 'Katolsk Forum' i Oslo, 7·2·1961." *Catholica*
       (1961): 18, 49-62.

3280. Raven, Charles E. "Orthodoxy and Science." Item 501,
       pp. 50-59.
          Also Item 497, pp. 50-59.

3281. ————. "Réflexions sur l'évolution." *Revue Teilhard
       de Chardin* (1961): 5, 3-6.

3282. ————. *Teilhard de Chardin, Scientist and Seer.* Lon-
       don: Collins, 1962.
          Also New York: Harper & Row, 1963.

3283. Ravera, Silvio. *Due profili: Pierre Teilhard de Chardin. Primo Mazzolari.* Vicenza: La Locusta, 1971.

3284. Raverdy, Pierre-Ives. "Teilhard de Chardin du P. Wildiers." *Cahiers de vie franciscaine* (1962): 33, 33–35.

3285. Ravier, André. "Garric et Teilhard de Chardin." *Revue de la Haute-Auvergne* (1968): 183–186.

3286. ————. "Homélie pour la Messe du Xe anniversaire de la mort du P. Teilhard de Chardin." Item 4883, pp. 155–163. "La dernière Pâque de Teilhard de Chardin." *Ecclesia* (1966): 205, 181–186. Also *La mystique et les mystiques*. Paris: Desclée de Brouwer, 1965.

3287. ————. "Teilhard de Chardin et l'éxperience mystique d'après ses notes intimes." Item 3950, pp. 212–232.

3288. ————. "Teilhard mystique?" *Revue des deux mondes* (1972): 3, 619–623.

3289. "Recherches paléo-anthropologiques en Afrique." *Revue Teilhard de Chardin* (1962): 10, 23–26.

3290. Redlich, Virgil. "Das Religiöse bei Teilhard de Chardin." *Seckauer Hefte* (1962): 25, 54–57.

3291. Reedy, Gerard. "Metaphor in 'The Phenomenon of Man.'" *Thought* (1971): 46, 247–261.

3292. *Réflexions sur la bonheur*. Paris: Seuil, 1960. Contains Items 83, 149, 287, 291, 324, 424, 508, 754, 1641, 1768, 1923, 2022, 2381, 2385, 2401, 3126, 3149, 3311, 3402, 3461, 3953, 4026, 4502, 4750.

3293. Refoule, F. "Teilhard de Chardin et Bultmann." *Parole et mission* (1964): 7, 602–621.

3294. Rehmann, E. "Gibt es 'kirchliche Kunst'?" *Schweizer Rundschau* (1966): 65, 328–341.

3295. Reid, Leslie. "Teilhard and the Tree of Life." *The Teilhard Review* (1969): 1, 40–45.

3296. Reilly, James P., Jr. "A Student of the 'Phenomena.'" Item 1544, pp. 49–63.

3297. Reilly, Michael C. "Teilhard de Chardin: Synthetical Appraisal." *Philippine Scholastic* (1962): 4, 152-161.

3298. Reinalter, Helmut. "Der Einfluss Kardinal Newmans auf Teilhard de Chardin." Item 3299, pp. 77-94.

3299. ———. *Evolution der Welt. Versuche über Teilhard de Chardin.* Innsbruck: Inn-Verlag, 1973. Contains Items 617, 1110, 1846, 1915, 2157, 3298, 3589.

3300. Reinhard, Edmund. *Teilhard de Chardin. Sein Weltbild im Blickfeld der Religionsphilosophie Mathilde Ludendorffs.* Pähl/Obb: Franz von Bebenburg, 1966.

3301. Reinhard, Pierre. "'Passons aux barbares.'" *Cahiers de vie franciscaine* (1962): 33, 36-49.

3302. Remane, Adolf. "Entwicklungslinie in der levenden Natur." Item 1213, pp. 181-198.

3303. Renwart, L. "Du nouveau sur Teilhard." *Nouvelle revue théologique* (1962): 84, 632-634.

3304. Rétif, André. "Construire en avant. Ce que le Père Teilhard de Chardin conseillait à une veuve." *Offertoire* (1966): 119/120, 27-32.

3305. ———. "La pensée missionnaire de Teilhard de Chardin." *Mission de l'Eglise* (1959): 15, 193-196.

3306. ———. "Teilhard missionaire." *Cahiers d'éducation missionaire* (1965): 12, 5-12.

3307. ———, and Louis Rétif. *Teilhard et l'evangélisation des temps nouveaux. Un aspect peu connu de la personnalité de Teilhard de Chardin.* Paris: Éditions ouvrières, 1970.

3308. Revel, Jean-François. *La cabale des dévots. Pourquoi des philosophes?* Paris: R. Julliard, 1962. See pp. 75-87.
       Also Paris: J.J. Pauvert, 1965. See pp. 82-96.

3309. Revel, M. "Création et révélation." *Trait d'union* (1962): 96, 15-17.

3310. Revol, Enrique Luis. *Símbolo y evolución humana.* Córdoba, Argentina: Universidad Nacional de Córdoba, Facultad de filosofía y humanidades, 1970.

3311.   Reymond, André. "La Croisière Jaune, souvenirs." Item
         3292, pp. 167-172.

3312.   ———. "Réponse." *Itinéraires* (1965): 96, 105-106.
         Reply to questionnaire in Item 3259.

3313.   Rezek, Roman. *Álarc nélkül (Teilhard élete és látomása)*.
         [Without a Mask (The Life and Vision of Teilhard).]
         São Paulo: Ahogy lehet, 1969.

3314.   ———. "Bibliographie des écrits de Teilhard de Char-
         din." Mimeographed. São Paulo: Rezek, 1972.

3315.   ———. "Como êle crê? Reflexões sobre o primeiro
         volume da 'Teologia especulativa e prática' de Teil-
         hard de Chardin." *Credo para amanhã*. Petrópolis:
         Vozes, 1970, vol. 1, pp. 135-156.

3315a.   ———. "Contribuicão do pensamento de Teilhard de Char-
         din para os direitos humanos." *A teologia em diálogo*.
         I. Direitos humanos. São Paulo: Edições Paulinas,
         1978, pp. 84-90.
         "The Contribution of Teilhard's Vision of Human
         Rights." *Forum for Correspondence and Contact* (1978):
         9, 101-106.

3316.   ———. "Contribuições de Teilhard de Chardin para a
         pedagogia do homem moderno." *Cadernos monásticos*
         (1971): 8, 29-41.

3317.   ———. "De la physique à l'hyperphysique." *Leopold-
         ianum* (1975): 1, 9-18.
         "From Physics to Hyperphysics." *Forum for Corre-
         spondence and Contact* (1976): 7, 34-38.

3318.   ———. *Egzistentializmus, marxzismus, Teilhard*. São
         Paulo: Ahogy lehet, 1967.

3319.   ———. *Ellene? vagy mellette? Teilhard de Chardin
         világképenék értékelése francia nyelvü könyvekben*.
         Könyvészeti tanulmányvázlat. [Against? or for Him?
         Teilhard de Chardin's Vision of the World According
         to the French Literature. Bibliographic Essay.]
         São Paulo: Rezek, 1965.
         Also *Katolikus Szemle* (1965): 3, 222-260.

3320. ————. "Az eucharisztia Teilhard szintézisében."
[The Eucharist in the Teilhardian Synthesis.] *Szolgálat* (1969): 4, 59-70.

3321. ————. *Francia-magyar Teilhard-bibliográfia*. [French
and Hungarian Teilhard Bibliography.] São Paulo:
Ahogy lehet, 1969.

3322. ————. "Os fundamentos epistemológicos e gnoseológicos
da cosmovisão de Teilhard de Chardin." *Leopoldianum*
(1976): 7, 11-38.

3323. ————. "Hogyan szenvedett Teilhard?" [How did Teilhard Suffer?] *Délamerikai Magyar Hirlap Evkönyve*
(1967): 193-214.

3324. ————. "'A Jövo zarandoka'--a 'Sondolkodó Nadszabról.'"
Ahogy lehet (1963): 132, 3-20.

3325. ————. "Madártávlatból húsz évröl. Néhány tanulság
as 1945-1965 közötti francia filozófiából." [Teach-
ings of French Philosophy Between 1945 and 1965.]
Délamerikai Magyar Hirlap Evkönyve (1965): 49-70.

3226. ————. "Magyarok Teilhard világképéröl. Könyvészeti
adattár. I. 1966 végéig. II. 1967-1970. III. 1971-
1974." [The Hungarians in Teilhard's Vision of the
World. Bibliographic List.] Mimeographed cards.
São Paulo: Rezek, 1973-75.

3227. ————. "'Megértenek--e engem valaha?' Teilhard nap-
lóinak elsö kötete." ["Doesn't Anyone Understand
Me?" The First Volume of Teilhard's Journal.] *Vigilia* (1975): 40, 741-748.

3328. ————. "Miért Teilhard?" [Why Teilhard?] *Délamerikai
Magyar Hirlap Evkönyve* (1966): 113-130.

3328a. ————. "'Nagy viharok szakadnak rám.' Teilhard bi-
zalmas leveleinek elsö kötete." ["Great Storms Await
Me." The First Volume of Teilhard's Private Letters.]
Vigilia (1976): 41, 804-816.

3329. ————. "Nyugatiak harca Teilhard körül." [The Struggle
of Westerners with Regard to Teilhard.] *Vigilia* (1970):
35, 231-239.

3330. ———. *Az örök nöi Teilhard életében es irásaiban.*
[The Eternal Feminine in the Life and Writings of
Teilhard.] São Paulo: Ahogy lehet, 1968.
Also 2d ed., 1972.

3331. ———. "Les premières 15 années. Bibliographie des
oeuvres et articles français sur Pierre Teilhard de
Chardin parus jusqu'à fin décembre 1970." Mimeographed. São Paulo: Rezek, 1972.

3332. ———. *A Rossz (a szenvedés, a bün és a halál Teilhard világképében).* [Evil (Suffering, Sin and Death
in Teilhard's Thought).] São Paulo: Ahogy lehet,
1967.

3333. ———. "Sartre existencialista humanizmusa--Teilhard
de Chardin keresztény humanizmusa." [Sartre's Exis-
tential Humanism, Teilhard's Christian Humanism.]
Délamerikai Magyar Hirlap Evkönyve (1964): 91-100.

3334. ———. *Szeretet/kozmikus energia Teilhard világ-
képében.* *Szövegközlés és értékelés.* [Love/Cosmic
Energy in Teilhard's Universe. Texts and Commentary.]
São Paulo: Ahogy lehet, 1967.

3335. ———. "Teilhard-breviárum a munka teológiájához."
[Teilhard-Breviary for the Theology of Work.] *Teológia* (1973): 7, 147-154.

3336. ———. "Teilhard de Chardin belsö dialógusa." [Teil-
hard de Chardin's Interior Dialogue.] *Teológia* (1972):
6, 152-158.

3337. ———. *Teilhard de Chardin. Bibliographie des plus
importantes études de langue française sur sa vie et
son oeuvre.* São Paulo: Ahogy lehet, 1967.

3338. ———. *Teilhard de Chardin és a filozófia.* [Teilhard
de Chardin and Philosophy.] São Paulo: Ahogy lehet,
1967.

3339. ———. *Teilhard de Chardin "pantheizmusa" és "mon-
izmusa."* [Teilhard de Chardin's "Pantheism" and "Monism."] São Paulo: Ahogy lehet, 1967.

3340. ———. "Teilhard élete és látomása." [Teilhard's Life
and Vision.] *Teológia* (1971): 5, 74-83.

3341. ————. *Teilhard és Pascal (Párhuzam és szembesítés).*
[Teilhard and Pascal (Comparison and Contrasts).]
São Paulo: Ahogy lehet, 1970.

3342. ————. "Teilhard 'folyton növekvo' Krisztusa." [The
"Ever Greater" Christ of Teilhard.] *Teológia* (1974):
8, 201-206.

3343. ————. "Teilhard hüperfizikája." [Teilhard's Hyper-
physics.] Mimeographed. São Paulo: Rezek, 1971.

3344. ————. "Teilhard hüperfizikája." [Teilhard's Hyper-
physics.] Mimeographed. 5 vols., São Paulo: Rezek,
1974.

3345. ————. "Teilhard imádságaiból." [Some of Teilhard's
Prayers.] *Vigilia* (1973): 38, 161-168.

3346. ————. *Teilhard körül--Tanulmányok.* [Studies Concerning Teilhard.] 2 vols; São Paulo: Ahogy lehet,
1968-72.

3347. ————. *Teilhard 'sodródó világa.'* [Teilhard's World
in Evolution.] Mimeographed. São Paulo: Rezek, 1968.

3348. ————. "Teilhard tudományos munkái." [Teilhard's
Scientific Works.] *Vigilia* (1974): 39, 80-85.

3349. ————. "Teilhard viszontagságai (Az emberi jelenség
körül)." [The Turmoil about Teilhard (Concerning the
Phenomenon of Man).] *Vigilia* (1974): 39, 433-439.

3350. ————. *Utak az Omega felé. Isten-"érvek" Teilhard
szintézisében.* [Roads to Omega--The Proofs of God
in Teilhard's Synthesis.] 7 vols., São Paulo: Ahogy
lehet, 1968-71.

3351. ————. "'Vou para Aquêle que ven.' Sobre a morte do
P. Teilhard de Chardin." *Credo para amanhã.* Petrópolis: Vozes, 1970, vol. 1,pp. 157-160.

3352. Riaza, Fernando. "Aportaciones teilhardianas a una
filosofía de la técnica." *Pensamiento* (1968): 24,
109-124.

3353. ————. "El hombre como fenómeno evolutivo según Teilhard de Chardin." *Arbor* (1967): 257, 5-21.

3354. ———. "La intuición de la reflexión en Teilhard de Chardin." Item 1396, pp. 87-110.

3355. ———. "Notas para un analisis formal de la fenomenologia teilhardiana." *Pensamiento* (1970): 26, 163-179.

3356. ———. *Teilhard de Chardin y la evolucion biológica.* Madrid: Ediciones Alcala, 1968.

3357. ———. "Teilhard y lo femenino." *Razón y fe* (1968): 850, 311-337.

3358. ———. *Teilhard y el trabajo.* Madrid: Editorial Zyx, 1967. Also Madrid: ICAI, 1971.

3359. Rich, Arthur. "Kritische Erwägungen vom Evolutionismus bei Teilhard de Chardin." *Reformatio* (1965): 14, 499-509.

3360. Richard, André. "Non pas en deça de Teilhard mais au delà." *L'homme nouveau*, June, 1967.

3361. ———. "Teilhard contre le teilhardisme." *L'homme nouveau*, September 1, 1963, pp. 8-9.

3362. Richard, Michel. *La pensée contemporaine. Les grands courants.* Lyon: Chronique Sociale de France, 1977. See pp. 119-124.

3363. Richards, Michael. "An Unreal Contrast? Teilhard de Chardin and the Future of Man." *Tablet* (1966): 6592.

3364. Richter, Josef. "Die überindividuellen Ganzheiten bei Teilhard de Chardin." *Perspektiven der Zukunft* (1971): 1, 5-6.

3365. Rideau, Émile. "Attualità del pensiero sociale di Teilhard de Chardin." *Aggiornamenti sociali* (1975): 26, 539-558.

3366. ———. "L'avenir de l'homme vu par le Père Teilhard de Chardin." *Responsables* (1960): 2, 36-43.

3367. ———. "Die Bedeutung Teilhard de Chardins für die Gegenwart." Item 3924, pp. 147-176.

3368. ———. "Connivences de Teilhard." *Informations cath-oliques internationales* (1965): 237, 3+.

3369. ———. "Controverse sur Teilhard de Chardin." *Bulletin du Cercle thomiste Saint-Nicolas de Caen* (1965): 32, 9-21.

3370. ———. "L'egouement pour Teilhard." *Choisir* (1965): 66, 15-18.

3371. ———. "El hombre y el cosmos en la fenomenologia teilhardiana." *Hechos y dichos* (1966): 274-281.

3372. ———. "Un homme qui a aimé l'homme." *Responsables* (1962): 3, 11-14.
   Also *Revue Teilhard de Chardin* (1962): 11, 3-5.

3373. ———. "Influssi di Teilhard sulla cultura moderna." *Futuro dell'uomo* (1977): 2, 9-19.

3374. ———. "Lettre." *Bulletin du Cercle thomiste Saint-Nicolas de Caen* (1965): 32, 10+.

3375. ———. "Das Menschenbild bei Teilhard de Chardin." *Dokumente* (1965): 21, 181-190.
   Also *Der grosse Entschluss* (1965-66): 21, 28-30, 53-57.
   "Ahogyan Teilhard az embert látta." *Vigilia* (1966): 31, 801-809.

3376. ———. "Pater Teilhard de Chardin." *Orientierung* (1958): 22, 195-196, 239-242; (1959): 23, 4-8.

3377. ———. "Péguy et Teilhard de Chardin." *Amitié Charles Péguy*, August, 1967, pp. 3-24.

3378. ———. *La pensée du Père Teilhard de Chardin*. Paris: Seuil, 1965. See Item 4086.
   O pensamento de Teilhard de Chardin. Lisboa: Livraria Morais, 1965.
   Teilhard de Chardin: A Guide to His Thought. London: Collins, 1968.
   The Thought of Teilhard de Chardin. New York: Harper & Row, 1967.
   El pensamiento de Teilhard de Chardin. Barcelona: Peninsula, 1968.

3379. ———. "Le 'phénomène Teilhard.'" *Informations cath-oliques internationales* (1965): 237, 19-29.

3380. ———. "La sexualité selon le Père Teilhard de Char- · din." *Nouvelle revue théologique* (1968): 90, 173-190. Also *Fiches documentaires du C.L.E.R.* (1967): 43, 67-69.

3381. ———. "La spiritualité missionnaire du Père Teilhard de Chardin." *Mission de l'Eglise* (1965): 3, 117-129.

3382. ———. "Teilhard de Chardin." *Panorama chrétien* (1962): 60, 8-17.

3383. ———. "Teilhard de Chardin et le travail." *Choisir* (1962): 37, 23-29. Also *Responsables* (1962): 53, 31-39.

3384. ———. "Teilhard de Chardin: L'avenir de l'homme.'" *Choisir* (1960): 6, 10-14.

3385. ———. "Teilhard de Chardin, l'inconnu ou le méconnu." *Promesses*, October, 1965, pp. 19-24; November, 1965, pp. 13-18.

3386. ———. *Teilhard oui ou non?* Paris: Fayard, 1967. *Teilhard de Chardin--ja oder nein?* München: Ars sacra, 1968. *Teilhard, ¿si o no?* Barcelona: Casal i Vall, 1968. *Si o no a Teilhard de Chardin.* Catania: Edizioni Paoline, 1969.

3387. ———. "Teilhards Botschaft der Hoffnung. Ihre Mög-lichkeiten und Grenzen." *Dokumente* (1966): 22, 187-200.

3388. Riedlinger, Helmut. "Die kosmische Königsherrschaft Christi." *Concilium* (1966): 2, 43-62. "How Universal is Christ's Kingship?" *Concilium* (1966): 1, 56-66. "El dominio cosmico de Cristo." *Concilium* (1966): 1, 108-126. "La royauté cosmique du Christ." *Concilium* (1966): 11, 95-113. "La regalità cosmica di Cristo." *Concilium* (1966): 1, 125-149. "Het kosmische koningschap van Christus." *Concilium*

(1966): 1, 98-118.
"O reinado cósmico de Cristo." *Concilium* (1966): 1, 91-111.

3389. Riefstahl, Hermann. "Neue Literatur von und über Pierre Teilhard de Chardin." *Zeitschrift für philosophische Forschung* (1968): 221, 111-130.

3390. Rigaud, Msgr. "A propos du Père Teilhard de Chardin." *Responsables* (1962): 8, 46-47.

3391. ————. "Monitum." *Bulletin diocésain de Pamiers.* August 16, 1962, pp. 147-148.

3392. Riggan, G.A. "A Selected Bibliography of the Works of Teilhard de Chardin." *Zygon* (1968): 3, 314-322.

3393. ————. "Testing the Teilhardian Foundations." *Zygon* (1968): 3, 259-313.

3394. Riley, P.G. "Evolution Still on Trial: The Witness of Father Teilhard de Chardin." *Catholic Educational Review*, September, 1962, pp. 53-56+.

3395. Riley, W. James. "Teilhard de Chardin and 'The Secular City.'" *Focus* (1966): 1, 89-99.

3396. Rillet, Jean. "Teilhard de Chardin definit le bonheur: un effort pour se joindre au mouvement éternel de la vie." *La Tribune de Genève*, January 4, 1961.

3397. Rimet, Michel. "De Teilhard de Chardin à André Lamouche." *Synthèses* (1965): 233, 76-89.

3398. Riquet, Michel. "De Renan à Teilhard de Chardin." *Saint-Luc. Evangile et médecine* (1964): 70, 100-114.

3399. *Riscoperta dell'uomo.* Milano: A. Mondadori, 1967.

3400. Rivera de Ventosa, E. "¿Mas luz en torno a Teilhard de Chardin?" *Augustinus* (1966): 11, 417-422.

3401. Rivet, Paul. "Mon ami Teilhard de Chardin." *France-observateur*, April, 1955, pp. 17-18.

3402. ————. "Souvenirs sur le Père Teilhard de Chardin." Item 3292, pp. 139-142.

3403. Rivière, Claude. "Baptême sous le cristal bleu du ciel de Pékin." *Revue Teilhard de Chardin* (1968): 39, 11-13. Excerpt from Item 3405.

3404. ———. *En Chine avec Teilhard de Chardin.* Paris: Seuil, 1968. *En China con Teilhard y cartas inéditas.* Madrid: Taurus, 1970.

3405. ———. "Une grande figure de foi et d'espérance. Le Père Teilhard de Chardin tel que je l'ai connu." *Faits et idées* (1956): 55, 32-36. Also *Rives d'azur*, July, 1956.

3406. ———. "Paul Claudel, François Mauriac et le Père Teilhard de Chardin." *Revue Teilhard de Chardin* (1962): 10, 11-13. Excerpt from Item 3407.

3407. ———. *Teilhard, Claudel et Mauriac.* Paris: Éditions universitaires, 1963. *Teilhard, Claudel e Mauriac.* Petrópolis: Vozes, 1967.

3408. Rizzo, Enrico. *La problematica di Teilhard de Chardin. Aspetti e sua attualità alla luce della critica.* Bologna: Pàtron, 1965.

3409. Roach, James Richard. "Some Theological Concepts in the Work of Pierre Teilhard de Chardin and the Faith and Order Commission of the World Council of Churches in Ecumenical Perspective." Doctoral dissertation, Boston University, 1972.

3410. Robert, G. "La vision de Teilhard de Chardin." *Maintenant*, November, 1962, pp. 391-392.

3411. Robin, Gérard-Alfred-Michel. "La place de la médecine dans la pensée du Père Teilhard de Chardin." *Le progrès médical* (1964): 3, 99.

3412. Robinson, John. "Man 'Is' What He Is Open to. A Comment on Garaudy's 'Freedom and Creativity.'" *The Teilhard Review* (1968-69): 2, 50-51. See Item 1593.

3413. Rocca, Francesca. "La dialettica nel pensiero del Padre Teilhard de Chardin." Typescript. Facoltà di lettere e filosofia dell'Università degli studi di Padova, 1968.

3414. Roche, Somin. "Teilhard de Chardin." *Renouveau* (1963):
       29, 3-6.

3415. Rochefoucauld, Édouard de la. "1928 à Paris, rencontres
       avec le Père Teilhard." *La table ronde* (1955): 90,
       72-74.

3416. Rodrigues, Afonso. *Teilhard de Chardin. Sintetização
       e justificativa filosóficas.* São Paulo: Faculdade de
       Filosofía. N.S. Medianeira, 1970.

3416a. Rodríguez, Enrique. "Punto Omega y Cristo cósmico. De
       la fenomenología preteológica a la cristología de
       Teilhard de Chardin." *Mayéutica* (1978): 4, 69-95.

3417. Rodríguez Rubio, Andrés. "La evolución, fenómeno cósmico
       en Teilhard de Chardin." *Horizontes* (1967): 10, 45-
       59.

3418. Rof Carballo, Juan. "Sobre la idea del amor en el Padre
       Teilhard de Chardin." Item 1396, pp. 41-67.

3419. Rogel, H. "El humanismo de Teilhard de Chardin." *In-
       stituto superior de estudios eclesiásticos.* Libro
       anual (1973-74): 165-180.

3420. Roig Gironella, J. "Sentido y alcance de la obra de
       Teilhard de Chardin según sus criticos." *Cristiandad*
       (1964): 21, 177-180, 257-261; (1965): 22, 78-81.
       Also *Espíritu* (1964): 13, 38-63.

3421. Rolandetti, Vittorino. "Introduzione alla lettura dell
       'epistolario di Pierre Teilhard de Chardin: la fede."
       Ricerche religiose (1968): 2, 34-50.

3422. ————. "Pensieri introduttivi alla lettura dell'epist-
       olario di Pierre Teilhard de Chardin." *Ricerche
       religiose* (1968): 1, 24-28.

3423. Roldan, A. "La respuesta ignaciana a la crisis cien-
       tífico-filosófica actual." *Razón y fe* (1958): 726-
       727, 41-54.

3424. Rolland, Édouard. "L'oeuvre de Pierre Teilhard de Char-
       din et la pensée catholique." *Enseignement chrétien*
       (1960-61): 1, 7-12.

3425. "Das römische Monitum." *Wort und Wahrheit* (1962): 17, 485-486.

3426. Rónay, György. "Möglichkeiten und Grenzen der Konvergenz." *Acta teilhardiana* (1970): 1, 45-58.

3427. ———. "Pour nous chrétiens de l'Est." *Informations catholiques internationales* (1965): 237, 22-23.

3428. ———. *Szentek, írók, irányok, Tanulmányok.* [Saints, Writers, Orientations. Essays.] Budapest: Szent István Társulat az Apostoli Szentszék Könyvkiajóda, 1970. Contains Items 3429, 3430, 3432.

3429. ———. "Teilhard de Chardin." Item 4512, pp. 7-26. Also *Vigilia* (1969): 34, 219-226. Also Item 3428, pp. 186-199.

3430. ———. "Teilhard en démocratie populaire." Item 1284, pp. 356-360.
"Teilhard en democracia popular." Item 1284 trans., pp. 93-99.
"Teilhard de Chardin in democrazia populare." *Nuovo osservatore* (1965): 6, 378-380.
"Teilhard a szocialismusban." Item 3428, pp. 200-204.

3431. ———. "Teilhard et les catholiques d'Europe orientale." *Cahiers littéraires* (1965): 13, 29-36.

3432. ———. "Teilhard et l'histoire." *Europe* (1965): 431/432, 119-128. See Item 218.
"Teilhard és a történelem." Item 3428, pp. 205-216.

3433. Rondeau, Marie-Josèphe. "Evangélisation et humanisme contemporain." *Bulletin du Cercle Saint-Jean-Baptiste* (1963): 23, 33-41.

3434. Rondet, Henri. "Hart van kerk en wereld. Teilhard de Chardin en het Hart van Christus." *De Heraut* (1967): 97, 176-179.

3435. ———. "Note sur Teilhard, Bruzbicki et la dévotion au Sacré-Coeur." *Revue d'ascétique et de mystique* (1969): 45, 451-452.
Also *Notre vie* (1970): 129, 51-53.

3436. Röösli, Josef. "Evolution und Metaphysik. Eine Antwort an Dr. Ladislaus Boros." *Schweizerische Kirchenzeitung* (1962): 130, 26-28, 42-46.

3437. ————. "Die Idee der Evolution von P. Teilhard de Chardin." *Schweizerische Kirchenzeitung* (1961): 41, 481-484; 42, 487-498; 43, 509-511; 44, 522-525; 45, 537-538.

3438. ————. "Teilhard de Chardin, ein neuer Weg des Wissens?" *Schweizerische Kirchenzeitung* (1965): 132, 143-145.

3439. Rooy, Jacques de. "Wetenschap als weg naar God. Leve van Teilhard de Chardin." *De Heraut* (1967): 89, 265-268.

3440. Roquer, Ramón. "Guión de espiritualidad. Teilhard de Chardin SJ." *Revista* (1956): 204, 9.

3441. Rosazza, Peter. "Camus and Teilhard." Item 607, pp. 101-110,

3442. Rosnay, Joël de. *Les origines de la vie.* Paris: Seuil, 1966. See pp. 87-94.

3443. Rossborn, Stern. "Fenomenet människam." [The Phenomenon of Man.] *Forum theologicum* (1963): 20, 119-132.

3444. Rosset, Clément. *Lettre sur les chimpanzés. Plaidoyer pour une humanité totale.* Paris: Gallimard, 1965. See pp. 77-96.

3445. Rossi, Mario. *I laici e la coscienze dell'evoluzione.* Vicenza: Laici per tempi nuovi, 1964.

3446. ————. "Quand les Italiens découvrent Teilhard." *Témoignage chrétien*, March 1, 1963, p. 12.

3447. ————. "La 'sanctificazione dello sforzo umano' in Teilhard de Chardin." Item 2744, pp. 181-189.
"La sanctification de l'effort humain chez Teilhard de Chardin considerée dans la perspective d'un humanisme marxiste." Item 2744 trans., pp. 173-180.

3448. Rossini, Anita. *Natura e soprannatura in Teilhard de Chardin.* Alba: Edizioni Paoline, 1971.

3449. Rostand, Jean. "L'idée de progrès chez le Père Teilhard de Chardin." *Revue du Tarn* (1960): 20, 380-392.

3450. ———. *Una mistificazione. Il caso Teilhard de Chardin.* Roma: Frattina, 1969.

3450a. ———. "La molécule et le philosophe." *Les nouvelles littéraires* (1963): 1894, 7.

3451. ———. "Que deviendra l'homme sur la terre?" *Le Figaro littéraire*, March 18, 1961.

3452. ———. "Le secret de l'évolution. Réponse de Jean Rostand." *Itinéraires* (1965): 96, 107-123. Reply to questionnaire in 3259.

3453. ———. "Sur l'optimisme de Teilhard de Chardin." *Forum international* (1965).
Also *Hommes d'autrefois et d'aujourd'hui*. Paris: Gallimard, 1966, pp. 124-141 *passim*.

3454. ———. "Teilhard de Chardin a-t-il eclairé le problème de l'évolution? Jean Rostand s'en prend à Teilhard de Chardin." *Le Figaro littéraire*, September 23 and 29, October 14 and 20, 1965.
Also *Hommes d'autrefois et d'aujourd'hui*. Paris: Gallimard, 1966, pp. 124-141 *passim*.

3455. ———. "Teilhard de Chardin le penseur, le moraliste, l'écrivain." *Bible et vie chrétienne* (1966): 71, 23-27.

3456. Number deleted.

3457. Roth, Robert. "The Importance of Matter. An Assessment of Pierre Teilhard de Chardin's Appeal for the American Mind." *America*, December 21, 1963, pp. 792-794.
Also Item 3514, pp. 22-32.

3458. Rotta, H., and R. Schmid. "Der mögliche Entwicklungstrend der Menschheit. Eine Vorschau auf die Jahrhundertwende." *Naturwissenschaftliche Rundschau* (1967): 7, 278+.

3459. Rousseau, M. "L'arbre de la vie, vivante image de l'évolution chez le Père Teilhard de Chardin." *Revue de Synthèse* (1963): 9/10, 113-121.

3460. Rousseau, René. "Le message de Teilhard de Chardin in-
       spirera à Nice le VIe congrès des 'Amitiés philosoph-
       iques internationales.'" *Le Figaro*, March 20, 1968,
       p. 32.

3461. Rousseaux, André. "En avant avec le Père Teilhard de
       Chardin." Item 3292, pp. 117-124.

3462. ————. "Mise en valeur du Père Teilhard de Chardin."
       Le Figaro littéraire, December 22, 1958.

3463. ————. "'Le phénomène humain.'" *Le Figaro littéraire*,
       December 24, 1955.

3464. ————. "La stature du Père Teilhard de Chardin." *Lit-
       terature du XXe siècle*. Paris: Albin Michel, 1958-64,
       vol. 7, pp. 105-114.

3465. ————. "La vision du Père Teilhard de Chardin." *Lit-
       terature du XXe siècle*. Paris: Albin Michel, 1958-64,
       vol. 6, pp. 155-174.
       "Wizja o Teilharda de Chardin." *Życie i myśl* (1963):
       111/112, 143-150.

3466. Roussel, Jean. "Teilhard de Chardin." *Larousse mensuel.
       Revue encyclopédique* (1955): 490, 669-670.

3467. Roussos, Michael. *"Pisteûô stòn kósmo." Pierre Teil-
       hard de Chardin*. Athênai: "Dionúsios ho Areopagítês,"
       1973.

3468. Rovati, Lucio. "L'evoluzionismo di Teilhard de Chardin."
       Critica sociale (1969): 61, 674-675.

3469. Roy, Michel. "Approche élémentaire d'une oeuvre. Notes
       sur le Père Teilhard de Chardin." *Les cahiers Albert
       le Grand* (1964): 70, 5-15.

3470. ————. "Teilhard de Chardin. Sein Leben und sein
       Werk." *Albertus-Magnus-Blätter* (1966): 13, 1033-
       1040.

3471. Royer, Robert. *La montée en Dieu par et à travers le
       monde, selon Teilhard de Chardin*. Bruxelles: Royer,
       1976.

3472. Rubio Carracedo, José. *La antropologia educativa de
       Teilhard de Chardin*. Madrid: Rubio Carracedo, 1970.
       Contains Item 3480.

3473. ————. "La antropología educativa de Teilhard de Chardin." *Revista de la Universidad de Madrid* (1970): 76,
83-84.

3474. ————. *Antropologia prospectiva, inspirado en los ensayos de Teilhard de Chardin.* Madrid: Studium, 1973.

3475. ————. "Bibliografía castellana sobre Teilhard de Chardin 1950-1970." *Estudio agustiniano* (1970): 5, 655-
670.

3476. ————. "El cristianismo del futuro según Teilhard de
Chardin." *Estudio agustiniano* (1971): 6, 439-472.

3477. ————. "Incredulidad moderna y cristianismo según
Teilhard de Chardin." *Estudio agustiniano* (1971): 6,
215-237.

3478. ————. "Para leer a Teilhard de Chardin. La dialéctica
teilhardiana." *Archivo teológico agustiniano* (1967):
2, 589-594.

3479. ————. "Quince años después: Del teilhardismo a Teilhard." *Arbor* (1970): 76, 43-46.

3480. ————. "Teilhard de Chardin y su 'frente humano.'"
Estudio agustiniano (1969): 5, 373-392.
Also in Item 3472.

3481. ————. "Teilhard, pensador religioso." *Arbor* (1971):
80, 309-319.

3482. ————. "La trasposición del cristianismo en Teilhard
de Chardin." Mimeographed. Valladolid: Rubio Carracedo, 1971.
*El cristianismo futuro. Su trasposición evolutiva
en Teilhard de Chardin.* Madrid: Studium, 1973.

3483. Ruffray, Patrick de. "A la découverte du Père Teilhard
de Chardin en lisant ses lettres de guerre." *Ecclesia*
(1962): 156, 109-114.

3484. Rugis, Jonas. "Pierre Teilhard de Chardin ir mūsu laiai."
Aidai (1964): 177-183.

3485. Rummel, Horst. "Ernst Jüngers 'Weltstaat' und Teilhard
de Chardins Gedanken über die Zukunft des Menschen."
Perspektiven der Zukunft (1967): 2, 7-8.

3486. Ruprecht, Horst. "Teilhards Beitrag zur Erziehung."
       Acta teilhardiana (1968): 5, 3-15.

3487. Russell, Bertrand. "L'humanité a-t-elle un avenir?"
       Univers (1965): 2, 91-94.

3488. Russell, John L. "The Concept of Natural Law." *The
       Heythrop Journal* (1965): 4, 434-446.

3489. ————. "Priest and Scientist." *The Catholic Herald*,
       November 30, 1962.

3490. ————. "The Principle of Finality in the Philosophy
       of Aristotle and Teilhard de Chardin." *The Heythrop
       Journal* (1962): 3, 347-357; (1963): 4, 32-41.

3491. ————. "Teilhard de Chardin: The Phenomenon of Man."
       The Heythrop Journal (1960): 4, 271-284; (1961): 1,
       3-13.
            Also in *Pax Romana*. *SQIS Bulletin* (1961): 25, 23-
       25.

3492. Russo, François. "A propos du livre de Teilhard de
       Chardin." *Études* (1956): 305.

3493. ————. "L'analyse des techniques et de leur évolution."
       Cahiers de l'Institut de science économique appliqué
       (1965): 158, 232-238.

3494. ————. "Apostolat scientifique." *Christus* (1958):
       17, 112-121.

3495. ————. "Autour d'une pensée contestée." *Études* (1959):
       118-120.

3495a. ————. "Une conférence de l'union rationaliste sur
       le Père Teilhard de Chardin." *Union catholique des
       scientifiques français. Bulletin* (1960): 54, 4-5.

3495b. ————. "Une double expérience spirituelle et scien-
       tifique." *Le Monde*, April 11-12, 1965, p. 13.
            Also in Item 2744 trans., pp.11-14.
            "Una doppia esperienza spirituale e scientifica."
       In Item 2744, pp.13-16.

3496. ————. Études récentes sur le Père Teilhard de Char-
       din." *Union catholique des scientifiques français.
       Bulletin* (1957): 40, 7-20.

3497. ———. "Fear of Scientific Progress." *Pax Romana Journal* (1967): 2, 7-8.

3498. ———. "Information une et diverse." *Revue de l'action populaire* (1963): 172, 1027-1042.

3499. ———. "La méthode du Père Teilhard de Chardin." *Recherches et débats* (1962): 40, 13-23.

3500. ———. "L'oeuvre du Père Teilhard de Chardin." *Union catholique des scientifiques français. Bulletin* (1957): 41, 9-12.

3501. ———. "L'oeuvre scientifique de P. Teilhard de Chardin." *Choisir* (1960): 14, 13-15.

3502. ———. "La pensée du P. Teilhard de Chardin." Typescript. Paris: Fondation Teilhard de Chardin, 1957.

3503. ———. "La persona nel fenomeno della socializzazione." Item 1300, pp. 263-287.

3504. ———. "Le phénomène humain. Actualités, le Père Teilhard de Chardin." *Études* (1955): 285, 254-259.
Also *Union catholique des scientifiques français. Bulletin* (1955): 17, 3-9.
"El Padre Teilhard de Chardin." *Criterio* (1955): 1243, 666-667.
Also *Mensaje* (1960): 95, 514-520.
"The Phenomenon of Man." *America* (1960): 5, 185-189.
Also Item 3514, pp. 1-21.

3505. ———. "Réflexions sur une leçon inaugurale au Collège de France." *Études* (1968): 191-198.

3505a. ———. "Une réunion privée au CCIF le 11 janvier 1958. Notes prises par le P. Russo." Typescript. Paris: Fondation Teilhard de Chardin, 1958.

3506. ———. "Science et foi." *Recherches et débats* (1966): 54, 36-48.

3507. ———. "La socialisation selon Teilhard." *Revue de l'Action populaire* (1962): 163, 1157-1170.
Also *Revue Teilhard de Chardin* (1963): 15, 7-12.
Also Item 1015, pp. 171-187.
"La socializzazione secondo Teilhard." *Civiltà*

delle machine (1963): 6, 84, 86-88.
"A socialização segundo Teilhard de Chardin." *O
tempo e o modo* (1963): 2, 27-38.

3508. ———. "Le système des sciences et sa structure."
Revue des questions scientifiques (1961): 234-251.

3509. ———. "La tâche apostolique dans le monde scientifique et technique selon le Père Teilhard de Chardin."
Responsables (1962): 8, 40-45.

3510. ———. "Trois études. Science et théologie." *Le
Monde*, June 6, 1967, p. 13.

3511-13. Numbers deleted.

3514. ———, and Robert J. Roth. *The Meaning of Teilhard
de Chardin*. New York: America Press, 1964. Contains
Items 3457, 3504.

3515. Rustan, Marie-Josèphe. "L'idée de progrès chez le Père
Teilhard de Chardin." *Revue du Tarn* (1960): 20, 380-
392.

3516. Rutten, N. "Teilhard de Chardin." *Le Vaillant* (1965):
44, 3.

3517. Ruyssen, Théodore. "Le système philosophique du Père
Teilhard de Chardin." *Rencontre Orient-Occident*
(1965): 4, 3-11; (1969-70): 2, 9-13; 3, 6-9.

3518. Ruytinx, Jacques. "A propos de Teilhard de Chardin."
Revue de l'Université de Bruxelles (1965): 239-250.

3519. ———. "Teilhard de Chardins wijsbegeerte in verband
met de idee van een eenheidswetenschap." *Handelingen
van het XXVe Vlaamse Filologencongres*. Zellik: Secretariaat van de Vlaamse Filologencongressen, 1967, pp.
41-47.

3520. Rybak, Boris. "Les origines de l'homme." *France-
observateur*, May 29, 1958.

3521. ———. "Y-a-t-il une science de droite?" *Les lettres
nouvelles* (1958): 900-907.

3522. Rylska, Teresa. "Ewolucja ludzkosci wg Pierre Teilharda de Chardin." *Znak* (1968): 20, 287-297. Also Item 3888, pp. 80-92. "Die Evolution der Menschheit nach Pierre Teilhard de Chardin." *Acta teilhardiana* (1973): 1, 5-13.

3523. ————. "Kierunkowość ewolucji kosmicznej w ujęciu O. Pierre Teilhard de Chardin." [The Direction of Cosmic Evolution According to Father Pierre Teilhard de Chardin.] *Zeszyty Naukowe Katolickiego Uniwersytetu Lubelskiego* (1969): 1, 43-52. Also Item 3888, pp. 28-40.

3524. ————. "Teilhard i o teilhardzie w tlomaczeniu polskim." [Works By and About Teilhard de Chardin in Polish.] *Znak* (1965): 17, 660-669.

3525. Sabarthez, Henri A. "Sur Teilhard de Chardin." *Citadelle* (1963): 4, 9-10.

3526. Sackarndt, Paul von. "Sind wir noch Krone der Schöpfung?" *Echo der Zeit* (1961): 14, 9-14.

3527. Saemisch, Ernst. "Der Mensch im Universum. Zum Werk Teilhard de Chardin." *Zeitwende* (1961): 32, 756-764.

3528. Sáez, J.I. "El concepto evolutivo de la muerte en Teilhard de Chardin." *Verdad y vida* (1968): 26, 475-506.

3529. Safford, D.W. "Teilhard de Chardin and the Phenomenon of Man." *Religion in Life* (1961): 30, 345-356.

3530. ————. "Teilhard de Chardin: A Vision of the Past and of the Future." *American Theological Review* (1964): 46, 286-297.

3531. Saget, Jules. *Décadence ou progrès. Gobineau et Teilhard de Chardin.* Douai: G. Sannier, 1964.

3532. Sahagún Lucas Hernandez, Juan. "La acción creadora vista por Teilhard de Chardin." *Verdad y vida* (1970): 28, 493-518.

3533. ————. "Convergencia y personalización en la obra de P. Teilhard de Chardin." *Antropologías del siglo XX.* Salamanca: Sígueme, 1976, pp. 58-78.

3534. ———. "En torno a los estudios eclesiásticos."
       Seminarios (1968): 35, 275-294.

3535. ———. "La evolución de la castidad y el Padre Teil-
       hard de Chardin." *Incunable* (1968): 35-36, 99-100.

3536. ———. *El hombre social en el pensamiento de Teilhard
       de Chardin.* Barcelona: Fontanella, 1969.

3537. ———. *Persona y evolución. El desarrollo des ser
       personal en el pensamiento de Teilhard de Chardin.*
       Burgos: Aldecoa, 1974.

3538. ———. "Precisiones en torno a Teilhard." *Verdad y
       vida* (1967): 535-554. Discusses Item 2727.

3539. ———. "La socialización en Teilhard." *Verdad y
       vida* (1968): 5-47, 91-138.

3540. ———. "Teilhard de Chardin y el estatuto del ser."
       Pensamiento (1973): 29, 73-104.

3541. ———. "Teilhard de Chardin y el panteismo." *Pensa-
       miento* (1970): 26, pp. 213-235.

3542. ———. "Teilhard de Chardin y la paz." *Razón y fe*
       (1969): 179, 623-636.

3543. ———. *La unificación de los seres en Teilhard de
       Chardin.* Madrid: Verdad y vida, 1968.

3544. Saher, P.J. "Östliche Weisheit und abendländisches
       Denken. Versuch einer Synthese der religionsphilo-
       sophischen Parallelen unter besonderer Berücksichti-
       gung von Aurobindo und Teilhard de Chardin." *Evolu-
       tion und Gottesidee. Studien zur Geschichte der
       philosophischen Gegenwartsströmungen zwischen Asien
       und dem Abendland.* Ratingen bei Düsseldorf: A. Henn,
       1967, pp. 65-82.

3545. ———. "Theologische Umdeutung der Abstammungslehre
       (Pierre Teilhard de Chardin, 1881-1955)." *Evolution
       und Gottesidee. Studien zur Geschichte der philo-
       sophischen Gegenwartsströmungen zwischen Asien und
       dem Abendland.* Ratingen bei Düsseldorf: A. Henn,
       1967, pp. 43-53.

3546. Saint-Amour, Jeanne-Marie. "Transcendence in Teilhard and Blondel." Doctoral dissertation, University of Missouri at Columbia, 1972.

3547. Saint-John-Stevas, Norman. "A Cosmic Optimist." *London Sunday Times*, February 27, 1966.

3548. Sakamoto, Y. "Teilhard to Kagawa Toyohiko." [Teilhard and Kagawa Toyohiko.] *Convergence* (1973): 3, 24-32.

3549. Salaberry, Étienne. "La messe sur le pays basque." *Gure Herria* (1964): 1, 34-36.

3550. Saldarriaga, Alberto. "La danza de las esferas o panorama del pensamiento de Pierre Teilhard de Chardin." *Universidad de Antioquia* (1967): 43, 245-319, 399-448; 44, 3-73.

3551. Salgado, A. "The Truth on Teilhard de Chardin." *Philippiniana sacra* (1968): 3, 28-51.

3552. Salleron, Louis. "A propos du 'Groupe zoologique humain.'" *Itinéraires*, May, 1966.

3553. ————. "Conte truffé de morceaux choisis. Bossuet lecteur de Teilhard." *Itinéraires* (1963): 75, 149-154.

3554. ————. *Contre Teilhard de Chardin.* Nancy: Berger-Levrault, 1967. Bound with Item 2789.
Anti Teilhard. Torino: Borla, 1967. Bound with Item 2789 trans.
En contra de Teilhard de Chardin. Barcelona: Pomaire, 1967. Bound with Item 2789 trans.
Also Santiago de Chile: Pomaire, 1967.
Teilhard de Chardin. Contra. Lisboa: Livros do Brasil, 1969. Bound with Item 2789 trans.

3555. ————. "De l'arianisme à Teilhard et à John A.T. Robinson. Pour la seconde fois le monde va-t-il se réveiller arien?" *Itinéraires* (1964): 80, 17-30.

3556. ————. "Encore Teilhard: 'Teilhard ou la foi au monde' de Jean Onimus." *Itinéraires* (1963): 73.

3557. ————. "En lisant 'Le phénomène humain' du Père Teilhard de Chardin." *Itinéraires* (1956): 1, 27-36.

3558. ———. "Le gnosticisme de Teilhard de Chardin."
      Itinéraires (1967): 109, 111-133.

3559. ———. "Le 'journal' de Teilhard." *Pensée catholique*
      (1975): 157, 63-72.

3560. ———. "Le message du Père Teilhard de Chardin." *Re-
      vue des deux mondes*, May, 1962, 29-42.

3561. ———. "Parenthèse sur le Père Teilhard de Chardin."
      Itinéraires (1958): 26, 24-33.

3562. ———. "La pensée du Père Teilhard de Chardin con-
      stitue-t-elle un dépassement de la pensée de Marx?"
      Exposés et travaux du Bureau d'études CEPEC (1958):
      5, 5-23.

3563. ———. "Réponse." Item 1243, pp. 127-129.

3564. Salzman, Gerhard. "Der Optimismus des Teilhard de Char-
      din." *Albertus-Magnus-Blätter* (1963): 37, 688-695.

3565. Samacoïtz, Jean-Georges. "Jésus et Oméga." *L'Alsace*,
      April 14, 1965, p. 5.

3566. Sanchez, Mateo. "The Scientific Basis of Teilhard de
      Chardin's Direction of Evolution." *Philippine Scho-
      lastic* (1962): 4, 139-151.

3567. Sanguinetti, F. "L'immagine del mondo di P. Teilhard
      de Chardin ed il teilhardismo." *Vichiana* (1969):
      6, 56-74.

3568. Sanjosé, Enrique. "Teilhard, acontecimiento espiritual
      del siglo." *Incunable* (1965): 91, 11-16.

3569. Sanmiguel Eguiluz, Jesus. *Teilhard de Chardin, señal
      de contradicción.* Bilbao: Gráficas Sigma, 1967.

3570. Santagostini, Claire. "Le thème du pour: R.P. Teilhard
      de Chardin." *Les cahiers astrologiques* (1958): 278-
      284.

3571. Sanz Criado, Luis M. "Dios-mundo. Dialéctica teilhard-
      iana de inmanencia y transcendencia." Item 1396, pp.
      111-128.

3572. Sanz Tena, J.M. "Humanismo de Teilhard de Chardin."
      Liceo franciscano (1966): 19, 93-123.

3573. Sanzo, Eileen. "The Convergence of Blake and Teilhard."
      The Teilhard Review (1977): 12, 73-78.

3574. Sasaki, Muneo. "Butsurigaku no tachiba kara mita Genshô
      to shite no ningen." [The "Phenomenon of Man" Seen by
      a Physician.] *Misuzu* (1964): 61, 19-21.

3575. Saslaw, William C. "Entropy and the Universe." *The
      Teilhard Review* (1968-69): 2, 76-79.

3576. Sauer, Adam. "Teilhard de Chardin im Widerstreit."
      Klerusblatt (1965): 2, 31-32.

3577. Sauter, M.R. "L'apparition de l'homme selon Teilhard
      de Chardin." *Journal de Genève*, March 9-10, 1957,
      p. 3.

3578. Sauvage, André. "La Croisière Jaune, souvenirs." Item
      3292, pp. 167-172.

3579. Sauvage, Michel. "Le catéchiste à l'école de Teilhard
      de Chardin?" *Catéchistes* (1965): 63, 255-279.

3580. Savonuzzi, Claudio. "Teilhard de Chardin: Il gesuita
      evoluzionista." *Il Resto di Carlino*, July, 1962, p. 7.

3581. Sawers, William King. "Changes in Jesuit Higher Educa-
      tion and the Influence of Teilhard de Chardin." Doc-
      toral dissertation, University of Southern California,
      1973.

3582. Sbisà, Antonio. "Dimensione pedagogica in Teilhard de
      Chardin." *Scuola e città* (1968): 4, 198-205.

3583. ———. "La possibilità del contestazione offerte
      dal pensiero politico di Teilhard de Chardin." *Hu-
      manitas* (1968): 23, 1005-1013.

3584. ———. *Il primo dissenso cattolico. Prospettive
      educative e sociali da Laberthonnière a Teilhard de
      Chardin.* Firenze: F. Le Monnier, 1976.

3585. Scabini, Eugenia. "Il mondo e Dio nel Milieu divin."
      Item 2744, pp. 155-158.
      "Le monde et Dieu dans le Milieu divin." Item 2744
      trans., pp. 144-147.

3586.   Scaltriti, Giacinto. "Père Teilhard de Chardin. 'La
        civiltà cattolica' e il teilhardismo." *Palestra del
        clero* (1965): 44, 939-951, 978-991.

3587.   ————. *Teilhard de Chardin tra il mito e l'eresia.*
        Roma: Idea, 1964. See Item 4076.
        Teilhard de Chardin: ¿Mito o herejia? Pamplona:
        T. Urdanoz, 1967.

3588.   Schaeuble, J. "Teilhard de Chardin." *Geschichte in
        Wissenschaft und Unterricht* (1968): 19, 457-467.

3589.   Schauberger, Walter. "Das Tongesetz und das Ereignis
        Teilhards de Chardin." Item 3299, pp. 95-111.

3590.   Scheets, Robert L. "Teilhard de Chardin and the De-
        velopment of Dogma." *Theological Studies* (1969):
        30, 445-462.

3591.   Scheffczyk, Leo. *Christliche Weltfrömmigkeit?* Essen/
        Werden: Fredebeul und Koenen, 1964.

3592.   ————. "Die 'Christogenese' Teilhard de Chardins und
        der kosmische Christus bei Paulus." *Tübinger theo-
        logische Quartalschrift* (1963): 143, 136-174.

3593.   ————. "Schöpfungswahrheit und Evolutionslehre."
        Theologie im Wandel. Freiburg-im-Breisgau: Erich
        Wewel, 1967, pp. 307-330.

3594.   ————. "Der 'Sonnengesang' des hl. Franziskus von
        Assisi und die 'Hymne an die Materie' des Teilhard
        de Chardin. Ein Vergleich zur Deutung der Struktur
        christlicher Schöpfungsfrömmigkeit." *Geist und Leben*
        (1962): 35, 219-233.

3595.   ————. "Zur Erbsünde-Auffassung Teilhard de Chardin."
        Münchener theologische Zeitschrift (1970): 21, 342-
        347.

3596.   Schellenbaum, Peter. *Le Christ dans l'energétique
        teilhardienne: Étude génétique.* Lyon: Faculté cath-
        olique de Lyon, 1969. Contains Item 3597.
        Also Paris: Cerf, 1971.

3597.   ————. "Le Christ dans l'energétique teilhardienne."
        Item 3653, pp. 25-59.
        Also in Item 3596.

3598. ———. "Die Christologie des Teilhard de Chardin."
Theologische Berichte. Zürich: Benziger, 1973, vol.
2, pp. 223-274.

3599. ———. "La foi, agent transformateur de la pensée et
de l'univers." *Etudes teilhardiennes* (1970): 3, 39-
50.

3600. Schenk, G. *L'homme*. Paris: Arthaud, 1963.

3601. Scherrer, Victor. "Hérésie teilhardienne?" *Le Vaillant*
(1965): 44, 2.

3602. Schilling, Othmar. *Geist und Materie in biblischer
Sicht. Ein exegetischer Beitrag zur Diskussion um
Teilhard de Chardin*. Stuttgart: Katholisches Bibel-
werk, 1967.

3603. Schilpp, Paul Arthur. "Toward a Super-Conscious To-
morrow." *Book Review*, December 19, 1964, p. 32.

3604. Schilson, Arno, and Walter Kasper. *Christologie im
Präsens. Kritische Sichtung neuer Entwurfe*. Freiburg-im-Breisgau: Herder, 1974. See pp. 72-80.

3605. Schlitt, Dale M. *Bibliography of Works About Teilhard
de Chardin*. Mississippi: Oblate Fathers' Seminary,
1966.

3606. Schlosser, B. "Construire la terre." *Isen* (1966): 15-
17.

3607. Schlüter-Hermkes, Maria. "Der Mensch--Sinn der Evolution. Einführung in das Werk Teilhards de Chardin."
Hochland (1958): 51, 115-131.

3608. Schmaus, Michael. "En general, hay que decir 'si' a
Teilhard de Chardin." *Incunable* (1965): 192, 7. See
Item 4078.

3609. Schmidt, Walter. "Hilft Teilhard de Chardin weiter?"
Christ und Welt (1968): 13, 12.

3610. Schmitt, Karl Heinz. "Der 'kritische Punkt der Hominisation' in der Aussage Pierre Teilhard de Chardins."
Mimeographed. Katholische Theologische Fakultät der
Rheinlandische Friedrich-Wilhelm-Universität Bonn,
1966. Contains Item 3611.

3611.   ———. "Der 'kritische Punkt der Hominisation' inner-
         halb der kosmischen Evolution in der Aussage Teilhards
         de Chardin." *Acta teilhardiana* (1967): 4, 60-74.
         Also in Item 3610.

3612.   Schmitt, William J. "The Vision of Teilhard de Chardin."
         Philippine Studies (1961): 9, 262-281.

3613.   Schmitz-Moorman, Karl. *Die Erbsünde. Überholte Vor-
         stellung, bleibender Glaube.* Olten/Freiburg-im-Breis-
         gau, 1969.

3614.   ———. "Nachwort." In Item 4343, pp. 170-192.

3614a.   ———. "The Scientific Writings of Teilhard." *The
         Teilhard Review* (1978): 13, 123-126.

3615.   ———. "Teilhard théologien." *Études teilhardiennes*
         (1970): 3, 63-69.

3615a.   ———. "Teologiska metoder i en värld stadd i utveck-
         ling." Item 1944, pp. 89-114.

3616.   ———. *Das Weltbild Teilhard de Chardins. Physik,
         Ultraphysik, Metaphysik: Untersuchungen zur Termin-
         ologie Teilhard de Chardins.* Köln/Opladen: West-
         deutscher Verlag, 1966.

3617.   Schneble, Beda. "Eine Million Irrtürmer. Zu den Über-
         setzungen der Schriften Teilhard de Chardins." *Der
         christliche Sonntag* (1966): 18, 277+.

3618.   ———. "Kommentar durch Übersetzung. Gedanken zu
         Grundsproblemen der Teilhardübersetzung." *Acta teil-
         hardiana* (1968): 5, 45-53.

3619.   Schneider, C.P. "Teilhard de Chardin et Édouard Schuré."
         Cahiers d'études cathares (1962): 13, 31-35.

3620.   Schneider, Klaus, and Alexander Gerkin. "Die Evolution
         und das Leid. Sein und Sendung." *Monatsschrift des
         katholischen Klerus* (1964): 29, 23-28.

3621.   Schneider, Mary Lea. "The Problem of Expiration in the
         Thought of Teilhard de Chardin: A Story of the Struc-
         tural Limitations of the Teilhardian Synthesis." Doc-
         toral dissertation, Marquette University, 1971.

3622. Schneider, Reinhold. "Schicksal und Landschaft." *Kommunität* (1961): 20, 204.

3623. Schneider, Stefan. "Vom Sinn der Menschwerdung bei Nikolas Cusanus und Teilhard de Chardin." *Acta teilhardiana* (1972): 1, 30-60.

3624. Schnitzer, Alois. "Deszendenzlehre oder Schöpfungsglaube. Eine Studie zum Natur- und Menschenbild Teilhard de Chardins." *Pädagogische Welt* (1968): 22, 338-347.

3625. ――――. "Die Lehre von der Evolution bei Teilhard de Chardin." *Pädagogische Welt* (1966): 20, 626-637.

3626. Schoof, T.M. *Aggiornamento. De doorbraak van een nieuwe katholieke theologie.* Baarn: Het Wereldvenster, 1968. See pp. 127-131.
Der Durchbruch der neuen katholischen Theologie. Ursprung, Wege, Struktur. Freiburg-im-Breisgau: Herder, 1969. See pp. 157-161.

3627. Schoonenberg, Piet. "Evolutie." *Bijdragen* (1962): 23, 109-137.
Also *Gods wordende wereld. Vijf theologische essays.* Tielt/Den Haag: Lannoo, 1963, pp. 9-38.
"Evolution." *God's World in the Making.* Pittsburgh: Duquesne University Press, 1964, pp. 1-35.
Also Dublin: Gill & Son, 1965, pp. 11-50.
"Evolución." *El mundo de Dios en evolución.* Buenos Aires: C. Lohle, 1966.
"Ewolucja i stworzenie." *Znak* (1966): 18, 1346-1359.
"Evolution." *Le monde de Dieu en devenir.* Paris: Centurion, 1967, pp. 11-54.
"L'evoluzione." *Il mondo di Dio en evoluzione.* Brescia: Queriniana, 1968, pp. 27-67.

3628. ――――. "De Menswording." *Verbum* (1960): 12, 453-466.

3629. Schrader, Wiebke. "Über Teilhard de Chardin und die Metaphysik." *Schelling-Studien. Festgabe für Manfred Schroder.* München/Wien: Oldenbourg, 1965, pp. 131-151.

3630. Schubert-Soldern, Rainer. *Der Evolutionismus Teilhards de Chardin. Eine kritische Studie.* Wien: Wiener katholische Akademie, 1970.

3631. Schutz, Paul. *Parusia. Hoffnung und Prophetie.* Heidel-
       berg: I. Schneider, 1960. See pp. 445-466.

3632. "Science at Vatican II." *America,* November 14, 1964,
       p. 583.

3633. "Science et christianisme." *La voix de Saint-Pierre*
       (1962): 48, 2.

3634. "Science et foi. Teilhard de Chardin." *Rencontre* (1962):
       1-22.

3635. "Science et synthèse. Colloque à l'UNESCO sur Einstein
       et Teilhard de Chardin." *Cahiers universitaires
       catholiques* (1966): 5, 239-241.

3636. *Science et synthèse.* Paris: Gallimard, 1967.
           Science and Synthesis. Berlin/New York: Springer
       Verlag, 1971.

3637. "La science, l'univers et la grâce." *Christianisme
       social* (1960): 1/2, 21-23.

3638. Scott, James. "The Vision of Teilhard de Chardin."
       Doctrine and Life (1967): 17, 144-155.

3639. Secrétan, Philibert. "Confronté avec Pascal. Teilhard
       de Chardin est-il le prophète d'un âge totalitaire?"
       La Tribune de Genève, December 3, 1963, p. 1.

3640. Seelen, A. "Dante en Teilhard. Twee wereldbeelden."
       Debazuin, July 10, 1965, pp. 6-7.

3641. Segaar, J. "De gedachtenwereld van Teilhard de Chardin.
       De natuur als geschiednis." *Adelbert* (1963): 135-138.

3642. ―――. "Teilhard na zeven jaar: Een kritische be-
       schouwing." *Wending* (1962): 17, 213-229.

3643. Segaar, P. "Recherche biologique et foi chrétienne."
       Foi et vie (1958): 55.

3644. Seiler, Hermann. "Den kristne i var tid. Himmelens och
       jordens manniska." [The Christian in Our Times. Heav-
       enly and Earthly Man.] *Credo* (1962): 43, 216-230.

3645. Semerano, Scipione. "Comment je crois. Il problema
       della filosofia della religione in Teilhard de Char-
       din." Typescript. Università Cattolica Sacro Cuore
       Milano, 1967.

3646. Sendaydiego, Henry B. "Indefinite Prolongation of Terminal Human Life." *Journal of the West Virginia Philosophical Society* (1975): 9, 24-27.

3647. Senghor, Léopold Sédar. "La francophone comme culture." Item 1259, pp. 100-113.

3648. ————. "Hommage à Teilhard de Chardin." *Afrique documents* (1965): 80, 157-160.
Also Item 1259, pp. 29-35.
"Teilhard de Chardin e kenzu." *Convergence* (1972): 2, 14-20.

3649. ————. "Itinéraires africains." *Développement et civilisations* (1962): 9, 18-24.

3650. ————. "Message aux amis du Père Teilhard de Chardin." *Revue Teilhard de Chardin* (1960): 1/2, 26.

3651. ————. "Pierre Teilhard de Chardin e la politica africana." *Politica africana*. Roma: Cinquelune, 1962, pp. 163-213.
"Teilhard de Chardin et la politique africaine." In Item 3920.
Pierre Teilhard de Chardin und die afrikanische Politik. Köln: M. Dumont Schauberg, 1968.
"Pierre Teilhard de Chardin en de afrikaanische politiek." Item 3724, pp. 9-51.

3652. ————. "Teilhard et le socialisme africain." *Cahiers littéraires* (1965): 13, 30-35.

3653. *Sens humain et sens divin. Inédits, études, conférences*. Paris: Seuil, 1971. Contains Items 1380, 1648, 1649, 2666, 3168, 3597.

3654. Sérant, Paul. "Lettre à Louis Salleron." *Centre d'études politiques. Dossier* (1958): 5, 25-28.

3655. Serracino-Inglott, Peter. "Teilhard de Chardin. Disputed Questions." *Scientia* (1964): 30, 173-185; (1965): 31, 36-45.

3656. Serrahima, Maurici. "El món concret, coses noves sota el sol." *Serra d'or* (1960): 9, 7-9.

3657. Serrou, Robert. "Teilhard de Chardin et le Saint-Office." *Le spectacle du monde* (1962): 5.

3658.   Sertillanges, Antonin. "L'évolution selon saint Thomas
        et Teilhard de Chardin." *L'univers et l'âme*. Paris:
        Éditions Ouvrières, 1965, pp. 19-50.

3659.   Servier, Jean. "Le progrès humain n'exist pas!" *Arts*
        1964): 963, 1, 17.

3660.   ————. "Teilhard de Chardin, ou le drame de l'human-
        isme bourgeios." *Revue de poche* (1965): 4, 155-166.

3661.   Seuntjens, Hubert. "Le pas de la réflexion dans Pierre
        Teilhard de Chardin." *Balisage* (1961): 16/17, 17-19.

3662.   ————. "Témoignage." *Revue Teilhard de Chardin*
        (1961): 5, 26-27.

3663.   Sève, Lucien. "Le Père Teilhard et le coeur du prob-
        lème." *La philosophie française contemporaine et
        sa genèse de 1789 à nos jours*. Paris: Éditions
        Sociales, 1962, pp. 268-282.

3664.   "The Seventh Colloquium at Vézelay." *The Teilhard Re-
        view* (1966-67): 2, 58-60.

3665.   Severin, Frank T. "The Humanistic Psychology of Teil-
        hard de Chardin." *The Challenge of Humanistic Psy-
        chology*, ed. by J.F.T. Bugenthal. New York: McGraw-
        Hill, 1967, pp. 151-158.
        "Teilhard de Chardin and the Science of Man." *Psy-
        chological Scene* (1968): 1-13.

3666.   ————. "Teilhard's Methodology for the Study of Cos-
        mic Psychology." *Catholic Psychological Record* (1967):
        5, 1-7.

3667.   Shaddy, Virginia M. "New Dimensions of Spirit in Man's
        Development." Item 2158, pp. 99-117.
        "Nuove dimensioni dello spirito nello sviluppo
        dell'uomo." Item 2158 trans., pp. 141-164.

3668.   Sheed, Wilfrid. "L'axe de l'évolution considéré par
        Teilhard." *Revue Teilhard de Chardin* (1961): 5, 11-
        14.

3669.   ————. "Père Teilhard's View of Evolution. A Jesuit
        Paleontologist Presents a Unique Statement About Man's
        Place on the Evolutionary Scale." *Jubilee* (1959): 8,
        42-49.

3670. Sheets, J. "Teilhard de Chardin and the Development of Dogma." *Theological Studies* (1969): 30, 445-462.

3671. Shimazaki, Toshio. "J.S. Huxley to Teilhard de Chardin." [Julian Huxley and Teilhard de Chardin.] *Riso* (1969): 7, 37-44.

3672. ————. "Teilhard de Chardin, sono hito to shisô." [Teilhard de Chardin, the Man and His Thought.] *Shunjû* (1970): 109, 1-5.

3673. Shimoyama, Tokujii. "Bunkyôgakuteki ningen—Chardin no hito to shisô." [Symphonic Man: The Man Teilhard de Chardin and His Thought.] *Misuzu* (1964): 61, 21-24.

3674. Shugô, Hiroshi. "Teilhard de Chardin hito to sono ningenkan. Watashi no tameno nôto." [Man and His Concept According to Teilhard de Chardin. Lecture Notes.] *Shisô* (1965): 8, 99-109.

3675. Sicard, Henri. "L'hominisation et ses problèmes." *Revue Teilhard de Chardin* (1966): 26, 14-22.

3676. ————. "Revolution teilhardienne." *Revue Teilhard de Chardin* (1973): 56, 5-12; 57, 7-27.

3677. Siczek, Stefan. "Tadeusz Pluzanski o P. Teilhardzie de Chardin." [Tadeusz Pluzanski on Pierre Teilhard de Chardin.] *Collectanea theologica* (1973): 2, 163-167.

3678. Siegmund, Georg. "Pierre Teilhard de Chardin im Widerstreit der Meinungen." *Anzeiger für die katholische Geistlichkeit* (1962): 71, 334-340; (1963): 72, 178-184.
   Also *Die Anregung. Korrespondenz- und Werkblatt für den Klerus* (1962): 14, 164-174.

3679. Silen, Sven. "Fraga mera. Inledning till en discussion med Père Teilhard de Chardin." [Many Questions. Introduction to a Discussion With Father Teilhard de Chardin.] *Var Lösen* (1961): 52, 70-74.

3680. Siles, J. "Las dos fuentes de la revolución contemporanea. El pensamiento filosófico y religioso de Teilhard de Chardin." *Finis terrae* (1962): 9, 86-94.

3681. Simon, Charlie May. *Faith Has Need of All the Truth: A Life of Pierre Teilhard de Chardin.* New York: Dutton, 1974.

3682. Simon, Janos Attila. "Teilhard de Chardin magyaror-
       szági hatásáról." [On the Influence of Teilhard de
       Chardin in Hungary.] *Vigilia* (1971): 36, 802-809.

3683. Simon, Pierre-Henri. "Le billet de Pierre-Henri Simon."
       Choisir (1960): 14, 32.

3684. ———. "L'humanisme de Pierre Teilhard de Chardin."
       Annales des Hautes Études de Gand (1960): 4, 17-45.

3685. ———. *Questions aux savants.* Paris: Seuil, 1969.

3686. Simonis, Michel. "Teilhard de Chardin et son public
       (Étude de psychologie religieuse)." Mimeographed.
       Institut de psychologie appliquée de l'Université
       catholique de Louvain, 1964.

3687. Simpson, George Gaylord. "The Divine 'Non Sequitur.'"
       Item 528, pp. 88-102.

3688. ———. "On the Remarkable Testament of the Jesuit
       Paleontologist Pierre Teilhard de Chardin." *Scien-
       tific American* (1960): 202, 201-207.

3689. ———. "Réponse." *Itinéraires* (1965): 96, 124-126.
       Reply to questionnaire in 3259.

3690. Sinéty, R. de. "La vie de la biosphère." *Archives de
       philosophie* (1936): 7, 125-132.

3691. Singleton, Michael. "Teilhard on Camus." *International
       Philosophical Quarterly* (1969): 9, 236-247.

3692. Sîrbu, Corneliu. "Sistemul teologic al lui Teilhard de
       Chardin." [Teilhard de Chardin's Theological System.]
       Ortodoxia (1973): 25, 516-545.

3693. Sitzmann, Gerhard-Helmut. "Die Entmythologisierung der
       Zukunft. Zur Bedeutung des Fortschritts im Geschichts-
       denken Teilhards." *Albertus-Magnus-Blätter* (1967): 14,
       1230-1236.

3694. ———. "Interdisziplinäre Anthropologie. Zur neuen
       Wissenschaft Teilhards de Chardin." Item 1473, pp.
       183-191.

3695. ———. "Mensch und Natur bei Teilhard de Chardin."
       Acta teilhardiana (1974): 11, 123-132.

3696. ———. "Der Optimismus bei Teilhard de Chardin." *Albertus-Magnus-Blätter* (1962-63): 10, 688-697. "L'optimisme de Teilhard." *Les cahiers Albert le Grand* (1964): 70, 17-29.

3697. ———. "Teilhard-Bibliographie des deutschen Sprachraums für das Jahr 1970." *Acta teilhardiana* (1972): 2, 100-103. See also Items 4071, 4072.

3698. ———. "Teilhard im deutschen Sprachraum." *Acta teilhardiana* (1970): 2, 63-81.

3699. ———. "Zur philosophischen Grundlegung der Anthropologie Teilhards." *Acta teilhardiana* (1967): 4, 74-76.

3700. Skeldioo, J. "La jesuito Tejar de Sarden." [The Jesuit Teilhard de Chardin.] *Sennacieca* (1963): 11-12.

3701. Skolimowski, Henryk. "Teilhard, Soleri and Evolution." *The Teilhard Review* (1975): 3, 79-86.

3702. Skvorc, Mijo. "'Slucaj' Teilhard de Chardin." [The Teilhard de Chardin "Case."] *Bogoslovska Smotra* (1963): 2, 96-107.

3703. ———. "Teilhard de Chardin vizionar modernog svijeta." [Teilhard de Chardin, Visionary of the Modern World.] *Glas Koncila* (1965): 12, 3.

3704. Ślaga, Szczepan W. "Świadomość ludzka wedlug Teilharda de Chardin." [The Human Conscience of Teilhard de Chardin.] *W nurcie zagadnień posoborowych* (1968): 2, 79-95.

3705. Smit, P. "Gedachten over het Verschilnsej Mens." *Vakblad voor biologen* (1962): 10, 1-13.

3706. Smith, Basil. "The Phenomenon of Man." *Theology* (1960): 476, 80-82.

3707. Smith, Robert B. "Analogy in an Evolutionary Perspective." *Anglican Theological Review* (1976): 58, 280-293.

3708. ———. "God and Evolutive Creation." Item 1919, pp. 41-58.

3709. ———. "Orthogenesis and God-Omega." *Harvard Theolog-*
       ical Review (1969): 62, 397-410.

3710. ———. "The Place of Evil in a World of Evolution."
       Item 1919, pp. 59-77.

3711. ———. "Towards the Discovery of God. A Study in the
       Thought of Teilhard de Chardin." Mimeographed. De-
       partment of Theology, University of Exeter, 1968.

3712. Smulders, Pieter. "Het christelijk evolutionisme van
       Teilhard de Chardin." *Nederlandse Katholieke Stemmen*
       (1963): 59, 144-158.

3713. ———. "De evolutie naar de toekomst: Teilhard de Char-
       din." *Katholiek Artsenblad* (1962): 41, 16-20.

3714. ———. "Evolutieleer en toekomstverwachting bij Teil-
       hard de Chardin." *Theologische Bezinning* (1960): 3,
       233-277.
       Also *Bijdragen* (1960): 3, 233-280.
       French summary in *Pax Romana. Bulletin du SIQS*
       (1961): 62, 8-11.

3715. ———. "The Optimism of Teilhard and Vatican II."
       Pax Romana Journal (1967): 2, 17-19.

3716. ———. "Rechzetting over Teilhard de Chardin." *Bijd-*
       ragen (1961): 22, 86-88.

3717. ———. "Schöpfung. Entwicklung und Vollendung. Zum
       Anliegen Teilhard de Chardins." *Wissenschaft und Weis-*
       heit (1964): 27, 12-29.

3718. ———. "Teilhard and the Future of Faith." *Theology*
       Digest (1969): 17, 326-337.

3719. ———. *Het visioen van Teilhard de Chardin. Poging*
       tot Theologische Waardering. Bruges: Desclée de
       Brouwer, 1962.
       Also 5th ed., 1966.
       Theologie und Evolution. Versuch über Teilhard de
       Chardin. Essen: Hans Driewer, 1963.
       La vision de Teilhard de Chardin. Essai de réflex-
       ion théologique. Paris: Desclée de Brouwer, 1964.
       A visão de Teilhard de Chardin. Ensaio de reflexão
       teológica. Petrópolis: Vozes, 1965.
       Also 4th ed., 1969.
       La visió de Teilhard de Chardin. Barcelona: Ediciones

62, 1966.
La visión de Teilhard de Chardin. Problemas teológicos de actualidad. Bilbao: Desclée de Brouwer, 1967.
The Design of Teilhard de Chardin. An Essay in Theological Reflexion. Westminster, Md.: Newman, 1967.

3720. Snape, H.C. "Two Jesuits and Their Church: Teilhard and Tyrrell." *Modern Churchman* (1961): 5, 255-260.

3721. Soborn, Bernard. "L'apport de Teilhard de Chardin à la pensée religieuse moderne." *Revue de l'évangelisation* (1959): 15, 115-131.

3722. Sobosan, Jeffrey G. "Seeing and Dying: An Approach to Chardin." *Journal of Religion and Health* (1974): 186-193.

3723. Sobrino, Juan. "Teilhard de Chardin en sus cartas." *Estudios centroamericanos* (1965): 20, 223-228.

3724. *Sociale politiek in de wereldbeschouwing van Teilhard de Chardin.* Utrecht/Antwerpen: Spectrum, 1968. Contains Items 239, 714, 1170, 3651.

3725. Šoka, Silvester. "Teilhard a teilhardizmus." *Duchovný Pastier* (1970): 45, 447-450.

3726. Sola, Francisco de P. "¿Teilhard de Chardin es Teilhard de Chardin?" *Espiritu* (1965): 14, 30-47.

3727. Solages, Bruno de. "La pensée chrétienne face à l'évolution." *Bulletin de la littérature ecclésiastique* (1947): 48.
"De christlijke gedachte ten opzichte van de evolutie." Item 3978, pp. 95-113.
"Christianity and Evolution." *Cross Currents* (1951): 4, 26-37.

3728. ————. "Pour l'honneur de la théologie." *Bulletin de littérature ecclésiastique* (1947): 46, 64-84.

3729. ————. "Les preuves teilhardiennes de Dieu." *L'homme devant Dieu.* Paris: Aubier, 1964, vol. 3, pp. 125-132.

3730. ————. "Progrès modernes dans la connaissance de
       l'humanité." *Chronique* (1956): 1, 6-16.

3731. ————. "Le R.P. Teilhard de Chardin." *Bulletin de
       littérature ecclésiastique* (1955): 2, 107.

3732. ————. "La sociologie de Teilhard de Chardin." *Mé-
       langes offert à Jean Brethe de la Gressage.* Bordeaux:
       Bière, 1967, pp. 777-780.

3733. ————. *Teilhard de Chardin. Témoignage et étude sur
       le développement de sa pensée.* Toulouse: Privat, 1967.

3734. ————. "L'univers de la science s'ouvrant à la foi des
       croyants: Le Père Teilhard de Chardin." *Lo calel*
       (1962): 29, 15.

3735. Solaguren, Celestino. "Ciencia, método y presupuesto
       en el pensamiento de Teilhard de Chardin." *Verdad y
       vida* (1962): 80, 509-531.

3736. ————. "El cristocentrismo cosmico de Teilhard de
       Chardin." *Verdad y vida* (1961): 19, 131-143.

3737. ————. "La cristologia del P. Teilhard de Chardin y
       el Principio Fundamento de san Ignacio." *Manresa*
       (1963): 134, 5-24.

3738. ————. "En torno a la 'peligrosidad' de Teilhard de
       Chardin." *Verdad y vida* (1963): 21, 323-355.

3739. Soley, Ramon. "De soziale Perspektive im Denken von
       Teilhard de Chardin." *Perspektiven der Zukunft*
       (1967): 4, 8-9.

3740. Sombra, José de Carvalho. "'La courbe conique du temps.'
       La notion de temps chez Teilhard de Chardin." Mimeo-
       graphed. Paris: Université de Paris I, 1972.

3741. Somerville, J.M. "Teilhard and Blondel." *Continuum*
       (1967): 2, 439-440.

3742. Sorber, W. "A propos de Teilhard de Chardin." *Syn-
       dicalisme*, January 31, 1967.

3743. Sorč, A., and A. Strle. "Teilhard de Chardin o 'večni
       ženskosti' in njegov pomen za naš čas." [Teilhard de
       Chardin on the "Eternal Feminine" and His Significance

for Our Times.] *Bogoslovni Vestnik* (1973): 33, 130-138.

3744. Soreil, Arsène. *Face au prophétisme de Teilhard de Chardin.* Bruxelles: Charles Dessart, 1963. Contains Items 851, 1036, 1133, 1208, 1489, 1546, 2740, 3745.

3745. ———. "D'une fascination de la vie." In Item 3744.

3746. Soreval, Eduardo Abranches de. "'O fenomeno humano' do P. Teilhard de Chardin. Reflexões críticas." *Universidade do Porto. Revista da Faculdade de Letras. Série de Filosofia* (1971): 1, 135-160.

3747. Soria, Mario. *Cuestiones disputadas del catolicismo contemporaneo.* Barcelona: L. de Caralt, 1967.

3748. ———. "Nuevo asedio a Teilhard de Chardin." *Punta Europa* (1966): 2, 40-67.

3749. ———. "Puntualizaciones sobre Teilhard de Chardin." *Punta Europa* (1967): 1, 44-50.

3750. ———. "Teilhard de Chardin ¿scientífico o hereje?" *Nueva época,* July 11, 1964, pp. 19-20.

3751. Sorokin, Pitrim A. "Discussion: Teilhard de Chardin and Sociology." *American Catholic Sociological Review* (1962): 4, 330-335.

3752. Souckova, Milada. "Setkání s P. Teilhardem." [Encounter with Teilhard.] *Studie* (1967): 13, 44-48.

3753. Soucy, Claude. *Pensée logique et pensée politique chez Teilhard de Chardin.* Paris: Presses Universitaires de France, 1967.

3754. ———. "Teilhard de Chardin est-il un philosophe?" *Recherches et débats* (1962): 40, 24-44.

3755. ———. "Teilhard, les personnalistes et l'État." Item 1284, pp. 387-401.
"Teilhard, los personalistas y el Estado." Item 1284 trans., pp. 137-157.
"Teilhard, i personaggi e lo Stato." *Nuovo osservatore* (1965): 6, 392-399.

3756. "La souffrance vue par Teilhard de Chardin: Énergie
       spirituelle; signification et valeur constitutrice."
       Horizons missionnaires, Autumn, 1969, pp. 4-10.

3757. Soulages, Gérard. "Le Père Teilhard de Chardin et Mar-
       cel Légaut." *Revue Teilhard de Chardin* (1962): 11,
       22-25.

3758. ————. "Teilhard de Chardin zu 'Humani generis.'"
       Internationale katholische Zeitschrift (1976): 5,
       42-45.

3759. Souviron, José Maria. "Una evolución en torno a la
       evolución." *El colombiano literario* (1958): 1, 8.
       Also *La estafeta literaria* (1964): 290, 12-13.

3760. Souza, Remy de. *Teilhard e Hesíodo, um possível para-
       lelo*. Salvador, Bahia: Mensageiro da fé, 1970.

3761. ————. "Teilhard poeta?" *Vida católica*, June 26,
       1967.

3762. ————. "Tomás de Aquino e Teilhard." *Semana católica*,
       April 30, 1967.

3763. Spaandonk, J.W.M. van. "Teilhard de Chardin. Drempelo-
       verschrijdingen tussen weten en denken." *Rekenschap*
       (1962): 9, 156-161.

3764. Spark, Muriel. "A Foretaste of Eternity. Le milieu
       divin by Pierre Teilhard de Chardin." *London Observ-
       er*, December 18, 1960.

3765. Speaight, Robert. "Best So Far on Teilhard de Chardin."
       The Catholic Herald, November 12, 1965.

3766. ————. "In Praise of Teilhard." *Tablet*, October 2,
       1965, pp. 1087-1088.

3767. ————. "Talking About Teilhard." *Tablet*, February
       11, 1967, pp. 158-159.

3768. ————. "Teilhard and the Jesuits." *The Month* (1967):
       4, 201-208.
       "Teilhard y los jesuitas." *Razón y fe* (1967): 831,
       423-430.
       "Teilhard und die Jesuiten." *Der groose Entschluss*
       (1967-68): 23, 82-86.

3769. ———. *Teilhard de Chardin: A Biography.* London: Collins, 1967. Contains Items 3772, 3773.
The Life of Teilhard de Chardin. New York: Harper & Row, 1967.
La vie de Pierre Teilhard de Chardin. Paris: Seuil, 1970.
Teilhard de Chardin. Biografía. Santander: Sal terrae, 1972.

3770. ———. "Teilhard de Chardin and Neo-Modernism. M. Maritain Speaks His Mind." *Tablet* (1967): 149-150. See Item 2647.

3771. ———. *Teilhard de Chardin: Remythologization.* Chicago: Argus Communications, 1970.

3772. ———. "Teilhard de Chardin: The Ending." *Tablet* (1967): 6645, 1013-1014. Also in Item 3769.

3773. ———. "Teilhard: The Last Years." *Tablet* (1967): 6644, 992-993. Also in Item 3769.

3774. ———. "Teilhardians in Congress: Intellectual Convergence." *Tablet* (1966): 6596, 1181.

3775. Speyer, Paul. "Débat sur le P. Teilhard." *Revue Teilhard de Chardin* (1961): 6, 32-33.

3776. Spoorenberg, J. "Teilhard utan McLuhan?" [Teilhard After McLuhan?"] *Mérleg* (1968): 3, 239-242.

3777. Sproxton, Vernon. *Teilhard de Chardin.* London: SCM Press, 1971.

3778. Spülbeck, Otto. "Teilhard de Chardin und die Pastoralkonstitution." *Die Autorität der Freiheit.* München: Kösel, 1967, vol. 3, pp. 86-97.

3779. Stadelmaier, Franz. "Teilhard de Chardin—Glaube an die Zukunft." *Zukunfts- und Friedenforschung, Information* (1971): 2, 57-61.

3780. Staico, Anselmo [pseud. Dino Calvo]. "Teilhard de Chardin, quindici anni dopo." *Testimonianze* (1970): 13, 801-807.

3781. Staico, Ubaldo. "B. Croce e P. Teilhard de Chardin:
       Due storicismi." *Studi senesi* (1973): 75, 475-511.

3782. ————. "Note sulla epistemologia di Teilhard de Char-
       din." *Atti e memoria dell'Academia toscana di sci-
       enze e lettere La Colombaria* (1974): 39, 87-124.

3783. ————. *Il pensiero politico di Teilhard de Chardin e
       la critica della democrazia.* Milano: A. Giuffrè, 1976.

3784. Stark, Werner. "Teilhard and the Problem of Human Au-
       tonomy." Item 3247, pp. 77-92.

3785. Stárková, Vera. "Střed v Bohu a Boží protředi. Ke
       knize P. Teilharda de Chardin 'Le milieu divin.'"
       [The Center in God and the Divine Milieu. In the
       Margin of Teilhard de Chardin's Book, "The Divine
       Milieu."] *Studie* (1967): 13, 49-54.

3786. Starzyński, Janusz. "O Teilhardzie--we wroclawskim
       K.I.K." [On Teilhard: The Colloquium of the Club
       of Catholic Intellectuals at Wroclaw.] *Weži* (1963):
       1, 150-153.

3787. Steck, K.G. "'Omega.' Bemerkungen zu Pierre Teilhard
       de Chardin: Der Mensch im Kosmos." *Evangelische
       Theologie* (1962): 22, 109-112.

3788. Stefano, Marcello de. "Teilhard de Chardin e la Re-
       sistenza. Note sul Centro di Ricerche e Studi di
       Undine." *Momento* (1966): 1, 86-87.

3789. Sténou, Y. "Christianisme et humanisme selon Teilhard
       de Chardin." *Catho-journal*, February, 1963, pp. 15-
       23.

3790. ————. "Christianisme évolutif de Teilhard de Chardin."
       Citadelle, June, 1963, pp. 20-21.

3791. Stephenson, Kerry. "New Paperbacks." *The Catholic
       Herald*, October 28, 1966, p. 10.

3792. Stern, Karl. "Great and Controversial Priest and
       Scientist." *Commonweal*, January 1, 1960, pp. 400-
       401. See Item 2972.

3793. ————. "Saint Augustine and Teilhard." Item 501, pp.
       67-68.
          Also Item 497, pp. 67-68.

3794. ————. "Universum Dei: An Augustinian Approach to Natural History." Item 1544, pp. 40-48.

3795. Stevens, Weston A. "The Sacred and the Profane as Found in Teilhard de Chardin and Abraham Maslow." *Religious Humanism* (1972): 6, 15-19.

3796. Stewart, E.M., and E.I. Watkin. "On Reading Père Teilhard de Chardin." *Tablet*, June 11, 1960, p. 564.

3797. Stiefvater, Alois. "Sinnziel der Welt. Hermann Schell und Teilhard de Chardin." *Perspektiven der Zukunft* (1973): 2, 4-6.

3798. Stiernotte, Alfred P. "An Interpretation of Teilhard as Reflected in Recent Literature." *Zygon* (1968): 4, 377-425.

3799. ————. "Process Philosophies and Mysticism." *International Philosophical Quarterly* (1969): 9, 560-571.

3800. Stock, Michael E. "The Phenomenon of Man." *The Thomist* (1960): 2, 295-303.

3801. ————. "Scientific vs. Phenomenological Evolution: A Critique of Teilhard de Chardin." *New Scholasticism* (1962): 36, 368-380.

3802. Stockhausen, Alma von. "Entwicklung und Verwandlung der Geist-Materie nach Teilhard de Chardin." *Perspektiven der Zukunft* (1973): 4, 3-6.

3803. ————. "Das Phänomen der Materie bei Teilhard de Chardin." *Perspektiven der Zukunft* (1967): 3, 2-4.

3804. Stoeckle, Bernhard. *Ich glaube an die Schöpfung.* Einsiedeln: Benziger, 1966. See pp. 67-70.

3805. Stoessel, François. "L'aujourd'hui du monde: Socialisation et relgiion selon le Père Teilhard de Chardin." Typescript. Faculté catholique de théologie de Lyon, 1966.

3806. Stolpe, Sven. "Teilhard de Chardin." *Credo* (1958): 39, 24-29.

3807.   Stoltz, M. Magdalena. "Zum 'Ewig-Weiblichen' bei Teil-
        hard de Chardin und Goethe." *Acta teilhardiana* (1971):
        2, 49-84.

3807a. Stolz, Walter. "Der 'Punkt Omega.' Teilhard de Chardin
        und Leidenschaft zur Erde." *Echo der Zeit* (1959): 24,
        10.

3808.   Straniero, Giorgio. *L'ontologia fenomenologica di Teil-
        hard de Chardin.* Milano: Vita e pensiero, 1969.

3809.   ————. "La prospettiva storica evolutiva di Teilhard
        de Chardin." *Vita e pensiero* (1970): 53, 703-711,
        715-716.

3810.   ————. "Teilhard de Chardin e il Fenomeno humano."
        Vita e pensiero (1969): 52, 791-798.

3811.   Streignart, J. "L'esthétique de Pierre Teilhard de Char-
        din et quelques eaux-fortes de Rembrandt." *Humanités
        chrétiennes* (1968-69): 3, 7-15.

3812.   ————. "Le tableau, 'une histoire comme Benson' de
        Pierre Teilhard de Chardin." *Humanités chrétiennes*
        (1968-69): 2, 1-12.

3812a. Strlè, A. "Neponarejeni Pierre Teilhard de Chardin."
        [Pierre Teilhard de Chardin Unfalsified.] *Bogoslovni
        Vestnik* (1978): 38, 355-364.

3813.   Strojnowski, Jerzy. "Dialektyka osoby i spoleczeństwa
        u Teilharda de Chardin i Ericha Fromm." *Życie i myśl*
        (1971): 10, 57-68.
              Also Item 3888, pp. 214-233.
        "Die Dialektik der Person und Gesellschaft bei
        Teilhard de Chardin und Erich Fromm." *Acta teilhard-
        iana* (1973): 1, 14-28.

3814.   ————. "Geneza i rzwój psychismu w ujęciu O. Teilharda
        de Chardin." [Genesis and Development of Psychism
        According to Father Teilhard de Chardin.] *Znak* (1968):
        20, 298-312.
              Also Item 3888, pp. 41-58.

3815.   ————. "Teilhard po polsku i po niemiecku." [Teil-
        hard in Polish and German.] *Więź* (1973): 4, 109-115.

3816. ————. "Teologowie polscy o Teilhardzie." [Polish
Theologians on Teilhard.] *Więź* (1975): 1, 140-145.

3817. Number deleted.

3818. Stróżewski, Wladyslaw. "Ku metafizyce ewolucji. Ary-
stoteles, Tomasz z Akwinu, Teilhard de Chardin." [On
the Metaphysics of Evolution: Aristotle, Thomas Aquinas,
Teilhard de Chardin.] *Znak* (1966): 18, 1360-1384.

3819. ————. "Na marginesie 'Czlowieka' Teilharda de Chardin." [In the Margin of Teilhard de Chardin's "Phenomenon of Man."] *Znak* (1963): 15, 1314-1338.

3820. Stuart, Alan L. "The Sciences and the Deity." *British
Journal for the Philosophy of Science* (1961-62): 12,
235-245.

3821. Suares, Carlo. "Teilhard de Chardin ou le ciel à l'heure
de la terre." *De quelques apprentis-sorciers*. Bruxelles: Être libre, 1965, pp. 70-94.
Also Paris: Courrier du livre, 1965.

3822. Sugi, R. Ya. "A propos de Teilhard." *La pensée* (1965):
494.

3823. Sûgô, Hiroshi. "Teilhard de Chardin oboegaki." [Some
Notes on Teilhard de Chardin.] *Risô* (1969): 7, 45-56.

3824. Sugranyes de Franch, Ramon. "Discours d'introduction."
Item 1015, pp. 15-16.

3825. Sullivan, Dan. "Psychosexuality: The Teilhard Lacunae."
Continuum (1967): 2, 254-278. See Item 1129.

3826. Sumner, Claude. "Pierre Teilhard de Chardin." *The
Philosophy of Man. II. From Kant to the Situation in
1962*. Addis Ababa: Central Printing Press, 1974, pp.
181-242.

3827. Swan, Lucile. "Exil in Peking." *Perspektiven der Zukunft* (1973): 3, 4-7; 4, 11-13; 5, 11-12.

3828. ————. "Une leçon d'esperance: Pierre Teilhard de
Chardin." *La table ronde* (1958): 129, 100-105.

3829. ————. "Memories and Letters." Item 501, pp. 40-49.
Also Item 497, pp. 40-49.

3829a. ———. *Memories and Letters--The Wind and the Rain.*
An Easterbook for 1962. London: Swan, 1962.

3830. ———. "With Teilhard in Peking." *The Month* (1962):
1, 5-15.

3831. Sykes, C. "Teilhard de Chardin and the Cosmic Christ."
Theology (1975): 78, 467-474.

3832. "Symphony to Chardin." *London Times*, October 12, 1967.

3833. "Systema Teilhard de Chardin ad Theologicam trutinam
revocatum." *Divinitas* (1959): 3, 219-364. Contains
Items 44, 1831, 2101, 2690, 3121.

3834. Szabó, Ferenc. "L'indétermination nécessaire de la notion d'origine selon Teilhard de Chardin." *Le monde
et la foi* (1960): 2, 13-17.

3835. ———. "Egy keresztény evolucionista." [A Christian
Evolutionist.] *Katolikus Szemle* (1962): 14, 39-48.

3836. ———. "A kétségbevont Teilhard de Chardin." [The
Controversial Teilhard de Chardin.] *Ahogy lehet*
(1962): 130, 3-17.

3837. ———. "Marxtól Teilhard de Chardin." [From Marx to
Teilhard de Chardin.] *Ahogy lehet* (1962): 131, 3-21.

3838. ———. "Megszentelni az emberi erőfeszítést. Gon-
dolatok Teilhard de Chardin műveiből." [Consecrating
Human Efforts. Thoughts on the Works of Teilhard de
Chardin.] *Szolgálat* (1977): 35, 77-79.

3839. ———. "Le 'phénomène Teilhard' et son arrière-plan."
Documentation sur l'Europe centrale (1963): 5, 30-31.

3840. ———. "Személy és társadalmiasulás Teilhard szem-
létetében." [Person and Socialization According to
Teilhard de Chardin.] *Katolikus szemle* (1965): 3,
193-208.

3841. ———. "Teilhard de Chardin." *A szeretet hullámhos-
szán.* [The Wavelength of Love.] Roma: Szerző Kiadasa, 1977, pp. 251-271.

3842. ———. "Teilhard de Chardin. Bevezetés Az isteni
miliőhöz." [Teilhard de Chardin. Introduction to
The Divine Milieu.] Paris: Ahogy lehet, 1965.

3843. ————. "Teilhard de Chardin kereszteny humanizmusa."
[The Christian Humanism of Teilhard de Chardin.]
Vilagnezetek harca. [The Ideological Struggle.]
Louvain: Collegium Hungaricum Universitatis Lovan-
iensis, 1963, pp. 129-185.
Also *Ahogy lehet* (1963): 133/134, 3-14.

3844. ————. "Teilhard de Chardin papi lelke." [The Priestly Soul of Teilhard de Chardin.] *Magyar Papi Egyseg*
(1964): 27, 33-39; 28, 51-58.

3845. ————. "Teilhard de Chardin vallasos eszmevilaga."
[The Religious Ideology of Teilhard de Chardin.]
Ahogy lehet (1963): 135, 3-14.
Also *Tavlatok.* [Perspectives.] Roma: Szerzo Kia-
dasa, 1970, pp. 125-165.

3846. ————. "Teilhard lelki üzenete." [Teilhard's Spiritual Message.] *Parbeszed a hitrol.* [Dialogue on the
Faith.] Roma: Szerzo Kiadasa, 1975, pp. 291-298.

3847. ————. "Teilhard personalizmusa." [Teilhard's Personalism.] *Tavlatok.* [Perspectives.] Roma: Szerzo Kiadasa, 1970, pp. 166-185.

3848. Szatrun, Lidia. "Aneks do 'Glosow o Teilhardzie.'
Kartki z przedwczesnej autobiografii." [Annex to
"Opinions on Teilhard": Some Pages of a Premature
Autobiography.] *Znak* (1962): 22/23, 265-271.

3849. ————. "Dyskusja Teilhardowska w 'Nova et vetera.'"
[The Discussion of Teilhard in "Nova et vetera."]
Znak (1963): 103, 133-140.

3850. Szekeres, Attila. "De anti-metafysische tendenties in
de filosofie en Teilhard de Chardin." *Nederlands
Theologisch Tijdschrift* (1967): 22, 13-37.

3851. ————. *Le Christ cosmique de Teilhard de Chardin.*
Antwerpen: Uitgeverij de nederlandsche boekhandel,
1969. Contains Items 894, 995, 1074, 1429, 2433, 2844,
3853, 3854, 3857, 3865, 4258, 4418
Also Paris: Seuil, 1969.

3852. ————. "Denkbeelden van Teilhard de Chardin over de
kosmiche evolutie." *Hervormd Nederland*, April 17,
1965, p. 10.

3853. ———. "'Honest to God' de l'évêque Robinson et la
tâche véritable de la théologie contemporaine." Item
3851, pp. 403-434.
Dutch version in *Nederlands Theologisch Tijdschrift*
(1966): 20, 192-217.

3854. ———. "Introduction." Item 3851, pp. 5-12.

3855. ———. "Karl Barth und die natürliche Theologie."
Evangelische Theologie (1964): 229-242.

3856. ———. "De kosmisch-universelle evolutie." Item 1206,
pp. 569-571.

3857. ———. "La pensée religieuse de Teilhard de Chardin et
la signification théologique de son Christ cosmique."
Item 3851, pp. 333-402.

3858. ———. "Pierre Teilhard de Chardin." *Nederlands Theologisch Tijdschrift* (1962): 16, 291-314.
Also *De Stem*, April 3, 1965, p. 7.

3859. ———. "Schrift en Traditie." *Kerk en theologie* (1963):
4, 1-10.

3860. ———. "Teilhard de Chardin en het grondprobleem van
de filozofie." *Vox theologica* (1963-64): 1, 8-91.
Also *Hendelingen van het XXVe Vlaamse Filologencongres*. Zellik: Secretariaat van de Vlaamse Filologencongressen, 1967, pp. 47-53.

3861. ———. "Teilhard de Chardin en de kosmische evolutie."
Hervormd Nederland, April 10, 1965, p. 15.

3862. ———. "Teilhard de Chardin en de kosmisch-universele
evolutie." *De Vlaamse Gids* (1965): 49, 583-596.

3863. ———. "Teilhard de Chardin en wij protestanten."
De Protestant (1965): 5, 7-11.

3864. ———. "Teilhard de Chardin 'Kind des hemels en van
de aarde.'" *Het Laastste Nieuws*, April 10-11, 1965,
p. 2.

3865. ———. "Teilhard en de rooms-katholieke theologie."
Kerk en theologie (1963): 1-26, 169-194.
"Les théologiens catholiques et Teilhard de Char-
din." Item 3851, pp. 83-149.

3866. ————. "De theologische betekenis van Teilhard de Chardin." *Kerk en theologie* (1964): 4, 271-282.

3867. ————. "Het visioen van Teilhard de Chardin." *Nederlands Theologisch Tijdschrift* (1963-64): 5, 381-390.

3868. ————. "Voor en tegen Teilhard de Chardin." *De Vlaamse Gids*, April, 1970, pp. 33-36.

3869. ————. "Zum 10. Todestag von Pierre Teilhard de Chardin." *Kirchenbote. Blatt der Evangelischreformierten Kirche in Nordwestdeutschland* (1965): 4, 1-3.

3870. Szigetti, Endre. "Teilhard de Chardin husvétja." [Teilhard de Chardin's Easter.] *Uj Ember* (1965): 16, 7.

3871. Szydzik, Stanis Edmund. "Evolution und Hoffnung." *Kommunität* (1961): 20, 178-180.

3872. Tack, Pauline Matheiu. "Le Père Teilhard tel que je l'ai vu." *Revue Teilhard de Chardin* (1961): 8/9, 49.

3873. "Tactical Error: Banning of Books by Teilhard, Rynne, Kaiser, and Kung." *Ave Maria*, October 26, 1963.

3874. Takahashi, Takechi. "Teilhard de Chardin no kirisutokyôkan." [The Idea of Christianity According to Teilhard.] *Logos* (1961): 7, 166-185.

3875. Takayanagi, Chunichi. "Teilhard de Chardin no shûkyôsei." [Teilhard de Chardin and His Spirituality.] *Katorikku Shingaku* (1965): 4, 395-422.

3876. Találkozás Kelettel. "Teilhard de Chardin leveleidől." [Some Letters of Teilhard de Chardin.] *Vigilia* (1965): 30, 21-52.

3877. Talhouet, Jean de. *Le lyrisme et la mystique dans les oeuvres du Père Teilhard de Chardin.* Paris: Scorpion, 1959.

3878. "Talking of Teilhard." *Tablet*, July 16, 1966, p. 816.

3879. Tanalski, Dionizy. "Klopoty z Teilhardem." [Difficulties with Teilhard.] *Zeszyty Argumentów* (1967): 4, 114-121.

3880.   Tanner, Henri.   *Le grain de sénéve.   De la science à la religion avec Teilhard de Chardin.*   Saint-Maurice: Éditions Saint-Augustin, 1967.

3881.   Taschdjian, Edgar.   "Dobzhansky and Teilhard."   *Cross Currents* (1967): 17, 360-363.

3882.   Taufour, Bernard.   "Le monde audio-visuel dans ses dimensions humaines et planétaires."   *Revue Teilhard de Chardin* (1967): 31, 27-37.

3883.   Taylor, Hugh.   "The Phenomenon of Man."   *The American Scientist*, March, 1960, 56A-58A.

3884.   Tazbir, Mieczyslaw.   "Aktualność dziela Teilharda de Chardin."   [The Actuality of Teilhard de Chardin's Works.]   *Życie i myśl* (1963): 9/10, 121-123.
        Also Item 3888, pp. 7-12.

3885.   ————.   "L'art d'être teilhardien."   *Życie i myśl* (1965): 5, 2-14.
        Also Item 3888, pp. 13-27.

3886.   ————.   "Dzielo Teilharda de Chardin a dialog katolików z marksistami."   [Teilhard de Chardin's Work and the Dialogue Between Catholics and Marxists.]   *Życie i myśl* (1965): 10, 71-75.
        Also Item 3888, pp. 359-366.

3887.   ————.   "Il n'y a que peu d'endroits dans le monde où l'idée de dialogue soit realisée d'une façon aussi créatrice."   *Revue de la presse catholique en Pologne* (1965): 10, 12-13.

3888.   ————.   *Myśl O. Teilharda de Chardin w Polsce.*   [The Thought of Father Teilhard de Chardin in Poland.]   Warszawa: Pax, 1973.   Contains Items 395, 421, 1623, 2182, 3182, 3183, 3193, 3206, 3209, 3210, 3522, 3814, 3884, 3885, 3886, 3890, 4292, 4293, 4294.

3889.   ————.   "VIII Tydzień teilhardowski w Vézelay."   [The Eighth Teilhard Week at Vezelay.]   *Życie i myśl* (1968): 6/7, 163-175.

3890.   ————.   "Podstawowna bibligrafia obcojęzyczna."   [Basic Bibliography in Foreign Languages.]   Item 3888, pp. 415-418.

3891. ——. "Przyjaciele Teilharda w Vézelay." [Teilhard's Friends at Vézelay.] *Kierunki* (1964): 42, 3.

3892. ——. "'Religia nieba' i 'religia ziemi.'" ["Sky" Religion and "Earth" Religion.] *Stowo powszechne*, March 7, 1965, pp. 3-4.

3893. ——. "VII Tydzień teilhardowski w Vézelay." [The Seventh Teilhard Week at Vézelay.] *Życie i myśl* (1967): 1, 100-107.

3894. ——. "Swiadek jutra." [The Witness of the Future.] *Kierunki* (1963): 15.

3895. ——. "V-VI Sympozjum teilhardowskie." [Fifth and Sixth Teilhard Symposium.] *Życie i myśl* (1967): 1, 108-113.

3896. ——. "Sympozjum w Vézelay." [Symposium at Vézelay.] *Życie i myśl* (1964): 11/12, 156-164.

3897. ——. "Teilhardiana." *Życie i myśl* (1965): 125-139; (1968): 183-186.

3898. "Technocratisme en teilhardisme." Item 1206, pp. 571-573.

3899. "Teilhard: A Profile." *Christian Century*, January 16, 1963, p. 95.

3900. "Teilhard and Catholic Indifference. Letters to *Search*." *Search* (1962): 8, 315-316.

3901. "Teilhard and the Church." *America*, July 14, 1962, p. 480.

3902. "Teilhard and Teilhardism: A Plea for Moderation." *Tablet*, January 14, 1967, pp. 34-35; January 21, 1967, p. 78; February 4, 1967, p. 134; February 11, 1967, pp. 160-162.

3903. *Teilhard de Chardin*. Paris: Hachette, 1969. Contains Items 209, 282, 986, 1102, 1596, 2488, 2571, 3155.

3904. "Teilhard de Chardin." *Cahiers de vie franciscaine* (1962): 1-49. Contains Items 951, 3301.

3905. "Teilhard de Chardin." *Ciencia y fe* (1964): 1/3, 203–212.

3906. "Teilhard de Chardin." *Dialogue* (1964–65): 3, 341–384. Contains Items 61, 863, 1990, 2308.

3907. "Teilhard de Chardin." *Estudios* (1965): 54, 85–132. Contains Items 1358, 1378, 2552, 2951, 3075.

3908. "Teilhard de Chardin." *Hechos y dichos* (1966): 242–336. Contains Items 567, 793, 943, 1702, 2504, 3370, 3934.

3909. "Teilhard de Chardin." *Katolikus Szemle* (1965): 3, 193–264. Contains Items 546, 3204, 3319, 3840.

3910. "Teilhard de Chardin." *Livres de France* (1966): 4, 2–30. Contains Items 209, 988, 989, 1024, 3167, 4159, 4265, 4653.

3911. "Teilhard de Chardin." *Nuovo osservatore politico-economico-soziale* (1965): 6, 302–402.

3912. "Teilhard de Chardin." *Ons Geestelijk Leven* (1964–65): 41, 321–374. Contains Items 3, 484, 1646, 1669, 2079.

3913. "Teilhard de Chardin and Sociology." *American Catholic Sociological Review* (1962): 23, 291–337. Contains Items 740, 1034, 1527, 3751.

3914. "Teilhard de Chardin: Attention, danger." *Revue nouvelle*, September, 1962, pp. 188–189.

3915. "Teilhard de Chardin, dieci anni dopo." *Testimonianze* (1965): 8, 744–765. Contains Items 64, 1181, 2731.

3916. "Teilhard de Chardin dopo il Concilio." *Il Regno* (1966): 114, 125–127.

3917. *Teilhard de Chardin e a convergência das civilizações e das ciências.* Lisboa: Instituto Superior de Ciências Sociais e Política Ultramarina, 1964. Contains Items 1043, 1118, 1962, 2327, 2420, 3027, 4213, 4221.

3918. "Teilhard de Chardin: el testimonio de Henri de Lubac." *Criterio* (1966): 39, 803–807.

3919. "Teilhard de Chardin, entre origen y destino, entre la ciencia y la fe, entre biologia y humanismo." *La estafeta literaria* (1964): 290, 3-14. Contains Items 22, 590, 787, 923, 1262, 2860, 3211, 3759.

3920. *Teilhard de Chardin et la politique africaine.* Paris: Seuil, 1962. Contains Items 3651, 4341, 4389, 4803.

3921. "Teilhard de Chardin filósofo." *Pensamiento* (1970): 26, 139-275. Contains Items 805, 1396, 2681, 3037, 3355, 3541, 4098.

3922. "Teilhard de Chardin: Genshô to shite no ningen ni tsuite." [In regard to "The Phenomenon of Man" of Teilhard de Chardin.] *Misuzu* (1964): 6, 17-39. Contains Items 76, 1819, 2172, 3574, 3673, 4289.

3923. "Teilhard de Chardin im Dialog zwischen Katholiken und Marxisten." *Herder-Korrespondenz* (1967): 21, 214-217.

3924. *Teilhard de Chardin. Philosophische und theologische Probleme seines Denkens.* Würzburg: Echter-Verlag, 1967. Contains Items 1025, 1278, 1841, 1892, 2537, 3367.

3925. *Teilhard de Chardin, prêtre de la Compagnie de Jésus savant contre l'Evangile de Jésus-Christ el la science.* Landes: Seignosse, 1962.

3926. *Teilhard de Chardin. Studi e dibatti.* Bologna: Dehoniane, 1969.

3927. "Teilhard de Chardin und die Teilhardismus." *Dokumente* (1967): 23, 46-58. Contains Items 182, 682, 2651.

3928. "Teilhard de Chardin: Die Vision der einen Welt." *Civis* (1963): 9, 18-21.

3929. Teilhard de Chardin, Joseph. "Les annales de la famille Teilhard." *Revue Teilhard de Chardin* (1967-68): 33/34, 3-72.

3930. ———. "Mon frère Pierre." *Revue Teilhard de Chardin* (1969): 39, 1-4.

3931. ———. "Préface." In Item 1137.

3932. Teilhard de Chardin, Marguerite Marie. *L'energie spirituelle de la souffrance.* Paris: Seuil, 1958. Contains Item 4718.

3933. "Teilhard de Chardin's Centrogenetic Ontology." *The Teilhard Review* (1976): 11, 58-64.

3934. "Teilhard el hombre espiritual." *Hechos y dichos* (1966): 243-246.

3935. *Teilhard et la pensée chrétienne.* Montréal: Beauchemin, 1966. Contains Items 1320, 1321, 2354, 2355, 2464.

3936. "Teilhard et la religion." *Itinéraires* (1965): 91, 110-183. Contains Items 850, 3276.

3937. "Teilhard et la science." *Itinéraires* (1965): 96, 4-140. Contains Items 471, 1116, 1178, 2612, 2909, 3162, 3259, 3312, 3452, 3689.

3938. "Teilhard in Britain." *Tablet*, September 4, 1965, p. 982.

3939. "Teilhard in the Trenches." *Time*, April 14, 1975, p. 47.

3940. "Teilhard philosophe malgré lui...." *La France catholique* (1960): 772, 2.

3941. "Teilhard y Africa." *La Vanguardia española*, November 23, 1967, p. 31.

3942. "The Teilhardian Phenomenon After Twenty Years." *America*, April 12, 1975, pp. 270-273.

3943. "Teilhardiana." *Życie i myśl* (1967): 1, 114-118.

3944. "A Teilhardism Gathering." *The Ampleforth Journal* (1968): 73, 8.

3945. "El teilhardismo." *Historia de la filosofía. La filosofía burguesa contemporanea.* Grijalbo, México: Instituto de Filosofía, 1966, vol. 7.

3946. Teislv, Af Rick. "Ndviklingdlaeren i kristelig belysning." *Kristelight dagblad*, May 28, 1964.

3947. Teldy-Naim, Robert. *Faut-il brûler Teilhard de Chardin?* Paris: Calmann-Levy, 1959. *Auf den Scheiterhaufen mit Teilhard de Chardin?* München: List, 1964.

3948. "Témoignages." Item 3292, pp. 181–185.

3949. "Témoignages." Item 3041, pp. 132–150.

3950. *Terre promise*. Paris: Seuil, 1974. Contains Items 241, 553, 865, 1221, 3287, 4103, 4567.

3951. Terres, Ágoston. "Kosmisches Denken bei Hildegard von Bingen und Teilhard de Chardin." *Ebertin kosmobiologisches Jahrbuch* (1968): 33–50.

3952. Tertulian, Nicolae. "Colocviul Teilhard de la Vézelay." [The Teilhard Colloquium at Vézelay.] *Gazeta literaria* (1965): 43, 8.

3953. ————. "Marxismul si gîndirea lui Teilhard de Chardin." *Viaţa româneasca* (1965): 12, 182–193. "Der Marxismus und das Denken Teilhard de Chardins." *Perspektiven der Zukunft* (1967): 2, 146–153.

3954. ————. "Romain Rolland, Teilhard de Chardin si problema umanismulu in gîndirea contemporanâ." [Romain Rolland, Teilhard de Chardin and the Problem of Humanism in Contemporary Thought.] *Viaţa româneasca* (1967): 2, 146–147.

3955. Tessiore, Paolo. "La sanctification de l'effort humain en Teilhard de Chardin." *II Congressus Unionis Mundialis antiquorum Societatis Iesu alumnorum, Romae 1967*. Napoli: L'Arte tipografica, 1970, pp. 150–155.

3956. "Testimonianze su Teilhard de Chardin." *Leggere* (1962): 11, 6.

3957. Thatcher, Adrian. "Three Theologies of the Future: Moltmann, Teilhard de Chardin and A.N. Whitehead." *Baptist Quarterly* (1974): 25, 242–250.

3958. Thérive, André. "Lectures françaises. Histoire de demain." *Écrits de Paris*, April, 1960, pp. 119–127.

3959. ————. *Procès de langage*. Paris: Stock, 1962.

3960. ————. "Teilhardisme et progressisme." *Entours de la foi*. Paris: Grasset, 1966, pp. 201–247.

3961. Thibon, G. "Le christianisme évolutif de Teilhard de Chardin." *Citadelle*, June, 1963, pp. 20–21.

3962.   Thiele, Wolfgang. "Die Anthropologie des Teilhard de
        Chardin." *Münchener medizinische Wochenschrift* (1065):
        108, 1673-1677.

3963.   ———. "Bewusstsein, Seele und Geist in der Evolutions-
        theorie des Teilhard de Chardin." *Medizinische Welt*
        (1966): 831-834.

3964.   ———. "Das Leib-Seele-Verhältnis bei Teilhard de
        Chardin." *Münchener medizinische Wochenschrift* (1965):
        107, 1891-1894.

3965.   Thomas, Jacob K. "Introduction to the Phenomenon Teil-
        hard." *The Rally* (1966): 5/6, 25-34.

3966.   Thomas, L.V. "Pierre Teilhard de Chardin et les philo-
        sophes modernes." *Afrique documents* (1962): 61, 3-9.

3967.   ———. "Le socialisme de Léopold Sédar Senghor et l'âme
        africaine." *Afrique documents* (1964): 75, 167-193.

3968.   Thomasma, David. "The Synthesis of Teilhard de Chardin."
        Thomist (1968): 32, 213-237.

3969.   ———. "Teilhard and Theology." *Cross Currents* (1967):
        17, 372-375.

3970.   Thompson, W.R. "Teilhard: Neither Scientific nor Ortho-
        dox?" *Michael de la Bedoyere's Search* (1962): 1, 189-
        193. See Item 1662.

3971.   Thonnard, F.J. "Philosophie augustinienne et Phéno-
        mène humain." *Revue des sciences religieuses* (1957):
        31, 275-289.

3972.   Thorbecke, William J. *A New Dimension in Political
        Thinking*. Leyden/New York: A.W. Sijthoff, 1965.

3973.   Thran, Sally. "Fr. Ong Discusses the Influence of Teil-
        hard de Chardin's Thought." *St. Louis Review*, October,
        1965, p. 13.

3974.   ———. "Personal Memory of Father Teilhard." *St.
        Louis Review*, October, 1965, p. 17.

3975.   Thum, Beda. "Philosophie und Wissenschaft im Weltbild
        von Teilhard de Chardin." *Theologisch-praktische
        Quartalschrift* (1964): 112, 23-30.

3976. Thys, Albert. *Conscience, réflexion, collectivisation chez Teilhard.* Paris: Éditions Universitaires, 1964. *Consciência, reflexão, colectivização em Teilhard.* Petrópolis: Vozes, 1967. *Conciencia, reflexión y colectivización según Teilhard.* Buenos Aires: Columba, 1968.

3977. Tiberghien, P. "Le 'Phénomène humain' du Père Teilhard de Chardin." *Mélanges de science religieuse* (1956): 13, 219-230.

3978. *Tijdgenoten over Teilhard de Chardin.* Utrecht/Antwerpen: Spectrum, 1965. Contains Items 1384, 2027, 2413, 3160, 3727, 4007, 4026.

3979. Tilloy, A. *Teilhard de Chardin, père de l'église ou pseudo-prophète?* St-Cénère: Éditions St-Michel, 1968.

3980. Tisch, Joseph Lesage. "Religion for the Space Age." *Religious Humanism* (1969): 3, 161-166.

3981. Tobler, Walter. "Zum Gespräch über P. Teilhard de Chardin." *Reformatio* (1966): 15, 436-444.

3982. Todd, J.M. "On Reading Père Teilhard de Chardin." *Tablet*, May 28, 1960, p. 522.

3983. Tollenaere, J. de. "Weltschöpfung als Entwicklung. Teilhard de Chardins Vision und das christliche Dogma." *Wort und Wahrheit* (1961): 4, 273-282.

3984. Tomas, Albert. "Contemplació en l'acció. L'aportació del Padre Teilhard de Chardin." *Qüestions de vida cristiana* (1965): 27, 17-26.

3985. Tomas, Jordi A. "Reflexions crítiques a partir de l'evolució." *Qüestions de vida cristiana* (1969): 47, 35-45.

3986. Tomas Cabot, José. "El futuro del hombre. La teoria de Teilhard de Chardin." *Destino*, May 21, 1966, pp. 44-47.

3987. Toniolo Pasquali, Anna. "Pierre Teilhard de Chardin." *Studium* (1963): 15-24.

3988. Tordai, Zádor. "Aktywizacja energii a zwiakek miedzy ludzkim i ponadludzkim." *Zeszyty Argumentów* (1965): 19, 88-91. "L'ultra humain et l'activation des énergies." *Europa* (1965): 431/432, 140-151.

3989. ————. "Filosofija Teilharda de Chardina i sovre-
       mennaja ideologičeskaja borjba." [Teilhard's Philo-
       sophy and the Contemporary Ideological Struggle.]
       Voprosy naučnogo ateizma (1966): 364-389.

3990. ————. "Miért érdelki önt, a marzistát, Teilhard de
       Chardin?" [Why Does Teilhard de Chardin Interest
       You as a Marxist?] Item 4702 trans., pp. 5-36.
       Also *Vigilia* (1973): 38, 586-597.

3991. ————. "Teilhard de Chardin és a katolikus ideológia
       válsága." [Teilhard de Chardin and the Crisis of
       Catholic Ideology.] *Magyar Filozófiai Szemle* (1965):
       9, 292-297.

3992. ————. "Teilhard de Chardin természetképe." [Teil-
       hard de Chardin's Nature.] *Termeszettudományi köz-
       löny* (1967): 11, 49-52.

3993. Torlais, Jean. "L'avenir de l'homme. La recherche
       scientifique, phénomène à la mode." *Le progrès méd-
       ical* (1960): 6, 129-130, 133.

3994. ————. "Une biologie optimiste, le groupe zoologique
       humain du P. Teilhard de Chardin." *Le progrès médi-
       cal* (1957): 4, 83-86.

3995. ————. "'La vision du passé' de Pierre Teilhard de
       Chardin." *Le progrès médical* (1959): 2, 36-38.

3996. Török, István. "Teilhard és a protestánsok. In memor-
       iam prof. dr. Szekeres." [Teilhard and the Protes-
       tants. In Memory of Dr. Szekeres.] *Vigilia* (1976):
       41, 156-162.

3997. Torres Arias, Rafael. "Hombre y mito." *Communidad*
       (1967): 2, 697-701.

3998. Touceda, Raúl. "Origen y fundamentos de la ciencia
       socioantropológica. El fenómeno social (Gurvitch)
       y el fenómeno humano (Teilhard de Chardin)." *In-
       troducción a la socioantropología.* Buenos Aires:
       Abeledo-Perrot, 1962, pp. 45-66.

3999. ————. *Sistema de la vida.* Buenos Aires: Abeledo-
       Perrot, 1961.

4000. Toulat, Jean. "I settant'anni dell'illustre gesuita. Padre de Lubac ci parla di Teilhard de Chardin." *L'avvenire d'Italia*, February 25, 1966, p. 3.

4001. Toulmin, Stephen. "On Teilhard de Chardin." *Commentary* (1965): 39, 50-55.

4002. Tovar, Saúl Antonio. "La visión humana de Teilhard de Chardin." *Eidos* (1970): 2, 86-105.

4003. Tovar Conche, Diego. "Ubicación del pensamiento de Teilhard de Chardin." *El Siglo*, February 18, 1959, pp. 12-14.

4004. Towers, Bernard. *Concerning Teilhard and Other Writings on Science and Religion*. London: Collins, 1969.

4005. ————. "Human Embryology and the Law of Complexity-Consciousness." Item 1421, pp. 47-57.

4006. ————. "In het post-teilhardiaanse tijdvak." In Item 1206, pp. 573-574.

4007. ————. "Jung and Teilhard." Item 501, pp. 78-87. Also Item 497, pp. 78-87. "Jung en Teilhard." Item 3978, pp. 125-135.

4008. ————. "On Reading Père Teilhard de Chardin." *Tablet*, May 7, 1960, p. 451.

4009. ————. "Optimism-Pessimism in Contemporary Culture." *Pax Romana Journal* (1967): 2, 20-22.

4010. ————. "The Phenomenon of Man. Discussion avec P. Medawar. Émission radiophonique de la BBC (London 14·5·1960)." Mimeographed. Paris: Fondation Teilhard de Chardin, 1960.

4011. ————. "The Phenomenon of Man. Père Teilhard de Chardin in Translation." *Tablet*, November 7, 1959, pp. 962-963.

4012. ————. "Scientific Master versus Pioneer." *The Teilhard Review* (1966-67): 2, 50-54. Also *Listener* (1965): 73, 557-558, 563.

4013. ————. "The Significance of Teilhard de Chardin." *Blackfriars* (1959): 40, 126-129.

4014. ————. "Teilhard de Chardin." *Blackfriars* (1960):
       480, 119-126.

4015. ————. "Teilhard de Chardin." *Expository Times*
       (1968): 79, 276-278.

4016. ————. *Teilhard de Chardin*. London: Carey Kingsgate
       Press, 1966.
       Also Richmond: John Knox Press, 1966.

4017. ————. "Teilhard in Depth." *Tablet*, April 13, 1965,
       p. 292.

4018. ————. "Teilhard--More Letters." *Newman Association,
       Philosophy of Science Group, Bulletin* (1960): 35, 2-3.

4019. ————. "The Teilhard Movement in Britain." *The Month*
       (1966): 36, 188-196.

4020. ————. "The Teilhard Syndrome." *Tablet*, February
       20, 1965, pp. 208-209.

4021. ————. "Time and the Growth of Complexity." Item
       528, pp. 115-128.

4022. Toynbee, Arnold. "Message du Professeur Arnold Toyn-
       bee." *Revue Teilhard de Chardin* (1961): 8/9, 4.
       Also *Le Phare dimanche*, April 2, 1961, p. 5.

4023. ————. "Le phénomène humain." In *Revue Teilhard de
       Chardin* (1960): 3/4, 17-19.
       Also *Synthèses* (1959-60): 163/164, 112-114.

4024. ————. "Una testimonianza di Arnold Toynbee per
       Pierre Teilhard de Chardin." *L'Europa letteraria*
       (1961): 9/10, 20-21.

4025. ————. "Vers l'unité humaine." *Revue Teilhard de
       Chardin* (1963): 14, 3.

4026. ————. "The Vision of the Unity." *Daily Mail*, Novem-
       ber 22, 1959.
       "Vision de l'unité." Item 3292, pp. 125-128.
       "Visie van eenheid." Item 3978, pp. 121-123.

4027. Treat, Ida. "Le laboratoire du Museum d'histoire
       naturelle durant l'hiver 1924-1925." *Europe* (1965):
       431/432, 31-33.

4028. Trebs, Herbert. "Zur Teilhard-Rezeption in der DDR." *Perspektiven der Zukunft* (1968): 6, 5-6.

4029. Tresmontant, Claude. "A propos du Père Teilhard de Chardin." *Responsables* (1962): 8, 46-50.

4030. ———. *Comment se pose aujourd'hui le problème de l'existence de Dieu.* Paris: Seuil, 1966. See pp. 166-170, 279-287.

4031. ———. *Introduction à la pensée de Teilhard de Chardin.* Paris: Seuil, 1956.
Introducción al pensamiento de Teilhard de Chardin. México: Universidad Nacional Autonoma de México, 1958. Also Madrid: Taurus, 1960. Also 6th ed., 1968.
Pierre Teilhard de Chardin: His Thought. Baltimore: Helicon, 1959.
Einführung in das Denken Teilhard de Chardins. Frankfurt: Alber, 1963.
Introdução ao pensamento de Teilhard de Chardin. Petrópolis: Vozes, 1964.
Teiyaru do Sharadan. Tokyo: Shinchôcha, 1966.

4032. ———. "Introduction à la pensée de Teilhard de Chardin." *Recherches et débats* (1955): 13, 96-137. Also *Le Bulletin* (1956): 5, 25-29.
"Einführung in das Denken Pierre Teilhard de Chardins." *Kommunität* (1961): 20, 202-203.

4033. ———. "Une meditation savante sur la nature." *La quinzaine littéraire*, October 1-15, 1966, pp. 19-20.

4034. ———. "Note sur l'oeuvre de Teilhard de Chardin." *Les études philosophiques* (1955): 4, 592-605.

4035. ———. "Le Père Teilhard de Chardin et la théologie." *Lettre* (1962): 49/50, 1-53. Contains Item 4552.

4036. ———. "Pierre Teilhard de Chardin." *La revue nouvelle* (1955): 6, 614-627.

4037. ———. "Rapport entre l'oeuvre de Teilhard et la théologie de Saint Paul." Paris: Fondation Teilhard de Chardin, 1955.

4038. ———. "Realités présentes et approches de l'avenir. Grandeur et limites de l'oeuvre du Père Teilhard de

Chardin." *Association des cadres dirigeants de
l'industrie pour le progrès social et économique.
Bulletin* (1963): 184, 423-431.

4039.   ———. "Réflexions concernant l'oeuvre du R.P. Teilhard de Chardin." *Témoignage chrétien*, January 31,
1958, p. 3.

4040.   ———. "Remarques complémentaires." *Lettre* (1962):
52, 27-30.

4041.   ———. "Retour aux sources." *Revue Teilhard de Chardin* (1960): 1/2, 20-22.

4042.   ———. "Sur la théorie du P. Teilhard de Chardin."
Études de metaphysique biblique. Paris: Gabalda,
1955.

4043.   ———. "Teilhard, signe de contradiction." *Le bulletin* (1957): 18, 40-48.

4044.   ———. "Wnioski i refleksje." [Conclusions and Reflections.] *Życie i myśl* (1963): 9/10, 166-170.

4045.   Trevisan, Armindo. "O amor em Teilhard de Chardin."
Vozes (1968): 62, 663-675.

4046.   Trevisano, Bernardo. "Polemiche su Teilhard de Chardin."
Il Giornale d'Italia, February 22, 1966.

4047.   Trewick, O. "Collectivisation?" *The Teilhard Review*
(1970): 5, 44-50.

4048.   Tribouille, Armelle de la. "De Socrate à Teilhard de
Chardin. Où mène la socialisation?" *Cahiers de
Neuilly* (1963).

4049.   ———. "Session teilhardienne sur l'énergie humaine."
Cahiers de Neuilly (1963): 49-52.

4050.   Troisfontaines, Roger. "Où l'évolution rejoint le
créateur." *Le Figaro littéraire*, September 17, 1960,
p. 10.

4051.   Trotzig, Birgitta. "Teilhard de Chardin: Ett alter-
nativ." [Teilhard de Chardin: The Alternative.]
Bonniers litterara magasin (1961): 30, 27-41.
Also Item 1944, pp. 30-63.

4052. Truc, Gonzague. "Esprit et création d'après Teilhard de Chardin." *Écrits de Paris*, July–August, 1960, pp. 31–39.

4053. ————. "Le Père Teilhard de Chardin et la realité de l'esprit." *Écrits de Paris*, November, 1956, pp. 73–78.

4054. Truhlar, Karl Vladimir. *Teilhard und Solowjew. Dichtung und religiöse Erfahrung*. Freiburg/München: Alber, 1966. *Solovjev y Teilhard. Poesía y experiencia religiosa*. Madrid: Razón y fe, 1966. *Teilhard e Soloviev*. Roma: Edizioni paoline, 1967.

4055. ————. "Tragika Teilharda de Chardena." [The Tragedy of Teilhard de Chardin.] *Znamenje* (1973): 3, 301–306.

4056. Truyols, Jaume. "L'aparició de la humanitat com a realitat zoológica." *Qüestions de vida cristiana* (1969): 47, 19–33.

4057. Trystram, Bernard. "Une interprétation de l'histoire." *Revue Teilhard de Chardin* (1961): 6, 15–17.

4058. Trzebuchowski, P. "Dwie wizje historii: Karol Péguy i Piotr Teilhard de Chardin." [Two Visions of History: Charles Peguy and Pierre Teilhard de Chardin.] *Novum* (1970): 5, 77–84.

4059. Trznadel, Jacek. "'Kto wypowie ... nieśmiertelny Odpadek ...' (Na marginesie pracy 'Le Pretre' Teilharda de Chardin)." ["Who Will Explain Immortal Loss?" (Marginal Note on Teilhard's Work, "The Priest").] *Życie i myśl* (1971): 10, 51–56.

4060. Tunc, André. "Aspetti politici nel pensiero di Teilhard de Chardin." *Leggere* (1962): 11, 1–6.

4061. ————. "La contribution possible des études juridiques comparatives à une meilleure compréhension entre nations." *Revue internationale de droit comparé* (1964): 1.

4062. ————. "La montée du pensant." *La Croix*, June 14, 1968, p. 20.

4063. ————. "La planétisation à partir des communautés
       humaines." Item 741, pp. 86–112.

4064. ————. "Planétisation du droit." *Revue de l'action
       populaire* (1963): 173, 1187–1196.

4065. ————. "The Political Importance of Teilhard de Char-
       din's Concept of 'Noosphere.' Conférence donnée à
       l'Université de Pennsylvanie, USA, 1960." Typescript.
       Paris: Fondation Teilhard de Chardin, 1960.

4066. ————. "L'université devant les grands problèmes du
       monde contemporain." *Revue de l'Université de Brux-
       elles* (1960): 1/2.

4067. Turk, F.A. "The Idea of Biological and Social Progress
       in the System of Teilhard de Chardin." Item 1919, pp.
       1–32.

4068. Turoldo, Davide M. "Niente miti." Item 2744, pp. 275–
       280.
       "Pas de mythes." Item 2744 trans., pp. 255–260.

4069. Tveteras, Camilla. "Mennesket og evolusjonen. Fra
       Teilhards de Chardins etterlatte skriftee." [Man-
       kind in Evolution. From Teilhard de Chardin's Later
       Writings.] *Samtiden* (1965): 65, 596–605.

4070. Ubaldi, Pietro. "Incontro con Teilhard de Chardin."
       Centro ricerce biopsichiche (1964): 10, 3–15; 11,
       7–16; 12, 15–21; (1965): 9, 15–28, 47–58, 87–92,
       103–114.
       *Encontro com Teilhard de Chardin e evolucão das
       religiões.* São Vicente: Grupo E. Monismo, 1966.

4071. Uhde, Volker. "Teilhard-Bibliographie." *Acta teil-
       hardiana* (1967): 4, 100–113; (1968): 5, 105–115.
       See also Items 3697, 4072.

4072. ————, and Gerhard H. Sitzmann. "Teilhard-Biblio-
       graphie." *Acta teilhardiana* (1969): 6, 102–107;
       (1970): 7, 129–133. See also Items 3697, 4071.

4073. Ulrich, Lawrence Paul. "The Concept of Man in Teilhard
       de Chardin." Doctoral dissertation, University of
       Toronto, 1972.

4074. Ungaretti, Giuseppe. "Osservazioni su Teilhard." *Europa letteraria* (1963): 19, 189-190.

4075. Urbančič, Ivan. "Jereticki jezuit Pierre Teilhard de Chardin: Njegova misao celine." [Pierre Teilhard de Chardin, the Heretical Jesuit: Summary of His Thought.] *Filosofija* (1967): 4, 127-151.

4076. Urdanoz, T. "Dos obras de crítica en torno a Teilhard de Chardin." *Estudios filosóficos* (1966): 15, 137-147. See Items 649, 3587.

4077. Urosa Savino, Jorge. *El progreso y el reino de Dios en Teilhard de Chardin.* Maracaibo: Urosa Savino, 1976.

4078. Useros, Manuel. "Michael Schmaus: 'En general, hay que decir 'si' a Teilhard de Chardin.'" *Incunable* (1965): 192, 7. See Item 3608.

4079. U Thant. "Teilhard de Chardin longuement cité par U Thant." *Le Figaro,* June 28, 1965.

4080. Vacek, Edward V. "Ethical Ideas in Teilhard de Chardin." Doctoral dissertation, St. Louis University, 1968.

4081. Valabek, Redemptus Maria. "Three Recent Books on Teilhard." *Carmelus* (1971): 8, 293-297. See Items 3115, 3118.

4082. Valderrey, Carmen. "El misterio de lo femenino en el pensamiento de Teilhard de Chardin." *Arbor* (1973): 85, 421-441.

4083. Valensin, Auguste. *Textes et documents inédits.* Paris: Aubier-Montaigne, 1961.

4084. Valentie, Maria Eugenia. "A propósito de una recente publicación sobre Teilhard de Chardin." *La Gaceta,* March 19, 1967.

4085. ———. "Nueva respuesta." *La Gaceta,* April 30, 1967.

4086. Vallentin, J. "Note sur la pensée de Teilhard de Chardin." *Cahiers de Neuilly* (1965): 3, 49-52. See Item 3378.

4087. ———. "Prolongements oecuméniques de la pensée teilhardienne." *Cahiers de Neuilly* (1965): 2, 48-63.

4088. Vallois, H.V. "Le R.P. Teilhard de Chardin (1881-1955)." *Revue archéologique* (1956): 47, 200-202.

4089. Valls Masriera, C. "Sobre al pensamiento filosófico y teológico de Pedro Teilhard de Chardin." *Espíritu* (1963): 12, 31-38.

4090. Valnère, René. *Teilhard l'apostata*. Roma: Volpe, 1971.

4091. ———. "Voici Gilson contre Teilhard." *Le monde et la vie* (1966): 152, 29.

4092. Valverde Mucientes, Carlos. "Contemplación para alcanzar amor y Medio Divino." *Manresa* (1970): 42, 157-168.

4093. ———. "Dialéctica y subida de conciencia come sentidos de la historia." *Pensamiento* (1970): 26, 419-427.

4094. ———. "Evolucionismo teilhardiano y quinta via." *Actes du Congrès thomiste international de Rome*. Roma: Le Congrès, 1966, vol. 1, pp. 295-301.

4095. ———. "La flecha de la evolución. Opción humana y exigencia cósmica de lo divino en el pensamiento de Teilhard de Chardin." *Humanidades* (1966): 18, 377-396.

4096. ———. "¿Que hay que pensar sobre Teilhard de Chardin?" *Sal terrae* (1963): 51, 668-689.

4097. ———. "Recuerdo de Teilhard. A los diez años de su muerte." *Humanidades* (1965): 17, 380-386. Also *Revista javeriana* (1966): 66, 292-298.

4098. ———. "Teilhard de Chardin y la filosofía." Item 745, pp. 89-114.

4099. ———. "Teilhard de Chardin y el marxismo." *Pensamiento* (1970): 26, 251-253.

4100. Van Ai, Nguyen. *Khoa Hoc và Bùc Tin. Gioi-Thiêu tu Tuong Teilhard de Chardin*. [Science and Faith. Introduction to Teilhard de Chardin.] Saigon: Nam Chi Tung Thu, 1966.

4101. Vancourt, R. "Hacía el primado del conocimento científico." *El Siglo*, February 18, 1959, pp. 12-13.

4102. Vandange, Pierre Charles. *Teilhard de Chardin et la
révolte des apprentis (une raison de vivre pour les
jeunes)*. Paris: Vandange, 1971.

4103. Van de Ghinste, Josée. "La vision poétique de Teilhard
de Chardin." Item 3950, pp. 31-67.

4104. Vandel, Albert. "L'évolutionnisme du Père Teilhard de
Chardin." *Les études philosophiques* (1965): 20, 449-
464.

4105. ———. *L'homme et l'évolution*. Paris: Gallimard,
1958.

4106. ———. "Un humanisme scientifique." *Dialectica*
(1960): 1, 5-20.

4107. ———. "L'importance de l'Évolution créatrice dans
la genèse de la pensée moderne." *Revue de théologie
et de philosophie* (1960): 2, 85-108.

4108. ———. "Le Père Teilhard de Chardin." *Revue de Paris*
(1956): 63, 107-114.

4109. ———. "Le phénomène humain." In *Les processus
d'hominisation. Colloques internationaux du C.N.R.S.
Paris 19-23 mai 1958*. Paris: C.N.R.S., 1958, pp. 193-
205.

4110. Vanderpaal, Mark. "Aarde en mens." *De linie* (1955):
341, 1, 3.

4111. Van Dusen, Henry Pitney. "Teilhard de Chardin: An Ap-
preciation." *Religion in Life* (1972): 41, 543-553.

4112. Van Esbroeck, Guy. "Mise en garde contre Teilhard."
*II Congressus Unionis Mundialis antiquorum Soci-
etatis Iesu alumnorum, Romae 1967*. Napoli: L'Arte
tipografica, 1970, pp. 180-183.

4113. Van Gerdinge, René. "De Pascal à Teilhard de Chardin."
Lumière (1962): 101, 1, 3; 102, 1, 3.

4114. Van Loo, Esther. "Le Père Teilhard de Chardin (1881-
1955)." *Naturalia* (1956): 65, 55-59.

4115. Van Overbeke, P.M. "Philosophie du droit." *Revue
       thomiste* (1969): 69, 435-462.

4116. Van Til, C. "Pierre Teilhard de Chardin." *Westmin-
       ster Theological Journal* (1966): 28, 109-144.

4117. Van Vroenhoven, F.J.W. "Teilhard de Chardin en de
       maatschappelijk-economische ontwikkeling." *Annalen
       van het Tijdgenootschap* (1965): 53, 1-11.

4118. Van Waesberghe, Henri P.J.M. *Kosmos, Verbond en Ver-
       wachting. Een kennismaking met het wereldbeeld van
       Teilhard de Chardin.* Groningen: Van Waesberghe, 1965.
       Also 's Hertogenbosch: Geert Groote Genootschap,
       1965.

4119. Vanzin, Vittorino C. "La salvezza dell'umanità in una
       nuova prospettiva eonnica." *Fede e civiltà* (1964):
       4, 49-59.

4120. Varga, Iván. "A dialógus Ichetöségei. A Vézelay-i
       Teilhard konferenciaról." *Világosság* (1964): 12,
       750-753.

4121. ————. "Een gemeenschappelijk front...." Item 1206,
       pp. 566-568.

4122. ————. "Konferencja teilhardowska w Vézelay."
       [The Teilhard Conference at Vézelay.] *Zeszyty Argu-
       mentów* (1965): 2, 74-82.

4123. ————. "Megújhodás vagy esmey válság? A 'Teilhard-
       jelenség' és ami mögötte van." [Renaissance or Ideo-
       logical Crisis? The "Teilhard Case" and What Follows
       It.] *Világosság* (1963): 4, 265-273.

4124. ————. "Teilhard de Chardin és a katolicizmus kiut-
       keresése." [Teilhard de Chardin and Catholicism's
       Search for a Way Out.] *Társadalmi Szemle* (1968):
       8/9, 71-78.

4125. ————. "Teilhard, Marks i problem postepu spolec
       znego." *Zeszyty Argumentów* (1965): 2, 83-87.
       "Teilhard, Marx et la question du progrès social."
       Europe (1965): 431/432, 152-158.

4126. ————. "Válság és utkeresés a mai katolicismusban."
       [Crisis and Solution for Today's Catholicism.]
       Elet és irodalon, December 12, 1963, p. 9.

4127. Vass, George. "Teilhard de Chardin and Inward Vision."
       Heythrop Journal (1961): 2, 237-249.

4128. ————. "Teilhard de Chardins christologische Spiri-
       tualität." *Dokumente* (1959): 15, 353-363.

4129. Vaufrey, R. "Le Père Pierre Teilhard de Chardin."
       L'anthropologie (1955): 3/4, 347-352.

4130. ————. "Le Père Teilhard de Chardin, savant."
       L'anthropologie (1965): 3/4, 303-304.

4131. Vaz, Henrique Claudio de Lima. *Universo científico
       e visão crista em Teilhard de Chardin.* Petrópolis:
       Vozes, 1967.

4132. Velasco Ibarra, J.M. *Servidumbre y liberación. Del
       imperialismo atómico a la claridad del espíritu.*
       Buenos Aires: Americalee, 1965. See pp. 129-141.

4133. Velez Correa, Jaime. "¿Un jesuita evoluctionista?"
       Revista javeriana (1959): 253, 144-160.

4134. ————. "El pensamiento filosófico en la teoria de
       Teilhard de Chardin." *Revista javeriana* (1963): 59,
       156-175.

4135. Veloso, Agostinho. "Teilhardismo científico falhado."
       Lumen (1965): 69, 543-549, 655-666.

4136. Venckus, J. "Pierre Teilhard de Chardin S.I. (20 metų
       nuo jo mirties)." [Pierre Teilhard de Chardin SJ
       (Twenty Years After His Death).] *Laiskai Lietuviams*
       (1975): 16, 291-294.

4137. Verbist, Henri. "Teilhard de Chardin." *Les grandes
       controverses de l'Église contemporaine (1789-1965).*
       Lausanne: Éditions Rencontre, 1971, pp. 143-164.
       "Teilhard de Chardin." *Las grandes controversias
       de la Iglesia contemporánea de 1789 a nuestros días.*
       Barcelona: Plaza y Janes, 1973, pp. 137-158.

4138. Verdong, Ernest. "Le Dieu d'Albert Camus. Pour une
       réponse. Divinité du Christ et problème du mal."
       Foi vivante (1961): 7, 81-85.

4139. ————. "Teilhard et les 'ombres de la foi.'" *Foi
       vivante* (1966): 7, 111-117.

4140. Vercheny, Adam. "Les progressismes." *Contacts*, October/November, 1958, pp. 59-87. See pp. 64-66.

4141. ———. "Théologie et évolution." *Foi vivante* (1967): 244-250.

4142. Vergot, Antoine. *Psychologie religieuse*. Bruxelles: Dessart, 1966. See pp. 74-80.

4143. Verhoeven, Enrico. *Progresso e redenzione cosmica. Contributo alla teologia della storia*. Roma: P.U.G., 1969.

4144. Vernet, Maurice. "Le 'Christ cosmique' de Teilhard de Chardin n'est pas le Christ de l'Evangile." *Le monde et la vie* (1965): 144, 53.

4145. ———. *La grande illusion de Teilhard de Chardin*. Paris: Gedalge-Wast, 1964.

4146. ———. *Vernet contre Teilhard de Chardin, une démystification*. Paris: Gedalge-Wast, 1965.

4147. "Il vero volto del gesuita-scienziato." *Ai nostri amici* (1967): 38, 268-275. Contains Items 2983, 4166.

4148. Verschuuren, G.M.N. "Teilhard verwoordt een mensbeeld." *Streven* (1966-67): 20, 173-179.

4149. Vetta, Luigi. "Ancora su Teilhard." *Civiltà delle macchine* (1963): 5, 12-14.

4150. Veuthey, Leone. "La spiritualità di Teilhard de Chardin." *Città di vita* (1967): 22, 365-377.

4151. Veylon, Roger. "L'homme de Pékin ou les tribulations du sinanthrope en Chine." *Presse médicale* (1971): 79, 2297-2300.

Viallet, François-Albert. See Boskowits, Karl Friedrich.

4152. Vidal, Guy. "L'expérience décisive de Teilhard." *Antonianum* (1968): 43, 53-98.

4153. Vidoni, Egidio. *L'individuo e il collettivo nella durata secondo P. Teilhard de Chardin*. Milano: L'ufficio Moderno, 1966.

4154. "Vie de Teilhard de Chardin." *Livres de France* (1966): 4, 25-26.

4155. Vigli, Marcello. "Fortuna e funzioni del teilhardismo in Italia." *Questitalia* (1968): 11, 352-370.

4156. Vignali, Adriano. "L'idea di progresso in Teilhard de Chardin." Typescript. Facoltà di lettere e filosofia dell'Università Cattolica del Sacro Cuore, Milano, 1965.

4157. Vigorelli, Giancarlo. *Il gesuita proibito. Vita e opere di Père Teilhard de Chardin.* Milano: Il Saggiatore, 1963.

4158. Villain, Jean. "Le 'Phénomène humain' du Père Teilhard de Chardin." *Études* (1955): 287, 1401-1403.

4159. Villiers, Jean de. "L'univers magnifié." *Revue Teilhard de Chardin* (1962): 10, 27-30.

4160. Vincent, André. "La synthèse cosmogénétique de Teilhard de Chardin et le droit." *Archives de philosophie du droit* (1965): 10, 33-63.

4161. Vita-Finzi, Claudio. "Glad Tidings." *New Statesman,* October 22, 1965, p. 618.

4162. Vivant, C. "Teilhard de Chardin et les combats de la forêt de Villers-Cotterêts (juillet 1968)." *Mémoires de la Fédération des Sociétés d'histoire et d'archéologie de l'Aisne* (1967): 13, 168-172.

4163. Voelkle, Robert E. "Imagination and Symbolism in Theology: The Apologetics of Teilhard de Chardin." *Focus* (1966): 1, 45-56.

4164. Vollert, Cyril. "The Interplay of Prayer and Action in Teilhard de Chardin." *Review for Religious* (1970): 29, 238-245.

4165. ————. "The Phenomenon of Man." *The Modern Schoolman* (1960): 38, 72-76.

4166. ————. "The Spirituality of Teilhard de Chardin." *Jesuit Bulletin* (1967): 1, 3-5.
"La sua spiritualità." *Ai nostri amici* (1967): 38, 273-275.

4167. ————. "Teilhard in the Light of Vatican II." Item
       2158, pp. 147-167.
       "Teilhard alla luce del Vaticano II." Item 2158
       trans., pp. 204-232.

4168. ————. "Towards Omega. Man in the Vision of Teil-
       hard de Chardin." *The Month* (1960): 23, 261-269.
       Also *Catholic Mind* (1960): 58, 402-409.
       Also *Theology Digest* (1960): 8, 133-136.
       Also *Bulletin du SIQS. Pax Romana* (1961): 26-27.

4169. Vránǎ, Karel. *Pierre Teilhard de Chardin. Vědec a
       apolštol naseho věku.* [Pierre Teilhard de Chardin:
       Seer and Apostle of Our Time.] Rim: Studium L.P.,
       1968.

4170. ————. "Pierre Teilhard de Chardin: Vědec a apoštol
       naseho věku." *Novy zivot* (1966): 18, 146-150.

4171. ————. "Scienza, filosofia, poesia in Teilhard de
       Chardin." *Filosofia e vita* (1963): 4, 343-362.

4172. Vygen, Jacques. "De beteknis van de menselijke in-
       spanning in het oeuvre van P. Teilhard de Chardin."
       Mimeographed. Katholieke Universiteit te Leuven,
       1973.

4172a. Waesberghe, Henri van. "L'Église est-elle toujours
       porteuse des espérances des hommes dans les activités
       scientifiques et culturelles?" *XII Congresso Europeo
       Ex-alunni della Compagnia di Gesù.* Rome: Federazione
       Italiana, 1977, pp. 44-66.

4173. Wagar, W.W. *The City of Man.* London: Penguin, 1968.

4174. Wagener, James W. "From Instinct to Thought: Chardin's
       Evolutionary Theory of Knowledge." *Journal of Thought*
       (1970): 5, 18-29.

4175. Wagner, Geoffrey. "Teilhard in Fiction." Item 501,
       pp. 96-102.
       Also Item 497, pp. 96-101.

4176. Wagner, J.F. "Evolution. Teilhard and the Monitum."
       Catholic Educational Review, September, 1962, p. 4.

4177. Wahl, François. "Panorama de la philosophie française
       de l'existentialisme à Teilhard de Chardin." *Ten-
       dances* (1960): 74-104.

4178. Wahlert, Gerd von. *Teilhard de Chardin und die moderne Theorie der Evolution der Organismen.* Stuttgart: G. Fischer, 1966.

4179. Walcot, Stephen. "The Witness of Teilhard." *Michael de la Bedoyere's Search* (1962): 1, 227-229.

4180. Wall, Bernard. "Teilhard and Teilhardism: A Plea for Moderation." *Tablet*, January 14, 1967, pp. 34-35.

4181. ————. "Teilhard de Chardin." *Tablet*, March 13, 1965, pp. 300-301.

4182. Wallace, A.A. "The Cosmogony of Teilhard de Chardin." *The New Scholasticism* (1962): 36, 353-367.

4183. Walschap, Gerald. "Teilhard de Chardin." *Nieuw Vlaams Tijdschrift* (1963): 16, 181-196.

4184. Walsh, James V. "Toward a Post-Teilhardian Multiverse." *Cross Currents* (1966): 3, 378-379.

4185. Walsh, John V. "History in the 'Phenomenon of Man.'" Item 1544, pp. 131-145.

4186. Walsh, Liam. "The Relevance of Teilhard de Chardin for Modern Man." *Dominicana* (1966): 51, 338-349.

4187. Walter, Jean-Jacques. "Complexité-conscience aujourd-'hui." *Études teilhardiennes* (1969): 2, 136-148.

4188. Wang, Joseph. "Pierre Teilhard de Chardin: A Modern Prophet." *Universitas* (1968): 1, 1-12.

4189. Wang Mou Tao, Angèle. "Témoignage." *Revue Teilhard de Chardin* (1961): 6, 35.

4190. Ward, M. Eucharista. "Suffering as Passivity: Pierre Teilhard de Chardin as a Gloss on Gerard Manley Hopkins." *Victorian Poetry* (1972): 10, 321-331.

4191. Ward, Maisie. "Dag Hammarskjöld and Teilhard de Chardin." *Dublin Review* (1968): 203-215. Also *Catholic World*, January, 1970, pp. 159-164.

4192. Warner, Peter O. "Man's Future: Facts, Physics and Teilhard de Chardin." *Proceedings of the American Catholic Philosophical Association* (1973): 47, 160-169.

4193. "Warning Against the Dangers of Father Teilhard de Char-
       din." *Tablet*, July 7, 1962, p. 652.

4194. Watt, W. Montgomery. "Christianity and Islam in Teil-
       hardian Perspective." *The Teilhard Review* (1972):
       3, 72-78.

4195. Wciórka, Ludwik. "Religia i nauka w ujęciu Teilharda
       de Chardin." [Religion and Science According to
       Teilhard de Chardin.] *Collectanea theologica* (1969):
       4, 49-69.

4196. ————. "Stworzenie a ewolucja w ujęciu Teilharda de
       Chardin." [Creation and Evolution According to Teil-
       hard de Chardin.] *Katechetyka* (1970): 14, 49-57.

4197. ————. *Szkice o Teilhardzie.* [Essays on Teilhard.]
       Poznan: Księgarnia św. Wojciecha, 1973.

4198. Weber, Jean-Paul. "Une grande figure du XXe siècle.
       Qui était Teilhard de Chardin? Propos recueillis au
       congrès de Vézelay du 2 au 9 septembre 1960." *Le
       Figaro littéraire*, September 17, 1960, pp. 1, 10.

4199. Weier, R. "Erbsünde und Sünde der Welt. Probleme der
       Erbsündenlehre Piet Schoonenbergs und Teilhards de
       Chardin." *Trierer theologische Zeitschrift* (1973):
       82, 154-171.

4200. Weierich, André Jean. "The Relationship of Teilhard de
       Chardin's Law of Complexity-Consciousness to the Mech-
       anism-Vitalism Debate in Biology." Doctoral disserta-
       tion, Oregon State University, 1971.

4201. Weigel, Gustave. "The Phenomenon of Teilhard de Char-
       din." *Natural Law Forum* (1961): 6, 134-142.
       Also Item 1544, pp. 156-166.

4202. Weij, A. van der. *Grote filosofen over de mens: Van
       Plato tot Teilhard.* Utrecht: Bijleveld, 1971.

4203. Weil, Apolonio. "Père Teilhard de Chardin." *Vozes*
       (1964): 58, 514-524.

4204. Wenger, Antoine. "Le 'Phénomène humain' du P. Teilhard
       publié en traduction russe à Moscou." *La Croix*, No-
       vember 27-28, 1966.

4205. Wenish, P. "Teilhard de Chardin and the Devotion to the Sacred Heart." *Clergy Monthly* (1972): 36, 189-202.
Also *Apostleship of Prayer* (1972): 275-293.
"Teilhard de Chardin et devotio Cordis Iesu."
Nuntius Apostolatus Orationis (1972): 11, 1-11.
"Teilhard de Chardin y la devoción al Corazón de Jesus." *Cuaderno ACJ* (1973): 38, 1-4; 39, 1-9.
"Teilhard de Chardin to Jesusu no milokoro." *Mikokoro no shito* (1974): 258-266, 322-330.

4206. Weron, Eugeniusz. "Teilhardyzm i teologia laikatu."
[Teilhard and the Theology of the Laity.] *Collectanea theologica* (1973): 2, 155-158.

4207. Wespin, Dominique de [see also Magliore, Georges].
"Actualité de la pensée du Père Teilhard." *Revue Teilhard de Chardin* (1962): 10, 2.

4208. ———. "Aimons-nous les uns les autres." *Revue Teilhard de Chardin* (1962): 13, 2. Contains Item 4584.

4209. ———. "L'avenir de l'homme, témoignage capital du Père Teilhard de Chardin." *Synthèses* (1959): 14, 488-491.

4210. ———. "Comment être heureux selon Teilhard." *Synthèses* (1960): 175, 293-297.
"Cómo ser feliz según Teilhard de Chardin." *Indice* (1963): 172, 1.

4211. ———. "Dixième anniversaire de la mort du Père Teilhard de Chardin." *Perspectives* (1965): 23, 7-21.

4212. ———. "En el corazón del problema." *Indice* (1964): 186, 3-5.

4213. ———. "Une grande étape dans la carrière du Père Teilhard: La découverte du sinanthrope." Item 3917, pp. 27-32.

4214. ———. "Mort et immortalité dans l'optique de Pierre Teilhard de Chardin." *Revue Teilhard de Chardin* (1970): 43, 2-8.

4215. ———. "Notes marginales." *Revue Teilhard de Chardin* (1962): 13, 39.

4216. ————. "Notes pékinoises." *Revue Teilhard de Chardin* (1961): 8/9, 28-29.

4217. ————. "Pensées teilhardiennes." *Revue Teilhard de Chardin* (1977): 69, 1-3; 70, 21-22.

4218. ————. "Le Père Teilhard à Péking." *Revue Teilhard de Chardin* (1966): 29, 19-22; (1967): 32, 4-9; (1968): 35, 12-20; (1969): 38, 7-15; (1971): 46, 13-18; 47/48, 44-49; (1972): 51, 11-16; 52/53, 49-57; (1973): 54/55, 52-59; 56, 33-43; 57, 34-47; (1974): 60, 7-18; (1975): 61/62, 5-16; (1976): 65, 18-28; 66, 2-11; 67/68, 33-41; (1977): 69, 28-32; 70, 10-15; 71/72, 37-44; (1978): 73, 16-20; 74, 27-32; 75/76, 46-51.

4219. ————. "Le Père Teilhard m'a dit...." *Balisage* (1961): 16/17, 36. Contains Item 4564.

4220. ————. "Pierre Teilhard de Chardin et le sinanthrope." *Revue Teilhard de Chardin* (1960): 3/4, 11-13.

4221. ————. "Pierre Teilhard de Chardin l'homme de la convergence." Item 3917, pp. 13-25.

4222. ————. "Sens de l'histoire et amorisation." *Revue Teilhard de Chardin* (1963): 3, 1-2.

4223. ————. "Les sociétés futures." *Revue Teilhard de Chardin* (1964): 14, 16-20.

4224. ————. "Teilhard et l'avenir de l'homme." *La vie collective* (1963): 330.

4225. ————. "Teilhard et son temps." *Revue Teilhard de Chardin* (1964): 20/21, 9-12.

4226. ————. "L'ultime mutation." *Revue Teilhard de Chardin* (1971): 49, 25-50.

4227. ————. "Unité de l'espèce humaine. 5e Symposium international Pierre Teilhard de Chardin." *Revue Teilhard de Chardin* (1965): 24/25, 3-9.

4228. ————. "L'unité de la vie." *Univers* (1966): 3, 6-10.

4229. ————. "Vu par Pierre Teilhard de Chardin l'avenir de l'homme paraît grandiose." *Le Phare dimanche*, July 26, 1957, p. 4.

4230. ———. "Wenn der Mensch denkt, verändert sich die Welt."
Frankfurter Hefte (1961): 16, 107-114.

4231. "What Is Not Condemned." *Tablet*, September 8, 1962.

4232. White, John. *Frontiers of Consciousness: The Meeting
Ground Between Inner and Outer Reality*. New York:
Julian Press, 1974.

4233. Whitla, William. "Sin and Redemption in Whitehead and
Teilhard de Chardin." *Anglican Theological Review*
(1965): 1, 81-93.

4234. Wijngaards, J.N.M. "Man's Nature and Destiny: Readings
in the Theology of Teilhard de Chardin." *Religion
and Society* (1973): 20, 64-72.

4235. Wilber, Charles. "The World of Teilhard." *Cross Currents* (1962): 1, 115-118.

4236. "Wildiers e Teilhard de Chardin." *Questitalia* (1963):
65/66, 90-92.

4237. Wildiers, Nico. "Natuurwetenschappen, techniek en
Teilhard." *Kultuurleven* (1965): 38, 359-367.

4238. Wildiers, Norbert M. "Die Aktualität von Pierre Teilhard de Chardin." *Geist und Zeit* (1957): 5, 174-178.
Also *Wetenschappelijke Tijdingen* (1957): 17, 197-
202.

4239. ———. "Avant-propos." Item 4806, pp. 1-24.

4240. ———. "Christendom en natuurwetenschappen." *Dietsche
Warande en Belfort* (1953): 1-15.

4241. ———. "L'experience fondamentale de Teilhard de Chardin." *La table ronde* (1955): 90, 41-54.
"De fundamentale ervaring van Pierre Teilhard de
Chardin (1881-1955)." *Dietsche Warande en Belfort*
(1956): 3-19.

4242. ———. "De figuur van Teilhard de Chardin. Heraut
van het levensvertrouwen." *De Standard der letteren*,
January 29, 1959.

4243. ———. "De gedachtenwereld van Teilhard de Chardin.
Is een christologische cosmologie mogelijk?" *Adelbert* (1963): 139-144.

4244. ———. "De gestalte van nieuwe kristen volgens Teilhard de Chardin." *Collectanea mechliniensia* (1966):
51, 149-165.
"The New Christian of Teilhard de Chardin." *Thought*
(1968): 43, 523-538.

4245. ———. "God en het Universum. De twee polen van Teilhards dialektik." *Revue Teilhard de Chardin* (1960):
1/2, 13-19.

4246. ———. "Grandeur de la science et de la technique selon Teilhard de Chardin." *Europe* (1965): 431/432,
39-40.

4247. ———. "Introduzione al Milieu divin di P. Teilhard de
Chardin." Item 2744, pp. 127-144.
"Introduction au Milieu divin." Item 2744 trans.,
pp. 119-133.

4248. ———. "Julian Huxley over Teilhard de Chardin. Plech-
tige herdenking te Parijs." *De Standaard*, April 29,
1959, p. 3.

4249. ———. *Ku chrześcijańskiemu neohumanizmowi.* [Toward
a Christian Neo-Humanism.] Warszawa: Pax, 1964.

4250. ———. "Marxisten en kristen. Do noodzakelijke dia-
loog." *De Standaard*, October 1-2, 1960.

4251. ———. *Des Menschen Zukunft und Aufgabe im Weltbild
Teilhard de Chardins.* Kevelaer: Butzon und Bercker,
1966.

4252. ———. "Nieuw licht op Teilhard de Chardin." *De
Standaard* (1962): 160/161, 9.

4253. ———. "P. Teilhard de Chardin 1881-1955." *Streven*
(1955): 9, 266-268.

4254. ———. "De religieuze visie van Teilhard de Chardin.
Texte d'une émission radiophonique du 20 juin 1961."
Typescript. Paris: Fondation Teilhard de Chardin,
1961.

4255. ———. "La religion universelle." Item 741, pp. 113-
120.

4256. ————. *Teilhàrd de Chardin.* Paris: Éditions Univer-
sitaires, 1960.
Einführung auf Teilhard de Chardin. Freiburg-im-
Breisgau: Herder, 1962.
Also 7th ed., 1966.
Introduzione a Teilhard de Chardin. Milano: Bom-
piani, 1962.
Also 4th ed., 1966.
Introducción a Teilhard de Chardin. Barcelona:
Fontanella, 1963.
Teilhard de Chardin. Een inleiding in zijn denken.
Antwerpen/Amsterdam: Standaard-Boekhandel, 1964.
An Introduction to Teilhard de Chardin. London:
Collins, 1968.
Also New York: Harper & Row, 1968.
Teilhard de Chardin, úvod do diela. Cambridge,
Ontario: Dobra kniha, 1974.

4257. ————. "Teilhard de Chardin en het christlijk humanisme." *Kultuurleven* (1960): 27, 410-417.

4258. ————. "Teilhard de Chardin et la théologie catholique." Item 3851, pp. 151-174.

4259. ————. "Teilhard de Chardin no kirisuto kyôkan."
[The Christian Thought of Teilhard de Chardin.]
Logos (1961): 7, 166-185.

4260. ————. "Teilhard de Chardin, penseur religieux."
Livres de France (1966): 4, 9-11.

4261. ————. "Úvod do štúdie Teilharda de Chardin." [Intro-
duction to the Study of Teilhard de Chardin.] *Echo*
(1973): 5, 3-13.

4262. ————. "Vers un néo-humanisme chrétien." *Le Phare
dimanche,* April 2, 1961, pp. 5-6.

4263. ————. "W strone chrześcijańskiego neohumanizmu."
[Towards Christian Neo-Humanism.] *Życie i myśl* (1963):
9/10, 158-165.

4264. ————. "Wereldbeeld en teologie in het werk van Teilhard de Chardin." *Wereldbeeld en teologie. Van de
middeleeuwen to vandaag.* Antwerpen/Amsterdam: Standaard-Boekhandel, 1973, pp. 333-369.

4265. ————. *Het wereldbeeld van Pierre Teilhard de Chardin.*
       Antwerpen/Amsterdam: Standaard-Boekhandel, 1960.

4266. William, Franz Michael. "Teilhard de Chardin und Kar-
       dinal Newman." *Orientierung* (1970): 34, 4-6, 25-28,
       36-38.

4267. Williams, Raphael. "Aristotle and Teilhard de Chardin."
       Tablet (1960): 214, 599-600.

4268. Wills, Garry. "Omega, the New Frontier." *Bare Ruined
       Choirs: Doubt, Prophecy, and Radical Religion.* Gar-
       den City, N.Y.: Doubleday, 1972, pp. 97-117.

4269. ————. "Truth on the Block." *National Review,* Decem-
       ber 3, 1960, pp. 351-352.

4270. ————. "Was Teilhard de Chardin a Racist?" *National
       Catholic Reporter* (1964): 3, 8.

4271. Wilson, Colin. *Beyond the Outsider.* London: Arthur
       Baker, 1965.

4272. Winkler, F.E. "Visionary." *Saturday Review,* December
       3, 1960, pp. 32-33.

4273. Winters, Francis Xavier. "The Evolutionary Ethics of
       Teilhard." *The Teilhard Review* (1976): 11, 53-58.

4274. ————. "Pierre Teilhard de Chardin's 'Morality of
       Movement.'" Doctoral dissertation, Fordham Univer-
       sity, 1973.

4275. "Wissenschaftlicher über Teilhard--der Paläontologe J.
       Piveteau, Paris; der Biologe T. Dobzhanski, New York;
       der Verhaltensforscher W.H. Thorpe, Cambridge." *Per-
       spektiven der Zukunft* (1970): 3, 2-6.

4276. Wojiechowski, Tadeusz. "Teilhardowska koncepcja tran-
       scendencji duszy ludzkiej i jej wplyw na chrześcijań-
       ską antropologie filozoficzna." [Transcendence of
       the Human Soul in the Conception of Teilhard.] *Slas-
       kie Studia Historyczno-Teologiczne* (1974): 7, 215-
       244.

4277. ————. "Transcendencja duszy ludzkiej w ujęciu Piotra
       Teilharda de Chardin." [Transcendence of the Human
       Soul in Teilhard de Chardin's Thought.] *Studia philo-
       sophiae christianae* (1969): 1, 259-262.

4278. Wouters, Jean de. "Parallèles et prolongements." *Synthèses* (1962): 189, 245-259.

4279. Wrede, Michael. *Die Einheit von Materie und Geist bei Teilhard de Chardin.* Limburg: Lahn, 1964.

4280. ———. "Geist und Materie bei Teilhard de Chardin." *Münchener theologische Zeitschrift* (1966): 17, 267-276.

4281. ———. "Der Mensch als Weg zu Gott. Zu Alexander Gosztonyi's Buch über die Anthropologie Teilhard de Chardins." *Perspektiven der Zukunft* (1969): 6, 3-5. See Item 1736.

4282. Wucherer-Huldenfeld, Augustinus Karl. "Zur Frage nach der Methode bei Teilhard de Chardin." *Entschluss* (1975): 333-342.

4283. Yamasaki, Yoîchirô. *Teiyâru do Sharudan.* Tokyo: Kodansha, 1971.

4284. Yasugi, Ryûichi. "'Miru koto.'" ["Comment je vois."] (1964): 6, 24-27.

4285. ———. "Ningen no idaisa to 'Miru koto.' Watashi no Teilhard nôto." [The Grandeur of Man and "Comment je vois." Teilhard's Lecture Notes.] *Shisô* (1965): 8, 110-118.

4286. ———. "Teilhard de Chardin to shinka." [Teilhard de Chardin and Evolution.] *Risô* (1969): 7, 18-24.

4287. Ydewalle, Pierre d'. "Ouverture du Symposium." *Revue Teilhard de Chardin* (1961): 8/9, 3.

4288. Yeiser, Frederick. "Pilgrim of the Future." *Cincinnati Enquirer*, July 7, 1962, p. 10.

4289. Young, Henry James. "Two Models of the Human Future: A Study in the Process Theism of Teilhard and Whitehead." Doctoral dissertation, The Hartford Seminary Foundation, 1974.

4290. Youngblut, John. "Evolution and Depth Psychology: Some Theological Implications." *The Teilhard Review* (1975): 2, 40-46.

4291. "Z dyskusji nad P. Teilhard de Chardin." [On the Dis-
       cussion About Teilhard de Chardin.] *Collectanea the-
       ologica* (1973): 2, 155-167. Contains Items 830, 3677,
       4211.

4292. Zaba, Zbigniew. "Ewolucjonistyczny personalizm Teil-
       harda de Chardin." [The Evolutionary Personalism of
       Teilhard de Chardin.] *Życie i myśl* (1965): 5, 15-29.
       Also Item 3888, pp. 152-169.

4293. ————. "Filosoficzne 'credo' O. Teilharda de Chardin."
       [The Philosophical Credo of Teilhard de Chardin.]
       Życie i myśl (1966): 9, 106-115.
       Also Item 3888, pp. 136-151.

4294. ————. "Hegel, Kierkegaard, Teilhard de Chardin, Trzy
       interpretacje opozycji: Jednostka a zbiorowość."
       [Hegel, Kierkegaard, Teilhard de Chardin. Three In-
       terpretations of Opposition: The Individual and the
       Collective.] Item 3888, pp. 192-213.

4295. Zablocki, Janusz. "Personalizm Teilhards i Mouniera."
       [The Personalism of Teilhard and Mounier.] *Wieź*
       (1963): 6, 87-91.

4296. Zabolotskij, N.A. "Teilhard de Chardin i cerkovnoučitel-
       'naja tradicija." [Teilhard de Chardin and the Church's
       Traditional Teaching.] *Messager de l'Exarchat du Patri-
       arche russe en Europe occidentale* (1970): 18, 266-287.

4297. Zaehner, Robert Charles. *Evolution in Religion: A Study
       in Sri Aurobindo and Pierre Teilhard de Chardin.* Ox-
       ford: Clarendon Press, 1971.

4298. ————. *Matter and Spirit: Their Convergence in Eastern
       Religions, Marx and Teilhard de Chardin.* New York:
       Harper & Row, 1963.
       The Convergent Spirit. London: Routledge and Kegan
       Paul, 1964.

4299. ————. "Teilhard and Eastern Religions." *The Teil-
       hard Review* (1967-68): 2, 41-53.

4300. Zanstra, Herman. "Is Religion Refuted by Physics or
       Astronomy?" *Vistas in Astronomy* (1968): 10, 1-21.
       See pp. 11-15.

4301. Zavadini, Giuliana. "Edizioni italiani su Teilhard de Chardin." *Civiltà delle macchine*, January-February, 1963, pp. 7-8.

4302. Zavala, Iris M. "La materia en Marx y en Teilhard de Chardin." *La palabra y el hombre* (1965): 33, 63-80.

4303. Zayed, Georges. "Pierre Teilhard de Chardin." *Revue du Caire* (1960): 234, 170-174.

4304. ————. "Teilhard de Chardin: Trois ans en Égypte." *L'Orient littéraire* (1962): 98, 3.

4305. Zbinden, Louis Albert. "Faut-il brûler le Père Teilhard de Chardin?" *Gazette de Lausanne*, March, 1959.

4305a. Zech, Albert. "Teilhard toujours parmi nous." *Revue Teilhard de Chardin* (1978): 74, 20-23.

4306. Zeegers, Victor. "Teilhard de Chardin et le 'Phénomène humain.'" *Revue générale belge* (1956): 92, 736-756.

Želivan, Pavel. See Vrána, Karel.

4307. Žigo, Milan. "Zoznamovanie sa s otcom Teilhardom." [Encounter with Teilhard.] *Slovenské Pohl'ady* (1967): 12, 136-138.

4308. Zilles, U. "Teilhard de Chardin: Criação e evolução." *Vozes* (1966): 60, 803-817.

4309. Zimmerman, Werner. "Pierre Teilhard de Chardin. Zu freien Ufern." *Monatschrift für Körper, Seele und Geist* (1963): 13, 568-571.

4310. Zimmermann, Theodorich. "Teilhard de Chardin--ein österlicher Mensch." *Seckauer Hefte* (1964): 27, 5-13.

4311. Zoghby, M. "The Cosmic Christ in Hopkins, Teilhard and Scotus." *Renascence* (1971-72): 24, 33-46.

4312. Zolla, Elemira. "A propósito de una más reciente publicación sobre Teilhard de Chardin." *La Gaceta*, March 30, 1967.

4313. ————. "Teilhard de Chardin o del futurismo cosmico."
       La Gaceta, March 12, 1967.

4314. Zolo, Danilo. "Dopo il 'Monitum' del Sant'Uffizio.
       (Lo status quaestionis su P. Teilhard de Chardin.)"
       Testimonianze (1963): 5, 193-204.

4315. ————. "Una messa a punto di P. de Lubac sull'inter-
       pretazione di Teilhard de Chardin." *Testimonianze*
       (1963): 6, 193-204.

4316. *Die Zukunft des Menschen in der Welt. Eine Tagung über
       die Zukunftserwartung bei Pierre Teilhard de Chardin.*
       Bad Boll: Evangelische Akademie, 1964. Contains Items
       965, 993, 1852.

4317. Zúñiga Valencia, Graciela. "Teilhard de Chardin y el
       amor (Incidentiv en lo educativo)." Typescript.
       Universidad Pontificia de Salamanca, 1973.

Works By Teilhard de Chardin

4318. "A propos du spiritisme: observations sur la synthèse expérimentale de l'esprit." [1920?] Typescript. 4 pp., double-spaced.

4319. *Accomplir l'homme. Lettres inédites (1926-1952).* Paris: B. Grasset, 1968.
Letters to Two Friends, 1926-1952. New York: New American Library, 1968.
Also London: Rapp & Whiting, 1970.
Also London: Collins, 1972.
Briefe an eine Marxistin (1926-1952). Briefe an eine Nichtchristin (1926-1952). 2 vols.; Olten: Walter-Verlag, 1971.
Realizzare l'uomo. Lettere inedite (1926-1952). Milan: Saggiatore, 1974.

4320. "Action et activation." [August 9, 1945.] Item 4805, pp. 219-234.

4321. *L'activation de l'énergie.* Paris: Seuil, 1963. Volume 7 of Item 4670. Contains Items 4322, 4335, 4344, 4350, 4369, 4400, 4411, 4441, 4442, 4453, 4458, 4500, 4510, 4611, 4699, 4707, 4715, 4718, 4727, 4748, 4751, 4754, 4808, 4810, 4835, 4862, 4869, 4878.
La activatión de la energia. Madrid: Taurus, 1965.
Also 2d ed., 1967.
Die lebendige Macht der Evolution: L'activation de l'énergie. Olten: Walter-Verlag, 1967.
Activation of Energy. London: Collins, 1970.
Also New York: Harcourt Brace Jovanovich, 1970.

4322. "L'activation de l'énergie humaine." [December 6, 1953.] Item 4321, pp. 407-416.

4323. "Afrique du sud, 1953." Item 4669, vol. 10, pp. 4486-4557.

4324. "L'Afrique et les origines humaines." *Revue des questions scientifiques* (1954): 126, 5-17.
Also Item 4337, pp. 277-291.

4325. "Allocution à l'ouverture de la réunion extraordinaire
      de 1925, en Alsace." *Compte-rendu Sommaire et Bul-
      letin de la Société géologique de France*, September
      11, 1925, p. 182.

4326. "Allocution de M.P. Teilhard de Chardin, conseiller du
      Service Géologique de Chine." *L'anthropologie* (1937):
      67, 599-60.
      Also Item 4669, vol. 6, pp. 2792-2793.

4327. "Allocution en souvenir de Davidson Black," *Bulletin
      of the Geological Society of China* (1934): 13, 322.

4328. "Allocution pour le mariage de Claude-Marie Haardt et de
      Mlle. Christine Dresch en l'église Notre Dame d'Au-
      euil." [December 21, 1948.] Item 4385, pp. 187-190.

4329. "Allocution pour son cinquantenaire de vie religieuse."
      March 19, 1949?

4330. "Allocution présidentielle." *Compte-rendu Sommaire et
      Bulletin de la Société géologique de France*, September
      11, 1925, p. 182.
      Also Item 4669, vol. 2, pp. 601-602.

4331. "Allocution présidentielle." *Compte-rendu Sommaire et
      Bulletin de la Société géologique de France*, January
      18, 1926, pp. 5-7.
      Also Item 4669, vol. 2, pp. 785-788.

4332. "Allocution prononcée devant les membres de la Croi-
      sière Jaune à la mission de Lian Tcheou (1er janv.
      1932)." *Sur la route de la soie*, by L. Audouin-
      Dubreuil. Paris: Plon, 1935, p. 225.

4333. "Allocution prononcée par le R.P. Teilhard de Chardin
      à l'occasion de la bénédiction nuptiale de Monsieur
      et Madame de la Goublaye de Menorval en l'église de
      Saint-Louis des Invalides le 15 juin 1935." Paris:
      Privately printed, 1935.
      Also Item 4385, pp. 165-170.

4334. "L'âme du monde." [Epiphany, 1918.] Item 4436, pp.
      177-190.

4335. "L'analyse de la vie." [June 10, 1945.] Item 4321,
      pp. 135-146.

4336. "The Antiquity and World Expansion of Human Culture."
Man's Role in Changing the Face of the Earth, ed. by
William L. Thomas, Jr. Chicago: University of Chicago
Press, 1956, pp. 103-112.
Also Item 4669, vol. 10, pp. 4580-4589.

4337. *L'apparition de l'homme.* Paris: Seuil, 1956. Volume
2 of Item 4670. Contains Items 4324, 4345, 4423, 4470,
4483, 4486, 4527, 4645, 4661, 4686, 4721, 4746, 4763,
4780, 4816, 4823, 3838.
La aparición del hombre. 4th ed.; Madrid: Taurus,
1964.
Das Auftreten des Menschen. Olten: Walter-Verlag,
1965.
The Appearance of Man. London: Collins, 1965.
Also New York: Harper & Row, 1965.

4338. "Appendice: (I) Observations géologiques en Chine."
(II) La préhistoire de l'Asie centrale." *La Croisière
Jaune Troisième Mission Haardt-Audouin-Dubreuil*, by
Georges Le Fèvre. Paris: Plon, 1933, pp. 357-366.
Also new ed., 1952.
Also Item 4669, vol. 5, pp. 2083-2092.

4339. "L'apport spirituel de l'Extrême-Orient." Typescript.
1 p., double-spaced. Notes taken from Fr. R. Girault
of a conference at the Institut catholique de Paris,
1947.

4340. "L'apport spirituel de l'Extrême-Orient. Quelques réflexions personnelles." *Revue de la pensée juive*
(1950): 5, 105-113.
Also *Monumenta nipponica* (1956): 12, 2-11.
Also Item 4431, pp. 147-160.

4341. "L'art dans la ligne de l'énergie humaine." Item 3920,
pp. 101-103.

4342. "L'Asie centrale, vue par le Dr. Erik Norin." *Revue
scientifique* (1947): 85, 981-982.
Also Item 4669, vol. 9, pp. 4237-4240.

4343. "L'atomisme de l'esprit. Un essai pour comprendre la
structure de l'étoffe de l'univers." [September 13,
1941.] Item 4321, pp. 27-67.

4344. "Australopithèques, Pithécanthropes et structure phylétique des Hominiens." *Compte-rendu de l'Académie*

des sciences (1952): 234, 377-379.
Also Item 4337, pp. 245-248.

4345. *Auswahl aus dem Werk.* Olten: Walter-Verlag, 1964.
        Also Frankfurt-am-Main: S. Fischer, 1967.

4346. *L'avenir de l'homme.* Paris: Seuil, 1959. Volume 5 of
        Item 4670. Contains Items 4386, 4390, 4430, 4452,
        4456, 4472, 4473, 4474, 4501, 4503, 4509, 4521, 4532,
        4600, 4636, 4710, 4737, 4738, 4743, 4755, 4756, 4829,
        4833, 4851, 4871.
        Die Zukunft des Menschen. Olten: Walter-Verlag,
        1963.
        The Future of Man. London: Collins, 1964.
        Also New York: Harper & Row, 1964.
        Also New York: Harper Torchbooks, 1969.
        El porvenir del hombre. 3d ed.; Madrid: Taurus,
        1965.

4347. "L'avenir de l'homme vu par un paléontologiste." *Cité
        nouvelle*, June 10, 1941, pp. 1107-1119.
        Also Item 4755, pp. 3-20.

4348. "L'avenir zoologique probable du groupe humain." Type-
        script. 5 pp., single-spaced. Notes taken by Edouard
        Boné, S.J., of a conference given October 24, 1950 at
        the C.I.E.F.R., Brussels.

4349. "Avertissement de *Geobiologia.*" *Geobiologia* (1943): 1,
        v.
            Also Item 4669, vol. 10, pp. 3747-3752.

4350. "Barrière de la mort et co-réflexion, ou de l'éveil
        imminent de la conscience humaine au sens de son
        irréversion." [January 1 & 5, 1955.] Item 4321, pp.
        417-429.

4351. "The Base of the Palaeozoic in Shansi: Metamorphism
        and Cycles." *Bulletin of the Geological Society of
        China* (1933): 13, 149-153.
        Also Item 4669, vol. 4, pp. 1848-1852.

4352. "Belle défense d'un Acridien." *Bulletin de la Société
        entomologique d'Égypte*, April-June, 1910, pp. 56-57.
        Also Item 4669, vol. 1, pp. 51-52.

4353. "La biologie, poussée à fond, peut-elle nous conduire
        à émerger dans le Transcendant?" [May 24, 1951.]
        Item 4805, pp. 277-280.

4354. "Les Bovinés fossiles en Chine du nord." *Compte-rendu Sommaire de la Société de biogéographie* (1933): 79, 1-2.
Also Item 4669, vol. 4, pp. 1858-1860.

4355. "Building the Earth." *Catholic Business Education Review*, Spring, 1966. Excerpt from Item 4408.

4356. "Building the Earth." *Jubilee*, December, 1965, pp. 8-11. Excerpt from Item 4408.

4357. *Building the Earth and the Psychological Conditions of Human Unification.* New York: Avon, 1969. Contains Items 4400, 4408.

4358. "Bulletin scientifique. La face de la terre." *Études* (1921): 169, 585-602.
Also Item 4873, pp. 43-74.

4359. "*Canis sinensis* et *Canis procyonides.*" *Compte-rendu Sommaire de la Société de biogéographie* (1928): 35, 10.

4360. "Les Carnassiers des phosphorites du Quercy." *Annales de paléontologie* (1914-1915): 9, 103-192.
Also Item 4669, vol. 1, pp. 89-198.

4361. "Carnet de retraites." Manuscript. Covers 1939, 1940, 1942 and 1943.

4362. "Carnet de retraites." Manuscript. Covers 1944, 1945, 1946, 1948, 1949, 1950, 1953 and 1954.

4363. "La carrière scientifique du P. Teilhard de Chardin." *Études* (1950): 266, 126-128.
Also Item 741, pp. 159-167.
Also Item 4385, pp. 191-196.
Also Item 4669, vol. 10, pp. 4273-4275.

4364. "Le cas de l'Homme de Piltdown." *Revue des questions scientifiques* (1920): 77, 149-155.
Also Item 4669, vol. 1, pp. 208-214.

4365. "Ce que le monde attend en ce moment de l'Église de Dieu: une généralisation et un approfondissement du sens de la croix." [September 14, 1952.] Item 4392, pp. 251-262.

4366.   "Ce que la science nous apprend de l'évolution: con-
        séquences pour notre apostolat." Typescript. 5 pp.,
        single-spaced. Notes taken by A. Millard of a con-
        ference at the Session études des Aumôniers fédéraux
        de l'Action catholique ouvrière, Versailles, Septem-
        ber 21, 1948.
            Also Typescript. 8 pp., single-spaced. Notes taken
        by Fr. Pihan.

4367.   "Cenozoic Vertebrate Fossils of E. Kansu and Inner Mon-
        golia." *Bulletin of the Geological Society of China*
        (1923): 2, 1-3.
            Also Item 4669, vol. 1, pp. 425-427.

4368.   "Le Cénozoïque de Chine centrale et méridionale."
        *Compte-rendu Sommaire et Bulletin de la Société géo-
        logique de France*, June 3, 1935, pp. 150-152.
            Also Item 4669, vol. 5, pp. 2148-2150.

4369.   "La centrologie. Essai d'une dialectique de l'union."
        [December 13, 1944.] Item 4321, pp. 103-134.

4370.   "China Gave a Lead to 'Missing Link.'" *New York Times*,
        March 19, 1937.

4371.   "Les Chloritoïdes des Western Hills près Pékin." *Annales
        Hébert et Haug* (1949): 7, 381-387.
            Item 4669, vol. 10, pp. 4258-4264.

4371a. "Choses mongoles." [June-October, 1923.] Item 1800,
        pp. 167-177.
            Also Item 4573, pp. 52-62.

4372.   "Le Christ dans la matière. Trois histoires comme Ben-
        son." [October 14, 1916.] In Item 4384.
            Also Item 4385 trans., pp. 61-66.
            Also in Item 501.
            Also in Item 4436.
            Also in Item 4523.
            Also *Ramparts*, November, 1962, pp. 18-20.

4373.   "Le Christ Évoluteur ou Un développement logique de la
        notion de rédemption." [October 8, 1942.] Item 741,
        pp. 17-28.
            Also Item 4392, pp. 161-176.

4374.   "Le christianisme dans le monde." [May, 1933.] Item
        4805, pp. 129-146.

4375. "Christianisme et évolution (Suggestions pour servir à une théologie nouvelle)." [November 10, 1945.] Item 4392, pp. 201-216.

4376. "Le christianisme et la science; P. Teilhard de Chardin." *Esprit*, (1946): 125, 253-256. "Catholicisme et science." Item 4805, pp. 235-242.

4377. "Le christique." [March, 1955.] Item 4385, pp. 93-118.

4378. "Christliche Engagement und kirchliche Gemeinde." *Perspektiven der Zukunft* (1969): 3, 1-3.

4379. "Christologie et Évolution." [Christmas, 1933.] Item 4392, pp. 93-114.

4380. Number deleted.

4381. "Chronologie des alluvions pléistocènes de Java." *L'anthropologie* (1935): 45, 707-708. Also Item 4669, vol. 5, pp. 2146-2147.

4382. "Chute, rédemption et géocentrie." [July 20, 1930.] Item 4392, pp. 47-58.

4383. "Climbing the Sacred Mountain." *Sign*, April, 1977, pp. 6-11.

4384. "Le coeur de la matière." [October 30, 1950.] Item 4385, pp. 19-92. Contains Items 4372, 4731.

4385. *Le coeur de la matière.* Paris: Seuil, 1976. Volume 13 of Item 4670. Contains Items 4328, 4333, 4363, 4372, 4377, 4384, 4591, 4602, 4613, 4663, 4703, 4713, 4731, 4860.
The Heart of Matter. London: Collins, 1978. Also New York: Harcourt Brace Jovanovich, 1979.

4386. "Le coeur du problème." [September 8, 1949.] Item 4346, pp. 339-349.

4387. "Les collections paléontologiques du Musée Hoang-ho-Pai-ho. Vertébrés." [May, 1937.] Item 4669, vol. 4, pp. 1841-1847.

4388. "Un colloque scientifique sur l'évolution." *Études* (1947): 253, 257-259. Also Item 4669, vol. 9, pp. 4234-4236.

4389. "Comment comprendre et utiliser l'art dans la ligne de
       l'énergie humaine. [March 13, 1939.] Item 4805, pp.
       93-98.
          Also Item 3920, pp. 101-103.
          Also *Idées et forces*, November-December, 1948, pp.
       32-34.
          "Une opinion du R.P. Teilhard de Chardin: 'Sur l'in-
       quiétude dans l'art d'aujourd'hui.'" *Le transhuman-
       isme, la semaine céphéenne*, June 1, 1939, p. 3.

4390. "Comment concevoir et espérer que se réalise sur terre
       l'unanimisation humaine?" [January 18, 1850.] Item
       4346, pp. 367-374.

4391. "Comment je crois." [October 28, 1934.] Item 4392,
       pp. 115-152.

4392. *Comment je crois*. Paris: Seuil, 1969. Volume 10 of
       Item 4670. Contains Items 4365, 4373, 4375, 4379,
       4382, 4391, 4409, 4429, 4533, 4610, 4632, 4635, 4637,
       4640, 4688, 4698, 4740, 4753, 4825, 4855.
          How I Believe. London: Collins, 1969.
          Also New York: Harper & Row, 1969.
          Christianity and Evolution. London: Collins, 1971.
          Also New York: Harcourt Brace Jovanovich, 1971.
          Also 1974.

4393. "Comment je vois." [August 12 and 26, 1948.] Item 4431,
       pp. 177-224.

4394. "Comment se pose aujourd'hui la question du transform-
       isme." *Études* (1921): 167, 524-544.
          Also Item 4873, pp. 17-40.

4395. "Commission chargée de reunir et de présenter (faire
       valoir) les preuves ou indices d'un déplacement bio-
       logique de l'humanité sur elle-même." [July 12,
       1951.] Manuscript. 1 p., single-spaced.

4396. "Communication. Anthropologie? Sur la place à donner
       en biologie au phénomène humain." [April 6, 1947?]
       Item 990, pp. 341-347.

4397. "Communication relative à des observations complémen-
       taires sur la géologie de l'Ordos (Chine)." *Compte-
       rendu Sommaire et Bulletin de la Société géologique
       de France*, November 17, 1924, pp. 162-163.
          Also Item 4669, vol. 2, pp. 509-510.

4398. "Comparative Observations on South Africa and Eastern
Asia (Northern China)." [1951.] Item 4669, vol. 10,
pp. 4406-4407.

4399. "Comptes rendus de la Congrégation des Grands du Col-
lège Notre-Dame de Mongré, Villefranche (Rhône)."
Notebook, Archives of the Jesuit Province of Lyon,
October-December, 1896, pp. 220-226.

4400. "Les conditions psychologiques de l'unification humaine."
Psyché (1948): 26, 1325-1332. Contains Item 4730.
Also *Psyché* (1955): 99/100, 73-80.
Also Item 4321, pp. 175-185.
Also in Item 4357.

4401. "Conférence." *L'Écho de Tientsin*, April 5, 1924.
Also Item 4669, vol. 2, pp. 782-784.

4402. "Conférence avec projections sur la géologie de la
Chine et le Sinanthropus pekinensis." *Compte-rendu
Sommaire et Bulletin de la Société géologique de
France*, December 15, 1930, pp. 207-208.
Also Item 4669, vol. 4, pp. 1479-1480.

4403. "Conférence du P. Teilhard de Chardin sur la Chine, la
Birmanie et Java." *La Moncelet*, January 12, 1939, pp.
4-5.

4404. "Congrès internationaux de philosophie des Sciences.
Colloque organisé par l'Association internationale
de philosophie des Sciences, et tenu dans les locaux
de l'U.N.E.S.C.O., sur l'évolution biologique, les
17-22 octobre 1949." *Études*, (1949): 213, 391-392.
The second paragraph is Teilhard's.
Also Item 4669, vol. 10, pp. 4265-4267.

4405. "Le Congrès universel des croyants." [1950.] Typescript. 1 p., single-spaced.

4406. "Consecration." *Catholic Digest*, June, 1968, pp. 58-
60. Excerpt from Item 4436.

4407. "La considération d'astres habités." 1917? Item 1341,
pp. 127-128.

4408. *Construire la terre*. Paris: Seuil, 1958. Contains
Items 4355, 4356.
Building the Earth. London/Dublin: Chapman, 1965.
Also Wilkes-Barre, Pa.: Dimension Books, 1965.
Also in Item 4357.

4409.   "Contingence de l'univers et goût humain de survivre,
        ou comment repenser, en conformité avec les lois de
        l'énergetique, la notion chrétienne de création."
        [May 1, 1953.] Item 4392, pp. 263-272.

4410.   "Contorted Structures in the Sinian Limestone." *Geo-
        biologia* (1943): 1, 53-55.
        Also Item 4669, vol. 9, pp. 3805-3810.

4411.   "La convergence de l'univers." [July 23, 1951.] Item
        4321, pp. 293-309.

4412.   "Conversation avec Marguerite Teilhard-Chambon." [After
        1950.] 3 pp.

4413.   "Conversations avec Grootaers." In "Journal de Willem
        A. Grootaers." Typescript. Single-spaced. See
        entries of March 27, April 1, May 10, June 28, August
        27, October 4, 19 and 27, November 4 and 7, December
        1, 1945, January 2 and 16, 1946.

4414.   "Conversations avec Roger Lévy." Manuscript. 5 pp.
        Notes taken by Lévy.

4415.   "Cosmologie et théologie." *Bulletin de Liaisons entre
        scientifiques S.J.*, January 19, 1947.

4416.   "Cosmos et cosmogénèse." [April 8, 1951.] In Item
        1010. See also Item 4810.

4417.   "Les couches de passage entre le Tertiaire et le
        Quaternaire en Chine septentrionale." *Compte-rendu
        Sommaire et Bulletin de la Société géologique de
        France*, January 23, 1928, pp. 12-14.
        Also Item 4669, vol. 2, pp. 859-861.

4418.   "Croix d'expiation et croix d'évolution." Item 3851,
        pp. 13-19.

4419.   "Les cycles sédimentaires (Pliocènes et plus récents)
        dans la Chine du nord." *Bulletin de l'Association de
        géographes française* (1933): 65, 3-7.
        Also Item 4669, vol. 4, pp. 1853-1857.

4420.   "Davidson Black, 1885-1934." *L'anthropologie* (1934):
        64, 424-426.
        Also Item 4669, vol. 5, pp. 2134-2136.

4421. "De l'arbitraire dans les lois, théories et principes de la physique." *Quodlibeta* (1905): 2, 247-274.
Also Item 4669, vol. 1, pp. 1-30.

4422. "La découverte du passé." *Études* (1935): 225, 469-478.
Also Item 4874, pp. 259-269.

4423. "La découverte du Sinanthrope." *Études* (1937): 232, 5-13.
Also Item 1800, pp. 180-190.
Also Item 4337, pp. 121-131.

4424. "Une défense de l'orthogénèse." [January, 1955.] *Colloques internationaux de Centre National de la Recherche Scientifique--LX. Problèmes actuels de paléontologie.* Paris: C.N.R.S., 1956, pp. 109-113.
Also Item 4873, pp. 381-391.

4425. "Le dernier symposium de la Wenner-Gren Foundation (Juin 1952). Quelques réflexions personnelles sur l'operation." Item 4669, vol. 10, pp. 4474-4477.

4426. "Description de Mammifères tertiaires de Chine et de Mongolie." *Annales de paléontologie* (1926): 15, 3-52.
Also Item 4669, vol. 2, pp. 665-727.

4427. "Deux nouveaux crânes de Sinanthrope." *L'anthropologie* (1936): 46, 716.
Also Item 4669, vol. 6, p. 2490.

4428. "Deuxièmes notes sur la paléontologie humaine en Asie Méridionale." *L'anthropologie* (1938): 48, 449-456.
Also Item 4669, vol. 7, pp. 2797-2804.

4429. "Le Dieu de l'évolution." [October 25, 1953.] Item 1259, pp. 11-17.
Also Item 4392, pp. 283-292.

4430. "Les directions et les conditions de l'avenir." *Psyché* (1948): 23/24, 981-991.
Also *Psyché* (1955): 99/100, 62-72.
Also Item 4346, pp. 293-305.

4431. *Les directions de l'avenir.* Paris: Seuil, 1973. Vol. 11 of Item 4670. Contains Items 4340, 4389, 4393, 4462, 4612, 4634, 4635, 4690, 4739, 4750, 4801, 4809, 4830, 4863.
Toward the Future. London: Collins, 1975.
Also New York: Harcourt Brace Jovanovich, 1975.

4432. "Discours prononcé ou devant être prononcé à Cahors 'De-
       puis que l'homme est homme....'" [June 21, 1950.]
       Typescript. 1 p., single-spaced.

4433. "Early Man in China." *Publication de l'Institut de géo-
       biologie de Pékin* (1941): 7, v-xi, 1-100.
       Also Item 4669, vol. 8, pp. 3261-3366.

4434. "The Early Man in China. Key to His Appearance and Dis-
       appearance is Found in Loess." *Dossiers de la Com-
       mission Synodale (Peiping)* (1929): 2, 904-906.
       Also Item 4669, vol. 3, pp. 1157-1159.

4435. "Éclaircissements à l'usage de ceux qui auront la
       charité de réviser ce livre." [February, 1941.]
       Typescript. 1 p., single-spaced. Regarding Item
       4702.

4436. *Écrits du temps de la guerre (1916-1919).* Paris: B.
       Grasset, 1965.
            Also Paris: Seuil, 1976. Volume 12 of Item 4670.
       Contains Items 4334, 4372, 4406, 4439, 4457, 4476,
       4478, 4489, 4502, 4588, 4592, 4604, 4608, 4625, 4626,
       4630, 4716, 4724, 4731, 4858, 4867, 4870.
            Writings in Time of War. London: Collins, 1968.
       Also New York: Harper & Row, 1968.
            Escritos do tempo de guerra. Lisboa: Portugália
       Editora, 1969.

4437. "Editor's Note." "A Preliminary Report of Archaeo-
       logical Investigations on the Sino-Tibetan Border
       of Szechwan," by Gordon T. Bowles. *Bulletin of the
       Geological Society of China* (1933-34): 13, 123.

4438. "L'education de l'amour." Typescript. 5 pp., single-
       spaced.

4439. "L'élément universel." [February 21, 1919.] Item
       4436, pp. 271-277.

4440. "En quoi consiste le corps humain?" [1919?] Item 4805,
       pp. 31-36.

4441. "En regardant un cyclotron. Réflexions sur le reploie-
       ment sur soi de l'énergie humaine." *Recherches et
       débats* (1953): 4, 123-130.
            Also Item 4321, pp. 365-377.

4442. "L'énergie d'évolution." [May 24, 1953.] Item 4321, pp. 379-393.

4443. "L'énergie humaine." [August 6-September 8, 1937.] Item 4444, pp. 141-200.

4444. *L'énergie humaine.* Paris: Seuil, 1962. Volume 6 of Item 4670. Contains Items 4443, 4451, 4454, 4616, 4704, 4813.
       Die menschliche Energie. Olten: Walter-Verlag, 1966.
       La energia humana. 2d ed.; Madrid: Taurus, 1967.
       Human Energy. London: Collins, 1969.
       Also New York: Harcourt Brace Jovanovich, 1971.

4445. "Enquête: Nouvelles littéraires, 1951." Typescript. 2 pp., single-spaced. See Item 517a.

4446. "Entretiens avec Claude Cuénot." Notes taken by Cuénot April 3, July 12, December 25, 1950, April 17, June 6, 1951, June 29, July 7, 1954. Manuscript. 17 pp.

4447. "Entretiens avec Fernand Lafargue." Notes taken by Lafargue in July, 1954, with Teilhard's outline of his philosophy.

4448. "Entretiens et propos de P. Teilhard de Chardin." In Item 2600.

4449. "L'Éocène des environs de Minieh." *Bulletin de l'Institut égyptien* (1909): 2, 116-121.
       Also Item 4669, vol. 1, pp. 41-46.

4450. "Eparchaean and Epi-Sinian Intervals in China." *Bulletin of the Geological Society of China* (1937): 17, 65-82.
       Also Item 4669, col. 6, pp. 2495-2511.

4451. "L'esprit de la terre." [March 9, 1931.] Item 4444, pp. 23-57.

4452. "L'esprit nouveau et le cône du temps." *Psyché* (1946): 17-37, 171-179.
       Also *Psyché* (1955): 99/100, 48-61.
       Also Item 4346, pp. 109-126.

4453. "Esquisse d'une dialectique de l'esprit." [November 25, 1946.] Item 4321, pp. 147-158.

4454. "Esquisse d'un univers personnel." [May 4, 1936.]
       Item 4444, pp. 67-114.

4455. "Essai d'intégration de l'homme dans l'univers." Four
       conferences given at Chaudefaud, November 19 and 27,
       December 3 and 10, 1930. Typescripts. 24 pp., 14
       pp., 14 pp.

4456. "L'essence de l'idée de democratie. Approche biologique
       du problème." [February 2, 1949.] Item 4346, pp. 309-
       315.

4457. "L'éternel féminin." [March 25, 1918.] Item 4436, pp.
       191-202.

4458. "L'étoffe de l'univers." [July 14, 1953.] Item 4321,
       pp. 395-406.

4459. *Être plus.* Paris: Seuil, 1968.
       Ser mas. Madrid: Taurus, 1970.

4460. "Étude géologique sur la region du Dalai-Noor." *Mé-
       moires de la Société géologique de France* (1926): 3,
       1-56.
       Also Item 4669, vol. 2, pp. 603-659.

4461. "L'évolution." *Courrier des Cercles d'études* (1911):
       227-232.
       Also Item 4669, vol. 1, pp. 69-74.

4462. "L'évolution de la chasteté." [February, 1934.] Item
       4431, pp. 65-92.

4463. "L'évolution de la responsabilité dans le monde."
       Psyché (1951): 57/58, 416-424.
       Also *Psyché* (1955): 99/100, 81-88.

4464. "Évolution zoologique et invention." *Paléontologie et
       transformisme.* Paris: Albin Michel, 1950.
       Also Item 4873, pp. 329-331.

4465. "Expedition scientifique en Chine." *Lettres de Jersey*
       (1926-27): 40, 89-90.
       Also Item 4669, vol. 2, pp. 854-855.

4466. "Extrait de la discussion suivant la conférence de
       M.C. Arambourg sur *l'extinction des Espèces et des
       Groupes.*" *Paléontologie et transformisme.* Paris:
       Albin Michel, 1950.
       Also Item 4669, vol. 10, p. 4281.

4467.   "Extraits de deux lettres (24 oct. 1907 et 12 mars 1908)."
        Relations d'Orient, May, 1908, pp. 178-179.
        Also Item 4669, vol. 1, pp. 39-40.

4468.   "Extraits de lettres de M.P. Teilhard de Chardin (trou-
        vailles anthropologiques en Chine.)" *L'anthropologie*
        (1937): 47, 655-656.
        Also Item 4669, vol. 6, pp. 2790-2791.

4469.   "Faire un 'lexique' de mes termes (notions)." [1951.]
        Item 990, p. 353.
        Also Item 971.

4470.   "La faune pléistocène et l'ancienneté de l'homme en
        Amérique du nord." *L'anthropologie* (1935): 45, 483-
        487.
        Also Item 4337, pp. 113-118.

4471.   "Le féminin et l'univers." Notes taken by Mme. Pelle-
        Douel of a conference given to "L'union spirituelle
        des femmes," 1939. Mimeographed. 3 pp., single-
        spaced.

4472.   "La fin de l'espèce." *Psyché* (1953): 76, 81-87.
        Also *Psyché* (1955): 99/100, 89-95.
        Also Item 4346, pp. 389-395.

4473.   "La foi en l'homme (World Congress of Faiths. Branche
        française, Musée Guimet)." [February, 1947.] Item
        4346, pp. 235-243.

4474.   "La foi en la paix." *Cahiers du monde nouveau* (1947):
        3, 1-5.
        Also *Dokumente* (1948): 576-580.
        Also Item 4346, pp. 191-197.
        "Faith in Peace." *Wiseman*, Winter, 1965, pp. 285-
        289.

4475.   "Foi humaine--foi spirituelle." Notes taken by L.
        Roinet of a conference at Paris, January 18, 1948.
        Manuscript. 1 p.
        Also notes taken my Mme. Solange Lemaitre. Manu-
        script. 13 pp.

4476.   "La foi qui opère." [September 27, 1918.] Item 4436,
        pp. 225-248.

4477. "Les fondements et le fond de l'idée d'évolution."
       [1926.] Item 4873, pp. 165-197.

4478. "Forma Christi." [December, 1918.] Item 4436, pp. 249-
       270.

4479. "La formation des déserts en Chine et Mongolie." In
       "La vie dans les régions désertiques nord tropicales
       de l'ancien monde." *Mémoires de la Société de bio-
       géographie* (1938): 6, 15-20.
       Also Item 4669, vol. 7, pp. 2971-2976.

4480. "Fossil Mammals from Locality 9 of Choukoutien."
       Paleontologica Sinica (1936): 7, 5-70.
       Also Item 4669, vol. 5, pp. 2257-2328.

4481. "Fossil Man in China and Mongolia." *Natural History*
       (1926): 26, 238-245.
       Also Item 4669, vol. 2, pp. 774-781

4482. "Fossil Man. On the Birth, Growth and Present Status
       of Our Idea of Fossil Man." *Inventory Paper for the
       Wenner-Gren Foundation International Symposium on
       Anthropology, #5.* New York: The Foundation, 1952.
       "The Idea of Fossil Man." *Anthropology Today*, ed.
       A.L. Krober. Chicago: University of Chicago Press,
       1953, pp. 93-100.
       Also Item 4669, vol. 10, pp. 4478-4485.

4483. *Fossil Men. Recent Discoveries and Present Problems.*
       Peking: Henri Vetch, 1943.
       "La question de l'homme fossile. Découvertes ré-
       centes et problèmes actuels." *Psyché* (1943): 126-
       134, 254-260, 423-433.
       Also Paris: Éditions Psyché, 1948.
       Also *Psyché* (1955): 99/100, 12-47.
       Also Item 4337, pp. 135-174.
       Also Item 4669, vol. 9, pp. 3905-3936.

4484. "The Fossils from Locality 12 of the Choukoutien."
       Paleontologica sinica (1938): 114, 1-47.
       Also Item 4669, vol. 7, pp. 2805-2856.

4485. "The Fossils from Locality 18, near Peking." *Paleon-
       tologica sinica* (1940): 124, 1-100.
       Also Item 4669, vol. 7, pp. 3111-3215.

4486. "Les fouilles préhistoriques de Péking." *Revue des questions scientifiques* (1934): 25, 181-193. Also Item 4337, pp. 99-110.

4487. "Fragments autobiographiques posthumes (inédits)." *Hermès. Recherches sur l'expérience spirituelle* (1964): 2, 19-36.

4488. "Franz Weidenreich." *L'anthropologie* (1949): 53, 328-330. Also Item 4669, vol. 10, pp. 4270-4272.

4489. *Frühe Schriften*. Freiburg-im-Breisgau/München: Karl Alber, 1968. Excerpts from Item 4436.

4490. *Genèse d'un pensée: lettres 1914-1919*. Paris: B. Grasset, 1961.
Entwurf und Enfaltung. Briefe aus den Jahren 1914-1919. Freiburg-im-Breisgau/München: Karl Alber, 1963. Contains Item 4875.
Genesis de un pensamiento, cartas (1914-1919). Madrid: Taurus, 1963. Also 3d ed., 1966.
Het voorspel 1914-1916. Het voorspel 1917-1919. 2 vols.; Utrecht/Antwerpen: Het Spectrum, 1963.
The Making of a Mind: Letters from a Soldier-Priest, 1914-1919. London: Collins, 1965. Also New York: Harper & Row, 1965.
Gênese de um pensamento. Cartas 1914-1919. Lisbon: Livraria Morais, 1966.
Genesi di un pensiero. Lettere dal fronte (1914-1919). Milan: Feltrinelli, 1966.
Genesi d'un pensament. Barcelona: Nova Terra, 1968.
Aru shisô no tanjô. Tokyo: Misuzu Shobô, 1969.

4491. "The Genesis of the Western Hills of Peking." *Geobiologia* (1943): 1, 17-49. Also Item 4669, vol. 9, pp. 3769-3801.

4492. "Géobiologie et Geobiologia." *Geobiologia* (1943): 1, 1-5. Also Item 4669, vol. 9, pp. 3753-3760.

4493. "Geological Observations in the Turfan Area." *Geografiska Annaler* (1935): 446-452. Item 4669, vol. 5, pp. 2243-2249.

4494. "The Geological Structure of the Shihmenchai Basin, near Shanhaikwan (North Hopei)." *Geobiologia* (1945): 2, 19-26.
Also Item 4669, vol. 9, pp. 4063-4070.

4495. "La géologie en Extrême-Orient pendant la guerre." *Compte-rendu Sommaire et Bulletin de la Société géologique de France* (1946): 11, 200-202.
Also Item 4669, vol. 10, pp. 4229-4231.

4496. "Geology of Northern Chihli and Eastern Mongolia." *Bulletin of the Geological Society of China* (1924): 3, 399-407.
Also Item 4669, vol. 2, pp. 451-460.

4497. "The Geology of the Weich'ang Area." *Bulletin of the Geological Society of China* (1932): 11, 1-46.
Also Item 4669, vol. 4, pp. 1646-1694.

4498. "The Geology of the Western Hills--Additional Notes." *Geobiologia* (1945): 2, 13-18.
Also Item 4669, vol. 9, pp. 4057-4062.

4499. "God is the Heart of Everything." *Catholic Messenger*, June 21, 1962, p. 10.

4500. "Le goût de vivre." [November, 1950.] Item 4321, pp. 237-251.

4501. "Un grand événement qui se dessine: la planétisation humaine." *Cahiers du monde nouveau* (1945-46): 2, 1-14.
Also Item 4346, pp. 159-175.

4502. "La grande monade." [February 15, 1918.] Item 3292, pp. 39-48.
Also in Item 4436.

4503. "La grande option." [1939.] *Cahiers du monde nouveau* (1945): 1, 247-263.
Also Item 4346, pp. 57-81.

4504. "The Granitization of China." *Publication de l'Institut de géobiologie. Pékin* (1940): 1, 1-33.
Also *Bulletin of the Geological Society of China* (1940): 19, 341-377.
Also Item 4669, vol. 7, pp. 3219-3255.

4505. "Les graviers plissés de Chine." *Bulletin de la société géologique de France* (1932): 2, 527-531. Item 4669, vol. 4, pp. 1832-1840.

4506. "A Great Reward for Hard Work." *The Leader Reprints* (1930): 51, 13-14. Also Item 4669, vol. 4, pp. 1481-1482.

4507. *Le groupe zoologique humain: structure et directions évolutives.* Paris: A. Michel, 1956.
La place de l'homme dans la nature: le groupe zoologique humain. Paris: Union Générale d'Éditions, 1962.
Also Paris: Seuil, 1963. Volume 8 of Item 4670.
Contains Items 4322, 4335, 4344, 4350, 4369, 4400, 4441, 4442, 4453, 4458, 4500, 4510, 4611, 4699, 4707, 4715, 4719, 4727, 4748, 4751, 4754, 4808, 4810, 4845, 4872, 4879, 4888.
El grupo zoológico humano: estructuras y sesgos evolutivos. Madrid: Taurus, 1957.
Also 5th ed., 1965.
Die Enststehung des Menschen. München: C.H. Beck, 1961.
Also 2d ed., 1963.
Czlowiek: Struktur i Kierunki Ewolucji Grupy Zoologicznej Ludzkiej. Warszawa: Pax, 1962.

4508. "Henry Fairfield Osborn, 1857-1935." *L'anthropologie* (1936): 46, 704-706.
Also item 4669, vol. 6, pp. 2491-2494.

4509. "Hérédité sociale et éducation. Notes sur la valeur humano-chrétienne de l'enseignement." [1938.]
Études (1945): 245, 84-94.
Also Item 4346, pp. 41-53.

4510. "L'heure de choisir—un sens possible de la guerre." [Christmas, 1939.] Item 4321, pp. 17-26.

4511. "L'histoire naturelle du monde. Réflexions sur la valeur et l'avenir de la systématique." *Scientia* (1925): 15-24.
Also Item 4873, pp. 145-157.

4512. *Hit az emberben.* [Faith in Man.] Budapest: Szent Istvan Társulat az Apostoli Szentszek Könyvkiadója, 1968.

4513. "L'hominisation. Introduction à une étude scientifique
       du phénomène humain." [May 6, 1925.] Item 4873, pp.
       77-111.

4514. "Homme. IV: L'homme devant les enseignements de l'Église
       et devant la philosophie spiritualiste." *Dictionnaire
       apologetique de la foi catholique.* Paris: Beauchesne,
       1912, vol. 2, cc. 510-514.

4515. "L'Homme de Pékin." *Écho de l'U.S.I.C.* (1931): 22, 51-
       52.
            Also Item 4669, vol. 4, pp. 1483-1484.

4516. "L'homme et la Paléontologie." Congrès de l'Union
       Française Universitaire, Besançon, August 14, 1946.
            "Au Congrès de l'Union Française Universitaire.
       Une heure avec le R.P. Teilhard de Chardin." *Le
       Franc-Comtois,* August 19, 1946, p. 1.
            "Quelques notes prises pendant la conférence faite
       par le Père Teilhard au cours des vacances de l'U.F.U.
       à Besancon, 14 août 1946." Notes taken by Jean Orcel.
       Typescript. 2 pp., single-spaced.

4517. "Hominisation et spéciation." *Revue scientifique* (1952):
       90, 434-438.
            Also Item 4873, pp. 365-379.

4518. "Homo-pekinensis I. une découverte chinoise en pré-
       histoire." *Dossiers de la Commission Synodale (Pei-
       ping)* (1929): 2, 938-939.
            Also Item 4669, vol. 4, pp. 1160-1161.

4519. "How and Where to Search [for] the Oldest Man in China."
       Bulletin of the Geological Society of China (1926):
       5, 201-206.
            Also Item 4669, vol. 2, pp. 737-742.

4520. "Huit jours au Fayoum." *Relations d'Orient* (1907):
       274-281.
            Also Item 4669, vol. 1, pp. 31-38.

4521. "L'humanité se meut-elle biologiquement sur elle-même?"
       Revue des questions scientifiques (1949): 120, 498-
       516.
            Also Item 4346, pp. 319-336.

4522. *Hymne an das Ewig Weibliche.* Einsiedeln: Johannes Ver-
       lag, 1968.

4523. *Hymne de l'univers.* Paris: Seuil, 1961. Contains Items
4372, 4602, 4731. See also Items 4524, 4525.
Also 1966.
Lobgesang des Alls. Olten/Freiburg-im-Breisgau:
Walter-Verlag, 1961.
Himno del universo. Madrid: Taurus, 1964.
Also 2d ed., 1967.
Hymn of the Universe. London: Collins, 1965.
Also New York: Harper & Row, 1969.
Also 1972.

4524. "Hymn of the Universe." *Critic* (1965): 23, 13-20.
Excerpt from Item 4523.

4525. "Hymn to Matter." *Catholic Mind* (1964): 62, 4-5. Excerpt from Item 4523.

4526. *Images et paroles.* Paris: Seuil, 1966.
Album. London: Collins, 1966.
Also New York: Harper & Row, 1967.
Imágenes y palabras. Madrid: Taurus, 1967.
Immagini e parole. Milan: A. Mondadori, 1968.

4527. "Une importante découverte en paléontologie humaine:
Le Sinanthropus pekinensis." *Revue des questions
scientifiques* (1930): 18, 5-16.
Also Item 4337, pp. 85-95.

4528. "L'incroyance moderne. Cause profonde et remède."
Vie intellectuelle, October 25, 1933, pp. 218-222.
Also Item 4805, pp. 147-154.

4529. "Inédits de Teilhard de Chardin." *Europe* (1965): 431/
432, 97-118.

4530. Inscription sur le livre d'or de l'Hostellerie Chavant,
Uzerche (Correze). July, 1954.

4531. "Instantanés du P. Teilhard." [1939, 1946, 1950.]
Dernière heure, April 28, 1960.

4532. "Une interprétation biologique plausible de l'histoire
humaine: la formation de la 'noosphère.'" *Revue des
questions scientifiques*, January, 1947, pp. 7-37.
Also Item 4346, pp. 201-231.

4533. "Introduction à la vie chrétienne." [June 29, 1944.]
Item 4392, pp. 177-200.

4534. "L'invasion de la télévision." *Études* (1950): 265, 251-
       252.
       Also Item 4669, vol. 10, p. 4284.

4535. *Je m'explique.* Paris: Seuil, 1966.
       Yo me explico. Madrid: Taurus, 1968.
       Let Me Explain. London: Collins, 1970.
       Also New York: Harper & Row, 1972.

4536. "Joint Geological and Prehistoric Studies in the Late
       Cenozoic in India." *Science* [Shanghai] (1936): 83,
       233-236.
       Also Item 4669, vol. 6, pp. 2457-2460.

4537. *Journal.* Vol. 1- ; Paris: Fayard, 1975- .
       Tagebücher. Vol. 1- ; Olten/Freiburg-im-Breisgau:
       Walter-Verlag, 1974- .
       Teilhard Naplója. Vol. 1- ; São Paulo: Rezek,
       1975- .

4538. "Late Cenozoic Gravels and Soils in Upper Burma." May,
       1938. Item 4669, vol. 7, pp. 2986-3014.

4539. "Léontine Zanta e no tegami." [Letters to Léontine
       Zanta.] *Convergence* (1973): 3, 34-40. Excerpts from
       Item 4569.

4540. "Letter from Egypt." *U.S. Catholic* (1965): 30, 25-31.
       Excerpt from Item 4572.

4541. *Lettere a un amico scienziato.* Torino: P. Gribaudi,
       1969.

4542. "Lettre à Alberto-Carlo Blanc." [July 18, 1946.]
       *Notizie sull'operosità scientifica e didattica di
       Alberto-Carlo Blanc* (1961): 28.

4543. "Lettre à Claude Cuenot." [November 30, 1952.] Item
       1009, p. 2.

4544. "Lettre à Jeanne Mortier." [August 14, 1951, July 13,
       1952.] *Europe*, March-April, 1965, pp. 28-31.

4545. "Lettre à K.P. Oakley." [November 28, 1953.] Item
       4669, vol. 10, pp. 4561-4567.

4546. "Lettre à Léon Lutand." [February 19, 1936.] *Revue
       Teilhard de Chardin* (1964): 20/21, 52.

4547. "Lettre à M. Costa." [November 10, 1924.] Typescript. 2 pp., double-spaced.

4548. "Lettre à M. Duprez." Item 1259, pp. 25-28.

4549. "Lettre à Mary Lecomte du Noüy." [October 15, 1947.] *Revue de Paris*, December, 1964, p. 150. Also Item 1259, pp. 20-24.

4550. "Lettre à Maryse Choisy." [May 15, 1953.] In Item 738a.

4551. "Lettre à Maxime Gorce." [October 4, 1950.] Item 1708, pp. 196-198.

4552. "Lettre à Mme. Jean Carlhian." [June 19, 1953.] Item 4035, p. 51. "Mal évolutif et péché originel." Typescript. 2 pp., single-spaced.

4553. "Lettre à Paul Fejos." [November 10, 1950.] Item 169, pp. 123-133.

4554. "Lettre à Paul Fejos." [August 1, 1951.] Item 4669, vol. 10, pp. 4408-4414.

4555. "Lettre à Pierre Lecomte de Noüy." September 15, 1947. *Revue de Paris*, December, 1964, p. 149. Also Item 1259, pp. 20-24.

4556. "Lettre au Dr. M.R. Sahn." [November 18, 1953.] *Journal of the Paleological Society of India* (1956): 1, xxxii. Also Item 4669, vol. 10, p. 4560. Also *Journal of the Paleological Society of India* (1957): 2, 23.

4557. "Lettre au P. Antonin-Gilbert Sertillanges." [February 4, 1934.] *Revue Teilhard de Chardin* (1960): 1/2, 12. Also Item 1800, pp. 178-179.

4558. "Lettre au P. Christian Burdo, S.J." [February 15, 1953.] Item 186, p. 13. Also Item 2507, p. 125.

4559. "Lettre au P. Henri de Lubac, S.J." July 31, 1930. *Mondes d'écrivains, destinées d'hommes* by Louis Barjon. Paris: Casterman, 1960.

4560. "Lettre au P. René d'Ouince, S.J." [December 21, 1950.]
       Item 3020, p. 343.

4561. "Lettre au T.R.P. Jean-Baptiste Janssens, S.J." [Sep-
       tember 25, 1947.] Item 3020, pp. 341-342.

4562. "Lettre au T.R.P. Jean-Baptiste Janssens, S.J." [Oc-
       tober 12, 1951.] Item 1800, pp. 213-215.
       Also Item 2413, pp. 55-60.

4563. "Une lettre inédite du Père Teilhard de Chardin à Madame
       G.-M. Haardt." Item 3910, p. 21.

4564. "Lettre inédite en guise d'éditorial, Pékin, 1945."
       Revue Teilhard de Chardin (1960): 3/4, 2; (1961): 5,
       2.
       Also *Le Phare dimanche*, April 2, 1961.
       Also Item 4219, p. 36.

4565. "Lettres à Arsène Henry." [November 24, 1943, Decem-
       ber 1943, January? 1946.] *Revue Teilhard de Chardin*
       (1962): 12, 4-5.

4566. "Lettres à George Brown Barbour." In Item 169.

4567. "Lettres à l'Abbe Christophe Gaudefroy." Item 3950,
       pp. 14-26.

4568. "Lettres à l'Abbe Christophe Gaudefroy." Item 1617a,
       pp. 3-8.

4569. *Lettres à Léontine Zanta.* Paris: Desclée de Brouwer,
       1965. Contains Item 4539.
            *Pelgrim van de toekomst. Brieven aan Léontine
       Zanta.* Brugge/Utrecht: Desclée de Brouwer, 1966.
            Briefe an Léontine Zanta. Freiburg: Herder, 1967.
            Cartas a Léontine Zanta. Lisbon: Livraria Morais,
       1967.
            Letters to Léontine Zanta. London: Collins, 1968.
            Convergence in alto. Lettere a Léontine Zanta.
       Milan: A. Mondadori, 1969.
            Cartes a Léontine Zanta. Barcelona: Nova Terra,
       1970.

4570. "Lettres au P. Jean-Paul Dallaire." [October 10 & 30,
       1942.] *Revue Teilhard de Chardin* (1964): 19, 19-31,
       33-34.

4571. "Lettres au P. Victor Fontoynent, S.J." [March 15 & July 22, 1916, July 26, 1917.] Item 2504, pp. 347-354.

4572. *Lettres d'Égypte (1905-1908)*: Aubier, 1963. Contains Item 4540.
Brieven uit Egypte, 1905-1908. Brugge/Utrecht: Desclée de Brouwer, 1965.
Briefe aus Ägypten, 1905-1908. Freiburg-im-Breisgau/München: K. Alber, 1965.
Letters from Egypt, 1905-1908. New York: Herder & Herder, 1965.
Lettere dall'Egitto, 1905-1908. Brescia: Morcelliana, 1966.
Cartas do Egipto (1905-1908). Lisbon: Livraria Morais, 1967.
Cartas de Egipto (1905-1908). Madrid: Taurus, 1967.

4573. *Lettres de voyage, 1923-1939*. Paris: B. Grasset, 1956. Contains Item 4371a.
Also in Item 4574.
Cartas de viaje (1923-1939). Madrid: Taurus, 1957.
Also 4th ed., 1966.
Geheimnis und Verheissung der Erde--Reisebriefe 1923-1939. Freiburg-im-Breisgau/München: K. Alber, 1958.
Also 4th ed., 1965.
Also Freiburg: Herder, 1968.
Cartas de viagem (1923-1939). Lisbon: Portugália, 1969.

4574. *Lettres de voyage (1923-1955)*. Paris: B. Grasset, 1961. Contains Items 4573, 4655.
Letters from a Traveller. London: Collins, 1962.
Also New York: Harper & Row, 1962.
Lettere di viaggio. Milan: Feltrinelli, 1962.
Reisbrieven, 1923-1955. Hilversum/Antwerp: P. Brand, 1963.
Tabi no tegami. Tokyo: Sisuzu Shobô, 1970.

4575. *Lettres d'Hastings et de Paris, 1908-1914*. Paris: Aubier-Montaigne, 1965. Contains Item 4577.
Lettere da Hastings e da Parigi, 1908-1914. Brescia: Morcelliana, 1967.
Cartas de Hastings e de Paris (1908-1914). Lisbon: Livraria Morais, 1967.
Letters from Hastings (1908-1912). *Letters from Paris (1912-1914)*. 2 vols.; London: Burns & Oates,

1967-68.
Also New York: Herder & Herder, 1967-68.
Cartas de Hastings y de París, 1908-1914. Madrid:
Taurus, 1968.

4576.   "Lettres du front (1914-1918.)" *Revue Teilhard de Chardin* (1960): 1/2, 2-10.

4577.   "Lettres du Père Teilhard sur la mort de sa soeur Françoise." Item 2504, pp. 360-361.

4578.   *Lettres familières de Pierre Teilhard de Chardin mon
ami. Les dernières années 1948-1955*, ed. by Pierre
Leroy. Paris: Centurion, 1976.

4579.   "Lettres inédites." *Revue générale belge* (1965): 11,
19-29.

4580.   "Lettres inédites d'un savant à ses amis." *Christus*
(1967): 14, 238-258.

4581.   "Lettres inédites du Père Teilhard de Chardin, enfance
et jeunesse." *Jésuites de l'assistance de France*
(1962): 3, 16-30.
Also in Item 4575.

4582.   *Lettres intimes à Auguste Valensin, Bruno de Solages,
Henri de Lubac.* Paris: Aubier Montaigne, 1972.
Also 2d ed., 1974.
*Cartas íntimas a Augusto Valensin, Bruno de So-
lages, Henri de Lubac.* Bilbao: Desclée de Brouwer,
1974.
*Bizalmas Levelei Auguste Valensin-hoz, Bruno de
Solages-hoz és Henri de Lubac-hoz.* São Paulo:
Rezek, 1976.

4583.   "Litanies au Sacré-coeur." In Item 896.
"Mes litanies." Item 4392, pp. 293ff.

4584.   "Logia." [1943.] In Item 4208.

4585.   "Logia et citations diverses." In Item 2604.

4586.   "La loi d'irréversibilite en évolution." *L'anthropologie* (1923): 33, 183-184.
Also Item 4873, pp. 73-74.

4587. "Lucien Cuénot (1867-1951.)" *Études* (1951): 267, 255-256.
 Also Item 4669, vol. 10, p. 4415.

4588. "La lutte contre la multitude." [February 26-March 22, 1917.] Item 4436, pp. 93-114.

4589. "The Lycoptera Beds and Sungari Series in Manchuria According to the Japanese Geologists." *Geobiologia* (1943): 1, 78-81.
 Also Item 4669, vol. 9, pp. 3832-3835.

4590. "M. Teilhard de Chardin présente une communication sur l'ancienneté de certains éléments des faunes continentales." *Compte-rendu Sommaire de la Société de biogéographie* (1925): 15, 111-113.
 Also Item 4669, vol. 2, pp. 598-600.

4591. "Ma position intellectuelle (réponse à une 'enquête,' et qui n'a jamais paru)." 1948. Item 1800, pp. 191-193.
 Also Item 4385, pp. 171-174.
 Also Item 4669, vol. 10, pp. 4568-4569.
 "La pensée du Père Teilhard de Chardin par lui-même, pour un article qui devait lui être consacré." *Les études philosophiques* (1955): 10, 580-581.

4592. "Machines à combiner et super-cerveaux." *Études* (1950): 264, 403-404.
 Also Item 4669, vol. 10, pp. 4282-4283.

4593. "La maîtrise du monde et le règne de Dieu." [September 15-20, 1916.] Item 4436, pp. 73-92.

4594. "Mammalian Paleontology. Survey of Pliocene Formations in North China." *Natural History* (1931): 31, 338-339.
 Also in Item 3010.

4595. "Les Mammifères de l'Éocène inférieur de la Belgique." *Mémoires du Musée royale d'histoire naturelle de Belgique* (1927): 36, 1-33.
 Also Item 4669, vol. 2, pp. 789-827.

4596. "Les Mammifères de l'Éocène inférieur français et leurs gisements." *Annales de paléontologie* (1921-22): 10, 9-116.
 Also Item 4669, vol. 1, pp. 253-385.

4597. "A Map of the Younger Eruptive Rocks in China." *Bulletin of the Geological Survey of China* (1937): 30, 1-52.
       Also Item 4669, vol. 6, pp. 2730-2781.

4598. "Le massif volcanique du Dalaï-Noor (Gobi-oriental)." *Bulletin volcanologique* (1925): 100-108.
       Also Item 4669, vol. 2, pp. 567-576.

4599. "Le massif volcanique du Dalaï-Noor (Gobi oriental)." *Compte-rendu du Congrès des Sociétés savantes et des departments tenu à Paris en 1925* (1926): 460-463.
       Also Item 4669, vol. 2, pp. 660-664.

4600. "The Maturing of the Species." *Critic*, August-September, 1964, pp. 31-34.

4601. "Memorandum au Dr. J. Huxley (à propos de son projet du 6 mars 51)." Typescript. 1 p., single-spaced.
       Also 1½ pp., single-spaced.

4602. *La Messe sur le monde.* [1923.] Sidi-Bel Abbes: Presses de la Légion Étrangère, 1961.
       Also Bruges: Desclée de Brouwer, 1965.
       Also Paris: Seuil, 1965.
       Also Item 4385, pp. 139-156.
       Also Item 4523, pp. 17-37.
       Also "*La Messe sur la monde*, Pierre Teilhard de Chardin, *Messa della domenica*, Girolamo Frescobaldi, église Saint-Jacques, Anvers, 12 mai 1961." Festival program, pp. 15-26.

4603. *Le milieu divin: essai de vie intérieure.* 1926-27. Paris: Seuil, 1957. Volume 4 of Item 4670.
       Le milieu divin: An Essay on the Interior Life. London: Collins, 1960.
       The Divine Milieu: An Essay on the Interior Life. New York: Harper, 1960.
       Also 1965.
       Der gottliche Bereich. Olten/Freiburg-im-Breisgau: Walter-Verlag, 1963.
       El medi divi. Assaig de vida interior. Barcelona: Nova Terra, 1964.
       El medio divino: ensayo de vida interior. 3d ed.; Madrid: Taurus, 1964.
       Also 6th ed., 1967.
       Benne élünk: az Isteni miliő. Tanulmány a belsö életröl. Paris: Ahogy lehet, 1965.

4604. "Le milieu mystique." [August 13, 1917.] Item 4436, pp. 115-149.

4605. "The Miocene Cervids from Shantung." *Bulletin of the Geological Society of China* (1939): 19, 269-278. Also Item 4669, vol. 7, pp. 3050-3059.

4606. "Les miracles de Lourdes et les enquêtes canoniques." *Études* (1909): 118, 161-183.

4607. "Mise en place et structure du groupe humain." [February, 1948.] Typescript. 3 pp., single-spaced.

4608. "Mon univers." [April 14, 1918.] In Item 4436.

4609. "Mon univers." [March 25, 1924.] Item 4805, pp. 63-114. Also Paris: Seuil, 1972.

4610. "Monogénisme et monophylétisme." [1950.] Item 4392, pp. 245-250.

4611. "La montée de l'autre." [January 20, 1942.] Item 4321, pp. 65-81.

4612. "La morale peut-elle se passer de soubassements métaphysiques avoués ou inavoués?" [April 23, 1945.] Item 4431, pp. 141-146.

4613. "Un mot d'explication sur mon attitude vis-à-vis de l'Église officielle." [January 5, 1921.] Item 4385, pp. 133-138.

4614. "Les mouvements de la vie." [April, 1928.] Item 4873, pp. 201-210.

4615. "The Movements of the Fauna Between Asia and North America Since the Lower Cretaceous." *Proceedings of the Sixth Pan-Pacific Scientific Congress.* California: University of California Press, 1939, vol. 3, pp. 647-649. Also Item 4669, vol. 7, pp. 3109-3110.

4616. "La mystique de la science." *Études* (1939): 238, 725-742. Also Item 4444, pp. 201-223.

4617. "Mystique orientale et mystique de l'ouest." Notes
       taken by L. Roinet of a conference at Paris, July
       4, 1948. Item 990, p. 361.

4618. "La nature et la succession des éruptions post-paléo-
       zoïques en Chine septentrionale." *Compte-rendu du
       l'Academia sinica* (1928): 186, 960-961.
       Also Item 4669, vol. 2, pp. 872-873.

4619. "Le Néolithic de la Chine d'après les découvertes du
       Dr. Andersson." *L'anthropologie* (1926): 36, 117-124.
       Also Item 4669, vol. 2, pp. 766-773.

4620. "The New Advances Made by Prehistory in South Africa."
       [March 14, 1952.] Item 4669, vol. 10, pp. 4420-
       4423.

4621. "New Continental Formations in Yunnan According to
       M.N. Bien and C.C. Young." *Geobiologia* (1943): 1,
       82-85.
       Also Item 4669, vol. 9, pp. 3836-3839.

4622. "New Observations on the Genus *Postschizotherium*, von
       Keonigswald." *Bulletin of the Geological Society of
       China* (1939): 19, 257-267.
       Also Item 4469, vol. 7, pp. 3037-3049.

4623. "New Observations on the Khangai Series of Mongolia
       and Some Other Allied Formations." *Bulletin of the
       Geological Society of China* (1932): 11, 395-409.
       Also Item 4669, vol. 4, pp. 1631-1645.

4624. "New Rodents of the Pliocene and Lower Pleistocene of
       North China." *Publication de l'Institut de Géobiologie
       de Pékin* (1942): 9, v-xiii, 1-101.
       Item 4669, vol. 8, pp. 3635-3746.

4625. "Les noms de la matière." [Easter 1919.] In Item 4436.

4626. "La nostalgie du front." *Études* (1917): 153, 458-467.
       Also in Item 4436.

4627. "Note complémentaire sur la faune de Mammifères du
       Tertiaire inférieure d'Orsmael." *Bulletin de l'Acadé-
       mie royale de Belgique* (1928): 14, 471-474.
       Also Item 4669, vol. 2, pp. 874-877.

4628. "Note pour servir à l'évangelisation des temps nouveaux."
[Epiphany, 1919.] Item 3041, pp. 11-21.
Also in Item 4436.

4629. "Note sur le Christ Universel." [1920.] Item 4805,
pp. 37-44.

4630. "Note sur l''élément universel' du monde." [December
22, 1918.] Item 4436, pp. 271-276.

4631. "Note sur l'essence du transformisme." [1921?] Typescript. 8 pp., double-spaced.

4632. "Note sur les modes de l'action divine dans l'univers."
[January, 1920.] Item 4392, pp. 33-46.

4633. "Note sur la nature synthétique de l'esprit et la
realité d'un centre d'union des monades." [Novem-
ber 10, 1917.] Manuscript.

4634. "Note sur la notion de perfection chrétienne." [1942.]
Item 4431, pp. 111-118.

4635. "Note sur la notion de transformisme créatrice." [1917?]
Item 4392, pp. 27-32.

4636. "Note sur le progrès." [August 10, 1920.] Item 4346,
pp. 23-27.

4637. "Note sur quelques représentations historiques possibles
du péché originel." [1922.] Item 4392, pp. 59-70.

4638. "Note sur la realité actuelle et la signification
évolutive d'une orthogénèse humaine." [May 5, 1951.]
Item 4873, pp. 353-362.

4639. "Note sur la structure des montagnes à l'ouest de
Linnming-kwan (Chihli méridional)." *Bulletin of the
Geological Society of China* (1924): 3, 393-397.
Also Item 4669, vol. 2, pp. 440-444.

4640. "Note sur l'union physique entre l'humanité du Christ
et les fidèles, au cours de la sanctification."
Item 4392, pp. 13-18.

4641. "Note-mémento sur la structure biologique de l'humanité." [August 3, 1948.] Typescript. 2 pp., single-
spaced.

4642. "Notes complementaires sur les roches éruptives de
       l'île de Jersey." In "Notes minéralogiques sur l'île
       de Jersey," by F. Pelletier. *Société Jersaise, Bul-
       letin annuel* (1910): 7, 108-111.
       Also Item 4669, vol. 1, pp. 66-68; vol. 10, pp. 293-
       294.

4643. "Notes de cours." Notes taken by Jean Cuvillier at the
       Institut catholique de Paris, 1921-1922.

4644. "Notes de lectures." Manuscript notebooks. [1945.] 105
       pp.; [1945.] 93 pp.; [After 1952.] 51 pp.

4645. "Notes de préhistoire Sud-africaine." [1951?] Item 4337,
       pp. 237-242.

4646. "Notes et esquisses." Manuscript notebooks. [1915-16.]
       75 pp,; [1916.] 20 pp.; [1916-17.] 18 pp.; [1917-18.]
       66 pp.; [1918-19.] 56 pp.; [1919.] 64 pp.; [1919-20.]
       72 pp.; [1920-22.] 113 pp.; [1922-25.] 99 pp.

4647. "Notes et esquisses." [1918.] Five detached pages in
       Item 4646 [1918-19.].

4648. Notes on a book, *Formation des continents et progression
       de la vie*, by H. & G. Termier. [1954.] Manuscript.
       1 p., both sides.

4649. "Notes on Continental Geology." *Bulletin of the Geolog-
       ical Society of China* (1936): 16, 195-220.
       Also Item 4669, vol. 6, pp. 2464-2489.

4650. "Notes prises au cours d'une conférence du R.P. Teilhard
       de Chardin sur le règne de Dieu dans le cadre des ex-
       ercices de S. Ignace." [July-August, 1946.] Notes
       taken by Fr. A. Lahogue. Typescript. 3 pp., single-
       spaced.

4651. "Notes scientifiques." [1952.] Item 4669, vol. 10, pp.
       4437-4474.

4652. "Notes sur la paléontologie humaine en Asie méridionale."
       L'anthropologie (1937): 47, 22-33.
       Also Item 4669, vol. 6, pp. 2520-2530.

4653. "Notre enquête sur les lectures spirituelles." [1948.]
       Interview by Robert Barrat. Typescript. 7 pp., double-
       spaced.

4654. "Nouveaux souvenirs d'enfance." [1939-46.] In Item 2598.

4655. *Nouvelles lettres de voyage (1939-1955).* Paris: B. Grasset, 1957.
Also in Item 4574.
Pilger der Zukunft, Reise im die Vergangenheit. Neue Reisebriefe 1939-1955. Freiburg/München: K. Alber, 1959.
Nuevas cartas de viaje (1939-1955). Madrid: Taurus: 1960.

4656. "Objet de recherche." [October 1, 1946.] Typescript. ½p., single-spaced.

4657. "Observations géologiques à travers les déserts d'Asie centrale de Kalgan à Hami." *Revue de géographie physique et de géologie dynamique* (1932): 5, 365-396.
Also Item 4669, vol. 4, pp. 1795-1831.

4658. "Observations géologiques en Somalie française et au Harrar." In "Études géologiques en Éthiope, Somalie et Arabie meridionale," *Mémoires de la Société Géologique de France* (1930): 4, 5-12.
Also Item 4669, vol. 4, pp. 1449-1456.

4659. "Observations nouvelles sur les Mammifères du Tertiaire inférieur de Belgique." *Bulletin de l'Académie royale de Belgique* (1925): 11, 48-50.
Also Item 4669, vol. 2, pp. 517-520.

4660. "Observations on the Elandsfontein Site near Hopefield." [1951.] Item 4669, vol. 10, pp. 4403-4405.

4661. "Observations sur les Australopithécinés." [March, 1952.] Item 4337, pp. 251-255.

4662. "Observations sur les changements de niveau marin dans la région d'Obock." *Compte-rendu Sommaire et Bulletin de la Société géologique de France*, November 7, 1932, pp. 180-181.
Also Item 4669, vol. 4, pp. 1695-1696.

4663. "Observations sur l'enseignement de la préhistoire." [September 23, 1948.] Item 4669, vol. 10, p. 4254.
"Sur l'enseignement de la préhistoire." Item 4385, pp. 175-178.

4664. "Observations sur la flore et la faune entre Urumchi
       et Aksu (sept. 1931)." In "Résultats scientifiques
       d'un voyage en Asie centrale," by A. Raymond. *Revue
       de géographie physique et de géologie dynamique*
       (1938): 71-73.
       Also Item 4669, vol. 6, pp. 2794-2796.

4665. "Observations sur la lenteur d'évolution des faunes de
       Mammifères continentales." *Paleobiologica* (1928):
       1, 55-60.
       Also Item 4669, vol. 2, pp. 862-867.

4666. "Observations sur les roches métamorphiques du plateau
       Somali près de Harrar." In "Études géologiques en
       Éthiopie, Somalie et Arabie méridionale." *Mémoires
       de la Société géologique de France* (1930): 4, 103.
       Also Item 4669, vol. 4, p. 1468.

4667. "Observations sur la signification et les conditions
       biologiques de la recherche." *Le Moncelet*, July 2,
       1939, p. 4.

4668. "Oecuménisme." [December 15, 1946.] Item 4805, pp.
       251-254.

4669. *L'oeuvre scientifique.* 10 vols.; Olten/Freiburg-im-Breis-
       gau: Walter Verlag, 1971. Contains Items 4323, 4326,
       4330, 4331, 4336, 4338, 4342, 4349, 4351, 4352, 4354,
       4360, 4363, 4364, 4367, 4368, 4371, 4381, 4387, 4388,
       4397, 4398, 4401, 4402, 4404, 4410, 4417, 4419, 4420,
       4421, 4425, 4426, 4427, 4428, 4433, 4434, 4449, 4450,
       4460, 4461, 4465, 4466, 4467, 4468, 4479, 4480, 4481,
       4482, 4483, 4484, 4485, 4488, 4491, 4492, 4493, 4494,
       4495, 4496, 4497, 4498, 4504, 4505, 4506, 4508, 4515,
       4518, 4519, 4520, 4534, 4536, 4538, 4545, 4554, 4556,
       4587, 4589, 4590, 4591, 4592, 4595, 4596, 4597, 4598,
       4599, 4605, 4615, 4618, 4619, 4620, 4621, 4622, 4623,
       4624, 4627, 4639, 4642, 4649, 4651, 4657, 4658, 4659,
       4660, 4662, 4663, 4664, 4665, 4666, 4671, 4674, 4675,
       4676, 4677, 4678, 4679, 4681, 4682, 4683, 4684, 4685,
       4687, 4691, 4692, 4694, 4695, 4708, 4711, 4712, 4719,
       4723, 4725, 4733, 4734, 4735, 4744, 4747, 4757, 4758,
       4765, 4766, 4767, 4768, 4769, 4770, 4771, 4772, 4773,
       4774, 4775, 4776, 4777, 4778, 4780, 4781, 4782, 4783,
       4784, 4785, 4786, 4787, 4788, 4789, 4790, 4791, 4792,
       4793, 4794, 4796, 4797, 4798, 4799, 4800, 4812, 4814,
       4817, 4818, 4820, 4824, 4831, 4836, 4837, 4841, 4842,
       4844, 4845, 4846, 4847, 4848, 4849, 4853, 4857, 4859,

4872, 4880, 4881, 4882, 4886, 4887, 4888, 4889, 4890,
4891, 4892, 4893, 4894, 4895, 4896, 4897, 4898, 4899,
4900, 4901, 4902, 4903, 4904, 4905, 4906, 4907, 4908,
4909, 4910, 4911, 4912, 4913, 4914, 4916, 4917, 4918,
4919, 4920, 4921, 4922, 4923, 4924, 4925, 4926, 4927,
4928, 4929, 4930, 4931, 4932, 4933, 4934, 4935, 4936,
4937, 4938.

4670. *Oeuvres.* 13 vols.; Paris: Seuil, 1956-1976. Contains
Items 4321, 4337, 4346, 4385, 4392, 4431, 4436, 4444,
4507, 4603, 4706, 4805, 4873.

4671. "On an Enigmatic Pteropod-like Fossil from the Lower
Cambrian of Southern Shansi, *Binoculites Grabaui*,
nov. gen., nov. sp." *Bulletin of the Geological
Society of China* (1931): 10, 179-184.
Also Item 4669, vol. 4, pp. 1496-1506.

4672. "On Human Suffering." *Continuum*, Fall, 1967, pp. 576-
580.

4673. "On the Biological Meaning of Human Socialisation."
[May 15, 1952.] Mimeographed. 5 pp., single-
spaced.

4674. "On the Occurrence of a Mongolian Eocene Perissodactyle
in the Red Sandstone of Sichuan, S.W. Honan." *Bulletin of the Geological Society of China* (1930): 9,
331-332.
Also Item 4669, vol. 3, pp. 1234-1236.

4675. "On the Presumable Existence of a World-Wide Subarctic
Sheet of Human Culture at the Dawn of the Neolithic."
Bulletin of the Geological Society of China (1939):
19, 333-339.
Also Item 4669, vol. 7, pp. 3060-3066.

4676. "On the Significance and Trend of Human Socialisation."
[February, 1951.] Item 4669, vol. 10, pp. 4291-4292.

4677. "On the Trend and Significance of Human Socialisation."
[April 9, 1948.] Item 4669, vol. 10, pp. 4243-4253.

4678. "On the Zoological Position and the Evolutionary Significance of Australopithecines." *Transactions of
the New York Academy of Science* (1952): 14, 208-210.
Also *Yearbook of Physical Anthropology for 1952*.
New York: Wenner-Gren Foundation, 1954, vol. 7, pp.
37-39.
Also Item 4669, vol. 10, pp. 4433-4436.

4679. "On Two Skulls of Machairodus from the Lower Pleis-
       tocene Beds of Choukoutien." *Bulletin of the Geo-
       logical Society of China* (1939): 19, 235-256.
       Also Item 4669, vol. 7, pp. 3015-3036.

4680. "Orient et Occident ou la mystique de la personnalité."
       Notes taken by Claude Cuénot of a conference at the
       École Normale Supérieure in 1952 or 1953. Item 990,
       pp. 174-175.

4681. "Le Paléolithique du Siam." *L'anthropologie* (1950):
       54, 547-549.
       Also Item 4669, vol. 10, pp. 4388-4390.

4682. "Le Paléolithique en Chine." *L'anthropologie* (1923):
       23, 630-632.
       Also Item 4669, vol. 10, pp. 4590-4592.

4683. "Le Paléolithique en Somalie française et en Abyssinie."
       L'anthropologie (1930): 40, 331-334.
       Also Item 4669, vol. 3, pp. 1175-1178.

4684. "Paleontological Notes." *Bulletin of the Geological
       Society of China* (1926): 5, pp. 57-59.
       Also Item 4669, vol. 2, pp. 734-736.

4685. "La paléontologie des Mammifères en Chine et l'oeuvre
       du Musée Hoangho-Paiho." *Revue scientifique* (1930):
       68, 360-362.
       Also Item 4669, vol. 4, pp. 1469-1475.

4686. "La paléontologie et l'apparation de l'homme." *Revue
       de Philosophie* (1923): 30, 144-173.
       Also Item 4337, pp. 53-81.

4687. "Paleontology of Mammifers in China." *Irish Eccles-
       iastical Record* (1930): 36, 363-369.
       Also Item 4669, vol. 3, pp. 1168-1174.

4688. "Panthéisme et Christianisme." [January 17, 1923.]
       Item 4392, pp. 71-92.

4689. "Le paradoxe transformiste. À propos de la dernière
       critique du transformisme par M. Vialleton." *Revue
       des questions scientifiques* (1925): 7, 53-80.
       Also Item 4873, pp. 115-142.

4690. "La parole attendue." [October 31, 1940.] Item 3041, pp. 22-29.
Also Item 4431, pp. 99-110.

4691. "The Past Climates of North China Since the Lower Cretaceous." *Proceedings of the Sixth Pan-Pacific Scientific Congress.* Berkeley: University of California Press, 1939, vol. 3, pp. 627-629.
Also Item 4669, vol. 7, pp. 3105-3108.

4692. "Peking Man: Our Most Apelike Relative." *Natural History* (1937): 40, 514-517.
Also Item 4669, vol. 6, pp. 2782-2789.

4693. "La pensée religieuse devant le fait de l'évolution, débat organisé par l'U.C.S.F. en février 1950." *Bulletin de l'U.C.S.F.* (1950): 12, 19-20.
Also Item 4873, pp. 347-349.

4694. "Le Père Teilhard de Chardin présente la note suivante de M. et Mme. Kelly sur un Gisement moustérien nouvellement decouvert à la Cave (Vilhoneur), (Charente)." *L'anthropologie* (1928): 38, 348.
Also Item 4669, vol. 3, p. 1098.

4695. "Le peuplement de l'Asie." *Bulletin de la Société des études indochinoises de Saigon* (1955): 30, 351-353.
Also Item 4669, vol. 10, pp. 4577-4579.

4696. "La peur existentielle." Notes taken by L. Roinet of a conference on January 29, 1949. Manuscript, 1 p.

4697. Number deleted.

4698. "Le phénomène chrétien." [May 10, 1950.] Item 4392, pp. 231-244.

4699. "Un phénomène de contre-evolution en biologie humaine ou la peur d'existence." [January 26, 1949.] Item 4321, pp. 187-202.

4700. "Le phénomène humain." [September, 1928.] Item 4805, pp. 115-128.

4701. "Le phénomène humain." *Revue des questions scientifiques* (1930): 18, 390-406.
Also Item 4873, pp. 227-243.

4702. *Le phénomène humain.* [1938-1940.] Paris: Seuil, 1955.
       Volume 1 of Item 4670.
          Also 1970.
          Der Mensch im Kosmos. 2d ed., München: C.H. Beck,
          1959.
          Also 1965.
          The Phenomenon of Man. London: Collins, 1960.
          Also New York: Harper, 1960.
          Also rev. ed., 1965.
          Het verschijnsel mens. Utrecht: Aula-Boeken, 1963.

4703. "Le phénomène humain (Comment, au-delà d'une 'anthro-
       pologie' philosophico-juridico-littéraire, établir
       une vraie science de l'homme, c'est-à-dire une anthro-
       podynamique et une anthropogénèse?)." [1954.] Item
       4385, pp. 197-200.

4704. "Le phénomène spirituel." [March, 1937.] Item 4444,
       pp. 115-139.

4704a. "The Phenomenon of (Colored) Man: The Teilhard Papers
       III, Excerpts from Letters." *Triumph*, January, 1972,
       pp. 28-30. See also Items 4759, 4855.

4705. "La place de l'homme dans la nature." *Revue des étudi-
       ants de l'Université nationale de Peiping* (1932):
       1-9.
          Also Item 4873, pp. 247-256.

4706. "La place de l'homme dans l'univers. Réflexions sur
       la complexité." [November 15, 1942.] Item 4873,
       pp. 305-326.

4707. "Place de la technique dans une biologie générale de
       l'humanité." [January 16, 1947.] Item 3421, pp.
       159-169.

4708. "The Pleistocene of China: Stratigraphy and Correla-
       tions." *Early Man*, by G.G. MacCurdy. Philadelphia:
       Lippincott, 1937, pp. 211-230.
          Also Item 4669, vol. 6, pp. 2531-2540.

4709. "Point de vue du P. Teilhard de Chardin à propos d'une
       conférence de Louis Lavelle au Centre catholique
       des intellectuels français 'Pourquoi un monde?'"
       [1947.] Typescript. 2 pp., double-spaced.

4710. "Position de l'homme et signification de la socialisation humaine dans la nature." *L'anthropologie* (1948):
52, 209-219.
Also Item 4346, pp. 275-289.

4711. "The Post-Villafranchian Interval in North China."
Bulletin of the Geological Society of China (1937):
17, 169-176.
Also Item 4669, vol. 6, pp. 2512-2519.

4712. "Pour fixer les traits d'un monde qui s'efface--La
semaine d'ethnologie religieuse de Louvain." *Le
Correspondant*, November 10, 1912, pp. 553-560.
Also Item 4669, vol. 1, pp. 75-82.

4713. "Pour Odette et pour Jean." [1928.] Item 4385, pp.
157-164.

4714. "Pour une théologie de la science moderne." *Esprit*,
November 1-2, 1947, pp. 10-11.
"Sur la valeur religieuse de la recherche." Item
4805, pp. 255-264.
Also Item 4864.

4715. "Pour y voir clair. Réflexions sur deux formes inverses
d'esprit." [July 25, 1950.] Item 4321, pp. 223-236.

4716. *The Prayer of the Universe*. London: Collins, 1973.
Excerpts from Item 4436.

4717. "Préface." In Item 4075.

4718. "Préface." Item 3932, pp. 9-12.
Also Item 4321, pp. 253-257.

4719. Preface of *Évolution et finalité*, unpublished work of
Oliver Costa de Beauregard, written under the pseudo-
nym of Jean Montassey. [February 12, 1948.] Item
4669, vol. 9, pp. 4255-4257.

4720. Preface to Romain Rolland's letters to a Catholic
friend [Jeanne Mortier]. *Europe* (1965): 431/432,
pp. 114-115.

4721. "La préhistoire et ses progrès." *Études* (1913): 134,
40-53.
Also Item 4337, pp. 23-28.

4722. "Pre-humain, humain, ultra-humain." *Idées et forces*
       (1949): 5, 59-69.

4723. "Présentation d'échantillons de quercyte (phosphocar-
       bonate de chaux)." *Bulletin de la Société géologique
       de France* (1914): 14, 9-10.
       Also Item 4669, vol. 1, pp. 86-88.

4724. *Le prêtre*. [1918.] Paris: Seuil, 1965.
       Also 1968.
       Also Item 4436, pp. 203-224.
       Also *Christus* (1964): 11, 393-401.
       Il Sacerdote. Brescia: Opera Sacerdotale, 1965.
       Also 2d ed., 1965.

4725. "Un problème de géologie asiatique: le faciès mongol."
       Geobiologia (1945): 2, 1-12.
       Also Item 4669, vol. 9, pp. 4045-4056.

4726. "Le problème du mal, réponse à un ami." Typescript.
       4 pp., single-spaced.

4727. "Un problème majeur pour l'anthropologie: y a-t-il,
       oui ou non, chez l'homme, prolongation et trans-
       formation du processus biologique de l'évolution?"
       [December 30, 1951.] Item 4321, pp. 325-332.

4728. "Profession de foi." [September 23, 1933.] Item 497,
       pp. 41-49.
       Also Item 501, pp. 41-49.
       Also Item 990, pp. 48-49.

4729. "Propos du Père Teilhard de Chardin." [June, 1954.]
       Journal, by Jean Guitton. Paris: Plon, 1959, pp.
       235-236.

4730. "The Psychological Conditions of Human Unification."
       Cross Currents, Fall, 1952, pp. 1-5. Excerpt from
       Item 4400.

4731. "La puissance spirituelle de la matière." [August 8,
       1919.] Item 4385, pp. 80-93.
       Also Item 4523, pp. 59-75.

4732. "Que faut-il penser du transformisme?" *Dossiers de
       la Commission Synodale (Peiping)* (1929): 2, 462-
       469.
       Also *Revue des questions scientifiques* (1930):

17, 89-99.
Also Item 4873, pp. 213-223.
Chinese version in *Tientsin University (Hautes Études)* (1929): 3, 61-66.

4733. "Quelques données nouvelles sur la mise en place de la faune moderne (Mammifères) en Chine septentrionale." *Compte-rendu Sommaire de la Société de biogéographie* (1928): 34, 1-3.
Also Item 4669, vol. 2, pp. 856-858.

4734. "Quelques observations biogéographiques en Chine." *Compte-rendu Sommaire de la Société de biogéographie* (1930): 60, 94-96.
Also Item 4669, vol. 4, pp. 1476-1479.

4735. "Quelques observations sur les terres jaunes (loess) de Chine et de Mongolie." *Société géologique de France, livre jubilaire 1830-1930* (1930): 2, 605-612.
Also Item 4669, vol. 3, pp. 1237-1244.

4736. "Quelques réflexions sur la conversion du monde." [October 9, 1936.] Item 4805, pp. 155-166.

4737. "Quelques réflexions sur les droits de l'homme." *Autour de la nouvelle Déclaration Universelle des Droits de l'Homme.* Paris: Sagittaire, 1949, pp. 88-89.
Also Item 4346, pp. 247-249.

4738. "Quelques réflexions sur le retenissement spirituel de la bombe atomique." *Études* (1946): 250, 223-230.
Also Item 4346, pp. 179-187.
"Some Reflections on the Spiritual Repercussions of the Atom Bomb." *Wiseman Review*, Winter, 1965, pp. 278-285.

4739. "Quelques remarques 'pour y voir clair' sur l'essence du sentiment mystique." [1951.] Item 4431, pp. 225-230.

4740. "Quelques vues générales sur l'essence du christianisme." [May, 1939.] Item 4392, pp. 153-160.

4741. "Qu'est-ce que la vie?" *Les Nouvelles littéraires*, March 2, 1950, col. 1.
Also *Panorama des idées contemporaines*, ed. by

Gaëtan Picon. Paris: Gallimard, 1957, p. 632.
Also Item 4805, pp. 273-276.

4742. "Rapport en vue d'obtenir un laboratoire des Hautes-
études pour des recherches de 'géologie continen-
tale' (considerée dans ses rapports avec la paléontologie humaine)." [October 1, 1937.] Item 193,
pp. 44-46.

4743. "Le rebondissement humain de l'évolution et ses con-
sequences." *Revue des questions scientifiques*
(1947): 119, 166-185.
Also Item 4346, pp. 253-271.

4744. "Les récents progrès de la préhistoire en Chine."
L'anthropologie (1935): 45, 735-740.
Also Item 4669, vol. 5, pp. 2250-2256.

4745. "Recherche, travail et adoration." [March, 1955.]
Item 4805, pp. 281-289.

4746. "Les recherches pour la découverte des origines humaines en Afrique, au sud du Sahara." *L'anthropologie* (1954): 58, 74-78.
Also Item 4337, pp. 265-275.

4747. "Les recherches préhistoriques en Extreme-Orient."
L'anthropologie (1939): 49, 251-252.
Also Item 4669, vol. 7, p. 3101.

4748. "La réflexion de l'énergie." *Revue des questions
scientifiques* (1952): 123, 481-497.
Also Item 4321, pp. 333-353.

4749. *Réflexions et prières dans l'espace-temps.* Paris:
Seuil, 1972.

4750. "Réflexions sur le bonheur." [December 28, 1943.]
Item 3292, pp. 53-70.
Also Item 4431, pp. 119-140.

4751. "Réflexions sur la compression humaine." *Psyché* (1953):
83, 1-6.
Also Item 4321, pp. 355-363.

4752. "Réflexions sur la gravité." Manuscript. 2 pp.,
single-spaced.

4753. "Réflexions sur le péché originel." [November 15, 1947.] Item 4392, pp. 217-230.

4754. "Réflexions sur la probabilité scientifique et les conséquences religieuses d'un ultra-humain." [March 25, 1951.] Item 4321, pp. 279-291.

4755. *Réflexions sur le progrès.* Peking: Privately printed, 1941. Contains Items 4346, 4347, 4829.

4756. "Réflexions sur l'ultra-humain ou 'les phases d'une planète vivant.'" [April 27, 1950.] Mimeographed. 17 pp., double-spaced; 10 pp., single-spaced.
"Du préhumain à l'ultrahumain." *Almanach des Sciences* (1951): 149-155.
"Du préhumain à l'ultra-humain ou 'les phases d'une planète vivante.'" Item 4346, pp. 377-385.

4757. "Remarques sur les flexures continentales de Chine." *Bulletin de la Société géologique de France* (1946): 16, 497-502.
Also Item 4669, vol. 10, pp. 4223-4228.

4758. "Remerciements de M. Teilhard de Chardin." [On receiving the Prix Viquesnel.] *Compte-rendu Sommaire et Bulletin de la Société géologique de France* (1922): 22, 131.
Also Item 4669, vol. 1, pp. 420-422.

4759. "Replacing Christianity: The Teilhard Papers II, The Human Sense." *Triumph*, December, 1971, pp. 28-31+.
See also Items 4704a, 4855.

4760. "Réponse aux critiques du R.P. Garrigou-Lagrange, O.P." [1947.] Typescript. 2 pp., double-spaced.

4761. "Réponses au Questionnaire du C.N.R.S." 1948-1952. Manuscripts. Five half-pages, single-spaced.

4762. "Les résultats scientifiques de l'expédition Citroën-centre Asie." *La géographie (Terre, air, mer)* (1932): 58, 379-390.
Also Item 4669, vol. 4, pp. 1697-1708.

4763. Review, "Les Australopithèques et le chainon manquant (ou "Missing Link") de l'évolution," of *Finding the Missing Link*, by R. Broom. *Études* (1950): 265, 340-343.
Also Item 4337, pp. 177-183.

4764. Review of *Catalyse et biologie*, by Frédéric Gillot.
       [February 10, 1950.] Typescript. 1 p., single-
       spaced.

4765. Review, "The Continental Basement of the Western Tarim
       Basin According to Dr. Erik Norin." *Geobiologia*
       (1943): 1, 73-77.
       Also Item 4669, vol. 9, pp. 3827-3831.

4766. Review of *Diluviale Menschenfund in Obercassel bei
       Bonn*, by Max Verworn, R. Bonnet and G. Steinmann.
       L'anthropologie (1921): 31, 533-536.
       Also Item 4669, vol. 1, pp. 249-252.

4767. Review of *Der diluviale Menschenfund von Obercassel
       bei Bonn*, by M. Verworn, R. Bonnet and G. Stein-
       mann. *L'anthropologie* (1923): 33, 206-208.
       Also Item 4669, vol. 2, pp. 429-431.

4768. Review of *Essai sur la théorie psychologique de la vie*,
       by Dr. Tilicheef. *Études* (1950): 266, 285.
       Also Item 4669, vol. 10, p. 4290.

4769. Review of *Études sur l'époque glaciaire dans l'Inde
       et sur les cultures humaines trouvées en association
       (Studies on the Ice Age in India and Associated Human
       Cultures)*, by H. de Terra and T.T. Paterson. *L'anthro-
       pologie* (1939): 49, 729-731.
       Also Item 4669, vol. 7, pp. 3256-3258.
       "The Quaternary Sequence in North India According
       to Dr. de Terra." *Geobiologia* (1943): 1, 97-101.
       Also Item 4669, vol. 7, pp. 3851-3855.

4770. Review, "L'évolution rédemptrice du P. Teilhard de
       Chardin," par ***. *Études* (1950): 266, 284.
       Also Item 4669, vol. 10, p. 4290.

4771   Review of *L'exigence idéaliste et le fait de l'évolu-
       tion*, by Édouard Le Roy. Published under the title,
       "La pensée dans la science," and the pseudonym, Max
       Bégouën, in *La Vie catholique en France et à l'étran-
       ger*, August 18, 1928, p. 5.

4772. Review, "The Flora and Climate of Northwestern China
       During the Miocene According to Dr. Ralph W. Chaney."
       Geobiologia (1943): 1, 86-91.
       Item 4669, vol. 9, pp. 3840-3845.

4773. Review of *Formation des continents et progression de la vie*, by H. and G. Termier. *Études* (1955): 284, 419.
Also Item 4669, vol. 10, pp. 4570-4572.

4774. Review of *La genèse des montagnes*, by M. Roubault. *Études* (1950): 264, 279-280.
Also Item 4669, vol. 10, pp. 4285-4286.

4775. Review, "The Genesis of the Japanese Islands as Seen by Dr. T. Kobayashi." *Geobiologia* (1943): 1, 63-72.
Also Item 4669, vol. 9, pp. 3817-3826.

4776. Review of *Géologie de l'Afrique*, by Raymond Furon. *Études* (1950): 266, 132-133.
Also Item 4669, vol. 10, p. 4289.

4777. Review of *La grotte de l'observatoire à Monaco*, by M. Boule and L. de Villeneuve. *L'anthropologie* (1928): 38, 150-153.
Also Item 4669, vol. 3, pp. 1102-1106.

4778. Review of *Histoire géologique de la biosphère*, by H. and G. Termier. *Études* (1953): 277, 425-426.
Also Item 4669, vol. 10, pp. 4558-4559.

4779. Review of *History of the Conflict Between Religion and Science*, by J.W. Draper. Typescript. 1 p., single-spaced.

4780. Review, "Les hommes fossiles. A propos d'un livre récent," of *Les hommes fossiles, éléments de paléontologie humaine*. by Marcellin Boule. *Études* (1921): 166, 570-577.
Also Item 4337, pp. 41-50.
"Fossil Man." *The Living Age* (1922): 221, 415-419.
Also Item 4669, vol. 1, pp. 402-406.

4781 Review of *Les hommes fossiles, éléments de paléontologie humaine*, by M. Boule and H. Vallois. *Études* (1947): 252, 122-123.
Also Item 4669, vol. 9, pp. 4232-4233.

4782. Review of *Die menschlichen Skeletreste aus dem Kampfe-'schen Bruch im Travertin von Ehringsdorf bei Weimar*, by Hans Virchow. *L'anthropologie* (1922): 32, 129-132.
Also Item 4669, vol. 1, pp. 407-410.

4783.   Review of *Note préliminaire sur les formations cénozoïques et plus récentes de la chaine annamitique septentrionale et du Haut-Laos (stratigéographie, préhistoire, anthropologie)*, by J. Fromaget and E. Saurin. *L'anthropologie* (1939): 49, 137-138. Also Item 4669, vol. 7, pp. 3259-3260.

4784.   Review of *On the Occurrence of Aboriginal Stone Implements of Unusual Types in the Tablelands of Central Australia*, by W. Howchin. *L'anthropologie* (1922): 32, 547-548. Also Item 4669, vol. 1, pp. 418-419.

4785.   Review of *The Origin and Evolution of the Human Dentition. A Paleontological Review*, by William K. Gregory. *L'anthropologie* (1922): 32, 285-288. Also Item 4669, vol. 1, pp. 411-414.

4786.   Review of *La planète au pillage*, by F. Osborn. *Études* (1949): 263, 402-403. Also Item 4669, vol. 10, pp. 4268-4269.

4787.   Review, "The Pleistocene of Hsikang According to Dr. J.G. Andersson." *Geobiologia* (1943): 1, 92-94. Also Item 4669, vol. 9, pp. 3846-3848.

4788.   Review, "The Pleistocene Sequence of Taiwan (Formosa) According to Dr. Hayasaka." *Geobiologia* (1943): 1, 95-96. Also Item 4669, vol. 9, pp. 3849-3850.

4789.   Review of *La préhistoire*, by A. Vayson de Pradenne, *Études* (1939): 238, 564-565. Also Item 4669, vol. 7, p. 3104.

4790.   Review of *Problématique de l'évolution*, by François Meyer. *Bulletin de l'U.C.S.F.* (1955): 25, 15-17. Also Item 4669, vol. 10, pp. 4574-4575.

4791.   Review of *Problématique de l'évolution*, by François Meyer. *Études* (1955): 285, 279. Also Item 4669, vol. 10, p. 4576.

4792.   Review, "Quantitative Zoology According to G.G. Simpson." *Geobiologia* (1943): 1, 139-141. Also Item 4669, vol. 9, pp. 3893-3904.

4793. Review of *Qu'est-ce que la vie?* by E. Schrödinger. *Études* (1951): 268, 275-276. Also Item 4669, vol. 10, pp. 4418-4419.

4794. Review of *Les religions de la préhistoire. L'âge paléolithique*, by Th. Mainage. *L'anthropologie* (1922): 32, 525-526. Also Item 4669, vol. 1, pp. 415-416.

4795. Review of *Rythme et modalités de l'évolution*, by G.G. Simpson. *L'anthropologie* (1951): 54, 460-461.

4796. Review of *Rythme et modalités de l'évolution*, by G.G. Simpson. *Études* (1950): 265, 278. Also Item 4669, vol. 10, pp. 4416-4417.

4797. Review of *Sa Majesté le pétrole*, by Georges Le Fevre. *Études* (1950): 266, 130. Also Item 4669, vol. 10, p. 4288.

4798. Review of *The Status of the Dingo*, by F. Wood-Jones. *L'anthropologie* (1922): 32, 546-547. Also Item 4669, vol. 1, pp. 546-547.

4799. Review of *Über einen bei Ehringsdorf in der Nähe von Weimar gefundende Unterkiefer des "Homo primigenius,"* by G. Schwalbe. *L'anthropologie* (1921): 31, 531-533. Also Item 4669, vol. 1, pp. 247-248.

4800. "Les roches éruptives post-paléozoïques du nord de la Chine." *Bulletin of the Geological Society of China* (1928): 7, 1-11. Also Item 4669, vol. 2, pp. 878-888.

4801. "La route de l'Ouest. Vers une mystique nouvelle." [September 8, 1932.] Item 4431, pp. 45-64.

4802. "Le royaume de Dieu." [July, 1954.] In Item 1587a.

4803. "Sauvons l'humanité." [November 11, 1936.] Mimeographed. 34 pp., double-spaced. Also Malakoff (Seine): G. Durassié, 1940. Also Item 3920, pp. 65-97. Also Item 4805, pp. 167-192. "La crise presente. Réflexions d'un naturaliste." *Études* (1937): 233, 145-165. "Les colonnes d'avenir." *Pensée française*, November 15, 1956, pp. 7-11.

4804. "Schéma (l'évolution vers Oméga)." Item 462, p. 215.

4805. *Science et Christ.* Paris: Seuil, 1965. Volume 9 of
        Item 4670. Contains Items 4320, 4353, 4374, 4376,
        4389, 4440, 4528, 4609, 4629, 4668, 4700, 4714, 4736,
        4741, 4745, 4803, 4806, 4826, 4843.
            Science and Christ. London: Collins, 1968.
            Also New York: Harper & Row, 1968.

4806. "Science et Christ (ou analyse et synthèse). Re-
        marques sur la manière dont l'étude scientifique
        de la matière peut et doit servir à remonter jusqu'
        au centre divin." [February 27, 1921.] Item 4805,
        pp. 45-62.

4807. "Le sens de la croix." [December 24, 1917.] Manuscript.
        2 pp., single-spaced.

4808. "Le sens de l'espèce chez l'homme." [May 31, 1949.]
        Item 4321, pp. 203-210.

4809. "Le sens humain." [February 12, 1929.] Item 4431,
        pp. 19-44.

4810. "Un seuil mental sous nos pas: du cosmos à la cosmo-
        génèse." [March 15, 1951.] Item 4321, pp. 259-
        277. See also Item 4416.

4811. "La seule tactique digne des plus hautes traditions
        de la Compagnie." [January, 1931.] Manuscript. 9
        lines, single-spaced.

4812. "The Significance of Piedmont Gravels in Continental
        Geology (with an Application to Northern and Western
        China)." *Report of XVI International Geological Con-
        gress, Washington.* Washington: The Congress, 1935,
        vol. 2, pp. 1031-1039.
            Also Item 4669, vol. 5, pp. 2137-2145.

4813. "La signification et la valeur constructrice de la
        souffrance." *Le trait d'union C.M.* (1933): 45,
        6-11.
            Also *Jubilee*, June, 1962, pp. 21-23.
            Also in Item 501.
            Also Item 4444, pp. 59-66.

4814. "Le Sinanthropus de Péking. État actuel de nos con-
        naissances sur le fossile et son gisement." *L'anthro-
        pologie* (1931): 41, 1-11.
            Also Item 4669, vol. 4, pp. 1485-1495.

4815. "Sinanthropus pekinensis." *Primitive Man* (1930): 3, 46-48.

4816. "Les singularités de l'espèce humaine." *Annales de paléontologie* (1954): 41, 1-54. Also Item 4337, pp. 295-375.

4817. "Some Observations on the Archaeological Material Collected by Mr. A.S. Lukashkin near Tsitsikar." *Bulletin of the Geological Society of China* (1931): 11, 183-200. Also Item 4669, vol. 4, pp. 1507-1524.

4818. "Un sommaire de ma perspective 'phénomenologique' du monde." [January, 1954.] *Les études philosophiques* (1955): 10, 569-571. Also Item 1800, pp. 216-219. Also Item 4669, vol. 10, pp. 4570-4572.

4819. "Sommaire des titres scientifiques de P. Teilhard de Chardin." [October 1, 1946.] Typescript. 1 p., single-spaced.

4820. "South African Archaeological Society." [October, 1951.] Typescript. 2 pp., single-spaced. Also Item 4669, vol. 10, pp. 4406-4407.

4821. "Souvenirs d'enfance." In Item 2597.

4822. "Spiritualistic Evolution." Speech at Villanova University on receiving the Mendel Medal, 1937. Chapbook I, Woodstock College Library, pp. 16-19.

4823. "La structure phylétique du groupe humain." *Annales de paléontologie* (1951): 37, 49-79. Also Item 4337, pp. 187-234.

4824. "La succession des faunes de Mammifères en Chine depuis le Tertiaire." *Compte-rendu Sommaire de la Société de biogéographie* (1939): 134, 27-29. Also Item 4669, vol. 7, pp. 3102-3103.

4825. "Une suite au problème des origenes humaines--La multiplicité des mondes habités." [June 5, 1953.] Item 4392, pp. 273-282.

4826. "Super-humanité, super-Christ, super-charité. De nouvelles dimensions pour l'avenir." [August, 1943.]

Item 4805, pp. 193-218.
"Super-humanity, Super-Christ, Super-charity."
Critic (1968-69): 27, 60-64.

4827. *Sur l'amour.* Paris: Seuil, 1967.
       On Love. London: Collins, 1972.
       Also New York: Harper & Row, 1972.

4828. "Sur l'apparence nécessairement discontinué de toute
       série évolutive." *L'anthropologie* (1926): 36, 320-
       321.
       Also Item 4873, pp. 161-162.

4829. "Sur les bases possibles d'un credo humain commun."
       Item 4755, pp. 21-27.
       Also in Item 4346.

4830. *Sur le bonheur.* Paris: Seuil, 1966.
       Also in Item 4431.
       On Happiness. London: Collins, 1973.

4831. "Sur la découverte de couches mézozoïques à poissons
       dans la région de Hailar." *Publication de la Musée
       Hoangho-Paiho* (1936): 33, 1-36.
       Also Item 4669, vol. 6, pp. 2461-2463.

4832. "Sur les degrés de certitude scientifique de l'idée
       d'évolution." *Atti del Congresso internazionale
       de filosofia promosso dall'istituto de studi filo-
       sofici*, Rome, November 15-20, 1946. Milan: Castel-
       lani, 1948, vol. 2, pp. 537-539.

4833. "Sur l'existence probable, en avant de nous, d'un
       'ultra-humain' (réflexions d'un biologiste)." Jan-
       uary 6, 1950. Item 4346, pp. 353-364.

4834. "Sur les miracles." *Dictionnaire des saints de tous
       les jours*, by Philippe Rouillard. Revest-Saint-
       Martin (Basses-Alpes): R. Morel, 1963.
       Also rev. ed.; Les Hautes Plaines de Mane: R.
       Morel, 1969.

4835. "Sur la nature du phénomène social humain, et ses
       relations cachées avec la gravité." [April 23,
       1948.] Item 4321, pp. 171-174.

4836. "Sur la nature et la signification des Collenia pré-
cambriennes." *Compte-rendu d'Académie des sciences*
(1952): 245, 845-847.
Also Item 4669, vol. 10, pp. 4430-4432.

4837. "Sur le présence d'un tarsier dans les phosphorites
du Quercy et sur l'origine tarsienne de l'homme."
L'anthropologie (1921): 31, 329-330.
Also Item 4669, vol. 1, pp. 215-216.

4838. "Sur la probabilité d'une bifurcation précoce du phy-
lum humain au voisinage immediat de ses origines."
Compte-rendu d'Académie des sciences (1953): 237,
1293-1294.
Also Item 4337, pp. 259-261.

4839. "Sur le progrès." [April 24, 1921.] Manuscript. 15
pp., single-spaced.

4840. *Sur la souffrance.* Paris: Seuil, 1974.
On Suffering. London: Collins, 1974. Contains
Item 4854.
Also London: Collins, 1975.

4841. "Sur la structure de l'île de Jersey." *Bulletin de la
Société géologique de France* (1920): 19, 273-278.
Also Item 4669, vol. 1, pp. 199-204.

4842. "Sur la succession des faunes de Mammifère dans l'Éocène inférieur européen." *Compte-rendu de l'Académie des sciences* (1920): 171, 1161-1162.
Also Item 4669, vol. 1, pp. 205-207.

4843. "Sur la valeur religieuse de la recherche." [August
20, 1947.] Item 4805, pp. 255-264.

4844. "Sur quelques Mammifères nouveaux du Tertiaire de la
Belgique." *Bulletin de l'Académie royale de Belgique*
(1926): 12, 210-215.
Also Item 4669, vol. 2, pp. 728-733.

4845. "Sur quelques primates des phosphorites du Quercy."
Annales de paléontologie (1916): 10, 1-20.
Also Item 4669, vol. 1, pp. 221-246.

4846. "Sur un cas remarquable d'orthogenèse de groupe:
l'évolution des Siphnéidés." *Paléontologie et*

transformisme. Paris: A. Michel, 1950.
Also Item 4669, vol. 10, pp. 4276-4280.

4847. "Sur une faune de Mammifères pontiens provenant de la
Chine septentrionale." *Compte-rendu de l'Académie
des sciences* (1922): 175, 979-981
Also Item 4669, vol. 1, pp. 386-388.

4848. "Sur une formation de carbono-phosphate de chaux d'âge
paléolithique." *Compte-rendu de l'Académie des sciences* (1913): 157, 1077-1079.
Also Item 4669, vol. 1, pp. 83-85.

4849. "Sur une mandible de Meganthropus." *Comte-rendu Sommaire et Bulletin de la Société géologique de France*
(1947): 309-310.
Also Item 4669, vol. 10, pp. 4241-4242.

4850. *Teilhard de Chardin levelei (Reszletek).* [Selected
Letters of Teilhard de Chardin.] São Paulo: Ahogy
lehet, 1967.

4851. "Teilhard de Chardin on Education." *Ave Maria*, October 10, 1964, p. 17. Exerpt from Item 4346.

4852. "Teilhard de Chardin's Note on a Discovery He Made in
the Ancient Deposits of the Vaal River at Harrisdale
near Barkly West." [August 25, 1951.] Manuscript.
5 lines.

4853. "Teilhard 1951 (S.A.)." Item 4669, vol. 10, pp. 4293-
4387.

4854. "Teilhard on Death." *Commonweal*, September 27, 1974,
p. 514. Excerpt from Item 4840.

4855. "The Teilhard Papers." *Triumph*, November, 1971, pp.
11-14+. Excerpt from Item 4392.

4856. "Témoignage fraternel." *Le trait d'union C.M.*, October, 1936, pp. 6-9.

4857. "Les tendances intellectuelles de la Chine moderne."
Dossiers de la Commission Synodale (Peiping) (1928):
1, 127-130.
Also Item 4669, vol. 2, pp. 868-871.

4858. "Terre promise." [February, 1919.] Item 4436, pp. 277-288.

4859. "The Times of the Loess and Early Man in China." In "Some Problems of Earth History." *Contributions of the Department of Geography and Geology (Yenching University)* (1929): 27, 14-16. Also Item 4669, vol. 3, pp. 1154-1156.

4860. "Titres et travaux de Pierre Teilhard de Chardin." [April, 1948.] Item 4385, pp. 201-224.

4861. *Toujours en avant.* Tournai: Desclée, 1970.

4862. "Transformisme et prologement en l'homme du mécanisme de l'évolution." [November 19, 1951.] Item 4321, pp. 311-323.

4863. "Trois choses que je vois ou: Une Weltanschauung en trois points." [February, 1948.] Item 4431, pp. 161-176.

4864. "Trois lettres de Chardin à Mounier." *Bulletin des Amis d'Emmanuel Mounier* (1966): 26, 29-32. Contains Item 4714.

4865. "Twenty-Three of the Chief Fossil Collecting Areas of China, 1885-1931, as Indicated by Teilhard." Item 3010, pp. 12-13.

4866. "L'ultra-humain." Notes taken by L. Roinet of a conference on October 16, 1949. Manuscript. 1 p.

4867. "L'union créatrice." [November 10, 1917.] Item 4436, pp. 151-176.

4868. "Les unités humaines naturelles. Essai d'une biologie et d'une morale des races." *Études* (1939): 240, 6-30. Also Item 4873, pp. 273-301.

4869. "Universalisation et union: un effort pour voir clair." [March 20, 1942.] Item 4321, pp. 83-101.

4870. "La vie cosmique." [April 24, 1916.] Item 4436, pp. 13-72.

4871. *Vie et planètes. Que se passe-t-il en ce moment sur la terre?* Peking: Catholic University Press, 1945. Also *Études* (1946): 249, 145-169. Also Item 4346, pp. 129-156.

4872.   "Le Villafranchien d'Asie et la question du Villa-
        franchien." *Compte-rendu Sommaire et Bulletin de
        la Société géologique de France* (1938): 325-327.
        Also Item 4669, vol. 7, pp. 2968-2970.

4873.   *La vision du passé.* Paris: Seuil, 1957. Volume 3
        of Item 4670. Contains 4358, 4394, 4424, 4464, 4477,
        4511, 4513, 4517, 4586, 4614, 4638, 4689, 4693, 4701,
        4705, 4706, 4732, 4828, 4868, 4874.
            La vision del pasado. Madrid: Taurus, 1958.
        Also 6th ed., 1967.
            Die Schau in die Vergangenheit. Olten/Freiburg-
        im-Breisgau: Walter-Verlag, 1965.
            The Vision of the Past. London: Collins, 1966.
        Also New York: Harper & Row, 1966.

4874.   "La vision du passé. Ce qu'elle apporte à la science
        et ce qu'elle lui ôte." *Études* (1949): 263, 308-
        315.
            Also Item 4873, pp. 335-343.
            "La vision de passé: ce qu'elle nous apporte, et
        ce qu'elle nous enlève." *Actualités scientifiques
        et industrielle.* Paris: Hermann, 1951, pp. 71-74.

4875.   "Werdegang eines Denkens. Briefe aus dem Feld."
        Dokumente (1962): 18, 171-182. Exerpts from Item
        4490.

4876.   *Worte des Glaubens.* Freiburg: Herder, 1976.

4877.   *Wybór pism.* [Selected Writings.] Warsaw: Pax, 1966.

4878.   "The Zest for Living." *Critic*, July-August, 1971,
        pp. 48-55. Excerpt from Item 4321.

4879.   with Andersson, Johan Gunnar. *Dans le sillage des
        sinanthropes. Lettres inédites de Pierre Teilhard
        de Chardin et Johan Gunnar Andersson, 1926-1934.*
        Paris: Fayard, 1971.

4880.   with Barbour, G.B., and E. Licent. "Geological Study
        of the Deposits of the Sang-kan-ho Basin." *Bulletin
        of the Geological Society of China* (1926): 5, 263-
        280.
            Also Item 4669, vol. 2, pp. 743-758.

4881.   with Barbour, G.B., and M.N. Bien. A Geological Re-
        connaissance Across the Eastern Tsinling." *Compte-*

rendu *Sommaire et Bulletin de la Société géologique de France*, June 3, 1935, p. 149.
Also Item 4669, vol. 5, p. 2181.

4882. with Barbour, G.B., and M.N. Bien. "A Geological Reconnaissance Across the Eastern Tsinling (Between Loyang and Hsichuan, Honan)." *Bulletin of the Geological Survey of China* (1935): 25, 9-37.
Also Item 4669, vol. 5, pp. 2152-2180.

4883. with Blondel, M. *Blondel et Teilhard de Chardin. Correspondance.* Paris: Beauchesne, 1965. Contains Items 2493, 2497, 3286.
Pierre Teilhard de Chardin, Maurice Blondel. Correspondence. London: Burns & Oates, 1967.
Also New York: Herder, 1967.
Blondel és Teilhard de Chardin levélvéltasa (magyarázatokkal). São Paulo: Rezek, 1967.
Maurice Blondel-Pierre Teilhard de Chardin. Briefwechsel. Freiburg-im-Breisgau/München: Alber, 1967.
Corrispondenza di Maurice Blondel et Pierre Teilhard de Chardin. Turin: Borla, 1968.
Blondel e Teilhard de Chardin. Correspondência. Lisbon: Livraria Morais, 1968.
Blondel y Teilhard. Correspondencia. Zaragoza: Hechos y Dichos, 1968.

4884. with Blondel, M. "Maurice Blondel et le P. Teilhard de Chardin, mémoires échangés en décembre 1919." *Archives de philosophie* (1961): 24, 123-156. Contains Item 4885.

4885. with Blondel, M. "Maurice Blondel et le Père Teilhard de Chardin." *Bulletin de l'U.C.S.F.* (1962): 66, 9-11. Excerpts from Item 4884.

4886. with Boule, M., H. Breuil, and E. Licent. "Le paléolithique de la Chine." *Archives de l'Institut de paléontologie humaine* (1928): 4, 1-139.
Also Item 4669, vol. 3, pp. 889-1097.

4887. with Breuil, H., and P. Wernert. "Les industries lithiques de Somalie française." *L'anthropologie* (1939): 49, 497-522.
Also Item 4669, vol. 7, pp. 3067-3092.

4888. with Breuil, G., and P. Wernert. "Le paléolithique du Harrar." *L'anthropologie* (1951): 55, 219-230.
Also Item 4669, vol. 10, pp. 4391-4402.

4889. with Davidson Black, P., C.C. Young, and W.C. Pei.
       "Fossil Man in China. The Choukoutien Cave Deposits
       with a Synopsis of Our Present Knowledge of the Late
       Cenozoic in China." *Memoirs of the Geological Sur-
       vey of China* (1933): 11, i-xi, 1-166.
       Also Item 4669, vol. 5, pp. 1903-2080.

4890. with De Terra, H. "Observations on the Upper Siwalik
       Formation and Later Pleistocene Deposits in India."
       Proceedings of the American Philosophical Society
       (1936): 76, 791-882.
       Also Item 4669, vol. 6, pp. 2425-2456.

4891. with De Terra, H. and H.L. Movius. "Geological and
       Archaeological Aspects of South-Eastern Asia."
       Nature (1938): 142, 275-278.
       Also Item 4669, vol. 7, pp. 2977-2985.

4892. with Dollo, L. "Les gisements de Mammifères paléo-
       cènes de la Belgique." *Quarterly Journal of the
       Geological Society of London* (1924): 80, 12-16.
       Also Item 4669, vol. 2, pp. 511-516.
       "The Deposits of Paleocene Mammalia in Belgium."
       Proceedings of the Geological Society of London
       (1924): 103.

4893. with Fraipont, C. "Note sur la présence dans le
       Tertiaire inférieur de Belgique d'un Condylarthré
       appartenant au groupe des Hyposodus." *Bulletin de
       l'Académie royale de Belgique* (1921): 7, 357-360.
       Also Item 4669, vol. 1, pp. 217-220.

4894. with Fritel, P.H. "Note sur quelques grès Mézozoïques
       à plantes de la Chine septentrionale." *Bulletin de
       la Société géologique de France* (1925): 25, 523-540.
       Also Item 4669, vol. 1, pp. 577-597.

4895. with Jodot, P., L. Joleand, and P. Lemoine. "Observa-
       tions sur le calcaire pisolithique de Vertus et du
       Mont Aimé (Marne)." *Bulletin de la Société géolog-
       ique de France* (1922): 22, 164-176.
       Also Item 4669, vol. 1, pp. 389-401.

4896. with Lamare, P. "Le cañon de l'Aouache et le volcan
       Fantalé." In "Études géologiques en Ethiopie, Soma-
       lie et Arabie meridionelle." *Mémoires de la Société
       géologique de France* (1930): 4, 13-20.
       Also Item 4669, vol. 4, pp. 1457-1467.

4897. with Lapparent, A. de. "Sur la découverte d'un rongeur du genre Paramys dans l'Éocène inférieur de Provence." *Compte-rendu Sommaire et Bulletin de la Société géologique de France*, February 6, 1933, pp. 26-27. Also Item 4669, vol. 5, pp. 2081-2082.

4898. with Lemoine, P. "Les gros blocs Quaternaires du port de Bonneuil." *La nature* (1923): 2560, 272. Also Item 4669, vol. 1, p. 428.

4899. with Leroy, P. "Chinese Fossil Mammals. A Complete Bibliography Analysed, Tabulated, Annotated and Indexed." *Publication de l'Institut de géobiologie Pékin* (1942): 8, 1-142. Also Item 4669, vol. 8, pp. 3491-3634.

4900. with Leroy, P. "Les Félidés de Chine." *Publication de l'Institut de géobiologie. Pékin* (1945): 11, v-vii, 1-58. Also Item 4669, vol. 9, pp. 4095-4158.

4901. with Leroy, P. "Les Mustélidés de Chine." *Publication de l'Institut de géobiologie. Pékin* (1945): 12, v-viii, 1-56. Also Item 4669, vol. 9, pp. 4159-4222.

4902. with Licent, É. "Geological Observations in Northern Manchuria and Barga (Hailar)." *Bulletin of the Geological Society of China* (1930): 9, 23-35. Also Item 4669, vol. 4, pp. 1429-1441.

4903. with Licent, É. "New Remains of Postschizotherium from S.E. Shanhi." *Bulletin of the Geological Society of China* (1936): 15, 421-427. Also Item 4669, vol. 6, pp. 2417-2424.

4904. with Licent, É. "Note sur deux instruments agricoles du Néolithique de Chine." *L'anthropologie* (1925): 35, 62-74. Also Item 4669, vol. 2, pp. 521-532.

4905. with Licent, É. "Observations complementaires sur la géologie de l'Ordos." *Bulletin de la Société géologique de France* (1924): 24, 462-464. Also Item 4669, vol. 2, pp. 504-508.

4906. with Licent, É. "Observations géologiques sur la bordure occidentale et meridionale de l'Ordos."

Bulletin de la Société géologique de France (1924):
24, 49-91.
Also Item 4669, vol. 2, pp. 461-503.

4907. with Licent, É. "Observations sur les formations quat-
        ernaires et tertiaires supérieures du Honan septen-
        trional et du Chansi meridional." *Bulletin of the
        Geological Society of China* (1927): 6, 129-148.
        Also Item 4669, vol. 2, pp. 834-853.

4908. with Licent, É. "On the Basal Beds of the Sedimen-
        tary Series in South-Western Shansi." *Bulletin of
        the Geological Society of China* (1927): 6, 61-65.
        Also Item 4669, vol. 2, pp. 828-831.

4909. with Licent, É. "On the Discovery of a Paleolithic
        Industry in Northern China." *Bulletin of the Geo-
        logical Society of China* (1924): 3, 45-50.
        Also Item 4669, vol. 2, pp. 445-450.

4910. with Licent, É. "On the Geology of the Northern, West-
        ern and Southern Borders of the Odros, China." *Bul-
        letin of the Geological Society of China* (1924): 3,
        37-44.
        Also Item 4669, vol. 2, pp. 432-439.

4911. with Licent, É. "On the Recent Marine Beds, and the
        Underlying Fresh-Water Deposits in Tientsin." *Bul-
        letin of the Geological Society of China* (1927): 6,
        127-128.
        Also Item 4669, vol. 2, pp. 832-833.

4912. with Licent, É. "Le paléolithique de la Chine."
        L'anthropologie (1925): 35, 201-234.
        Also Item 4669, vol. 2, pp. 533-566.

4913. with Licent, É., and P. Davidson Black. "On a Pre-
        sumably Pleistocene Human Tooth from the Sjara-Osso-
        Gol (South-Eastern Ordos) Deposits." *Bulletin of
        the Geological Society of China* (1926): 5, 285-290.
        Also Item 4669, vol. 2, pp. 759-765.

4914. with Licent, É., and M. Trassaert. "The Pliocene
        Lacustrine Series in Central Shansi." *Bulletin of
        the Geological Society of China* (1935): 14, 211-219.
        Also Item 4669, vol. 5, pp. 2232-2242.

4915. with Marcel, Gabriel. "Équipe 'Science et conscience': Débat entre le Père Teilhard de Chardin et Gabriel Marcel." [January 21, 1947.] Typescript. 6 pp., single-spaced.

4916. with Pei, W.C. "The Fossil Mammals from Locality 13 of Choukoutien." *Paleontologica sinica* (1941): 126, 1-106.
Also Item 4669, vol. 8, pp. 3367-3490.

4917. with Pei, W.C. "The Lithic Industry of the Sinanthropus Deposits in Choukoutien." *Bulletin of the Geological Society of China* (1932): 11, 315-364.
Also Item 4669, vol. 4, pp. 1721-1771.

4918. with Pei, W.C. "Le néolithique de la Chine." *Publication de l'Institut de géobiologie. Pékin* (1944): 10, ix-xiv, 1-100.
Also Item 4669, vol. 9, pp. 3937-4042.

4919. with Pei, W.C. "New Discoveries in Choukoutien, 1933-1934." *Bulletin of the Geological Society of China* (1934): 13, 369-394.
Also Item 4669, vol. 5, pp. 2093-2119.

4920. with Piveteau, J. "Les Mammifères fossiles de Nihowan (Chine)." *Annales de paleontologie* (1930): 19, 3-134.
Also Item 4669, vol. 3, pp. 1245-1427.

4921. with Piveteau, J. "Nouvelle étude sur le Cervus Ertborni Dub. des argiles de la Campine." *Bulletin du Musée royal d'histoire naturelle de Belgique* (1932): 8: 1-12.
Also Item 4669, vol. 4, pp. 1709-1720.

4922. with Piveteau, J. "P. Teilhard de Chardin et J. Piveteau offrent leur mémoire: Les Mammifères fossiles de Nihowan (Chine)." *Compte-rendu Sommaire et Bulletin de la Société géologique de France* (1930): 182-183.
Also Item 4669, vol. 3, p. 1428.

4923. with Stirton, R.A. "A Correlation of Some Miocene and Pliocene Mammalian Assemblages in North America and Asia with a Discussion of the Mio-Pliocene Boundary." *Publication of the University of California, Bulletin of the Department of Geological Science* (1934): 23, 277-290.
Also Item 4669, vol. 5, pp. 2120-2133.

4924. with Trassaert, M. "Cavicornia of South-Eastern Shansi."
       Paleontologica sinica (1938): 115, 1-106.
       Also Item 4669, vol. 7, pp. 2857-2967.

4925. with Trassaert, M. "The Pliocene Camelidae, Giraf-
       fidae and Cervidae of South-Eastern Shansi." *Paleon-
       tologica sinica* (1937): 102, 1-56.
       Also Item 4669, vol. 6, pp. 2653-2729.

4926. with Trassaert, M. "The Proboscidians of South-Eastern
       Shansi (Yushe Basin)." *Paleontologica sinica* (1937):
       13, 1-58.
       Also Item 4669, vol. 6, pp. 2565-2652.

4927. with Yang Kieh. "The Structural Geology of Eastern
       Shantung (Between Tsingtao and Yung Ch'eng)." *Bul-
       letin of the Geological Survey of China* (1937): 29,
       85-108.
       Also Item 4669, vol. 6, pp. 2541-2564.

4928. with Young, C.C. "The Cenozoic Sequence in the Yang-
       tze Valley." *Bulletin of the Geological Society of
       China* (1935): 14, 161-178.
       Also Item 4669, vol. 5, pp. 2182-2199.

4929. with Young, C.C. "Fossil Mammals from the Late Ceno-
       zoic of Northern China." *Paleontologica sinica*
       (1931): 9, 1-88.
       Also Item 4669, vol. 4, pp. 1525-1617.

4930. with Young, C.C. "The Late Cenozoic Formations of
       South-Eastern Shansi." *Bulletin of the Geological
       Society of China* (1933): 12, 207-248.
       Also Item 4669, vol. 5, pp. 1861-1902.

4931. with Young, C.C. "A Mongolian Amblypod in the Red Beds
       of Ichang (Hupeh)." *Bulletin of the Geological Soci-
       ety of China* (1936): 15, 217-223.
       Also Item 4669, vol. 6, pp. 2410-2416.

4932. with Young, C.C. "On the Mammalian Remains from the
       Archaeological Site of Anyang." *Paleontologica
       sinica* (1936): 12, 5-78.
       Also Item 4669, vol. 6, pp. 2329-2409.

4933. with Young, C.C. "On Some Neolithic and Possibly
       Paleolithic Finds in Mongolia, Sinkiang and West

China." *Bulletin of the Geological Society of China*
(1932): 12, 83-104.
Also Item 4669, vol. 4, pp. 1772-1794.

4934. with Young, C.C. "On Some Traces of Vertebrate Life
in the Jurassic and Triassic Beds of Shansi and Shensi." *Bulletin of the Geological Society of China*
(1929): 8, 131-133.
Also Item 4669, vol. 3, pp. 1107-1111.

4935. with Young, C.C. "Preliminary Observations on the Pre-
loessic and Postpontian Formations in Western Shansi
and Northern Shensi." *Geological Memoirs* (1930): 8,
1-54.
Also Item 4669, vol. 3, pp. 1179-1233.

4936. with Young, C.C. "Preliminary Report on the Choukoutien Fossiliferous Deposits." *Bulletin of the Geological Society of China* (1929): 8, 173-202.
Also Item 4669, vol. 3, pp. 1112-1153.

4937. with Young, C.C. "Some Correlation Between the Geology
of China Proper and the Geology of Mongolia." *Bulletin of the Geological Society of China* (1930): 9,
119-125.
Also Item 4669, vol. 4, pp. 1442-1448.

4938. with Young, C.C., W.C. Pei, and H.C. Chang. "On the
Cenozoic Formations of Kwangsi and Kwangtung." *Bulletin of the Geological Society of China* (1935): 14,
179-210.
Also Item 4669, vol. 5, pp. 2200-2231.

Indexes

INDEX TO WORKS
ABOUT TEILHARD DE CHARDIN

Evolution (cont.)

Mary, Blessed Virgin, 1305
Maslow, A., 3795
Mass on the World, 1817, 1822, 1823, 1929
Massignon, L., 2382
Massis, H., 576
Materialism, 114, 2122, 2128, 2651, 3015
Matter, 233, 431, 549, 678, 765, 852, 961, 1066, 1251, 1395,
     1437, 1441, 1694, 1731, 1862, 1948, 2214, 2273, 2456,
     2537, 2538, 2700, 3143, 3457, 3602, 3802, 3803, 4279,
     4280, 4298, 4302
Maturity, 2708
Mauriac, F., 2701, 3407
Meaning, 1591
Mechanism, 2779, 4200
Medawar, P.B., 4010
Medicine, 3411
Memory, 722
Mercier, G., 1654
Metaphor, 1571, 3291
Metaphysics, 90, 181, 375, 442, 1701, 1893, 2113, 2181, 2558,
     2656, 2657, 2914, 2922, 3097, 3317, 3343, 3436, 3616,
     3629, 3850
Method, 107, 165, 212, 230, 241, 269, 384, 385, 560, 572, 710,
     1166, 1175, 1185, 1229, 1318, 1331, 1405, 1438, 1679,
     2002, 2043, 2185, 2358, 2539, 2544, 2574, 2619, 2657,
     2837, 3000, 3173, 3499, 3666, 3735, 4282
Michelangelo, 2037
Microcosmos, 928
Missionary Activity, 1138, 1520, 3305, 3306, 3381, 3433
Modernism, 63, 876, 881
Molina, L., 2064
Moltmann, J., 113, 3957
Monod, J., 1271, 1687, 2993
Montaigne, M. de, 1386
Monchanin, Abbé, 2500
Monism, 3339
Monogenism, 1050, 2186
Morality, 34, 393, 410, 511, 975, 1049, 1094, 1234, 1769,
     1770, 2738, 2739, 2762, 2767, 2788, 2868, 2996, 3188
Morgan, L., 1902
Mortier de Chardin, Mademoiselle, 8, 36
Mounier, E., 437, 1759
Muller, A., 748
Mumford, L., 1749
Music, 2295
Mysticism, 202, 216, 231, 709, 773, 774, 1013, 1133, 1221,
     1366, 1398, 1503, 1674-1676, 1693, 1718, 1757, 1972,
     2017, 2086, 2170, 2199, 2394, 2466, 2517, 2531, 2534,

Relativism, 2378
Religion, 741, 744, 747, 850, 1046, 1056, 1067, 1103, 1136,
    1179, 1241, 1264, 1311, 1323, 1334, 1362, 1481, 1551,
    1821, 1865, 1914, 1926, 1952, 2166, 2214, 2343, 2345,
    2355, 2504, 2560, 2695, 2869, 2916, 2987, 3006, 3021,
    3136, 3143, 3217, 3219, 3252, 3261, 3280, 3290, 3481,
    3680, 3686, 3721, 3805, 3845, 3880, 3892, 3936, 3980,
    4004, 4054, 4070, 4089, 4195, 4254, 4255, 4260, 4297,
    4300
Religious Education, 868, 1443
Renan, J.E., 3398
Renewal, 2516
Republicanism, 2148
Resurrection, 1470
Revelation, 1904, 3309
Revitalization, 1776
Rights, 3521
Risk, 2821, 2827
Robinson, J., 2780, 2853
Rolland, R., 3954
Rostand, J., 725, 2364, 2400, 3454
Rousseau, J.J., 1386
Royce, J., 481
Rynne, X., 3873

Sacrament, 2598
Sacred, 706, 1766, 3795
Sacred Heart, 71a, 3434, 3435, 4203
Saint Exupéry, A. de, 1237, 2843
Salleron, L., 3654
Salvation, 2224, 2618, 4119
Sartre, J.P., 94, 613, 3333
Scheler, M., 2942
Schell, H., 2872, 3797
Schmaus, M., 4078
Schoonenberg, P., 4199
Schuré, E., 123, 3619
Schweitzer, A., 2853
Science, 53-55, 61, 122, 127, 147, 148, 179, 260, 270, 374,
    397, 550, 569, 595, 636, 700, 701, 708, 709, 721, 855,
    878, 882, 890, 893, 911, 932, 935, 953, 977, 1002, 1003,
    1044, 1058, 1086, 1109, 1136, 1160, 1179, 1181, 1183,
    1196, 1266, 1267, 1292, 1348, 1407, 1418, 1580, 1636,
    1657, 1788, 1801, 1821, 1863, 1865, 1882, 1914, 1925,
    1941, 1951, 1956, 1957, 1985, 1997, 2008, 2031a, 2048,
    2090, 2091, 2102, 2124, 2146, 2199, 2209, 2232, 2300,
    2356, 2363, 2416, 2465, 2517, 2519, 2543, 2549a, 2583,
    2610, 2639, 2646, 2679, 2686, 2749, 2777, 2803, 2805,

INDEX TO WORKS
BY TEILHARD DE CHARDIN